STRATEGIC ENTREPRENEURSHIP

Strategic Management Society Book Series

The Strategic Management Book Series is a cooperative effort between the Strategic Management Society and Blackwell Publishers. The purpose of the series is to present information on cutting-edge concepts and topics in strategic management theory and practice. The books emphasize building and maintaining bridges between strategic management theory and practice. The work published in these books generates and tests new theories of strategic management. Additionally, work published in this series also demonstrates how to learn, understand and apply these theories in practice. The content of the series represents the newest and critical thinking in the field of strategic management. As a result, the books in this series provide valuable knowledge for strategic management scholars, consultants and executives.

This book highlights a new concept, strategic entrepreneurship. Strategic entrepreneurship integrates theory and research from the strategic management and entrepreneurship fields. In practice it combines opportunity-seeking and advantage-seeking behaviors. Thus strategic entrepreneurship involves identifying and exploiting opportunities to achieve a competitive advantage and thereby create wealth. This book includes chapters by top scholars in strategic management and entrepreneurship. The chapters use complementary work in strategic management and entrepreneurship to examine six separate domains. These domains include resources, innovation, strategic alliances and networks, strategic leadership and growth. Three author teams also explore the integration of the theory and research in the two disciplines. These works were presented at a specially invited mini-conference co-sponsored by the Strategic Management Society, Kauffmann Foundation, Arizona State University and the University of Richmond. The authors used feedback from the conference and from the co-editors to develop thought-provoking and creative explorations of their topics. This book is an important reference for scholars and thoughtful executives interested in the cutting edge of theory and research in strategic management and entrepreneurship.

Michael A. Hitt
Series Editor

Strategic Entrepreneurship

Creating a New Mindset

Edited by

Michael A. Hitt
R. Duane Ireland
S. Michael Camp
Donald L. Sexton

Blackwell Publishing

© 2002 by Blackwell Publishing Ltd
except for editorial arrangement and introduction © 2002 by Michael A. Hitt, R. Duane Ireland,
S. Michael Camp, and Donald L. Sexton

BLACKWELL PUBLISHING
350 Main Street, Malden, MA 02148-5020, USA
9600 Garsington Road, Oxford OX4 2DQ, UK
550 Swanston Street, Carlton, Victoria 3053, Australia

First published 2002 by Blackwell Publishing Ltd

3   2006

Library of Congress Cataloging-in-Publication Data

Strategic entrepreneurship : creating a new integrated mindset / edited by Michael A. Hitt ... [et al.].
        p. cm. — (Strategic Management Society book series)
    Includes bibliographical references and index.
    ISBN 0-631-23410-1 (hb : alk. paper)
    1. Entrepreneurship. 2. Strategic planning. 3. Industrial management. I. Hitt, Michael A. II. Series.

    HB615 .S768 2002
    658.4′21—dc21

                                                                        2002020890

ISBN-13: 978-0-631-23410-4 (hb : alk. paper)

A catalogue record for this title is available from the British Library.

The publisher's policy is to use permanent paper from mills that operate a sustainable forestry policy, and
which has been manufactured from pulp processed using acid-free and elementary chlorine-free practices.
Furthermore, the publisher ensures that the text paper and cover board used have met acceptable
environmental accreditation standards.

For further information on
Blackwell Publishing, visit our website:
www.blackwellpublishing.com

Contents

Figures

Tables

Contributors

Alvarez, Sharon A.
Ohio State University
e-mail: *alvarez@cob.ohio-state.edu*

Barkema, Harry
Tilburg University
e-mail: *barkema@kub.nl*

Barney, Jay B.
Ohio State University
e-mail: *barney.8@osu.edu*

Busenitz, Lowell W.
University of Oklahoma
e-mail: *Busenitz@ou.edu*

Camp, S. Michael
Kauffman Center for Entrepreneurship Leadership
e-mail: *mcamp@emkf.org*

Chvyrkov, Oleg
Tilburg University
e-mail: *O.Chvyrkov@kub.nl*

Cooper, Arnold C.
Purdue University
e-mail: *coopera@mgmt.purdue.edu*

Covin, Jeffrey G.
Indiana University
e-mail: *covin@indiana.edu*

Davidsson, Per
Jönköping International Business School
e-mail: *p.davidsson@qut.edu.au*

Delmar, Frédéric
Entrepreneurship and Small Business Research Institute
e-mail: *Frederic.Delmar@esbri.se*

Di Gregario, Dante
University of Maryland
e-mail: *ddigrego@rhsmith.umd.edu*

Drazin, Robert
Emory University
e-mail: *Robert_Drazin@bus.emory.edu*

George, Gerard
University of Wisconsin-Madison
e-mail: *Gegeorge@syr.edu*

Glynn, Mary Ann
Emory University
e-mail: *maryann_glynn@bus.emory.edu*

Hagedoorn, John
University of Maastricht
e-mail: *j.hagedoorn@mw.unimaas.nl*

Hitt, Michael A.
Arizona State University
e-mail: *michael.hitt@asu.edu*

Hoskisson, Robert E.
University of Oklahoma
e-mail: *rhoskiss@ou.edu*

Ireland, R. Duane
University of Richmond
e-mail: *direland@richmond.edu*

Johnson, Scott
University of Minnesota
e-mail: *sjohnson3@csom.umn.edu*

Kazanjian, Robert K.
Emory University
e-mail: *kazanjian@bus.emory.edu*

Meeks, Michael D.
University of Colorado at Boulder
e-mail: *mmeeks@Colorado.edu*

Meyer, G. Dale
University of Colorado at Boulder
e-mail: *g.meyer@Colorado.edu*

Michael, Steven
University of Illinois
e-mail: *smichael@uiuc.edu*

Mosakowski, Elaine
Purdue University
e-mail: *emosakowski@mgmt.purdue.edu*

Neck, Heidi M.
Babson College
e-mail: *hneck@babson.edu*

Roijakkers, Nadine
University of Maastricht
e-mail: *n.roijakkers@mw.unimaas.nl*

Sexton, Donald L.
(Retired)
e-mail: *dlsexton@aol.com*

Slevin, Dennis P.
University of Pittsburgh
e-mail: *dpslevin@katz.business.pitt.edu*

Smith, Ken G.
University of Maryland
e-mail: *kgsmith@bmgtmail.umd.edu*

Storey, David
University of Warwick
e-mail: *smeds@wbs.warwick.ac.uk*

Thomas, Howard
University of Warwick
e-mail: *deanht@wbs.warwick.ac.uk*

Van de Ven, Andrew H.
University of Minnesota
e-mail: *avandeven@csom.umn.edu*

Wiklund, Johan
Jönköping International Business School
e-mail: *johan.wiklund@jibs.hj.se*

Zahra, Shaker A.
Georgia State University
e-mail: *szahra@gsu.edu*

CHAPTER ONE

Strategic Entrepreneurship: Integrating Entrepreneurial and Strategic Management Perspectives

Michael A. Hitt, R. Duane Ireland, S. Michael Camp, Donald L. Sexton

A new competitive landscape developed in the 1990s (Hitt, Ireland, and Hoskisson, 2001d). Filled with threats to existing patterns of successful competition as well as opportunities to form competitive advantages through innovations that create new industries and markets, this landscape was characterized by substantial and often frame-breaking change, a series of temporary, rather than sustainable competitive advantages for individual firms, the criticality of speed in making and implementing strategic decisions, shortened product life cycles, and new forms of competition among global competitors (Bettis and Hitt, 1995; Hitt, 2000; Hitt et al., 2001c; Hitt, Keats, and DeMarie, 1998; Ireland and Hitt, 1999).

The essence of the new competitive landscape remains a dominant influence on firm success in the twenty-first century. Indeed, the landscape's characteristics combine and interact to create an environment in which revolutionaries (entrepreneurial actors) have the potential to (1) capture existing markets in some instances while creating new ones in others, (2) take market share from less aggressive and innovative competitors, and (3) take the customers, assets, and even the employees of staid existing firms (Hamel, 2000). In this setting, entrepreneurial strategies for both new ventures and established firms are becoming increasingly important as their link to firm success receives additional validation (Bettis and Hitt, 1995; Hitt et al., 2001c; Ireland et al., 2001a). Entrepreneurial strategies are the embodiment of what some view as an entrepreneurial revolution occurring in nations across the globe, including some countries characterized as emerging economies (Morris, Kuratko, and Schindehutte, 2001; Zahra, Ireland, and Hitt, 2000b). An entrepreneurial mindset is required for firms to compete successfully in the new competitive landscape through use of carefully selected and implemented entrepreneurial strategies. An entrepreneurial mindset denotes a way of thinking about business and its opportunities that captures the benefits of uncertainty. These benefits are captured as individuals search for and attempt to exploit high potential opportunities that are commonly associated with uncertain business environments (McGrath and MacMillan, 2000).

The twenty-first century's competitive landscape and the vital entrepreneurial strategies for competitive success demand effective strategic and entrepreneurial actions (Ireland et al., 2001a; Kuratko, Ireland, and Hornsby, 2001; Porter, 2001). *Strategic actions* are those through which companies develop and exploit current competitive advantages while supporting entrepreneurial actions that exploit opportunities that will help create competitive advantages for the firm in the future. A *competitive advantage* results from an enduring value differential in the minds of customers between one firm's good or service and those of its rivals (Duncan, Ginter, and Swayne, 1998). *Entrepreneurial actions* are actions through which companies identify and then seek to exploit entrepreneurial opportunities rivals have not noticed or fully exploited (Ireland et al., 2001a). *Entrepreneurial opportunities* are external environmental conditions suggesting the viability of introducing and selling new products, services, raw materials and organizing methods at prices exceeding their production costs (Casson, 1982; Shane and Venkataraman, 2000). Relying on earlier arguments (e.g., Casson, 1982; Kirzner, 1973), Alvarez and Barney (2001) argue that entrepreneurial opportunities surface when actors have insights about the value of resources or a combination of resources that are unknown to others.

Strategic entrepreneurship is the integration of entrepreneurial (i.e., opportunity-seeking actions) and strategic (i.e., advantage-seeking actions) perspectives to design and implement entrepreneurial strategies that create wealth (Hitt et al., 2001c). Thus, strategic entrepreneurship is entrepreneurial action that is taken with a strategic perspective. Venkataraman and Sarasvathy (2001) referred to such activity as Romeo (entrepreneur) on the balcony (strategy).

Integrating entrepreneurial and strategic actions is necessary for firms to create maximum wealth (Ireland et al., 2001a). Entrepreneurial and strategic actions are complementary, not interchangeable (McGrath and MacMillan, 2000; Meyer and Heppard, 2000). Entrepreneurial action is designed to identify and pursue entrepreneurial opportunities. Thus, it is valuable in dynamic and uncertain environments such as the new competitive landscape because entrepreneurial opportunities arise from uncertainty. Entrepreneurial action using a strategic perspective is helpful to identify the most appropriate opportunities to exploit and then facilitate the exploitation to establish competitive advantages (hopefully ones that are sustainable for a reasonable period of time).

Because of its value to firms competing in a competitive landscape characterized by uncertainty, discontinuities, and rapid change, this book focuses on strategic entrepreneurship. Several domains important to both strategic management and entrepreneurship are examined herein. Individual chapters identify entrepreneurial strategies and how they can be effectively implemented to create new ventures (either independent startups or new units within established organizations) that produce enhanced wealth. Herein, outstanding entrepreneurship and strategic management scholars advance novel and path-breaking ideas that have the potential to meaningfully contribute to both fields and inform our understanding of wealth creation in organizations.

Our book begins with two chapters in which the intersections and interrelationships between the entrepreneurship and strategic management fields are examined. Following these chapters is one presenting different perspectives about entrepreneurial strategies.

Entrepreneurship and Strategic Management

Entrepreneurs create goods and services and managers seek to establish a competitive advantage with the goods and services created. Thus, entrepreneurial and strategic actions are complementary and can achieve the greatest wealth when integrated. In their chapter, Meyer, Neck, and Meeks explain the intersection between entrepreneurship and strategic management while simultaneously emphasizing the differences. They suggest, for example, that entrepreneurship focuses on creation while strategic management focuses on building a competitive advantage (firm performance). Additionally, they note that the entrepreneurship and strategic management fields have had different foci in the size of firms. Entrepreneurship has largely examined small businesses while strategic management concentrates on large businesses. However, they emphasize that the primary interface is creation–performance. In the framework presented earlier, the creation–performance relationship involves both opportunity-seeking and advantage-seeking actions, the integration of which we refer to as strategic entrepreneurship. Meyer et al. also suggest that two other intersections requiring further study are corporate entrepreneurship and the strategies and resulting performance of small and medium-sized businesses. Important issues, both are explored in other chapters in this book.

Michael, Storey, and Thomas's chapter also examines the intersection of strategic management and entrepreneurship. Reaching a conclusion that differs from that of Meyer et al., they suggest that strategic management represents the "unrecognized union" between two fields – one concentrating on coordination and prevention of loss and the other focusing on the creation of future businesses. They refer to these fields as administrative management and entrepreneurial management, respectively. Additionally, Michael and his colleagues argue that most strategic management research has emphasized administrative management. This conclusion is supported by the results of an analysis of journal publications that Meyer et al. completed. They found little emphasis in the strategic management literature on entrepreneurial firms or on research questions important to them. Michael et al. argue that future strategic management research should emphasize entrepreneurial management because of its importance. While we see the fields of strategic management and entrepreneurship as independent, in agreement with Meyer and his colleagues, we agree on the importance of research on entrepreneurial management issues. We also suggest that these fields intersect in important areas and that the integration of theory and research in them is vital. The two aforementioned chapters provide interesting and thought-provoking arguments, ideas, and directions for entrepreneurship and strategic management scholars.

The third chapter in the first part presents a framework for entrepreneurial strategies. Developed by Johnson and Van de Ven, the framework provides four different models of entrepreneurial strategy. The emphasis is different in each model. Highlighting the different foci are the theoretical lenses used to explain and support each model. As described by Johnson and Van de Ven, the models of entrepreneurial strategy (and their theoretical lenses) focus on (1) opportunity recognition (population ecology model), (2) achieving legitimacy (institutionalism model), (3) achieving fitness (industrial communities model), and (4) actions taken related to resource endowments, institutional arrangements, proprietary activities, and market consumption (industrial communities model). Johnson and Van de Ven appropriately suggest that each model requires a different entrepreneurial mindset. This requirement is consistent with arguments advanced by McGrath and MacMillan (2000). However, this perspective varies from the more common view that there is a single entrepreneurial mindset with a particular set of characteristics.

Johnson and Van de Ven also suggest that the most important type of entrepreneurial action identifies entrepreneurial opportunities that in turn lead to the development of new industries. The integration of entrepreneurial actions and complementary strategic actions that results in the creation of new industries through marketplace competition is a critical area of future theoretical and empirical research for strategic management and entrepreneurship scholars. In particular, there is need for future research on what differentiates a successful from an unsuccessful entrepreneurial firm and for understanding the sources of competitive advantage among entrepreneurial firms in the creation of new technology. Johnson and Van de Ven note that most new industries are forged not by single entrepreneurs but by numerous entrepreneurs collectively building an infrastructure.

Entrepreneurial actions that create a competitive advantage based on firms' tangible and intangible resources are the topics of the book's second major part.

Entrepreneurial Resources

Entrepreneurs (people acting independently or as part of a corporate system to create new organizations or to instigate renewal or innovation within an existing company – Sharma and Chrisman, 1999) and entrepreneurial firms identify and exploit opportunities that rivals have not observed or have underexploited. An appropriate set of resources is required to identify entrepreneurial opportunities with the greatest potential returns and to use a disciplined approach to exploit them (McGrath and MacMillan, 2000). Thus, the tenets of the resource-based view are applicable to both entrepreneurial ventures and established firms. The entrepreneurial and strategic actions linked to wealth creation are products of the firm's resources (Hitt et al., 2001b). To build and maintain a competitive advantage through which entrepreneurial opportunities can be identified and exploited, firms must hold or have access to heterogeneous and idiosyncratic resources that current and potential rivals cannot easily duplicate (Amit and Schoemaker, 1993; Barney, 1991). Recent evidence supports this argument. For example, Baum, Locke, and Smith (2001) found that a new venture's internal capabilities are an important predictor of its performance. Likewise, Lee, Lee, and Pennings (2001) found that technology-based new ventures created value using their internal capabilities. Compared to tangible resources, intangible resources are more likely to contribute to a competitive advantage because they are socially complex and difficult for current and potential rivals to understand and imitate (Hitt et al., 2001a). Oftentimes, entrepreneurial firms' most competitively valuable resources are intangible, such as unique knowledge or proprietary technology. In their chapter, Alvarez and Barney suggest that entrepreneurs frequently have an idiosyncratic resource in the unique cognitive models that they use to make strategic decisions. In fact, entrepreneurs often apply heuristics unknown to others in their decision processes. Alvarez and Barney also argue that these heuristics allow the entrepreneur to achieve unique and higher-level learning, thereby enhancing their knowledge base.

To identify entrepreneurial opportunities, Alvarez and Barney highlight the importance of entrepreneurial alertness, another entrepreneurial resource. In particular, they call on Kirzner's (1973) arguments suggesting that entrepreneurs often have special insight into potential market disequilibrium opportunities. Alvarez and Barney suggest that entrepreneurial alertness is motivated largely by the lure of profits. Their arguments strongly support the belief that wealth creation is a driving force for entrepreneurs – both those engaged in startup ventures and those working entrepreneurially in an established organization (Ireland, Hitt and Vaidyanath, 2001b).

Knowledge, which is justified true belief, is a critical intangible resource that helps firms to identify and especially exploit opportunities to establish competitive advantages (von Krogh, Ichijo, and Nonaka, 2000). Alvarez and Barney use Schumpeter's arguments to suggest that entrepreneurs integrate disparate knowledge to accomplish these tasks (which include both entrepreneurial and strategic actions). They note that entrepreneurial knowledge includes where to obtain undervalued resources and how to exploit them. In effect, entrepreneurs bundle resources in new ways to create value. Entrepreneurs, then, exploit uncertainty about the true value of the bundle of resources (Poppo and Weigelt, 2000). As a result, they create disequilibrium in the market.

In contrast, Mosakowski's chapter explains how entrepreneurs overcome an inherent resource disadvantage to create wealth. She also argues that firms with large resource endowments experience problems such as core rigidities, reduced experimentation, lower incentives to develop new resources, and enhanced strategic transparency to competitors. In effect, Mosakowski argues that entrepreneurial action exercised in startup ventures is unlikely to suffer from these problems. In these settings, entrepreneurs are motivated to seek resources or to create them in order to produce wealth. Because of having fewer resources, they experiment more, have greater incentives to act, and are less transparent to potential competitors. Lower transparency increases the difficulty for rivals to understand and imitate a competitor's entrepreneurial and strategic actions. The approach to entrepreneurial action commonly observed in new ventures and less-established organizations demonstrates more of a dynamic capabilities or competencies approach (i.e., Lei, Hitt, and Bettis, 1996; Teece, Pisano, and Shuen, 1997).

One of the problems with firms having large resource endowments is that they may become less motivated to develop or seek new resources. Alternatively, entrepreneurial firms do so and thus create new resources or obtain and combine existing resources in unique ways to invent and innovate (Schumpeter, 1934). As such, they create disequilibrium in the market, often reducing the value of the established and stable firm's resources. Microsoft CEO Steve Ballmer explains the problem in the following observation: "being big or small isn't the crucial issue. If you don't move, you don't move . . . Now what is interesting is that in pharmaceuticals, the company that leads a therapeutic category in one generation is very seldom the leader the next generation" (Anders, 2001). Reasons for these competitive outcomes relative to market leadership are noted briefly above and are more thoroughly explained in Mosakowski's chapter.

Thus, entrepreneurial resources are important in the creation of innovation as well as to the development of alliances and networks. We discuss the first relationship in the next part; analysis of the second one appears in a later part.

Innovation

The essence of entrepreneurship is creation (Lumpkin and Dess, 1996; Shane and Venkataraman, 2000). Innovation, often the foundation of creations, is critical for any firm (large or small) to compete effectively in the twenty-first century's landscape (Hamel, 2000). Building on the importance of entrepreneurial action, Smith and Di Gregorio explain that the essence of entrepreneurship is newness: new resources, new customers, new markets, and/or new combinations of existing resources, customers, or markets. Further, they differentiate equilibrating and disequilibrating actions, using the same Austrian framework that served as a basis for many of Alvarez and Barney's arguments. They suggest that equilibrating actions are based on the combination of existing and related resources that revise existing knowledge about markets. In contrast, disequilibrating actions are based on a combination of existing but unrelated resources that are incompatible with prevailing mental models. Smith and Di Gregorio argue that entrepreneurial firms can use bisociation to produce a creative action. Essentially, bisociation is the combination of two unrelated sets of information and resources. In fact, the extent to which bisociation is used differentiates the integrated entrepreneurial and strategic actions taken. They suggest that the variance in levels of knowledge across buyers and sellers presents entrepreneurial opportunities. Alert entrepreneurs and firms subsequently identify these opportunities and take strategic actions to exploit them.

Smith and Di Gregorio argue that disequilibrating actions can produce long-term competitive advantages because they are complex and will be difficult for competitors to identify and especially to imitate. Because the bisociative process occurs with individuals, organizational characteristics and processes can greatly affect it. For example, the reward system and expectations are likely to affect individual motivation and resulting behaviors (Ireland et al., 2001a). Firms with greater slack can invest that slack in the development of more radical innovation projects (i.e., take greater risks). The experience (e.g., tacit knowledge) of managers and the internal social networks along with connections to external networks may provide information inputs to the bisociation process. Thus, both individual and organizational factors affect entrepreneurial and strategic actions that are taken by organizations.

While individual entrepreneurs produce many innovations, Hoskisson and Busenitz note that 80 percent of the research and development conducted in developed nations takes place in large firms. Yet, according to them, these large firms account for less than half of recorded patents. Thus, while large firms can be entrepreneurial, they are not able to take advantage of a significant amount of entrepreneurial opportunities. In light of this evidence, Hoskisson and Busenitz conclude that smaller entrepreneurial firms account for a significant amount of technological progress. However, this is a critical issue because research has shown that corporate entrepreneurship can have substantial effects on the performance and growth of established firms (Barringer and Bluedorn, 1999). In short, innovation is required for most firms to compete in local and global markets (Hamel, 2000; Hitt et al., 1998; Ireland and Hitt, 1999).

Alternatively, Ahuja and Lampert (2001) suggest that larger established firms are producing or certainly contributing to the production of radical or "breakthrough" innovation much more than is recognized. Further, they argue that large firms can and at least some do develop routines that enable the production of major innovations that represent significant technological breakthroughs.

These ideas suggest the importance of understanding how large established companies can become entrepreneurial through effective integration of entrepreneurial and strategic actions. This area of focus is often referred to as corporate entrepreneurship. The Hoskisson and Busenitz chapter examines the strategic actions firms can take to engage in corporate entrepreneurship. In particular, they explain the most appropriate mode of entering new areas that take advantage of entrepreneurial opportunities. For example, they suggest that acquisitions may be the most effective mode of entering markets new to the firm when market uncertainty is low but there are greater amounts of learning the firm must undertake (high learning distance) to develop new capabilities necessary to compete effectively in this new market. When market uncertainty is higher and the learning distance low, they recommend that the firm develop a new internal venture. In other words, the firm has the necessary capabilities to compete in the market and other firms are unlikely to have an advantage because of high uncertainty. Finally, Hoskisson and Busenitz suggest that a joint venture may be the best approach to enter new markets when market uncertainty and learning distance are both high. A joint venture affords the greatest amount of flexibility to firms. Significant amounts of flexibility can be especially valuable in uncertain markets. However, we also emphasize that the learning distance cannot be too high or the joint venture may fail. The firms need to have complementary resources for the joint venture to be successful (Hitt et al., 2000). Also, if the partner firms are to learn from each other, they must have adequate absorptive capacity to do so (Cohen and Levinthal, 1990). This means that the capabilities cannot be too dissimilar; that is, the learning distance cannot be too great or the partners will not be able to learn from each other (Lane and Lubatkin, 1998). In this case, the joint venture may be unsuccessful. Current research also suggests that relatedness in knowledge bases will help produce more innovations from acquisitions (Ahuja and Katila, 2001).

Implementation of corporate entrepreneurship strategies is important and can play a major role in the success (or lack thereof) of efforts to produce innovation in firms (Hitt et al., 1999). Kazanjian, Drazin, and Glynn, in their chapter, explore the strategies used to implement corporate entrepreneurship. In particular, they relate the use of knowledge in corporate entrepreneurship. For example, they suggest that product-line extensions are implemented largely by exploiting the firm's existing knowledge. Alternatively, the development of a new platform requires the recombination of existing knowledge along with extensions of it. Finally, creating new businesses requires new knowledge. New knowledge is necessary in these cases because new businesses often are based on technologies different from those the firm currently employs. Additionally, these new businesses operate in new markets, making it necessary for the firm to develop knowledge of how to use the new technology and how to compete effectively in the new market. Their work helps explain the inertia that sometimes occurs with larger successful firms that is described by Mosakowski in her chapter. To develop other than product-line extensions, the firm's knowledge base must be extended or new knowledge must be added. Even when developing new platforms, new combinations of current knowledge must be effectively developed. Ahuja and Lampert (2001) and Floyd and Wooldridge (1999) argue that firms seeking to engage in corporate entrepreneurship must seek a delicate balance between activities that use what is currently known and those requiring the generation of new knowledge. New knowledge is vital to organizational renewal (Sharma and Chrisman, 1999). In essence, this delicate balance is concerned with the equally important tasks of simultaneously exploring (e.g., experimentation, discovery, and flexibility) for new knowledge while exploiting (e.g., efficiency, refinement, and execution) existing knowledge to create wealth (March, 1991).

Increasingly, firms are using alliances and networks to build knowledge that is important for innovation (i.e., exploration) and for the implementation (i.e., exploitation) of corporate entrepreneurship strategies (Kale, Singh, and Perlmutter, 2000). As such, our next topic examines the growing use of alliances and networks for entrepreneurial efforts.

Alliances and Networks

Alliances and networks have emerged as a major form of organizing to acquire the resources and capabilities necessary to compete effectively in markets (Hitt et al., 2001a) and therefore, wealth creation (Ireland et al., 2001b). Furthermore, Gulati, Nohria, and Zaheer (2000) argue that strategic alliances and strategic networks can help firms develop resources and capabilities that are difficult to imitate, leading to a competitive advantage. Strategic networks may be even more important for entrepreneurial firms, partly because of the need for resources in order to compete effectively against other entrepreneurial and established firms. The chapter by Cooper examines the interrelationship among alliances, strategic networks, and successful entrepreneurship.

Alliances and networks provide access to information, resources, technology and markets (Hitt et al., 2001c). Cooper suggests that networks may serve even more competitively critical purposes for entrepreneurial firms. For example, networks create legitimacy for entrepreneurial firms when they partner with a well-known and respected company. This is especially true for independent new ventures focused on creating a new market or a niche within an established market. Additionally, Cooper suggests that alliances can lead to exchange relationships with entrepreneurial firms' customers. Furthermore, the creation of new independent ventures frequently is based either on the network ties of an individual entrepreneur or of entrepreneurial teams in the case of ventures by larger firms. In particular, sources of ideas for new ventures often come from social networks. Thus, networks are sources of entrepreneurial opportunities. Perhaps most importantly, some of the critical resources to create and operate a new venture are obtained through network ties. As such, according to Cooper's review of the research, the number and extent of network ties are positively related to entrepreneurial firm performance.

Complementing Cooper's work, Hagedoorn and Roijakkers' chapter examines alliances between small entrepreneurial firms and larger established companies. In fact, Hagedoorn and Roijakkers report the results of empirical research on inter-firm networks of R&D partnerships in the biotechnology industry. Their research shows that the small firms largely provided the new technology and the large firms provided the financial resources, manufacturing capabilities and the marketing and distribution systems for the new products. Thus, the large established pharmaceutical firms and the smaller biotechnology firms had complementary resources and capabilities. In point of fact, the smaller entrepreneurial biotechnology firms created technological discontinuities in the Schumpeterian tradition. Furthermore, over time, the larger pharmaceutical firms increased their relative investment in R&D. This suggests that these firms have learned from their alliance with the smaller biotechnology firms. These results are supported by Rothaermel's (2001) study of the same industry. He argued that the smaller biotechnology firms created a technological discontinuity in the pharmaceutical industry. However, through the alliances, the larger pharmaceutical firms learned new capabilities and adapted to the new technology.

Strategic alliances and strategic networks have become a highly popular means of entering international markets. Of late, entrepreneurial firms have been entering international markets in record numbers, often through international alliances (Hitt et al., 2001c; Ireland et al., 2001a). Therefore, we consider the concept of international entrepreneurship.

International Entrepreneurship

During the decade of the 1990s and continuing into the twenty-first century, the global economic landscape has been undergoing substantial changes (Zahra et al., 2000a). The increasing globalization has produced and continues to produce a number of outcomes, some of which are unprecedented. Clearly, there is substantial global competition in most economically developed markets, particularly in the US. For example, for the period of 1998–2000, foreign firms spent over $900 billion to acquire US businesses. During the same time period, US firms spent $418 billion to acquire foreign firms (Jones, 2001). Certainly, many large firms regardless of their home base are generating an increasing amount of their sales revenue from international markets. For example, approximately 50 percent of Toyota's sales come from markets outside of Japan, while over 60 percent of McDonald's annual revenue comes from markets outside of the US (Ireland et al., 2001a). Because of the significant potential returns, internationalization has become a primary driver of the competitive landscape (Hitt, Hoskisson, and Kim, 1997; Hitt et al., 2001d).

Internationalization also has accelerated among smaller and newer firms (McDougall and Oviatt, 2000). In fact, many new firms have been born international, particularly those using the Internet to conduct business transactions (Semadeni, Hitt, and Uhlenbruck, 2001). International markets present new entrepreneurial opportunities. Thus, Lu and Beamish (2001) argue that entry into international markets is an entrepreneurial act undertaken at least in part to identify and pursue entrepreneurial opportunities.

The chapter by Zahra and George examines the domain of international entrepreneurship, its evolution, and current important dimensions. Reviewing the international entrepreneurship domain and examining the work on it, they define international entrepreneurship as the process of creatively discovering and exploiting opportunities outside of the firm's domestic market for the purpose of achieving a competitive advantage. Zahra and George examine the research on the dimensions of international entrepreneurship to include the degree of internationalization, the scope, and the speed of market entry. Importantly, they develop an integrated model of international entrepreneurship. The model suggests that the primary factors in moving into international markets are the firm's resources, the characteristics of the top management team (e.g., international experience/exposure), and other firm characteristics such as age, size, location, and home base. However, Zahra and George suggest that there are also important moderators of the relationship between organizational factors and international entrepreneurship. The two prominent moderators are environmental factors and strategic factors. Environmental factors such as competitive forces, national culture, and institutional environment may affect the extent to which an entrepreneurial firm engages in international entrepreneurship as well as the markets it chooses to enter. Additionally, its general firm strategies and the market entry strategies used may also affect the extent and location of international entrepreneurship of a firm.

Zahra and George also review some of the theoretical explanations for international entrepreneurship. Of course, there are established theories (e.g., Dunning's 1988 eclectic theory for foreign direct investment, transaction cost, and organizational learning theories) that researchers have used to examine questions related to international entrepreneurship. For example, Zahra et al. (2000b) used organizational learning theory to explain the depth, breadth, and speed of technological learning from international market entries by new ventures. They found that firms with greater depth, breadth, and speed of technological learning enjoyed higher returns. Zahra and George conclude that there is much opportunity for research in international entrepreneurship.

Top management teams are critically important for the exercise of strategic entrepreneurship. Hambrick and Mason (1984) suggested that organizations are reflections of their top managers. Furthermore, top executives play a critical role in the development and implementation of the firm's strategy (Finkelstein and Hambrick, 1996). Daily, Certo, and Dalton (2000) suggest that top managers represent a unique resource for the firm. In fact, recent research has found this resource to be positively related to firm performance (Hitt et al., 2001b). Entrepreneurial organizations depend even more strongly on their top managers for success.

Likewise, Barkema and Chvyrkov in their chapter argue that the top management team is critically important in internationally diversified firms. In fact, they suggest that internationally diversified firms require well-developed social networks and the capability to process substantial amounts of information to be critical to top executives' efforts to act entrepreneurially. Barkema and Chvyrkov explain that managing a large, internationally diversified firm is highly complex and challenging. These managers must decide which and how many international markets to enter. In addition, Barkema and Chvyrkov argue that top managers in internationally diversified firms facilitate the horizontal flow of vast streams of people and information often across unit, region, and country boundaries. They must monitor and manage a variety of subsidiaries in many countries and cultures. Finally, they still must deal with the usual challenges of business such as responding to competition and satisfying customers but in a more complex milieu of cultures and institutional infrastructures (i.e., Newman, 2000).

Barkema and Chevyrkov conducted a longitudinal study of the top management team in 25 firms for the years 1966–98. They found that firms with longer-tenured CEOs and top management teams were also more internationally diversified. Top managers with more experience in the firm are better able to coordinate and link its diverse internal groups. These managers have strong internal networks and relationships. They also found that top management teams with greater heterogeneity in tenure and education were more likely to operate effectively in internationally diversified firms. The heterogeneity is important to deal with the substantial complexity encountered in internationally diversified firms. The top managers must be entrepreneurial, identifying and exploiting opportunities. As we have explained and as Barkema and Chvyrkov demonstrate, top managers are important in internationally diversified firms. However, this set of organizational actors plays a critical role in terms of wealth creation in all types of firms, including independent new ventures. Furthermore, these executives and the leadership they provide are vital to the survival and performance of entrepreneurial firms. A critical indicator of performance in new ventures is growth. The strategic leadership that contributes to growth and subsequently, the creation of wealth along with the components of independent new ventures' growth are the foundation of the next section.

Strategic Leadership and Growth

The top managers and top entrepreneurs for the year 2000 were profiled in the January 2001 issue of *Business Week*. Interestingly, many of those recognized as top managers (for large and established companies) are also known to be entrepreneurial. Examples of these successful executives include the well-known Herb Kelleher, former CEO of Southwest Airlines, and the less well-known Keji Tachikawa, CEO of DoCoMo, the Japanese wireless communications company that is becoming a household name. Alternatively, the top entrepreneurs were not only creating new products that were in demand but also building businesses that had "staying power." Therefore, the top corporate managers and entrepreneurs seem to be exhibiting many of the same behaviors – behaviors that demonstrate strategic entrepreneurship.

In their chapter, Covin and Slevin analyze the entrepreneurial imperatives of strategic leadership. They emphasize the definition of strategic leadership posed by Hitt et al. (2001d) and emphasized by Ireland and Hitt (1999). This definition suggests that strategic leadership is the ability to anticipate, envision, maintain flexibility, and empower others to create strategic change as necessary. This form of leadership is similar to the entrepreneurial manager described in the chapter by Michael, Storey, and Thomas. In addition to the domains of strategic leadership described by Hitt et al. (2001d) and Ireland and Hitt (1999), Covin and Slevin argue that these individuals must have an entrepreneurial mindset. An entrepreneurial mindset is similar to the concept of entrepreneurial dominant logic presented by Meyer and Heppard (2000). An entrepreneurial mindset or dominant logic is prepared to take advantage of uncertainty by being flexible, building a strong capacity for innovation in order to preempt competitors to exploit product market opportunities and receptivity to novel and promising new business models.

The heart of Covin and Slevin's chapter focuses on the entrepreneurial imperatives of strategic leadership. These include nourishing entrepreneurial capabilities, nurturing innovations that threaten the firm's current business model, keeping the organization's boundaries broad enough to encompass promising opportunities, being prepared to question the current dominant logic focus on the deceptively simple questions, and linking entrepreneurship and strategy. We focus only on a couple of these crucially important imperatives.

It is common for managers to protect the firm's business model and when they are in a protective mode, they are likely to reject innovations that may disrupt the business model. However, this is absolutely the wrong action. Organizations acting in this manner are not seeking entrepreneurial opportunities. If the firm either is not aware of or chooses to reject an innovation that changes its business model, a more flexible competitor is likely to accept and implement it. Hamel (2000) suggests that revolutionaries are firms that will sequentially take other firms' customers and markets followed by their assets and best employees, leaving very little of value for the non-revolutionary competitor. In a similar vein, the firm's boundaries should not be too narrow so as to preclude promising opportunities. Jack Welch recently admitted that his requirement for all of GE's businesses to be number one or two in their markets forced managers to define their markets too narrowly. As a result, they missed excellent opportunities that others exploited. Therefore, this requirement for GE's businesses has been eliminated.

Of major importance to most new ventures is the ability to grow and develop assets and resources. Indeed, commitment to growth and rates of growth have emerged as primary factors distinguishing entrepreneurial ventures from small business organizations (Sexton and Smilor, 1997). Their importance can cause those leading new ventures to seek growth even at the expense of profits, especially in the early years of the venture's life. Davidsson, Delmar, and Wiklund explain the importance of entrepreneurial growth in their chapter. They argue that growth is a reasonable indicator of entrepreneurship for younger and smaller firms but not necessarily so for larger and more mature firms. All three of the coauthors are highly qualified to focus on this topic as each of the three wrote his dissertation on entrepreneurship and small firm growth. These authors suggest that if one considers entrepreneurship as the creation of new economic activity, entrepreneurship is growth. But, all growth is not entrepreneurship. For example, growth of existing economic activity (e.g., through acquisitions of other firms or increasing sales of current product lines) is not entrepreneurship. Thus, a primary strategic objective of firms should be to create new economic activity. Entrepreneurial strategies that lead to high growth are of particular importance.

Conclusions

This book is about a new concept, strategic entrepreneurship. Strategic entrepreneurship is applicable to smaller newer firms and older established companies as well. As we have explained herein and as is addressed in different fashions by the scholars whose work appears in this book, at its most basic, strategic entrepreneurship is comprised of entrepreneurial actions that are taken using a strategic perspective. In more depth, this concept details the strategic discipline through which exploration is used to identify entrepreneurial opportunities by which these opportunities are exploited to create firm wealth. Thus, strategic entrepreneurship facilitates firms' efforts to identify the best opportunities (matched to their resources and with the highest potential returns) and then to exploit them with the discipline of a strategic business plan. The goal of strategic entrepreneurship is to continuously create competitive advantages that lead to maximum wealth creation.

This book explores strategic entrepreneurship by integrating the concepts of firm actions that research in the entrepreneurship and strategic management literatures show to be relevant to the creation of wealth. Chapters herein explore how firms use their resources to explore for and then to identify the competitive value of and exploit entrepreneurial opportunities. They explore the use of alliances and networks in entrepreneurial processes. Other chapters examine innovation, that which is entrepreneurial and the necessity of it for survival and success. The chapters include discussions of corporate entrepreneurship and how it is implemented. International entrepreneurship is examined along with how top managers contribute entrepreneurial and strategic actions to facilitate and support internationalization of their firm. Finally, the exercise of strategic leadership and achievement of growth are explored in separate chapters. Of particular importance are the imperatives of entrepreneurship for strategic leadership.

The concept of strategic leadership has significant implications for the development and management of new ventures and larger established firms. These implications extend to the research and teaching in the disciplines of entrepreneurship and strategic management. Strategic entrepreneurship is a critically important business concept for the twenty-first century.

References

Ahuja, G. and Katila, R. 2001. Technological acquisitions and the innovation performance of acquiring firms: A longitudinal study. *Strategic Management Journal*, 22: 197–220.

Ahuja, G. and Lampert, C. M. 2001. Entrepreneurship in the large corporation: A longitudinal study of how established firms create breakthrough inventions. *Strategic Management Journal*, 22 (special issue): in press.

Alvarez, S. A. and Barney, J. B. 2001. How entrepreneurial firms can benefit from alliances with large partners. *Academy of Management Executive*, 15(1): 139–48.

Amit, R. and Schoemaker, P. J. H. 1993. Strategic assets and organizational rent. *Strategic Management Journal*, 14: 33–46.

Anders, G. 2001. Steve Ballmer's Big Moves. *Fast company*, March, 142–8.

Barney, J. B. 1991. Firm resources and sustained competitive advantage. *Journal of Management*, 17: 99–129.

Barringer, B. R. and Bluedorn, A. C. 1999. The relationship between corporate entrepreneurship and strategic management. *Strategic Management Journal*, 20: 421–44.

Baum, J. R., Locke, E. A., and Smith, K. G. 2001. A multi-dimensional model of venture growth. *Academy of Management Journal*, 44: in press.

Bettis, R. A. and Hitt, M. A. 1995. The new competitive landscape. *Strategic Management Journal*, 16(special issue): 7–20.

Business Week. 2001. The Top 25 Managers of the Year. January 8, 60–80.

Business Week. 2001. The Top Entrepreneurs. January 8, 83–4.

Casson, M. 1982. *The entrepreneur*. Totowa, N.J.: Barnes & Noble Books.

Cohen, W. M. and Levinthal, D. A. 1990. Absorptive capacity: A new perspective on learning and innovation. *Administrative Science Quarterly*, 35: 128–52.

Daily, C. M., Certo, S. T., and Dalton, D. R. 2000. A decade of corporate women: Some progress in the boardroom, none in the executive suite. *Strategic Management Journal*, 20: 93–9.

Duncan, W. J., Ginter, P. M., and Swayne, L. E. 1998. Competitive advantage and internal organizational assessment. *Academy of Management Executive*, 12(3): 6–16.

Dunning, J. H. 1988. The eclectic paradigm of international production: A restatement and some possible extensions. *Journal of International Business Studies*, 19(1): 1–31.

Finkelstein, S. and Hambrick, D. 1996. *Strategic leadership*. St. Paul: West Publishing Co.

Floyd, S. W. and Wooldridge, B. 1999. Knowledge creation and social networks in corporate entrepreneurship: The renewal of organizational capability. *Entrepreneurship Theory and Practice*, 23: 123–43.

Gulati, R., Nohria, N., and Zaheer, A. 2000. Strategic networks. *Strategic Management Journal*, 21 (special issue): 2003–15.

Hambrick, D. C. and Mason, P. 1984. Upper echelons: The organization as a reflection of its top managers. *Academy of Management Journal*, 14: 401–18.

Hamel, G. 2000. *Leading the revolution*. Boston, MA: Harvard Business School Press.

Hitt, M. A. 2000. The new frontier: Transformation of management for the new millennium. *Organizational Dynamics*, 28: 6–17.

Hitt, M. A., Ahlstrom, D., Dacin, M. T., and Levitas, E. 2001a. The economic and institutional context of international strategic alliance partner selection: China vs. Russia. Paper presented at the *Academy of Management* meetings, August, Washington, D.C.

Hitt, M. A., Bierman, L., Shimizu, K., and Kochhar, R. 2001b. Direct and moderating effects of human capital on strategy and performance in professional service firms: A resource-based perspective. *Academy of Management Journal*, 44: 13–28.

Hitt, M. A., Dacin, M. T., Levitas, E., Arregle, J.-L., and Borza, A. 2000. Partner selection in a merging and developed market context: Resource-based and organizational learning perspectives. *Academy of Management Journal*, 43: 449–467.

Hitt, M. A., Hoskisson, R. E., and Kim, H. 1997. International diversification: Effects on innovation and firm performance in product-diversified firms. *Academy of Management Journal*, 40: 767–98.

Hitt, M. A., Ireland, R. D., Camp, S. M., and Sexton, D. L. 2001c. Strategic entrepreneurship: Entrepreneurial strategies for wealth creation. *Strategic Management Journal*, 22 (special issue): 479–91.

Hitt, M. A., Ireland, R. D., and Hoskisson, R. E. 2001d. *Strategic management: Competitiveness and globalization*. Cincinnati, OH: South-Western College Publishing.

Hitt, M. A., Keats, B. W., and DeMarie, S. 1998. Navigating in the new competitive landscape: Building strategic flexibility and competitive advantage in the twenty-first century. *Academy of Management Executive*, 12(4): 22–42.

Hitt, M. A., Nixon, R. D., Hoskisson, R. E., and Kochhar, R. 1999. Corporate entrepreneurship and cross-functional fertilization: Activation, process, and disintegration of a new product design team. *Entrepreneurship Theory and Practice*, 23(3): 145–67.

Ireland, R. D. and Hitt, M. A. 1999. Achieving and maintaining strategic competitiveness in the twenty-first century: The role of strategic leadership. *Academy of Management Executive*, 13(1): 43–57.

Ireland, R. D., Hitt, M. A., Camp, S. M., and Sexton, D. L. 2001a. Integrating entrepreneurship and strategic management actions to create firm wealth. *Academy of Management Executive*, 15(1): 49–63.

Ireland, R. D., Hitt, M. A., and Vaidyanath, D. 2001b. Strategic alliances as a pathway to competitive success. *Journal of Management*, in press.

Jones, D. 2001. Foreign companies step up buyouts of US competitors. *The Arizona Republic*, March 11, D1, D4.

Kale, P., Singh, H., and Perlmutter, H. 2000. Learning and protection of proprietary assets in strategic alliances: Building relational capital. *Strategic Management Journal*, 21 (special issue): 217–37.

Kirzner, I. M. 1973. *Competition and entrepreneurship*. Chicago: University of Chicago Press.

Kuratko, D. F., Ireland, R. D., and Hornsby, J. S. 2001. Using entrepreneurial actions to increase firm performance: Insights from Acordia, Inc. *Academy of Management Executive*, 15: in press.

Lane, P. J. and Lubatkin, M. 1998. Relative absorptive capacity and interorganizational learning. *Strategic Management Journal*, 19: 461–77.

Lee, C., Lee, K., and Pennings, J. M. 2001. Internal capabilities, external networks, and performance: A study on technology-based ventures. *Strategic Management Journal*, 22 (special issue): 615–40.

Lei, D., Hitt, M. A., and Bettis, R. 1996. Dynamic core competences through meta-learning and strategic context. *Journal of Management*, 22: 549–69.

Lu, J. W. and Beamish, P. W. 2001. The internationalization and performance of SMEs. *Strategic Management Journal*, 22 (special issue): in press.

Lumpkin, G. T. and Dess, G. G. 1996. Clarifying the entrepreneurial orientation construct and linking it to performance. *Academy of Management Review*, 21: 135–72.

March, J. G. 1991. Exploration and exploitation in organizational learning. *Organization Science*, 2: 71–87.

McDougall, P. P. and Oviatt, B. M. 2000. International entrepreneurship: The intersection of two research paths. *Academy of Management Journal*, 43: 902–8.

McGrath, R. G. and MacMillan, I. 2000. *The entrepreneurial mindset*. Boston: Harvard Business School Press.

Meyer, G. D. and Heppard, K. A. 2000. *Entrepreneurship as strategy: Competing on the entrepreneurial edge*. Thousand Oaks, CA: Sage Publications.

Morris, M. H., Kuratko, D. F., and Schindehutte, M. 2001. Towards integration: Understanding entrepreneurship through frameworks. *International Journal of Entrepreneurship and Innovation*, 2 (1): 35–49.

Newman, K. L. 2000. Organizational transformation during institutional upheaval. *Academy of Management Review*, 25: 602–19.

Poppo, L. and Weigelt, K. 2000. A test of the resource-based model using baseball free agents. *Journal of Economics and Management Strategy*, 9: 585–614.

Porter, M. E. 2001. Strategy and the Internet. *Harvard Business Review*, 79(3): 62–78.

Rothaermel, F. T. 2001. Incumbent's advantage through exploiting complementary assets via interfirm cooperation. *Strategic Management Journal*, 22 (special issue): 687–99.

Schumpeter, J. A. 1934. *The theory of economic development*. Cambridge, MA: Harvard University Press.

Semadeni, M., Hitt, M. A., and Uhlenbruck, K. 2001. Born international/born electronic: The intersection of electronic commerce and international new ventures. Paper presented at the *Academy of Management* meetings, August, Washington, D.C.

Sexton, D. L. and Smilor, R. W. (eds) 1997. *Entrepreneurship 2000*. Chicago, IL: Upstart Publishing Company.

Shane, S. and Venkataraman, S. 2000. The promise of entrepreneurship as a field of research. *Academy of Management Review*, 25: 217–26.

Sharma, P. and Chrisman, J. J. 1999. Toward a reconciliation of the definitional issues in the field of corporate entrepreneurship. *Entrepreneurship Theory and Practice*, 23(3): 11–27.

Teece, D. J., Pisano, G., and Shuen, A. 1997. Dynamic capabilities in strategic management. *Strategic Management Journal*, 18: 509–34.

Venkataraman, S. and Sarasvathy, S. D. 2001. Strategy and entrepreneurship: Outlines of an untold story. In M. A. Hitt, E. Freeman and J. S. Harrison (eds). *Handbook of strategic management*. Oxford, UK: Blackwell, 650–68.

von Krogh, G., Ichijo, K., and Nonaka, I. 2000. *Enabling knowledge creation: How to unlock the mystery of tacit knowledge and release the power of innovation*. New York: Oxford University Press.

Zahra, S. A., Ireland, R. D., Gutierrez, I., and Hitt, M. A. 2000a. Privatization and entrepreneurial transformation: Emerging issues and a future research agenda. *Academy of Management Review*, 25: 509–24.

Zahra, S. A., Ireland, R. D., and Hitt, M. A. 2000b. International expansion by new venture firms: International diversity, mode of market entry, technological learning, and performance. *Academy of Management Journal*, 43: 925–50.

Entrepreneurship and Strategic Management

CHAPTER TWO

The Entrepreneurship–Strategic Management Interface

G. Dale Meyer, Heidi M. Neck, Michael D. Meeks

In the past 20 years the purview of strategic management scholars has been primarily to seek to understand which decisions and actions are needed to achieve competitive advantage (Hitt, Ireland, and Hoskisson, 2001). And entrepreneurship scholars have been greatly focused trying to understand how opportunities to bring into existence future goods and services are discovered and exploited to create and grow new ventures (Venkataraman, 1997). Strategic management researchers have been interested mostly in relatively large corporations. And entrepreneurship researchers have and continue to study mostly small and medium-sized enterprises. There is a seemingly increasing intersection of these fields of study. Whether this is an "integration" or more of an "interface" will be addressed in this chapter.

The creation aspect of entrepreneurship is a necessary antecedent to the performance-oriented process of strategic management. Given this alignment between the two fields, the intellectual boundaries of entrepreneurship and strategic management research appear to be blurring. Articles discussing the intersection of the fields have suggested numerous research topics shared by both fields (Sandberg, 1992; Day, 1992; Hitt and Ireland, 2000). In fact, Hitt and Ireland have called for more integrative entrepreneurship and strategic management research (2000: 58). But, integration, by definition, means to unite or blend into a whole. Taking the intersection conversations to the extreme, integration implies a need for the fields of entrepreneurship and strategic management to converge.

We believe that the intersection is growing into what we will later define as an interface. But we argue that integration (which implies little, if any, difference in the foci of the fields) is too strong a word to describe the changes afoot. Therefore, we offer an alternative view, the **Entrepreneurship–Strategic Management Interface** (ESMI). The purpose of the interface is to connect the creation aspect of entrepreneurship with the performance orientation of strategic management via four research spaces that are differentiated by firm size (small/large) and research focus (creation/ performance). Although no management discipline should operate remotely without some overlap with other functional areas, we feel entrepreneurship can have a unique intellectual platform from which to build knowledge. The ESMI developed in this chapter will encourage entrepreneurship to have a distinct domain but to also acknowledge and promote the contribution strategic management can have on the entrepreneurship field.

Each section of this chapter builds to our ESMI concept. We begin with a history of the entrepreneurship field and address the problems the field is having in developing a definition and domain. Then, we revisit the conversations on the intersection of the fields. Next, we acknowledge that there are forces and phenomena that are creating a potential for integrating the research domains of the two fields. The driving forces are a shared interest in firm performance, factors of the "new economy," and shifting strategic management paradigms, yet we conclude these forces are not sufficient cause for convergence. Finally we introduce the ESMI and conclude with the implications and future directions for the fields. To support our theses, throughout this chapter we report results from a content analysis of the *Journal of Business Venturing (JBV)* from 1985 to 2000, and the *Strategic Management Journal (SMJ)* from 1980 to 2000.[1]

Entrepreneurship as a Field of Academic Inquiry

History of the field

The initial era of entrepreneurship dates back to the concepts introduced by early economists, including Knight (1921) on risk and uncertainty, Schumpeter (1934) on new combinations and waves of creative destruction driven by entrepreneurs, and Penrose (1959) on entrepreneurial services and productive opportunities. The Austrian economists – Hayek, von Mises, and Kirzner – were instrumental in recognizing the impact of the individual on the economy. Hayek (1945) introduced mutual learning and market participant awareness, and von Mises (1944) introduced human action and the entrepreneur. Later, Kirzner (1973, 1997), a student of von Mises, expanded the work of his mentor and Hayek to introduce "entrepreneurial discovery." According to Kirzner (1973), entrepreneurs are not economizing individuals, but rather they have alertness to opportunities that already exist in the market. The Austrian view, one of human action as creative and active, is in direct opposition with the more mainstream Neoclassical view, which holds that human beings are passive, rational, and mechanical within ultimately efficient markets. While the Austrians argue disequilibrium as the prevailing state in an economy, Neoclassical economists theorize that economic forces alter equilibrium states but markets are assumed efficient at the equilibrium point.

Entrepreneurship as a field of study began to emerge in the 1970s. In 1974, Karl Vesper organized a special entrepreneurship interest group of the Academy of Management's Business Policy division, which became a separate division in 1987. The findings of David Birch (1979, 1987) highlighted entrepreneurship as the engine of growth in the economy. Prior to Birch's work, general political and economic beliefs assumed that large corporations created most of society's jobs, yet Birch uncovered counterintuitive statistics regarding job creation. During the period studied, 1981–5, small firms (1 to 19 employees) created 88 percent of all new jobs; firms with 20 to 99 employees created 27 percent of new jobs; large corporations (5,000+ employees) created 5 percent of new jobs; and firms with 100 to 4,999 employees lost 20 percent of the jobs created (Birch, 1987: 16). According to the *Global Entrepreneurship Monitor*, since 1980, *Fortune* 500 companies have lost more than five million jobs, but more than 34 million new jobs have been created (Reynolds, Hay, and Camp, 1999: 7). More recently, the OECD reported that 35 percent of new jobs created in 1995 were generated by organizations with only one to four employees (Arzeni, 1998).

The Birch studies and others (Kirchoff and Phillips, 1987, 1988; Reynolds, 1992; Reynolds, Hay, and Camp, 1999; Acs, 1999) revealed that the economic impact of entrepreneurship was not only attributed to business formation, but also to the growth of new businesses. Reynolds et al. (1999) reported that 15 percent of the highest growth firms in 1996 created 94 percent of new jobs. Because of the earlier findings relating entrepreneurship to firm growth, a movement began in the mid-1980s to separate entrepreneurship from small business management – the ultimate difference being the growth of the firm (Sexton and Smilor, 1997). Morris argues that, certainly in recent years, "The entrepreneurial firm is defined as one that proactively seeks to grow and is not constrained by resources under its control" (1998: 15). According to Sexton and Smilor, "significant differences exist between the problems associated with starting a business and growing one" (1997: 97) and they assert, "growth is the essence of entrepreneurship" (1997: 97). Thus, managing growth is fundamental and the problems inherent in high-growth firms are well documented (e.g., Penrose, 1959; Hambrick and Crozier, 1985; Kazanjian, 1988; Covin and Slevin, 1997; Welbourne, Meyer, and Neck, 1998), yet we believe more predictive studies are needed.

Entrepreneurship research, which began with the study of individual traits, has evolved into a comprehensive and complex phenomenon. Morris (1998) characterized the field as having seven perspectives that are quite representative of the evolution of the field while also emphasizing the apparent importance of "creation" on the field. These perspectives are: the creation of wealth, the creation of enterprise, the creation of innovation, the creation of change, the creation of employment, the creation of value, and the creation of growth (1998: 14). Though the entrepreneurship field is still emerging, we believe the field is taking its natural course similar to other fields that have emerged in the organization sciences. Overall, the field has been subjected to criticism regarding the rigor of the research being produced as well as questions regarding the focus of entrepreneurship research. Today scholars of entrepreneurship are attempting to establish boundaries, definitions, domains, and discover theory. The following section discusses these aspects as the field continues to struggle with its issues of legitimacy.

Definition and domain of entrepreneurship research

The 1990s was a decade of debate over the domain of entrepreneurship research, its legitimacy, and its contribution to management practice (Harrison and Leitch, 1996; Aldrich and Baker, 1997; Busenitz, et al. 2000). The establishment of entrepreneurship as a legitimate academic research domain has seen limited progress (Aldrich and Baker, 1997; Busenitz et al., 2000) and without an entrepreneurship research paradigm, the progress of the field and its legitimacy will be limited (Venkataraman, 1997).

Entrepreneurship research has been criticized for lack of rigor (Schendel, 1990), multiple levels of analysis (Venkataraman, 1997), and an absence of a unifying framework to guide the field's research. The large public databases such as PIMS or COMPUSTAT used in strategic management are not available for smaller, private, entrepreneurial firms. Consequently, data constraints, rather than research preference, may account partly for the nature of the work being done in entrepreneurship. But, even when databases for entrepreneurship research are available, sensitive financial information is not included (Phillips and Dennis, 1997), making it difficult to address performance queries. One could speculate that the lack of research progress in the field has resulted from our inability to define entrepreneurship using terms agreed upon by those in the field. And, Bygrave and Hofer (1991) contend that it is impossible to operationalize a construct that is not defined.

Table 2.1   Selected definitions of entrepreneurship

Author	Definition
Schumpeter (1934)	Entrepreneurship is seen as new combinations including the doing of new things or the doing of things that are already being done in a new way. New combinations include (1) introduction of new good, (2) new method of production, (3) opening of a new market, (4) new source of supply, (5) new organizations.
Kirzner (1973)	Entrepreneurship is the ability to perceive new opportunities. This recognition and seizing of the opportunity will tend to "correct" the market and bring it back toward equilibrium.
Drucker (1985)	Entrepreneurship is an act of innovation that involves endowing existing resources with new wealth-producing capacity.
Stevenson, Roberts, & Grousbeck (1985)	Entrepreneurship is the pursuit of an opportunity without concern for current resources or capabilities.
Rumelt (1987)	Entrepreneurship is the creation of new business, new business meaning that they do not exactly duplicate existing businesses but have some element of novelty.
Low & MacMillan (1988)	Entrepreneurship is the creation of new enterprise.
Gartner (1988)	Entrepreneurship is the creation of organizations, the process by which new organizations come into existence.
Timmons (1997)	Entrepreneurship is a way of thinking, reasoning, and acting that is opportunity obsessed, holistic in approach, and leadership balanced.
Venkataraman (1997)	Entrepreneurship research seeks to understand how opportunities to bring into existence future goods and services are discovered, created, and exploited, by whom, and with what consequences.
Morris (1998)	Entrepreneurship is the process through which individuals and teams create value by bringing together unique packages of resource inputs to exploit opportunities in the environment. It can occur in any organizational context and results in a variety of possible outcomes, including new ventures, products, services, processes, markets, and technologies.
Sharma & Chrisman (1999)	Entrepreneurship encompasses acts of organizational creation, renewal, or innovation that occur within or outside an existing organization.

Entrepreneurship has multiple definitions (see table 2.1 for a selected review) of which no one definition has been accepted by the field. Morris (1998) found 77 different definitions in a review of journal articles and textbooks over a five-year period. The lack of one definition leaves open multiple paths of inquiry and various perspectives of what entrepreneurship is. If not an agreed upon definition, then the field should at least establish a dominant paradigm from which to build knowledge. Without such a framework, the field lacks boundaries, structure, and a legitimate course of scientific inquiry. Scholars have been and continue to address the domain-paradigm-definition issue in the entrepreneurship field.

Gartner (1988) believes that entrepreneurship is the creation of new organizations while others argue that entrepreneurship encompasses organizational growth, strategic renewal, transformation, and innovation (Schendel and Hofer, 1979; Schendel, 1990; Day, 1992; Barringer and Bluedorn, 1999; Sexton and Smilor, 1997, Van de Ven et al., 1999; Hitt and Ireland, 2000). Entrepreneurship can take the form of a new venture or can occur inside an existing organization (Rumelt, 1987; Schendel, 1990; Guth and Ginsberg, 1990; Block and MacMillan, 1993; Morris and Sexton, 1996; Morris, 1998; Sharma and Chrisman, 1999; Shane and Venkataraman, 2000). We can study such topics as the individual entrepreneur (McClelland, 1961; Collins and Moore, 1970; Hornaday and Aboud, 1971; Hull, Bosley, and Udell, 1980), behaviors and actions (Gartner, 1988, Busenitz and Barney, 1997), opportunity recognition (Kirzner, 1973, 1979; Kaish and Gilad, 1991; Herron and Sapienza, 1992; Gaglio, 1997), populations of foundings (Aldrich, 1990, 1999; Aldrich and Wiedenmeyer, 1993), entrepreneurial teams (Slevin and Covin, 1992; Cooper and Daily, 1997; Ensley et al., 1999), organizational growth (Churchill and Lewis, 1983; Eisenhardt and Schoonhoven, 1990; Covin and Slevin, 1997), firm performance (Cooper, 1993; Chandler and Hanks, 1994; McDougall et al., 1994), and economic impact (Baumol, 1986; Birch, 1987; Kirchoff, 1991; Acs, 1999).

Without an overarching definition of entrepreneurship, however, each researcher's interpretation of entrepreneurship guides the research question, sample, and level of analysis. This limits the generalizability of findings and leads to an inability to replicate studies. Additionally, without an accumulation of empirically driven and consistent findings, we are unable to apply our knowledge in good faith to the practicing field of entrepreneurs in the real world. But, Gartner even admits to having difficulty arriving at a definition and the research domain of entrepreneurship. In commenting on the Domain Statement of the Entrepreneurship Division of the Academy of Management, he states:

> I am at a loss to ferret out the unique domain of entrepreneurship. . . . How is the study of "maintaining an enterprise" and "the creation and management of new businesses, small businesses and family businesses" different for entrepreneurship scholars than for [other] management scholars? (Gartner, 2000: 7)

Gartner goes on to state:

> I think the primary issue facing scholars interested in developing a domain statement for the field of entrepreneurship is the encroaching power of other academic disciplines. (Gartner, 2000: 7)

Scholars have significantly contributed to the literature in their attempt to define the domain of entrepreneurship research. For example, Bygrave and Hofer (1991) view entrepreneurship as a dynamic process that is an act of human volition analyzed at the firm level. The process is unique and dynamic with many antecedent variables, and these variables are sensitive to initial environmental conditions. Extending Bygrave's (1989) work on chaos theory, Bygrave and Hofer (1991) incorporated the notion of nonlinearity into the "process" of entrepreneurship. Later, Bull and Willard (1993) noted that the field should cease its attempt to define and redefine entrepreneurship because Schumpeter (1934, 1942) gave the field its domain many years ago. Schumpeter's (1934) notion of new combinations (new organizations, new markets, new sources of supply, new methods of production, new products and services) that disrupt markets and shift or destroy demand and supply curves is a rigorous and broad enough view for entrepreneurship research (Bull and Willard, 1993).

Morris (1998) proposed an interesting input–output process model of entrepreneurship that incorporated much of the literature to date in the field. Inputs to the entrepreneurial process include opportunities, individuals, organizational context, unique business concepts, and resources, while the output of the process (or outcome) can be a going venture, value creation, new products or services, processes, technologies, profits and/or personal benefits, and growth (Morris, 1998: 19). The inputs of the entrepreneurial process are both necessary and constant whereas the outputs that determine "entrepreneurial intensity" may vary. Accordingly, Morris proposes various dependent variables from which a researcher can choose depending on the research question of interest. Additionally, the definition of entrepreneurship proposed by Morris (see table 2.1) is sufficiently broad to include multiple levels of analysis, and organizational size does not constrain entrepreneurial activity.

Recently, Venkataraman (1997) and Shane and Venkataraman (2000) have been leading the challenge to establish a unique identity for the entrepreneurship field. Their view presumes a strong cognitive focus on opportunity identification, evaluation, and exploitation. Venkataraman defines the field of entrepreneurship as "a scholarly field that seeks to understand how opportunities to bring into existence future goods and services are developed, created, and exploited by whom and with what circumstances" (1997: 120). He is attempting to separate entrepreneurship from other disciplines, specifically strategic management, *vis-à-vis* a strong emphasis on the "emergence" of new businesses. Even though he includes both new and existing ventures in his definition, the break from strategic management is the analysis of opportunities from identification to commercialization with an emphasis on "future" goods and services.

Venkataraman (1997) regards absolute economic value and social wealth as the relevant benchmarks for entrepreneurship research. Economic value, or entrepreneurial rents, is profit in excess of the cost of time, effort, resources, and uncertainty. Without taking these opportunity costs into consideration, any profit and economic contribution resulting from the entrepreneurial venture is incomplete and misleading. The second benchmark, social wealth, is a byproduct of positive economic value. Through innovation, by way of self-interested opportunity exploitation and commercialization, entrepreneurs benefit society via new products, markets, and growth in demand and supply. Thus, entrepreneurial actions result in both personal and social wealth.

In 1999, Dale Meyer created the "Task Force on Doctoral Education in Entrepre-

---

Domain of Entrepreneurship Research
Draft as of December 18, 1999
Task force on Doctoral Education in Entrepreneurship

Entrepreneurship is about creation. Therefore, the research domain of the entrepreneurship field involves the:

- Creation of new ventures and organizations,
- Creation of new combinations of goods and services, methods of production, markets, and supply chains,
- Recognition and exploitation of new and existing opportunities, and
- Cognitive processes, behaviors and modes of action to exploit new and existing opportunities.

Entrepreneurship research examines these creation endeavors, the individuals and teams involved, the emergence of new ventures and organizations, and distinctive strategies utilized in the creation process; as well as the macroeconomic job and wealth creation impacts of entrepreneurial endeavor.

Entrepreneurship research can vary in context examined, such as new firms and organizations, existing corporations, family businesses, franchises and new international entrepreneurial activity.

Figure 2.1   Domain of entrepreneurship research (Meyer, Venkataraman, and Gartner, 1999)

neurship" as part of the Entrepreneurship Division of the Academy of Management. One of the primary challenges facing the Task Force is to develop a domain statement for research in entrepreneurship. The domain sub-committee comprised of Dale Meyer, S. Venkataraman, and William Gartner has been struggling to meet the challenge (Gartner, 2000). The most recent draft of the entrepreneurship research domain statement is reproduced in figure 2.1. Meyer, Venkataraman, and Gartner (1999) focus on entrepreneurship as creation but broadly define creation to encompass multiple and multidisciplinary topics for examination.

Scholars writing directly on the domain of entrepreneurship research are attempting to distinguish entrepreneurship from other disciplines – specifically strategic management. In summary, Gartner (1988) views entrepreneurship as the act of new venture creation where growth and survival are not topics of study. Bygrave and Hofer (1991) take a strong process view but their work is very broad and leaves a considerable amount of room for interpretation. Bull and Willard (1993) adhere to Schumpeter's view of new combinations as the impetus for creative destruction. Morris (1998) views entrepreneurship through an integrative input-output model where resource inputs are used to exploit opportunities that can result in various performance outcomes. Venkataraman (1997) and Shane and Venkataraman (2000) focus on creation *vis-à-vis* opportunity identification, evaluation, and exploitation. Finally, Meyer et al. (1999) view entrepreneurship as the examination of various creation endeavors.

All of these scholars have proposed domains to establish boundaries for entrepreneurship research, yet none have been fully accepted. The lack of agreement and ongoing conversation are evidence of the complexity of the entrepreneurial phenomenon as well as the youth of the field. Perhaps Baumol (1993) was correct when he implied (using the individual entrepreneur as opposed to the process of entrepreneurship) that whatever boundaries are placed on the field, someone will claim them as too restrictive.

> Any attempt at rigid definition of the term *entrepreneur* will be avoided assiduously here, because whatever attributes are selected, they are sure to prove excessively restrictive, ruling out some feature, activity, or accomplishment of this inherently subtle and elusive character. (Baumol, 1993: 7)

However, entrepreneurship's documented importance to and impact on the global economy challenges researchers to continue seeking answers to important questions pertaining to the birth, growth, failure, renewal, and transformation of organizations. Because the resulting economic impact is wealth and job creation, organizational performance becomes a critical factor. Just as the individual can affect the firm, the firm can affect the economy. Because strategic management is most often concerned with decisions and actions that lead to improved firm performance, it is reasonable to suggest, as some scholars have, that the fields of entrepreneurship and strategic management have a sizeable intersection.

The Intersection of Entrepreneurship and Strategic Management

As a child of the 1960s, strategic management has its roots in the efforts of early policy scholars to develop means of cross-disciplinary integration for the purposes of performance and increased efficiencies (Rumelt, Schendel, and Teece, 1995). The field has traversed four eras in its development during the past century, each with a distinctive paradigm built upon the one before. Strategic management thought began with the "Policy-Making" era in the early part of the century, then moved to a more proactive "Policy and Planning" approach after World War II, then to the "Initial Strategy" era of complex organizations operating over large geographic areas and serving a multitude of markets with numerous products, and finally to the current era of "Strategic Management" which deals with organizational performance and growth, and the systems and strategies used to achieve such growth (Schendel and Hofer, 1979; Summer et al., 1990).

But today, speed and action are the nucleus of the rapidly changing business environment. With increasing interest on speed and action, the new economy is an entrepreneurial economy. Therefore, all organizations regardless of age or size must be entrepreneurial to effectively compete and survive. Thus, strategic management has shifted much of its interest from static industry models and efficient markets (Bain, 1956; Caves, 1964; Porter, 1980) to more dynamic models of change and flexibility (Sanchez, 1993; Bowman and Hurry, 1993; Teece, Pisano, and Shuen, 1997; Brown and Eisenhardt, 1997, 1998). Performance differentiation is attributed not only to environmental or industry factors but also to distinctive competencies (Selznick, 1957; Snow and Hrebiniak, 1980; Hitt, Ireland, and Palia, 1982; Hitt and Ireland, 1985, 1986) or firm-specific resources (Nelson and Winter, 1982; Wernerfelt, 1984; Dierickx and Cool, 1989; Barney, 1991).

When conversations ensue around such topics as innovation, fast growth, internal venturing, flexibility, entrepreneurial strategy, resource scarcity, new venture top management teams, survival and failure, and organizational transformation (just to name a few), are these topics of concern for entrepreneurship or for strategic management scholars? This is a very difficult question to answer; yet a few seminal articles have been published espousing an intersection of entrepreneurship and strategic management – a place where the two fields overlap and share similar research agendas (Day, 1992; Sandberg, 1992; Hitt and Ireland, 2000).

Prior to this intersection work, however, earlier mainstream strategists referred to the importance of entrepreneurship to the study of strategic management. Schendel and Hofer defined strategic management as "a process that deals with the entrepreneurial work of the organization, with organizational renewal and growth, and more particularly, with developing and utilizing the strategy which is to guide the organization's operations" (1979: 11). They also suggested that entrepreneurship is the foundation from which strategy and functional integration emanates. Consider the following from Schendel and Hofer:

> The "key idea," that product of the entrepreneurial mind, is the central concept that is to be noted. Without it, there is no business, and indeed this same argument can easily be generalized to any type of purposive organization. This entrepreneurial choice is at the heart of the concept of strategy, and it is good strategy that insures the formation, renewal, and survival of the total enterprise, that in turn leads to an integration of the functional areas of the business and not the other way around. (1979: 6)

Later, Schendel (1990), in his editor's introduction to the special corporate entrepreneurship issue of the *Strategic Management Journal,* placed great emphasis on the topic of entrepreneurship and admitted that some would argue that entrepreneurship is at the very heart of strategic management. He wrote that entrepreneurial issues go beyond startup activities and entrepreneurs; questions addressing innovation, change, and the rebirth of existing firms are paramount to organizational strategy regardless of size or age. A few years later, Schendel (1995), writing on "Strategy Futures," discussed two components of strategy – the entrepreneurial component and the integrative component. The entrepreneurial component tells how the organization will be positioned in a competitive environment (scope and resource allocation). The integrative component is concerned with managing what entrepreneurship creates (policy, cultural norms, and administrative structure). Accordingly, the interplay of the entrepreneurial and integrative strategy components determines how businesses achieve competitive advantage (Slater and Olson, 2000). In this sense, entrepreneurship is seen simply as a subordinate component of strategic management – not necessarily intersecting.

Stevenson and Jarillo (1990) and Day (1992) were the first to address the "intersection" of entrepreneurship and strategic management, and each author used the term "entrepreneurial management" as the intersection of the fields. Specifically, Day defined entrepreneurial management as "all management actions and decisions concerning the creation of new businesses and the related development of innovations from new or reconfigured resources, regardless of the scope of such development efforts (i.e., from startups to large, established firms)" (1992: 117). She provides an extensive framework outlining specific topic areas in strategic management and general management that have relevance to entrepreneurship such as competitive strategy (founding conditions, first mover advantages, entry strategies), corporate strategy (theory of growth and growth stages, diversification, modes of venturing, strategic planning (role of uncertainty and risk, risk–return relationships, diffusion of innovations), strategic implementation (networks, structure, organizational designs, innovation processes), and general management (leadership, top management teams, succession planning).

Sandberg (1992) argued that the "locus of contact" between the fields of entrepreneurship and strategic management is corporate entrepreneurship. Each field can learn from the other, and there are specific areas in strategic management research and theory that can relate to several topics in entrepreneurship (implying strategic entrepreneurship). These include new business creation, innovation, opportunity seeking, and risk assumption. Most recently, Hitt and Ireland (2000) set forth six main content domains that lie at the intersection of entrepreneurship and strategic management (innovation, organizational networks, internationalization, organizational learning, top management teams and governance, and growth, flexibility, and change) and view entrepreneurship's contribution to strategic management in terms of fast-growth firms, arguing that the growth of the firm can be the difference between failure and long-term survival.

The above-mentioned articles offer great insight into the various topic areas that intersect both fields; however, there has been a recent shift from shared research topic areas to entrepreneurship as a "way of thinking." McGrath and MacMillan discuss strategy as discovery and the need for an entrepreneurial mindset – "a way of thinking about your business that captures the benefits of uncertainty" (2000: 1). Meyer and Heppard (2000) expand upon Prahalad and Bettis' work (1986; Bettis and Prahalad, 1995) proffering the concept of an entrepreneurial dominant logic that is pervasive throughout an organization and is the basis for entrepreneurial strategy. According to Meyer and Heppard, an entrepreneurial dominant logic "leads a firm and its members to constantly search and filter information for new product ideas and process innovations that will lead to greater profitability" (2000: 2).

In summary, whether one argues that strategic management subsumes entrepreneurship or that entrepreneurship subsumes strategic management, it is difficult to deny the continuing influence of strategic management on the field of entrepreneurship and the apparent intersection that exists. The issue at hand now becomes a question of integration. Given the logic behind the writings on the intersection of the fields and the changing competitive landscape under study, it would seem the integration (or unification) of the fields might be inevitable. In the section that follows we discuss the key factors driving the possible integration of the fields.

Driving Forces of Integration

As mentioned in the introduction of this chapter, integration by definition means to unite with something else or to blend into a whole. Separate from intersection, integration implies that entrepreneurship and strategic management are not separate fields – the fields share one domain. The strategic management literature indirectly considers entrepreneurship as a subset of strategy, and the historical evolution of the field, specifically that the Entrepreneurship Division of the Academy of Management was a spin-off from the Business Policy and Strategy Division, contributes to this "subset" image. We believe the most recent push for integration is being driven by three forces.

1 Researchers in both fields are using firm performance as the primary dependent variable.
2 The new economy and increasing dynamic nature of the competitive environment demand entrepreneurial qualities such as flexibility and real-time responsiveness.
3 Shifting paradigms in strategic management highlight the dynamic nature of organizations and the need for *all* organizations to be "entrepreneurial."

Firm performance as the dependent variable

Strategic management adopted firm performance as the primary dependent variable of the field (Summer et al., 1990). This performance orientation is at the heart of virtually all strategic management research whether it be collaborative strategy (Hamel et al., 1989), strategies for hostile environments (Hall, 1980), turnaround strategies (Hofer, 1980; Hambrick and Schecter, 1983), strategies for declining industries (Harrigan, 1981), strategies for stagnant industries (Hammermesh and Silk, 1979), new venture strategies (McDougall and Robinson, 1990; Carter et al., 1994), deliberate, or emergent strategies (Mintzberg and Waters, 1985). Clearly, firm-level performance remains the central theme behind the research of strategic management scholars. Venkataraman and Ramanujam point out the importance of performance to strategy researchers:

> For the strategy researcher, the option to move away from defining (and measuring) performance or effectiveness is not a viable one. This is because performance improvement is at the heart of strategic management. (1986: 801)

Our content analysis of the *Strategic Management Journal* (*SMJ*) from its inception in 1980 through June of 2000 revealed that of the 1,010 total editorial notes, refereed articles, and research notes, 86 percent had performance as a fundamental theme. Clearly strategic management focuses on the performance-oriented process by which businesses achieve competitive advantage.

Firm performance is similarly important for entrepreneurship. Entrepreneurship journals (such as *Journal of Business Venturing*, *Entrepreneurship Theory and Practice*, and

Journal of Small Business Management) have devoted significant attention to perform-ance-based research. Venkataraman, addressing his review of entrepreneurship jour-nals and the "disproportionate preoccupation" with performance, argues "the discriminating issues in these studies, or what purportedly makes them qualify as en-trepreneurship research, is that the questions are raised at the level of start-ups, small businesses, or corporate venture initiatives" (1994: 3).

Venkataraman (1997), positing an opportunity and exploitation focus, has called for wealth creation as the dependent variable in entrepreneurship research, and asserts firm performance is not a sufficient benchmark. Wealth creation from a macro-eco-nomic view aligns well with the potential impact of entrepreneurship on an economy. However, it does not seem appropriate to dismiss measuring firm performance in en-trepreneurship research because firm performance (organizational wealth) is an ante-cedent of societal wealth. By the same token, positive firm performance results in shareholder wealth that can also be considered a precursor of societal wealth. Regard-less of the position taken on the dependent variable issue in the entrepreneurship field, it is evident that the performance of entrepreneurial endeavors (i.e., new ventures and their growth) should be studied. It is to the benefit of any society that new businesses not only survive, but also thrive (Leibenstein, 1978; Baumol, 1996; Sen, 1999).

Our content analysis of the *Journal of Business Venturing* (*JBV*) and *Strategic Man-agement Journal* (*SMJ*) revealed that the primary dependent variable used in empirical articles is performance, 46 percent (193 of 419 articles) and 83 percent (838 of 1,010 articles) respectively. In addition, strategy played a role in 58 percent of the *JBV* arti-cles. Based on the high percentage of strategy-related *JBV* articles, the influence of its mother discipline, strategic management, is ever present. Although *SMJ*, in their state-ment of editorial policy (1980), lists entrepreneurship as one of 34 desired topic areas for publication, our content analysis revealed that less than 4 percent of the *SMJ* arti-cles, editorials, and research notes have addressed entrepreneurship and these were primarily corporate entrepreneurship articles. The point being that although much of the entrepreneurship research is strategy-based, the reverse is not found in the strate-gic management journals.

The new economy and increasingly dynamic nature of the environment

The boundaries between strategic management and entrepreneurship are becoming blurred due to the new competitive landscape (Bettis and Hitt, 1995) where the abil-ity to manage continuous change and maintain flexibility are necessary for survival. The fundamental structural transitions in a wide variety of industries, brought about by major catalysts such as deregulation, global competition, technological discontinuities, changing customer expectations, the Internet, are imposing new strains on managers around the world. Traditional business models no longer work and nor should they (Ridderståle and Nordström, 2000). Managers, concerned with restoring competitiveness of their firms, are abandoning traditional approaches to strategy; they are searching for new approaches that give guidance in a turbulent environment.

The strategic management literature has been inundated with researchers acknowl-edging the changes in the environment and the complexity of interaction. The litera-ture asserts we are operating in a postindustrial society (Lowendahl and Revang, 1998) where blurring boundaries of control (Hamel and Prahalad, 1996) combined with shifting dominant logics (Prahalad and Bettis, 1986) are forcing organizations to continuously change (Brown and Eisenhardt, 1997) and compete on the edge of structure and time (Brown and Eisenhardt, 1998) to make intense rapid strategic moves in order to generate continuous competitive advantages (D'Aveni, 1994) in the new competitive landscape (Bettis and Hitt, 1995). The difference between large corporations and small new ventures in terms of strategy, structure, processes, and performance are not really as different as one would intuitively believe (Stevenson and Jarillo, 1990). The bottom line is that the small, new venture, once considered the only type of entrepreneurial firm, may be facing the same problems as the large corporation undergoing strategic change, renewal, or transformation. The ultimate destination is the same for both, but they start from different positions (Eisenhardt, Brown, and Neck, 2000).

The convergence of entrepreneurship and strategic management is being driven partly by time and responsiveness – speed of innovation and actions taken in the marketplace. Entrepreneurial ventures are stereotyped as agile and capable of making decisions in real time. These time-compressed decision processes are created to meet the needs of customers, adapt to the environment, and compete in a continuously changing competitive landscape (Bettis and Hitt, 1995; Brown and Eisenhardt, 1998). Large corporations with foresight have a desire to be just as nimble and are recognizing the value of entrepreneurship and the need to have their own type of entrepreneurial organization in order to remain competitive.

Technology is allowing more for less, and more in less time. As a result, the process of information gathering, decision making based on available information, and action based on the decisions made, has been compressed to the point of virtually being "real time" (McKenna, 1997). Managers are now able to gather and use information, learn, innovate, make decisions, deploy resources, and react almost instantaneously. This ability is quickly becoming a necessity in hypercompetitive environments, and soon a requirement for survival (D'Aveni, 1994). Real time demands responsiveness, speed, quick strategic thinking and planning, and the capacity to break down bureaucratic slowness. Organizations must monitor, adapt, react, initiate, and verify based on real-time information exchanges (Brown and Eisenhardt, 1998). Any attempt to predict long-term trends or future consumer demands in rapidly changing markets is often a futile exercise.

The international impact of time and responsiveness cannot be ignored. For example, the concept of real-time management is more likely to be adopted and therefore provide a competitive advantage to those cultures (like the US) that value speed, competitive response, and adaptation. Such cultures are more likely to excel in this new environment. Wall Street rewards speed and consumers have grown to appreciate, and, in some cases, expect speed. First mover strategies, if accompanied with the ability to adapt quickly, will prove valuable in today's marketplace. Note that Deming's (1986) TQM/Keizen concept, so appropriately and effectively adopted and implemented by the Japanese, may no longer be effective in today's dynamic environment because it focuses on perfection (e.g., exhaustive testing before bringing a product to market).

These new mandates in strategic thinking have shifted the strategic management paradigms from essentially static to much more dynamic worldviews. Thus, attempts to change the corporate/bureaucratic mind to an entrepreneurial mindset are a high priority in corporations of all ages and sizes around the world.

Shifting paradigms in strategic management

According to Teece, Pisano, and Shuen (1997), there are three traditional approaches to strategic management – *Competitive Forces* (Porter, 1980, 1985), *Strategic Conflict* (Shapiro, 1989; Camerer, 1991), and the *Resource-Based View* (Wernerfelt, 1984, Dierickx and Cool, 1989; Barney, 1986; Peteraf, 1993). Two additional lenses have recently been introduced to help inform strategic management scholars: *Structured Chaos* (Brown and Eisenhardt, 1998) and *Dynamic Capabilities* (Teece et al., 1997). *Structured Chaos* is a combination of complexity and evolutionary theories, whereas *Dynamic Capabilities* is an extension of the resource-based view that incorporates evolutionary theory. These recent theoretical advancements in strategic management attempt to meet the challenge of operating in today's new business environments, and both are designed to address strategic change and the ability (or lack thereof) to adapt to rapidly shifting environments.

Structured Chaos views strategy as balancing structure and time (Brown and Eisenhardt, 1998). The "edge of structure" demands a minimal organization structure that is conducive for innovation, experimentation, improvisation, and leading change. The "edge of time" is a temporal balancing act where organizations establish a rhythm and internal change becomes standard operating procedure. The Dynamic Capabilities approach emphasizes core competencies that are shaped by firm-specific asset positions and the path-dependent accumulation of knowledge (Teece et al., 1997). Given the business world's current focus on continuous innovation, flexibility, and minimum structure, the implementation of these new perspectives in an entrepreneurship context is timely and appropriate.

We have attempted to illustrate thus far that there are many conversations taking place regarding entrepreneurship, its domain, its legitimacy, its intersection with strategic management, and the possible perceived convergence or integration with strategic management. However, we take the position that the fields are unique and that integration is not necessary or encouraged. There are topics outside of strategic management that are important to the entrepreneurship field (Sandberg, 1992); yet these may be difficult to see given the strong influence of strategic management scholars on this emerging field. If strategy scholars conduct entrepreneurship research and exploration, then the results will be biased by similar paradigms, similar research methods, similar outcome goals, and similar underlying theoretical arguments (Kuhn, 1962).

Entrepreneurship can and should stand on its own intellectual platform. However, we do not discount but rather encourage the apparent linkages between the fields. Rather than concentrating on the intersection where specific topics are shared by the fields, we feel a more fruitful exercise is to address the bounded space, or a place, where the fields communicate with one another. We call this space, to be discussed in the following section, the Entrepreneurship–Strategic Management Interface.

The Entrepreneurship–Strategic Management Interface (ESMI)

The intersection of entrepreneurship and strategic management is evident and logical, but discussions on shared topics do not necessarily appease the debate over what is entrepreneurship and what is strategic management. We believe it is time to move beyond "intersection" conversations. But, we do not advocate the extreme view of integrating the fields. Although no discipline can effectively function in isolation, we feel that the integration of the fields of strategic management and entrepreneurship will weaken the ability to describe, explain, and predict their respective business phenomena of interest. We do, however, recognize contributions that each field can provide the other. Furthermore, we acknowledge the changing business environments in which organizations compete and strategic management's attempt to create dynamic models to assist firms in this new competitive landscape.

Rather than intersection or integration, we offer an alternative view – that of an interface. Is this just an argument in semantics? We think not. Consider for a moment the following definitions from Webster's Dictionary:

> **Intersection**: The place or area where two or more things intersect; the set of elements common to two sets.
> **Integration**: To form or blend into a whole; to unite with something else.
> **Interface**: A surface forming a common boundary of two bodies, spaces, or phases; the place at which independent systems meet and act on or communicate with each other.

The Entrepreneurship–Strategic Management Interface (ESMI) establishes boundaries for the fields working together. Entrepreneurship is ultimately about creation and strategic management is predominantly about the process to achieve above-average performance via competitive advantage. It would be illogical to look at creation without looking at the outcome of such creation whether this is wealth creation, job creation, profitability, sales growth, or other similar outcome proposed by Morris (1998). Regardless, all of these "outcomes" are performance measures. So, rather than continuously thrashing out what field should research which topics (intersection), use what dependent variable and at what level of analysis, let us move to an interface view that illustrates our common boundaries. Figure 2.2 graphically depicts our view of the Entrepreneurship–Strategic Management Interface (ESMI).

Figure 2.2 indicates that entrepreneurship and strategic management do not intersect. Rather, the size of the firm under study (small/large) and the research focus (creation/performance) creates the spaces in which the fields communicate – the interface. Large corporations benefit from entrepreneurship (A) (e.g., corporate entrepreneurship) and large corporations obviously benefit from strategic management (C) (e.g., corporate performance and shareholder wealth); small and medium-sized enterprises (SMEs) benefit from entrepreneurship (B) (e.g., new venture creation), and new ventures and SMEs can certainly benefit from strategic management (D) (e.g., growth and performance). This line of thinking aligns well with those that believe entrepreneurship should be embraced and encouraged by all organizations

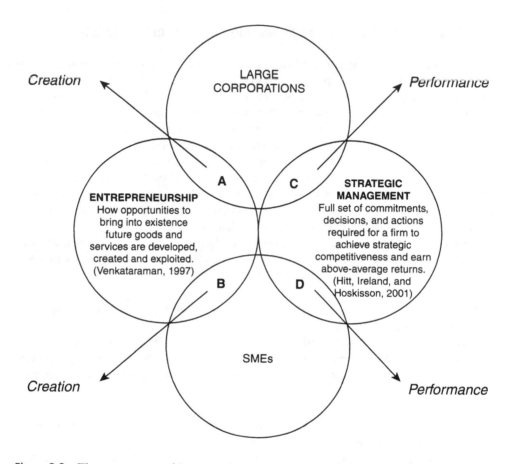

Figure 2.2   The entrepreneurship–strategic management interface

(Brown and Eisenhardt, 1998; Meyer and Heppard, 2000; McGrath and MacMillan, 2000).

The strategic management literature seems to lack research in the "D" space which, as indicated earlier in the chapter, is where the greatest economic impact is found in terms of job creation (Birch, 1987). Given the evolution of both fields, the size difference is a valid issue. Early views of entrepreneurship acknowledged only the new firm and small business. Likewise, the strategic management focus was on the large, multidivisional organization. Because strategic management scholars historically studied large established firms, new or emerging enterprises were virtually ignored in the mainstream strategy literature. With the exception of corporate entrepreneurship studies (e.g., Burgelman, 1983; Kuratko, Montagno, and Hornsby, 1990; Garud and Van de Ven, 1992; Zahra, 1996; Shrader and Simon, 1997), entrepreneurial firm performance has primarily been the domain of the entrepreneurship field.

Our content analysis found that of the 952 empirical *SMJ* articles that make some reference to firm size (even if only the type of firms sampled), 97 percent focused on large firms (as defined by greater than 500 employees – the Small Business Administration standard) while only 3 percent were SMEs. In fact, of the firms empirically studied in the *SMJ* articles, over 90 percent were of the *Fortune* 500 type. We further found that of the 349 empirical *JBV* articles, only 33 percent focused on large firms with 67 percent addressing small businesses and SMEs. Correcting for only those firms with management issues, that is firms with employees, the total number of US firms is approximately 5 million (Aldrich, 1999). However, over 95 percent of all empirical strategic management research represents less than 1 percent of the total population (Dennis, 1997; Aldrich, 1999). Strategy researchers are virtually ignoring the performance aspects of small businesses, and inclusive in that set are new ventures. There are roughly 850,000 US de novo startup firms each year (Dennis, 1997). These new ventures create almost all new net jobs (Birch, 1987; Kirchhoff and Phillips, 1988) and a better understanding of their performance is needed. Strategic management's preoccupation with the largest corporations leaves over 99 percent of America's firms unexamined in the context of success or failure (Aldrich, 1999; Dennis, 1997). We encourage more strategic management scholars to recognize the necessity and importance of studying these types of firms.

The ESMI (Figure 2.2) is where we believe creation connects with performance. If we accept Venkataraman's (1997) definition of entrepreneurship as the development, creation, and exploitation of future goods and services and the Hitt et al. (2001) definition of strategic management as a process of commitment, decision making, and action to achieve competitive advantage, then it becomes more convincing that the interface is a creation–performance connection. We acknowledge that the "exploitation" aspect of Venkataraman's definition seems indicative of strategy; however, the difference lies in his emphasis on "future" goods and services. How do you exploit something that does not exist in the present? If a product or service will not be created until some undetermined point in the future, market absence and creation must be explained (Arrow, 1974; Venkataraman, 1997). According to Venkataraman:

> Cognitive conditions, incentives, and creative processing vary among individuals and these differences matter. These variables strongly influence the search for and exploitation of an opportunity, and they also influence the success of the exploitation process. (1997: 124)

The ESMI connects the two fields bounded by four research spaces. As seen on figure 2.2, spaces labeled "A" and "B" represent the creation spaces and spaces labeled "C" and "D" represent the performance side of the interface. "A" can be viewed as corporate entrepreneurship or the creation of internal ventures, innovation in large firms, and new product development in large firms. "B" and "C" are representative of the traditional view of each field. New venture creation fills most of the "B" space while typical strategic management concepts (e.g., process, content, diversification, alliances, mergers, TMTs) occupy the "C" space. As previously indicated, the "D" space is the most under-researched aspect of the interface. This area is most concerned with the strategy and resulting performance of SMEs, whereas the "C" space is most concerned with large corporate performance.

We are not suggesting specific topic areas to study; however, our content analysis of *SMJ* and *JBV* does partly focus on research topics to illustrate that the four spaces of

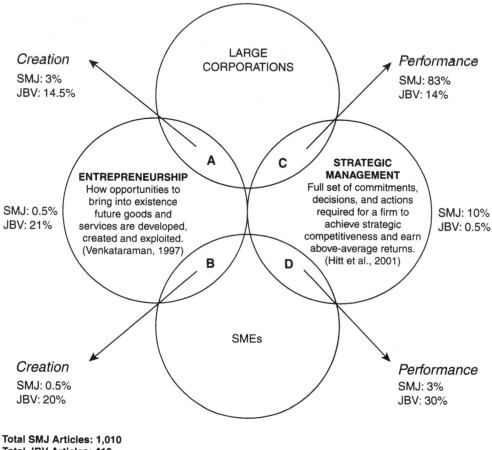

Creation
SMJ: 3%
JBV: 14.5%

Performance
SMJ: 83%
JBV: 14%

LARGE CORPORATIONS

A   **C**

ENTREPRENEURSHIP
How opportunities to bring into existence future goods and services are developed, created and exploited.
(Venkataraman, 1997)

STRATEGIC MANAGEMENT
Full set of commitments, decisions, and actions required for a firm to achieve strategic competitiveness and earn above-average returns.
(Hitt et al., 2001)

SMJ: 0.5%
JBV: 21%

SMJ: 10%
JBV: 0.5%

B   **D**

SMEs

Creation
SMJ: 0.5%
JBV: 20%

Performance
SMJ: 3%
JBV: 30%

Total SMJ Articles: 1,010
Total JBV Articles: 419

Figure 2.3   The entrepreneurship–strategic management interface: content analysis results

the ESMI do exist. Figure 2.3 and table 2.2 report our findings. Our results indicate that only 3.5 percent (A + B) of articles published in *SMJ* had some type of entrepreneurship interface component. Conversely, 44 percent (C + D) of articles published in *JBV* had some type of strategic management interface component. Additionally, only 3.5 percent of *SMJ* articles used small or emerging business as the size of firm studied, but 50 percent of the *JBV* articles as expected had researched small or emerging firms.

The ESMI is somewhat imbalanced when looking at the top journal in each field. It is apparent that entrepreneurship is particularly accepting of strategic management research but the reverse is not true. A reason for this may be due to the so-called lack of rigor and theory in entrepreneurship that opens the door for other fields to question the legitimacy, acceptability, and contribution of entrepreneurship research (Schendel, 1990). It is evident that each field can benefit the other, and given the maturity of the strategic management field, strategy scholars interfacing with entrepre-

Table 2.2 Content analysis results

Designation from figures 2.2 and 2.3	Interface[a]	Content analysis topics	% of articles published in SMJ[b]	% of articles published in JBV[c]
A	ENT × LB	corporate entrepreneurship; innovation in large firms; new product development in large firms	3.0	14.5
B	ENT × SB	new venture creation, new product development in small firms, innovation in small firms, opportunity recognition	0.5	20.0
C	SM × LB	strategy process and content, formulation and implementation, TMTs, diversification, mergers, acquisitions, alliances technology management, global strategy, control and reward systems, goals and objectives, corporate performance	83.0	14.0
D	SM × SB	new venture performance and strategy, small business performance and strategy, growth, small business strategic factors and resources	3.0	30.0
Non-interface				
	ENT (other)	research issues, entrepreneurship education, venture capitalists' decision processes, traits/characteristics of entrepreneurs, definition and domain issues, societal impact and wealth creation	0.5	21.0
	SM (other)	policy, teaching in the field, research issues, definition and domain issues	10.0	0.5

[a] ENT (entrepreneurship); SM (strategic management); LB (large business – 500 + employees); SB (small business and SMEs – 0–499 employees)
[b] A total of 1,010 articles, research notes, and editorials were reviewed from 1980 through July 2000 (vol. 21, No. 7).
[c] A total of 419 articles, research notes, and editorials were reviewed from 1985 through November 2000 (vol. 15, No. 6).

neurship could greatly contribute to the progression and legitimacy of the entrepreneurship field.

Conclusion: the New Mindset

Low and MacMillan (1988) observed that the range of disciplines represented in the entrepreneurship literature includes economics, sociology, anthropology, psychology, history, and finance. Therefore, Low and MacMillan concluded that it would be highly unlikely, given this broad and diverse array of sciences, that the entrepreneurship field would agree on the domain and/or definition of entrepreneurship. Perhaps the best we can do is to establish the space where the entrepreneurship and strategic management fields can connect, act on, or communicate with each other. After all, that is what those reading this book are most interested in. We have attempted to offer an alternative view, the *Entrepreneurship–Strategic Management Interface* (ESMI) that connects the two unique fields and recognizes the impact each can have on the other. Both creation and performance are essential to the study of organizations, yet this does not imply the need to integrate the fields. Quite the contrary; we believe each field has a unique history with "living" domains that are constantly subject to change given the nature of the changing competitive landscape. Although strategic management scholars may benefit by subsuming entrepreneurship, particularly in view of its popularity among business school students, practitioners, and popular press, entrepreneurship scholars, in their quest for legitimacy, would be ill served by integration. The interface presented in this chapter is a sufficient medium to move beyond intersection (shared topics), avoid integration (one field), while accepting the benefit of having a common boundary (interface) where research is concerned with both creation and performance. This we consider to be the new mindset in entrepreneurship and strategic management research.

Notes

1   Throughout this chapter we refer to a content analysis we conducted of the *Journal of Business Venturing* and the *Strategic Managment Journal*. We recognize that there are many other journals publishing entrepreneurship research (e.g., *Entrepreneurship Theory & Practice, Journal of Small Business Management*, and *Small Business Economics*). Katz (2000) lists 40 refereed journals publishing entrepreneurship research. Other reviews of journals examining published entrepreneurship research (e.g., Busenitz et al., 2000; Shane, 1997; MacMillan, 1994) have content analyzed numerous entrepreneurship journals and general management journals (*Academy of Management Journal, Academy of Management Review, Organization Science, Journal of Management, Administrative Science Quarterly*, and *Management Science*). Because this chapter focuses on the interface of entrepreneurship and strategic management research in hopes of persuading those in each field that integration is unnecessary, we chose the top discipline-specific journal in each field to build our interface argument. Given the quality reputation of each journal, the editors have a significant impact on establishing current and future directions of their respective field. A total of 1,010 *SMJ* articles, research notes, and editorials were reviewed from 1980 (the inception of the

journal through July 2000 (vol. 21, issue 7). A total of 419 *JBV* articles, research notes, and editorials were reviewed from 1985 (the inception of the journal) through November 2000 (vol. 15, issues 5–6). The content analysis was conducted by the third author with assistance from the second author to ensure interrater reliability. Titles and abstracts were reviewed to establish topic areas, and empirical articles were reviewed in greater detail to determine the types of firms (size) used in the study.

References

Acs, Z. J. 1999. *Are small firms important? Their role and impact.* Boston: Kluwer Academic Publishers.

Aldrich, H. E. 1990. Using an ecological perspective to study organization founding rates. *Entrepreneurship Theory and Practice*, 14(3): 7–24.

Aldrich, H. E. 1999. *Organizations evolving.* London: Sage.

Aldrich, H. E. and Wiedenmeyer, G. 1993. From traits to rates: An ecological perspective on organizational foundings. *Advances in Entrepreneurship, Firm Emergence, and Growth*, 1: 145–95.

Aldrich, H. E. and Baker, T. 1997. Blinded by the cites? Has there been progress in entrepreneurship research?. In D. L. Sexton and R. W. Smilor (eds), *Entrepreneurship 2000*, Chicago: Upstart Publishing, 377–400.

Arrow, K. J. 1974. Limited knowledge and economic analysis. *American Economic Review*, 64(1): 1–10.

Arzeni, S. 1998. Entrepreneurship and job creation. *The OECD Observer*, 209: 18–20.

Bain, J. S. 1956. *Barriers to new competition.* Cambridge, MA: Harvard University Press.

Barney, J. B. 1986. Strategic factor markets: Expectations, luck, and business strategy. *Management Science*, 32(10): 1231–41.

Barney, J. B. 1991. Firm resources and sustained competitive advantage. *Journal of Management*, 17: 99–120.

Barringer, B. R. and Bluedorn, A. C. 1999. The relationship between corporate entrepreneurship and strategic management. *Strategic Management Journal*, 20(5): 421–44.

Baumol, W. J. 1986. Entrepreneurship and a century of growth. *Journal of Business Venturing*, 1: 141–45.

Baumol, W. J. 1993. *Entrepreneurship, management, and the structure of payoffs.* Cambridge, MA: MIT Press.

Baumol, W. J. 1996. Entrepreneurship: Productive, unproductive, and destructive. *Journal of Business Venturing*, 11(1): 3–22.

Bettis, R. A. and Hitt, M. A. 1995. The new competitive landscape. *Strategic Management Journal*, 16 (special issue): 7–19.

Bettis, R. A. and Prahalad, C. K. 1995. The dominant logic: Retrospective and extension. *Strategic Management Journal*, 16: 5–14.

Birch, D. L. 1979. *The job generation process.* Cambridge: MIT Program on Neighborhood and Regional Change.

Birch, D. L. 1987. *Job creation in America: How our smallest companies put the most people to work.* New York: Free Press.

Block, Z. and MacMillan, I. 1993. *Corporate venturing: Creating new business within the firm.* Cambridge, MA: Harvard Business School Press.

Bowman, E. H. and Hurry, D. 1993. Strategy through the options lens: An integrated view of resource investments and the incremental-choice processes. *Academy of Management Review*, 18(4): 760–82.

Brown, S. L. and Eisenhardt, K. M. 1997. The art of continuous change: Linking complexity theory and time-paced evolution in relentlessly shifting organizations. *Administrative Science Quarterly*, 42(1): 1–34.

Brown, S. L. and Eisenhardt, K. M. 1998. *Competing on the edge: Strategy as structured chaos.* Boston: Harvard Business School Press.

Bull, I. and Willard, G. E. 1993. Towards a theory of entrepreneurship. *Journal of Business Venturing*, 8(3): 183–96.

Burgelman, R. A. 1983. A process model of internal corporate venturing in the diversified major firm. *Administrative Science Quarterly*, 28(2): 223–44

Busenitz, L. W., and Barney, J. B. 1997. Differences between entrepreneurs and managers in large organizations: Biases and heuristics in strategic decision-making. *Journal of Business Venturing*, 12(1): 9–30.

Busenitz, L., West, P., Shepherd, D., Zacharakis, A., Nelson, T., and Chandler, G. 2000. Entrepreneurship in emergence: Fourteen years of entrepreneurship research in management journals. Working paper for the Task Force on Doctoral Education in Entrepreneurship, Academy of Management, Entrepreneurship Division.

Bygrave, W. D. 1989. The entrepreneurship paradigm (II): Chaos and catastrophes among quantum jumps. *Entrepreneurship Theory and Practice*, 14(2): 7–30.

Bygrave, W. D. and Hofer, C. W. 1991. Theorizing about entrepreneurship. *Entrepreneurship Theory and Practice*, 16(2): 13–22.

Camerer, C. F. 1991. Does strategy research need game theory? *Strategic Management Journal*, 12 (special issue): 137–52.

Carter, N. M., Stearns, T. M., Reynolds, P. D., and Miller, B. A. 1994. New venture strategies: Theory development with an empirical basis. *Strategic Management Journal*, 15: 537–54.

Caves, R. 1964. *American industry: Structure, conduct, performance.* Foundations of Modern Economies Series, Englewood Cliffs, NJ: Prentice Hall.

Chandler, G. N. and Hanks, S. H. 1994. Market attractiveness, resource-based capabilities, venture strategies, and venture performance. *Journal of Business Venturing*, 9(4): 331–49.

Churchill, N. C. and Lewis, V. 1983. The five stages of small business growth. *Harvard Business Review*, 61(3): 30–50.

Collins, O. F. and Moore, D. G. 1970. *The organization makers.* New York: Appleton-Century-Crofts.

Cooper, A. C. 1993. Challenges in predicting new firm performance. *Journal of Business Venturing*, 8(3): 241–53.

Cooper, A. C. and Daily, C. M. 1997. Entrepreneurial teams. In D. L. Sexton and R. W. Smilor (eds), *Entrepreneurship 2000.* Chicago: Upstart Publishing 127–50.

Covin, J. G. and Slevin, D. P. 1997. High growth transitions: Theoretical perspectives. In D. L. Sexton and R. W. Smilor (eds), *Entrepreneurship 2000.* Chicago: Upstart Publishing, 99–126.

D'Aveni, R. 1994. *Hypercompetition: Managing the dynamics of strategic maneuvering.* New York: Free Press.

Day, D. L. 1992. Research linkages between entrepreneurship and strategic management. In D. L. Sexton and J. D. Kasarda (eds), *The State of the Art of Entrepreneurship.* Boston: PWS-Kent, 117–63.

Deming, W. E. 1986. *Out of crisis.* Cambridge, MA: MIT Press.

Dennis, W. 1997. More than you think: an inclusive estimate of business entries. *Journal of Business Venturing*, 12: 175–96.

Dierickx, I. and Cool, K., 1989. Asset stock accumulation and sustainability of competitive advantage. *Management Science*, 35(12): 1504–14.

Drucker, P. 1985. *Innovation and entrepreneurship.* New York: Harper and Row.

Eisenhardt, K. M., Brown, S., and Neck, H. M. 2000. Competing on the entrepreneurial edge. In G. D. Meyer and K. Heppard (eds), *Entrepreneurial strategies*. Thousand Oaks, CA: Sage Publications, 49–62.

Eisenhardt, K. M. and Schoonhoven, C. B. 1990. Organizational growth: Linking founding team, strategy, environment and growth among US semiconductor firms, 1978–1988. *Administrative Science Quarterly*, 35(3): 504–29.

Ensley, M. D., Carland, J. C., Carland, J. W., and Banks, M. 1999. Exploring the existence of entrepreneurial teams. *International Journal of Management*, 16(2): 276–86.

Gaglio, C. M. 1997. Opportunity identification: Review, critique and suggested research directions. In J. A. Katz (ed.), *Advances in entrepreneurship, firm emergence, and growth*. Greenwich, CT: JAI Press, 139–202.

Gartner, W. B. 1988. Who is an entrepreneur? Is the wrong question. *American Journal of Small Business*, 12(4): 11–32.

Gartner, W. B. 2000. I am nothing without you: The phenomenon of entrepreneurship as a disciplinary problem. Working paper for the Task Force on Doctoral Education in Entrepreneurship, Academy of Management, Entrepreneurship Division.

Garud, R. and Van de Ven, A. 1992. An empirical evaluation of the internal corporate venturing process. *Strategic Management Journal*, 13 (special issue): 93–109.

Guth, W. D. and Ginsberg, A. 1990. Guest editors' introduction: Corporate entrepreneurship. *Strategic Management Journal*, 11(summer): 5–15.

Hall, W. K. 1980. Survival strategies in a hostile environment. *Harvard Business Review*, 50(5): 75–85.

Hambrick, D. C. and Crozier, L. M. 1985. Stumblers and stars in the management of rapid growth. *Journal of Business Venturing*, 1(1): 31–45.

Hambrick, D. C. and Schecter, S. M. 1983. Turnaround strategies for mature industrial-product business units. *Academy of Management Journal*, 26(2): 231–48.

Hamel, G., Doz, Y.L., and Prahalad, C.K. 1989. Collaborate with your competitors – and win. *Harvard Business Review*. 58(1): 133–39.

Hamel, G. and Prahalad, C. K. 1996. Competing in the new economy: Managing out of bounds. *Strategic Management Journal*, 17: 237–42.

Hammermesh, R. G. and Silk, S.B. 1979. How to compete in stagnant industries. *Harvard Business Review*, 57(5): 161–68.

Harrigan, K. R. 1981. *Strategies for declining businesses*. Lexington, MA: Heath.

Harrison, R. T. and Leitch, C. M. 1996. Discipline emergence in entrepreneurship: Accumulative fragmentalism or paradigmatic science. *Entrepreneurship, Innovation, and Change*, 5(2): 65–83.

Hayek, F. A. 1945. The use of knowledge in society. *American Economic Review*, 35(4), 519–30.

Herron, L. and Sapienza, H. 1992. The entrepreneur and the initiation of new venture launch activities. *Entrepreneurship Theory and Practice*, 17(1): 49–55.

Hitt, M. A. and Ireland, R. D. 1985. Corporate distinctive competence, strategy, industry, and performance. *Strategic Management Journal*, 6: 273–93.

Hitt, M. A. and Ireland, R. D. 1986. Relationships among corporate level distinctive competencies, diversification strategy, corporate structure and performance. *Journal of Management Studies*, 23: 401–16.

Hitt, M. A. and Ireland, R. D. 2000. The intersection of entrepreneurship and strategic management research. In D. L. Sexton and H. Landstrom (eds), *Handbook of entrepreneurship*. Oxford: Blackwell, 45–63.

Hitt, M. A., Ireland, R. D., and Hoskisson, R. E. 2001. *Strategic management: Competitiveness and globalization* (4th edn). Cincinnati, OH: South-Western College Publishing.

Hitt, M. A., Ireland, R. D., and Palia, K. A. 1982. Industrial firms' grand strategy and functional importance: Moderating effects of technology and uncertainty. *Academy of Management Journal*, 25(2): 265–98.

Hofer, C. W. 1980. Turnaround strategies. *Journal of Business Strategy*, 1(1): 19–31.

Hornaday, J. and Aboud, J. 1971. Characteristics of successful entrepreneurs. *Personnel Psychology*, 23: 47–54.

Hull, D. L., Bosley, J. J., and Udell, G. G. 1980. Reviewing the heffalump: Identifying potential entrepreneurs by personality characteristics. *Journal of Small Business Management*, 18: 19–24.

Kaish, S. and Gilad, B. 1991. Characteristics of opportunities search of entrepreneurs versus executives: Sources, interests, general alertness. *Journal of Business Venturing*, 6(1): 45–61.

Katz, J. 2000. eWeb. www.slu.edu/eweb/

Kazanjian, R. K. 1988. Relation of dominant problems to stages of growth in technology-based new ventures. *Academy of Management Journal*, 31(2): 257–79.

Kirchoff, B. A. 1991. Entrepreneurship's contribution to economics. *Entrepreneurship Theory and Practice*, 16(2): 93–112.

Kirchoff, B. A. and Phillips, B. D. 1987. Examining entrepreneurship's role in economic growth. *Frontiers of Entrepreneurship Research*: 57–71.

Kirchoff, B. A. and Phillips, B. D. 1988. The effect of firm formation and growth on job creation in the United States. *Journal of Business Venturing*, 3(4): 261–72.

Kirzner, I. 1973. *Competition and entrepreneurship*. Chicago: University of Chicago Press.

Kirzner, I. 1979. *Perception, opportunity, and profit*. Chicago: University of Chicago Press.

Kirzner, I. 1997. Entrepreneurial discovery and the competitive market process: An Austrian approach. *Journal of Economic Literature*, 35(1): 60–85.

Knight, F. 1921. *Risk, uncertainty and profit*. New York: Augustus Kelley.

Kuhn, T. S. 1962. *The structure of scientific revolutions*. Chicago: University of Chicago Press.

Kuratko, D. F., Montagno, R. V., and Hornsby, J. S. 1990. Developing an entrepreneurial assessment instrument for an effective corporate entrepreneurial environment. *Strategic Management Journal*, 11(summer): 49–58.

Leibenstein, H. 1978. *General X-efficiency theory and economic development*. New York: Oxford University Press.

Low, M. B. and MacMillan, I. C. 1988. Entrepreneurship: Past research and future challenges. *Journal of Management*, 14(2): 139–61.

Lowendahl, B., and Revang, O. 1998. Challenges to existing strategy theory in a postindustrial society. *Strategic Management Journal*, 19: 755–73.

MacMillan, I. C. 1994. The emerging forum for business policy scholars. *Journal of Business Venturing*, 9: 85–9.

McClelland, D. 1961. *The achieving society*. Princeton, NJ: Van Nostrand.

McDougall, P. P., Covin, J. G., Robinson, R. B., Jr., and Herron, L. 1994. The effects of industry growth and strategic breadth on new venture performance and strategy content. *Strategic Management Journal*, 15(7): 537–54.

McDougall, P. and Robinson, R. 1990. New venture strategies: An empirical investigation of eight 'archetypes' of competitive strategy for new entry. *Strategic Management Journal*, 11(6): 447–67.

McGrath, R. G. and MacMillan, I. 2000. *The entrepreneurial mindset: Strategies for continuously creating opportunity in an age of uncertainty*. Boston: Harvard Business School Press.

McKenna, R. 1997. *Real time: Preparing for the age of the never satisfied customer*. Cambridge, MA: Harvard Business School Press.

Meyer, G. D. and Heppard, K. A. 2000. Entrepreneurial strategies: The dominant logic of entrepreneurship. In G. D. Meyer and K. A. Heppard (eds), *Entrepreneurship as strategy:*

Competing on the entrepreneurial edge, Thousand Oaks, CA: Sage Publications, 1–22.

Meyer, G. D., Venkataraman, S., and Gartner, W. 1999. Task force on doctoral education in entrepreneurship. Entrepreneurship Division of the Academy of Management.

Mintzberg, H. and Waters, J. A. 1985. Of strategies, deliberate and emergent. *Strategic Management Journal*, 6(3): 257–72.

Morris, M. H. 1998. *Entrepreneurial intensity: Sustainable advantages for individuals, organizations, and societies.* Westport, CT: Quorum.

Morris, M. H. and Sexton, D. L. 1996. The concept of entrepreneurial intensity: Implications for company performance. *Journal of Business Research*, 36: 5–13.

Nelson, R. R. and Winter, S. G. 1982. *An evolutionary theory of economic change.* Cambridge, MA: Harvard University Press.

Penrose, E. T. 1959. *The theory of the growth of the firm.* New York: John Wiley.

Peteraf, M. A. 1993. The cornerstones of competitive advantage: A resource-based view. *Strategic Management Journal*, 14(3): 179–91.

Phillips, B. D. and Dennis, W. J., Jr. 1997. Databases for small business analysis. In D. L. Sexton and R. W. Smilor (eds), *Entrepreneurship 2000.* Chicago: Upstart Publishing, 341–60.

Porter, M. E. 1980. *Competitive strategy: Techniques for analyzing industries and competitors.* New York: Free Press.

Porter, M. E. 1985. *Competitive advantage: Creating and sustaining superior performance.* New York: Free Press.

Prahalad, C. K. and Bettis, R. A. 1986. The dominant logic: A new linkage between diversity and performance. *Strategic Management Journal*, 7: 485–501.

Reynolds, P. D. 1992. Predicting new-firm births: Interactions of organizational and human populations. In D. L. Sexton and J. D. Kasarda (eds), *The state of the art of entrepreneurship.* Boston: PWS-Kent, 268–97.

Reynolds, P. D., Hay, M., and Camp, S. M. 1999. *Global entrepreneurship monitor: 1999 executive report.* Kauffman Center for Entrepreneurial Leadership, Ewing Marion Kauffman Foundation.

Ridderstråle, J. and Nordström, K. 2000. *Funky business: Talent makes capital. Financial Times/* Prentice-Hall Publishing.

Rumelt, R. P. 1987. Theory, strategy, and entrepreneurship. In D. J. Teece (ed.), *The competitive challenge.* Cambridge, MA: Ballinger, 137–58.

Rumelt, R. P., Schendel, D. E., and Teece, D. J. 1995. *Fundamental issues in strategy.* Cambridge, MA: Harvard Business School Press.

Sanchez, R. 1993. Strategic flexibility, firm organization, and managerial work in dynamic markets: A strategic options perspective. In P. Shrivastava, A. Huff and J. Dutton (eds), *Advances in strategic management*, vol. 9. Greenwich, CT: JAI Press, 251–91.

Sandberg, W. R. 1992. Strategic management's potential contributions to a theory of entrepreneurship. *Entrepreneurship Theory and Practice*, 16(3): 73–90.

Schendel, D. E. 1990. Introduction to the special issue on corporate entrepreneurship. *Strategic Management Journal*, 11(summer): 1–3.

Schendel, D. E. 1995. Strategy futures: What's left to worry about? *Advances in Strategic Management*, 11B: 143–88.

Schendel, D. E. and Hofer, C. W. 1979. *Strategic management: A new view of business policy and planning.* Boston: Little, Brown, and Company.

Schumpeter, J. 1934. *Theory of economic development.* Cambridge, MA: Harvard University Press.

Schumpeter, J. 1942. *Capitalism, socialism and democracy.* New York: Harper and Row.

Selznick, P. 1957. *Leadership in administration.* New York: Harper & Row.

Sen, A. 1999. *Development as freedom.* New York: Alfred Knopf Publishers.

Sexton, D. L. and Smilor, R. W. 1997. *Entrepreneurship 2000.* Chicago: Upstart Publishing, 401–8.

Shane, S. A. 1997. Who is publishing entrepreneurship research? *Journal of Management*, 23: 83–95.

Shane, S. and Venkataraman, S. 2000. The promise of entrepreneurship as a field of research. *Academy of Management Review*, 25(1): 217–26.

Shapiro, C. 1989. The theory of business strategy. *Rand Journal of Economics*, 20(1): 125–37.

Sharma, P. and Chrisman, J. J. 1999. Toward a reconciliation of the definitional issues in the field of corporate entrepreneurship. *Entrepreneurship Theory and Practice*, 23(3): 11–28.

Shrader, R. C. and Simon, M. 1997. Corporate versus independent new ventures: Resource, strategy, and performance differences. *Journal of Business Venturing*, 12(1): 47–66.

Slater, S. F. and Olson, E. M. 2000. Strategy type and performance. *Strategic Management Journal*, 21: 813–29.

Slevin, D. P. and Covin, J. G. 1992. Creating and maintaining high-performance teams. In D. L. Sexton and J. D. Kasarda (eds), *The state of the art of entrepreneurship*. Boston: PWS-Kent, 358–86,

Snow, C. C. and Hrebiniak, L. G. 1980. Strategy, distinctive competence, and organizational performance. *Administrative Science Quarterly*, 25(2): 317–36.

Stevenson, H. and Jarillo, J. C. 1990. A paradigm of entrepreneurship: Entrepreneurial management. *Strategic Management Journal*, 11(summer): 17–27.

Stevenson, H., Roberts, M., and Grousback, H. 1985. *New business ventures &the entrepreneur*. Homewood, IL: Irwin.

Summer, C. E., Bettis, R. A., Duhaime, I. H., Grant, J. H., Hambrick, D. C., Snow, C. C., and Zeithaml, C. P. 1990. Doctoral education in the field of business policy and strategy. *Journal of Management*, 16(2): 361–98.

Teece, D. J., Pisano, G., and Shuen, A. 1997. Dynamic capabilities and strategic management. *Strategic Management Journal*, 18(7): 509–33.

Timmons, J. A. 1997. *New venture creation: Entrepreneurship for the 21st century* (5th edn). Boston: Irwin McGraw-Hill.

Van de Ven, A. H., Polley, D. E., Garud, R., and Venkataraman, S. 1999. *The innovation journey*. New York: Oxford University Press.

Venkataraman, S. 1994. Associate editor's note. *Journal of Business Venturing*, 9(1): 3–6.

Venkataraman, S. 1997. The distinctive domain of entrepreneurship research. *Advances in entrepreneurship, firm emergence and growth*, 3: 119–38.

Venkataraman, N. and Ramanujam, V. 1986. Measurement of business performance in strategy research: A comparison of approaches. *Academy of Management Review*, 11(4): 801–14.

von Mises, L. 1944. *Bureaucracy*. New Haven: Yale University Press, 1944.

Welbourne, T. M., Meyer, G. D., and Neck, H. M. 1998. Getting past the "entrepreneurial growth ceiling": A longitudinal study of IPO firm growth through solution driven strategies. *Frontiers of Entrepreneurship Research*: 426–39.

Wernerfelt, B. 1984. A resource-based view of the firm. *Strategic Management Journal*, 5: 171–80.

Zahra, S. A. 1996. Governance, ownership, and corporate entrepreneurship: The moderating impact of industry technological opportunities. *Academy of Management Journal*, 39(6): 1713–35.

CHAPTER THREE

Discovery and Coordination in Strategic Management and Entrepreneurship

Steven Michael, David Storey, Howard Thomas

Strategic Management at the Mature Phase of the Research Life Cycle

Strategic management, a discipline with its origins in the national and global expansion of business in the twentieth century, is a young discipline as business disciplines go. The founding event is often identified with the publication in 1962 of Chandler's *Strategy and Structure*, describing the growth of large businesses into new product areas and new markets, both across the United States and to a lesser extent abroad, and the organizational changes such expansion required. In this work, Chandler offers the first working definition of strategy: "the determination of the basic long term goals and objectives of an enterprise, and the adoption of courses of action and the allocation of resources necessary for carrying out these goals" (1962: 13). Implied in this and other managerial writing (reviewed more fully below) is that the task of strategy (or strategic management) actually contains two distinct tasks. The first focuses on the coordination of activities within the firm, preventing loss, and supervising the use of resources. The second focuses on identifying opportunity and mobilizing resources to take the firm in new directions with new capabilities, products, or markets.

These two tasks, herein termed "administrative management" and "entrepreneurial management" respectively, for good historical and economic reasons were joined for the duration of the twentieth century. For the twenty-first century, however, a number of trends reviewed below have permitted a much greater separation between the two areas. A close reexamination of the research of strategic management suggests that many of the most significant achievements for both theory and practice have been in administrative management. Also, changes characterized as the new competitive landscape (Bettis and Hitt, 1995) have raised the return to entrepreneurial management. Entrepreneurial management is thus more important than ever but also much less researched than administrative management. At the same time, the successes of administrative management have imposed some (in our view) unnecessary limitations on research in entrepreneurial management. In order to develop the field of entrepreneurial management, in this chapter some (not all) existing research is examined and critiqued in light of the potential limitations created by the history of the field of strategic management. Directions for research are then suggested. Our purpose is to ruminate rather than review, to be thought provoking rather than encyclopedic, conversational and not comprehensive, on the grounds that the field can be most advanced through a creative reexamination of existing work in order to continue good conversation in the field.

Entrepreneurial and Administrative Management

Chandler (1962) is not the only author to recognize the basic distinction between administrative and entrepreneurial management. Peter Drucker, in a work published at a similar time, *Managing for Results* (1964), divides his book into three sections: "Understanding the Business" or administrative management; "Focus on Opportunity" or entrepreneurial management; and "A Program for Performance" or implementation of the two tasks.[1] In the economic literature, in an important but neglected article, Baumol (1968) distinguishes between the entrepreneurial and the managerial (what we term administrative) functions. "We may define the manager to be the individual who oversees the ongoing efficiency of continuing processes" (1968: 64). But Chandler (1994: 327–8) describes at length the two tasks of entrepreneurial and administrative management. We quote this recent restatement of his work:

> To fulfill this role the executives at the new headquarters had to carry out two closely related functions. One was entrepreneurial or value creating, that is, to determine strategies for maintaining and utilizing in the long term the firm's organizational skills, facilities, and capital and to allocate resources – capital and product specific technical and managerial skills – to pursue these strategies. The second was more administrative or loss preventive. It was to monitor the performance of the operating divisions; to check on the use of the resources allocated; and, when necessary, to redefine the product lines of the divisions so as to continue to use the firm's organizational capabilities effectively.
>
> The administrative tasks of monitoring were, of course, intimately related to the entrepreneurial task of strategic planning and resource allocation. Monitoring provided the essential information about changing technology and markets and about the nature and pace of competition in the different businesses. And it permitted a continuing evaluation of the performance of divisional operating managers. Indeed, management development has long been a critical function of the corporate headquarters. Of all the enterprise's resources, product specific and firm specific managerial skills are the most essential to maintaining the capabilities of its existing businesses and to taking the enterprise into new geographical and product markets where such capabilities give it a competitive advantage.

In summary, administrative management primarily focuses on loss prevention and coordination, while entrepreneurial management focuses on value creation, opportunity recognition, or discovering tomorrow's business today.[2]

Separating entrepreneurial from administrative management

Why the marriage of these two unlikely partners? If the tasks are as distinct as the above authors have suggested, why were they joined together in the twentieth century corporation? As quoted above, Chandler argued that these were joined because it was only through monitoring and feedback that the organization learned what to do next. But this conclusion came from observing four large American companies in the process of expanding operations along the value chain and into related products and markets across the US and across the world. The historical conditions that gave rise to this opportunity are probably unique. The technological advances of the time of transportation and communication (railroad, telegraph, telephone) coupled with the development of the vast potential of the American continent is unlikely to be repeated.[3] The current growth of business does not follow the same traditional paths of expansion into related areas and markets. In particular, three trends have made possible separating the skill of coordinating and administrative management from the skill of discovering new businesses, even though they both focus on creating value for the organization: the rise of control without ownership, the employment of information technology for coordination and monitoring in the new economy, and the advances of administrative management itself.

Whether termed strategic alliances, networked organizations, co-option, or other names, control without ownership through inter-firm cooperation is now an important part of business (e.g., Miles et al., 1997; Snow, Miles, and Coleman, 1992). Alliances now account for some 25 percent of corporate sales and income. They are likely to remain so for the foreseeable future. As noted by Dyer and Singh, 1998, they are an important source of resources that can secure competitive advantage. Both the facts and the theories driving this powerful trend are discussed more fully in Zenger and Hesterly, 1997. But information technology must be assigned one of the central roles. The role of information systems as a coordination and control mechanism must be emphasized. Malone and Rockart (1993), document that IT has facilitated the creation of totally new forms of coordination. For example, Wal-Mart, the largest US retailer, has developed a totally electronic value chain with suppliers. The integration of order systems and payment systems has lowered coordination costs, in turn leading to more efficient markets and more outsourcing. It is important to note that much of the IT investment is not transaction specific (Clemons, 1993). In the absence of transaction-specific investment, ownership to achieve control is not necessary (Williamson, 1985). Hence IT has fostered smaller firms and presumably greater outsourcing and networking (Brynjolfsson et al., 1994).

At the same time, monitoring has separated into two different tasks, usually termed financial control and strategic control (Hill 1998; Chandler, 1994; Goold and Campbell, 1987). The widespread use of management information systems has made monitoring of finances (or financial controls) more mechanical and much easier (Nolan, 1999). Financial feedback is available throughout an organization, facilitating loss prevention and administrative management. Networking technologies have also facilitated simple coordination and planning of activities in the value chain (Haeckel and Nolan, 1993). At the same time, the asset base the organization seeks to leverage through entrepreneurial management has shifted. The key assets are no longer plants and personnel, but instead technologies, science, and knowledge assets. Monitoring of those assets (or strategic control) is much more difficult, because the monitor must know as much as the monitored – an impossible task in technology-based industries (Fama and Jensen, 1983). Therefore, alternatives to the traditional loss prevention of administrative management must be found.

It is also worth noting that much of the progress in strategic management has been primarily progress in administrative management in terms of both efficiency and value creation. As this progress has become more diffused into boardrooms and classrooms, its ability to create competitive advantage has also diminished. In a sense, administrative management is a solved problem. Because this claim is more novel than the other factors identified, we discuss this in more detail.

Administrative management as a solved problem

Much of the research in strategic management has focused on administrative management through coordination. At the beginning of the field, a very active stream of research in the field related to strategic planning. Planning was seen as crucial to coordinate the disparate activities within firms, and to fit those activities to the needs of the environment (see, for example, Andrews, 1971; Hax and Majluf, 1984). Certainly for some time the field was perceived as strategic "planning" and not strategic "management." A more sophisticated understanding of the process of making strategy has led planning to be viewed as less important and less central than it once was (Mintzberg, 1987, 1994). Yet planning remains an important tool to achieve coordination in many large organizations – and there is some research demonstrating the positive effects of strategic planning on performance (e.g., Hopkins and Hopkins, 1997). A second advance in this area came with generic strategies, summarizing in a phrase the competitive positioning of the organization (Porter, 1980). This logic was further amplified by explicit prescription of how to "fit" the pieces of the organization with the strategy (Porter, 1985). With these tools, managers and scholars could see how to align internal functions, such as marketing and operations, to the generic strategy. Generic strategies become strategic intent (Hamel and Prahalad, 1994) that facilitate without explicit instructions all aspects of strategy implementation in the organization. For example, a firm engaged in a cost leadership strategy – and explicitly understood to be doing so by all employees – has implicitly offered guidance on everything from which media to use in advertising to which universities at which to recruit. And such strategies, grounded as they were in economics, were "guaranteed" to be profitable – the low cost producer or the differentiator always is. A related contribution came from the resource-based view of the firm (Barney, 1986; Wernerfelt, 1984). The resource-based view gave some framework and tools to identify what "fit with the organization" might mean. It also amplified the conditions under which fit (and with which resources) might lead to superior profitability. A powerful addition to this body of work in strategic management came from the introduction, or importation, of agency theory and transaction cost economics (e.g., Eisenhardt, 1989; Williamson, 1985). The separation of ownership and control creates clear incentive problems for managers, and requires special consideration. Both monitoring of managers coupled with incentives in the form of compensation and stock options reduces loss due to managerial malfeasance. In a more dynamic sense, organizational efficiency is usually improved when individuals in those organizations (or partners in a value chain) adapt themselves, each to the other, through transaction-specific investments. But those investments may create a holdup problem. To give individual economic agents incentive to make these investments, particular governance structures must be in place.

Added to these tools must be the knowledge and learning gained from research about the multibusiness company (Goold and Campbell, 1987; Govindarajan and Gupta, 1985; Hill and Hoskisson, 1987; Hoskisson, Hitt and Hill, 1993). The initial results suggest both what form of diversification is desirable and how to manage across divisions. Most recent efforts here are on the subjects of financial and strategic control. Financial control, with the help of information technology, helps us to manage to generate a satisfactory return on investment in separate divisions, while giving incentive through profit and loss responsibility to particular managers.

Strategic control helps managers to share resources across related lines of business. In summary, taken together these make a powerful set of tools for coordinating a large multibusiness, multinational firm. But much current research published in strategic management now reflects refinements of technique in topics of administrative management rather than developing entrepreneurial management. For example, consider real options theory (e.g., Kogut, 1991; Pindyck, 1990). In effect, research in this area has argued that existing calculations of economic payoff (through, say, net present value) are incorrect, because the option not to invest also has economic value. Adding this tool to the toolkit is powerful and valuable, but it does not change any of the existing static prescriptions of the field. The concept of framing decisions using real options techniques is, at least in part, a simple refinement of the payoff.

As a second example, cognitive science has been applied to the area of resource and strategic groups. Who competes with whom was primarily determined, at least according to the research community, by the pattern of sunk cost investment, shared customer or other resource bases. But social cognition seems to play a role as well (Porac et al., 1995), and who competes with whom is primarily a social construction. Again, this is important and relevant, but it does not change the fundamental logic of resource and strategic groups and their role in competition.

Added to these refinements of techniques, new areas of practical application of strategy have arisen. In the nineties, we saw the de-diversification, downscoping, and downsizing of many firms (e.g., Hoskisson and Hitt, 1994; Johnson, 1996). We have seen the rise of alliances, network organizations, and joint ventures (e.g., Kogut, 1991). More of the large firms traditionally the subject of strategy research are going global, facing new problems in organization and coordination, as well as relating to the business (and even the natural) environment. And a new area of research is in privatization and transition economies (as seen in the recent issues of the *Academy of Management Review* and *Academy of Management Journal*). All of these are important; good work is continuing and should continue in these areas.

As scholars we can take legitimate pride in what we've accomplished. The tools now part of strategy textbooks worldwide represent solid achievements and superb tools to run organizations better. Refining those solutions and advancing their implementation and application to broader areas is important and worthwhile. This counts to our credit in the quest to improve human life and human happiness. As a result of this now-almost-forty years of research, the fundamental framework of administrative management, of how to prevent loss, of coordination, of value creation, is in place.

Entrepreneurial Management as Discovering Tomorrow's Businesses

But a new challenge has arisen. The relative advances in administrative management, plus the forces operating in the world economy frequently summarized as the "new competitive landscape" (Bettis and Hitt, 1995) have raised the return to entrepreneurial management. Having discussed administrative management above, we briefly review the forces contributing to the new competitive landscape. *Globalization*, and in particular the decline of trade barriers among nations, has made economies of scale and scope easier to achieve by firms located anywhere while at the same time effectively inviting competitors from all nations. The advance of *technology* has had several effects. One is to raise the pace of competition. Through information technology and e-commerce, pricing power has been eroded. The rapid pace of technological development has shifted the task from management of existing resources to managing knowledge and intangible assets. And the advances in finance and the deregulation of financial markets have made capital more abundant and available than it once was. Therefore, good ideas are increasingly likely to be funded.

One reason for the heightened pressure of competition is the new modularity of design rules (Clark and Baldwin, 1997). Modularity in design makes possible the independent design of components of a system-based product underneath an overall architecture. Therefore any component of a system-based product can, in principle, be redesigned for improvement without requiring a redesign of the total product. As a result, competition becomes possible in components, spurring more and more innovation among independent suppliers. At the same time, the systems nature of many technology products creates a premium on design skills by allowing startups to reduce their investment in marketing and (perhaps) management and manufacturing that has historically been required by new companies (Chandler, 1990). Startups in general do better when they can deal with a few customers rather than a mass market (Bruderl, Preisendorfer, and Ziegler, 1992). Systems products and design rules create opportunity for design companies and startups rather than large-scale full line competitors.

A third area of change, less widely noted, is that, at least in the developed world, basic human needs have broadly speaking been met. Food, energy, transport, and clothing (several of the products of Chandler's four companies) are now available in good quality at reasonable prices throughout much of the world. The era of mass customization has begun. The new challenge is ever further refinement of satisfaction of customers by identification of new and advanced needs. For instance, one estimate suggests that there are at least 62 distinct market segments of citizens in the United States, and that finer and finer segmentation is inevitable (Labich, 1994). "Economic advancement may become not so much a matter of producing more with fewer resources, but rather a matter of better matching economic output to a progressively heterogeneous demand" (Fornell, 1995). In this environment the task of creating new products and services becomes much harder, because firms must discover new ways of meeting old needs, as well as create new needs. These require building tomorrow's business today; in short, they require entrepreneurial management.

The alternative explanation for the heightened interest by scholars in entrepreneurial management is rather more prosaic. There has always been competition between firms – even if the nature of that competition has changed in character in recent years. So competition is not new. Instead it is scholars and scholarship.

Scholars and scholarship

It is quite rational for Management scholars to focus their attention on understanding those managerial processes where added value per unit of input is greatest. It seems plausible to argue that large enterprises – the prime subject of Administrative Management – are the obvious initial focus of attention for Management scholars. Such firms are major influences in key marketplaces and significant providers of jobs and wealth.

To scholars, not only do large firms seem "relevant," but they also have several other key advantages. They are "credible," "accessible," and "easy." They are credible since they constitute the commanding heights, the "household names" in the economy. Scholars can then bask in the reflected glory of working with/advising such global names.

Such firms are accessible to scholars, often because the firms wish to recruit graduates and so wish to have strong links with academia. Furthermore, their managers are often alumni of top universities, so facilitating access and, of course, the managers themselves will recognize that the research conducted could benefit their own organization. Finally, data and information on these firms is much more likely to be in the public domain, making the scholar's work easier. The final benefit is that, because global enterprises have market power, they are capable of developing and implementing some form of strategy. Performance is more easily related to managerial actions and the stochastic component of performance is likely to be relatively small. Given the greater availability of information, the scholar's task of linking action and performance, over time, is easier the larger is the firm.

For all these reasons it is quite rational for the large global enterprise to be the natural focus of attention of students and scholars of management. But we have argued above that matters have begun to change, primarily because the returns to further investment in Administrative Management have declined. Instead there is now a recognition that the really important and challenging questions are those relating to rapidly growing, but generally smaller, entrepreneurial businesses.

Even the reader prepared to accept the concept that entrepreneurial firms are a legitimate subject for study might argue, with some justification, that the Administrative Management toolkit has been developed with care and skill. Surely, although the entrepreneurial firm may differ somewhat from the global firm, the basic issues of good management are common to both? Why throw the baby out with the bath water? Instead, why not modify the lessons of Administrative Management learned from the study of global giants, and apply them to entrepreneurial enterprises?

We reject this argument for the same reasons as those given by Edith Penrose (1959). She famously wrote that a small firm was no more a scaled-down version of a large firm than a caterpillar was a scaled-down version of a butterfly. As the Penrose analogy implies, the two look different, behave differently and, from our current perspective, respond differently to stimuli. In the context of enterprises the analogy implies that if we take out our large firm Administrative Management toolkit and apply it to the entrepreneurial firm there is a major risk of it being inappropriate.

Evidence on the entrepreneurial firm

To demonstrate the inherent dangers of "applying the lessons" of Administrative Management to the entrepreneurial firm, this section will review key results from a study by David Storey of rapidly growing middle-sized UK companies.

The study identifies all 7,203 independent UK companies with annual sales of between £5m and £100m with at least four years of financial records. It then ranks the companies in terms of their sales growth rates over four years and takes as Entrepreneurial those that achieved annual sales growth rates of at least 30 percent per annum over a four-year period. This was 708 companies – or 9.8 percent of the stock. For this reason the Entrepreneurial companies are known as The Ten Percenters. Samples of these Ten Percenters are then analyzed. First, 156 were contacted by telephone in 1996. A second sample of 46 were the subject of face-to-face interviews in 1997. Finally, two years later in 1999, the performance of the 46 was again documented.

To describe the findings the analogy of boats travelling down a river is used. The research examines the characteristics of those boats which travel quickest down the river – those that grow fastest. It is assumed there are only two ways in which the boat can travel. The first way is for the crew to be strong and coordinated. In this case the valid analogy is with Administrative Management. The firm exhibits the "textbook" characteristics of tight financial control, modern labor practices, sophisticated distribution and production methods, and the like.

The alternative strategy for moving the boat quickly down the river is for the captain of the boat to identify a fast-moving current. The analogy here is with the marketplace, with the firm being "sucked along" by the demand for its products or services. In some instances the captain is skillful enough to move the boat out of a slow-flowing stream into a fast-moving stream; in other instances the boat is swept along by the force of the current without the captain having to move streams.

In principle therefore, the research seeks to examine which are the more consistent influences on the speed at which the boat travels. Is it the skill of the captain in being able to organize and coordinate the crew, or is it the skill of the captain in being able enough, or fortunate enough, to ensure that the boat is in a fast-moving stream?

Key findings

The central finding of the research is that the coordination of the crew appears to be significantly less influential in influencing the speed with which the boat travels, than does the location of the boat within the current. Evidence for this statement is provided below:

1   When asked about the extent to which they perform better than their competitors, the Ten Percenters were most likely to emphasize a superiority in the areas

of "customer service," "understanding customer needs," and quality of product or services. Even within the Ten Percenter group those exhibiting spectacular sales growth were much more likely, even than the norm, to view their comparative advantage as in these areas. In contrast, Ten Percenters were much less likely to view their comparative advantage in "physical distribution," "lower selling prices," or "credit availability and terms." In terms of Administrative/ Entrepreneurial Management issues the Ten Percenters were much more likely to point to their Entrepreneurial Management, rather than their Administrative Management, expertise as the source of their comparative advantage.

2 Almost without exception, Ten Percenters were in markets which were rapidly expanding. Almost none achieved rapid sales growth by a substantial increase in market share. Where they had previously been in slow-growing or contracting markets the entrepreneurial firm had shifted.

3 The new markets in which Ten Percenters were found were generally "niches." The markets existed for a variety of reasons, including outsourcing, legislation, special local circumstances, as well as new technologies and changing tastes and social circumstances.

4 However, given their clever market positioning, the key struggle for the firms' leaders is to maintain the entrepreneurial and often freewheeling style of management that the owner(s) feel underlies their prior growth, with the requirement to become more formalized as the business develops. In many cases the business founders recognize the need for formality but fear that traveling down this route will douse the fires of entrepreneurship.

The picture that emerges of Administrative Management amongst Ten Percenters is that some are formalized; yet many others are not. Since, by definition, all Ten Percenters are highly successful, Administrative Management skills are neither a necessary nor sufficient condition for success. Three different Ten Percenters illustrate this diversity when asked about their objectives and accountabilities.

"The objectives and accountabilities of senior managers are ongoing. Any redefinitions happen frequently at informal meetings, normally in the local Indian restaurant on a Friday night."

"The objectives and accountabilities of senior managers are not written down. This is an entrepreneurial company and I wouldn't have ever recruited anyone who didn't know that their responsibility was to drive the company forward."

Another Ten Percenter, when asked about defining objectives and accountabilities, said:

"That's an interesting question . . . I suppose not at all; it's an ongoing process. In a company like ours it doesn't work like that but it goes on all the time, but I suppose we don't do it formally, because everything is moving so fast. If we came to a standstill I suppose we might formalize it then."

5   Management and performance. Given the face-to-face interviews which took place in 1997 a "management score" for each of the 46 participants was derived based upon 11 Administrative Management criteria including the use of non-executive directors, the tightness of financial control, the scale of staff training, the specification of job descriptions, etc.

In 1999 the performance of these 46 firms was examined. Twenty-nine percent continued to be rapidly growing, 46 percent had slowed their growth but survived, and 25 percent had departed. The average Administrative Management score for the three groups of firms was broadly the same. This suggests that it is difficult to link Administrative Management scores to subsequent performance.

Further evidence

In short, it appears that Administrative Management and Entrepreneurial Management, historically complements, are now substitutes. This substitution effect can be used to explain a number of empirical regularities observed in studies of established firms, of which we selectively highlight three. At the product level, Prusa and Schmitz (1994) show that, in software, sales of a company's first product are almost always larger than any subsequent product. At the industry level, Christensen (1997) demonstrates that established disk drive manufacturers always failed to lead the industry into the next generation of products (from 8 inch to 5.25 inch to 3.5 inch). Across industries, Cooper and Smith (1992) considered the response of 27 established industry leaders in the second third of the twentieth century to innovative technologies. Only 7 of the 27 succeeded in maintaining leadership into the next wave of technology.

Each of these studies has clear strengths and weaknesses. Taken as a whole, however, the results strongly suggest that established firms, grounded in Administrative Management, cannot successfully compete when Entrepreneurial Management is required, and that younger firms need to retain Entrepreneurial Management against the efforts to develop Administrative Management.

Implications for the entrepreneurial firm

At core, the above findings for entrepreneurial firms do not imply that "management doesn't matter," but rather that what is good management in an Administrative context may not be good management in an Entrepreneurial context.

Does this matter? We think so, and offer three examples. The first is the decisions of venture capital firms on whether or not to invest in fledgling businesses. Certainly in the UK the dominant player in the marketplace, 3I, emphasizes that its choice of investment is strongly influenced by what it believes to be the "quality" of the management. However, the bulk of 3I's funds are directed toward management buyouts and leveraged buyouts where the qualities sought from a team to continue the development of an existing, well-established, and comparatively large business are much closer to those of Administrative Management. In contrast, the skills of developing the new startup and directing its early growth are likely to demand Entrepreneurial Management talent. Since the bulk of their portfolio is directed towards the MBO market,

3I corporate philosophy is likely to place greater emphasis in its selection upon Administrative, rather than Entrepreneurial, Management. This means that fledgling firms with growth potential find it difficult to access funds.

The second implication is for what is taught in business schools. The implicit assumption is that graduates from business schools are likely to find employment as managers in large or middle-sized companies. In that case it was appropriate for them to be educated in Administrative Management since the key issue was "control." The major strategic issue was to ensure that, *within* the company, decisions made were implemented. This contrasts starkly with the issues facing a smaller firm, primarily those of a lack of legitimacy and market power.

The skills required to overcome lack of legitimacy, market power, and other uncertainties outside the firm are rarely taught in business schools. Indeed there is even a debate about whether they can be taught. For example, we observe the fundamental importance of "niches" in explaining the exceptional performance of entrepreneurial firms. We see that such firms are nearly always "leader driven" and that the leader is an individual who sees it to be their task to have the big picture. Yet, while every business school has courses on financial control and pricing, on HRM, on productions management, there remain virtually none on "Big Pictures," on "Niches," on "Moving the Boat," or on "Maintaining the Entrepreneurial Fires while growing the business." The third key implication is for the research community. It is the key research finding that those making the key decisions in entrepreneurial firms are, in practice, struggling to avoid the suffocating and controlling influences of Administrative Management. They want to avoid meetings, formality, procedures, plans and policies. Indeed many of them established their businesses to get away from such practices. Clearly, most recognize that increasing formality is inevitably associated with larger size, but the key issue for them is to ensure that the tail does not wag the dog. For them the business has experienced rapid growth because of its Entrepreneurialism, and not because of its expertise in Administrative Management.

A central research issue is therefore how this trade-off between Entrepreneurial and Administrative Management is delivered in practice and how it changes as the business grows. The problem is that, by the standards of Administrative Management, entrepreneurial firms look to be (often very) badly managed. However, we have argued that Administrative Management expertise is not an appropriate criterion on which to assess the management skills of entrepreneurial firms. Alternatively expressed, the Administrative Management toolkit does not currently contain the appropriate equipment for this analysis. It needs the explicit inclusion of the mindset of the Entrepreneur and Entrepreneurial Management.

Topics of Entrepreneurial Management

Existing research in entrepreneurial management has developed several distinct lines of inquiry without a unifying framework or theme. Several topics are reviewed here that form part of entrepreneurial management. Despite the obvious advances in these areas, they are to some extent handicapped by the previous approaches to administrative management. We discuss ways in which the research should be broadened, in some cases beyond the historic strategic management domain, in order to make further progress.

Knowledge management

How the firm organizes what its members know, and utilizes it across different projects and markets, is an important part of organizational innovation. It is also driven by an intensely practical problem and an intensely practical constituency: many consulting firms face exactly this problem, and have developed very sophisticated best practices databases and information-sharing devices.

This is important and good work. But the orientation is still fundamentally one of administrative management. The problem of knowledge management is usually expressed as a problem of coordination, how to allow individuals to link up their knowledge in order to take advantage of experience and, also, to transfer that research into organizational learning. This has the virtue of allowing research to build on the older phenomenon of the learning curve, and again of helping to solve an intensely practical problem. But the overall point of view is still one of efficiency. Existing literature in entrepreneurship has typically viewed the problem differently, as one of opportunity recognition. The analysis begins from the perspective of Austrian economics. Unlike Neoclassical economics, where information is assumed to be costless and common knowledge to market participants, Austrian economists note that information is in fact dispersed, uncovered at a cost, and in some cases not uncovered at all. Therefore the question becomes how people come into the knowledge of an opportunity – a human need not yet met that can be met by the proper application of technology.

This point of view is fundamentally different – and potentially more fruitful – than a knowledge management approach. Knowledge management presumes the knowledge is there – the entrepreneurial management approach presumes it is not. Knowledge management does not suggest market research, sessions on creativity, or experiments – all of which can help to uncover information previously unknown to the entrepreneurial manager.

Resource-based view of the firm

The basic insights of the resource-based view of the firm are well known. The resource-based view of the firm (RBV) has argued that the firm is best viewed as a bundle of resources or factors of production that management must deploy systematically to add value (Barney, 1991; Wernerfelt, 1984). Resources can yield sustained competitive advantage when they are relatively valuable, scarce, hard to imitate, and hard to replace (Barney, 1986; Mahoney and Pandian, 1992). In short, factors that yield sustainable competitive advantage are not easily traded on markets. The RBV is a powerful tool, and has yielded insights in many distinct areas. Typically, the existing application of this reasoning in entrepreneurial management has been to focus on managerial, marketing, operational, or technological resources, e.g., to measure those skills in some way in a new venture and examine their effects. For example, Deeds, DeCarolis, and Coombs (2000) examine whether technological resources (measured by the usual suspects of patent citations and CEOs with Ph.Ds) positively affect new product development. But this approach, however insightful, may be incomplete. Working in the traditional functional areas may blind us to the different resources and capabilities of entrepreneurial management. Studies in entrepreneurship repeatedly argue that crucial resources of the entrepreneur or startup are not captured by these functional models. Indeed, they first presume an organization. To what extent are we talking about the resources of an organization? The resources of entrepreneurial management include not just traditional functional areas (grounded in administrative management) but information, social capital, and startup experience. As one example, existing strategic management research often assumes that financing is or can be made available because of the hypothesis of perfect capital markets. Such a hypothesis is inappropriate in the case of entrepreneurial management. An additional resource may be the ability to gather funding.

In short, the resources of entrepreneurial management may be different from the resources of administrative management.

Organizing for innovation

The current literature on organizing for innovation as a part of entrepreneurial management contains at its heart a contradiction. A number of authors have argued that entrepreneurial management to facilitate innovation requires a different kind of organization than administrative management. The organization needs to empower individuals to act on opportunities (Amit, Brigham, and Markman, 2000). They need to develop creativity and an ability to improvise within rules (Eisenhardt, Brown and Neck, 2000). They need to develop the cellular organization (Miles et al., 1997), an organizational form in which each cell shares characteristics with the other cells. But a research stream with many different sources both old and new argues that these characteristics cannot coexist with the traditional organization. Burns and Stalker (1961) argued that organizations cannot be both "organic" and "mechanistic." Ghemawat and Ricart i Costa (1993) argued that an organization cannot be efficient in both a static sense and a dynamic sense. March (1991) argues that organizations must trade off gains in average performance through "exploration" (similar to discovery, or entrepreneurial management) against the reduction in variance in returns gained through "exploitation" (similar to coordination, or administrative management). Organizational learning increases the return to exploitation in the short run but is likely to weaken overall returns in the long run. And Baker, Gibbs, and Holmstrom (1994) argued that powerful forces in organizations limit the amount of salary dispersion tolerated in organizations, which may play against the need to compensate entrepreneurial managers with incentive compensation rather than traditional salary. Therefore, it may not be possible for an organization to be both administrative and entrepreneurial.

Limited as we are in focusing on existing organizations, preferably the *Fortune* 500, we may be missing the need to form new and independent organizations. This is obvious in the case of a startup venture, of course, but it is also true within existing organizations. If the above authors are correct, a new organization, outside the existing one, must be founded in order to take advantage of an opportunity. How should the two be joined? Only through an equity relationship? Shared personnel? Common personnel policies?

Organizational learning

Organizational learning is the creation of new knowledge within the firm that can improve performance (Hitt and Ireland, 2000). Many different conceptualizations of organizational learning exist (Miller, 1996). Perhaps the most significant of these models is learning by doing (see for example Lieberman, 1984; Darr, Argote and Epple, 1995). Beginning from observations on airframe production costs during wartime, the observed fact that costs decline with cumulative experience has been a staple of the strategy literature for many years (as well as the foundation of a successful consulting practice). A second model has emphasized organizational memory, the constant repetition of activities within organizations (Nelson and Winter, 1982). Such repetition and related codifications into rules and procedures allow for the lessons of experience to be retained and accumulated over time despite organizational transitions (Levitt and March, 1988). Such routines are necessary to develop dynamic core competencies in order to continue with innovation (Teece, Písano, and Shuen, 1997).

But the concept of organizational learning runs the risk of reifying the organization (Simon, 1964). It may be true that large organizations create through organized repetition. Smaller organizations, and in particular startups, with a team of perhaps five people, are likely to combine their knowledge without such complicated procedures. Repetition may be the death of creativity in such situations. At a broader level, how do small groups of individuals combine their collective experiences to identify new opportunities? Is it through formal or informal methods? How can these processes be facilitated?

The role of small groups as the fundamental creators of innovation creates considerable tension with the rest of the organization, as shown in the discussion of organizing for innovation. One key finding of entrepreneurial management is that small, autonomous groups must separate from the main body of (administrative) work of the firm for innovation, whether it is described as the innovator's dilemma (Christensen, 1997), an incentive problem (Holmstrom, 1989), or in other terms. Then how is organizational learning supposed to take place? How can dynamic core competencies be created in the organization? Indeed, how can they even exist if the inevitable pressure of a successful product brings with it the tendency toward administrative management?

Entrepreneurial finance

Strong links have been forged between finance and strategic management. One link not previously discussed has been the theory of efficient capital markets: firms can access capital at whatever level they need, given that information is available to convince investors to invest. All, or at least most, positive net present value projects are funded. This is implicit in the assumptions of many strategic management papers. For example, the widespread use of event studies assumes the market can price information correctly.

Whatever the merits of this in the context of larger firms and administrative management, it is not correct in the context of entrepreneurial management, and certainly not startups. Technology entrepreneurs in the UK reported significant financial constraints on their businesses (Westhead and Storey, 1996). And an analysis of US entrepreneurs found that entrepreneurs have access to capital that is only 50 percent beyond that of their personal wealth (Evans and Jovanovic, 1989). These empirical facts call attention to the theoretical difficulties involved in demonstrating the viability of an opportunity. Opportunities suffer from the paradox of information (Arrow, 1975), that the value of the information cannot be determined without revealing the information, and in turn making it possible for someone to use it without paying for it. In addition, individuals with opportunities face the problem of adverse selection, of credibly signaling their capabilities to execute the idea (Amit, Glosten, and Muller, 1990; Sahlman, 1990).

So funding and finance are different under entrepreneurial management.

Future Directions

To manage the transition from strategic management to entrepreneurial management, we have to make some changes.

First we must be willing to do some serious carpetbagging

Colleagues in technology management have developed useful tools in thinking about technology and how it changes both product design and competition. And colleagues in marketing can reintroduce us to the customer in order to understand human needs and opportunities better. As a consequence, we need to learn from them and adapt/ borrow their concepts and toolkit where necessary.

Next we have to be willing to abandon some long-cherished assumptions

The dominant role of economics may have to be reexamined. Economics is a valuable tool in any scholar's toolkit. But some of the basic assumptions of economics are untenable in the new competitive landscape. For example, information on specific existing product markets may be perfectly known to all, but information on potential products is not. Rational behavior makes sense only in the context of well-understood payoffs and probabilities. In the face of uncertainty, rational behavior (as currently operationalized in economics) is far less likely. At the present time, economics is built primarily on a static framework, assuming markets and technologies for existing goods and services rather than considering change.[4]

Second, we may need to make some clear choices dividing administrative from entrepreneurial management. One clear example is corporate governance. As discussed above, the organization required for entrepreneurial management and innovation is very different than the one required for administrative management. Indeed, there may not even be much of a formal organization. But, to even talk about governance, a corporation and a corporate board are presumed. More generally, wealth is not created through boards and board structures, but it can be destroyed. Good governance is about loss prevention. Therefore, governance is one topic that should be researched and studied within administrative management.

Third, we don't have to focus only on for profit companies. Much can be learned about developing new businesses from not-for-profits. Strategy has traditionally been the province of the diversified corporation and its close cousins, multinationals, alliances, etc. All of these are from the for-profit sector. But much entrepreneurship is NOT about building for profit organizations. What about the role of community builders, institution builders, that are not corporations? For example, the Jesuit religious order, founded by Ignatius of Loyola, has outlived most for-profit corporations and indeed most social and religious organizations. What can the Jesuit experience tell us about entrepreneurial management, specifically adaptation to change in organizational environments and human needs? Does, for example, a strong and sustainable culture create long-term competitive advantage?

Strategy needs to reinterpret older contributions and update them to the new competitive landscape

Strategy has stopped talking about growth as a desired goal although there was a time we did. Can we give good answers to individuals and firms who want to grow an organization? Can we tell them how to expand customers and markets – and, equally importantly, can we tell them how to organize to do it? At one time, the path was relatively clear. Consider Chandler – the prototypical growth path for the firm is single product, multiple geographies, or multiple product, single geographies, followed by vertical integration. In a related vein, we had a literature in retrenchment and turnaround, which is certainly not a popular research venue now. Can we give answers to firms, ventures, or individuals who find themselves over-extended?

An emphasis on entrepreneurial management will also need to rediscover the business environment. Do social, legal, cultural, or governmental forces foster entrepreneurial management? Baumol (1990) answered that societies that value rent creation more than rent seeking innovate faster. At a practical level, what drives the difference between a British entrepreneur like Branson and an American one like Bezos? And why are some universities entrepreneurial and not others? Even intra-European analysis might generate some insights. Does entrepreneurial management need strategic planning? Planning is itself subject to internal contradictions that make many in strategic management question its effectiveness (Mintzberg, 1994). In a rapidly changing environment, planning may not be possible, especially for entrepreneurs (Bhide, 1994). And entrepreneurial management emphasizes responsiveness and reaction to market conditions. On the other hand, every entrepreneurial venture is encouraged to develop a business plan, and ventures are not funded by venture capitalists without a plan. Is a business plan simply a financial document or does it have operational utility? More generally, do any of the older insights from planning extend to new venture formation and entrepreneurial management?

How will this impact our traditional research methods?

Strategic management research has evolved into a mature science, but that has come in large part through focus on methods that are acceptable to existing social sciences – in particular, through large-scale samples and statistical analysis. But the work in entrepreneurial management is relatively sparse, so methods that are less "mature" may be required. It was a work of business history (Chandler's *Strategy and Structure*) that began in large part the strategic management discipline; perhaps another work could further entrepreneurial management? As a founding scholar of entrepreneurship, Joseph Schumpeter, said, "A satisfactory analysis of economic change – to avoid the colored word "progress" – can only be achieved by historical work" (Swedberg, 1991: 408). A second alternative might be processual research, as exemplifed by Pettigrew's cradle to grave study of ICI (Pettigrew, 1985). As a third alternative, a seminal work in entrepreneurship, Gartner (1985), noted that differences among ventures may be more important than differences between ventures and established organizations. This suggests a need for taxonomy and classification.

In particular, the hazards of mortality and organizational failure may be so large as to suggest that serious harm might be done using simple cross-sectional analysis. After all, if most new ventures fail, then regression techniques are inadequate in a gross sense: estimating a conditional mean when the mean venture fails is not especially helpful.

Related to the question of how we change our research is how we change our teaching. Current management education is geared toward producing industrial civil servants. How do we encourage students to seek out opportunities and invest in them, to practice entrepreneurial management? Perhaps we need two courses, one in administrative management and one in entrepreneurial management.

Conclusion

In this chapter we argue that Strategic Management must be adapted to the new competitive landscape. The old style of Strategic Management, which we term Administrative Management, focused on the prevention of loss and coordination of activities, is less important. Instead, today, the focus has to be on "Entrepreneurial Management," which is more focused on discovery, development, and growth. We justify this on two grounds. First that, in economic terms, there are diminishing returns in further study of Administrative Management – basically the interesting problems have been solved. Second, the current technical revolution – the new competitive landscape – means the returns on a better understanding of Entrepreneurial Management are much higher.

But we also seek to demonstrate an even more radical point. Through observation of rapidly growing middle-sized UK companies, we conclude that their owners – "the entrepreneurs" – are fighting a constant battle as their business grows to avoid the shackles of Administrative Management. They recognize there is an explicit trade-off between Administrative and Entrepreneurial Management. This chapter provides some plausible, but not irrefutable, evidence justifying their concerns. First, the chapter demonstrates that the highly successful companies, in this size range, are those which excel in Entrepreneurial Management, but that their performance in Administrative Management is much more diverse. Second, the chapter demonstrates that current performance in Administrative Management is no guide to future performance. Third, other studies of established firms seeking to discover and innovate are cited to further support the contention that Administrative Management and Entrepreneurial Management are substitutes. The nature of the argument may suggest that this is primarily a scholarly debate, but operating results of real companies demonstrate that continued reinvention of the corporation through entrepreneurial activity is necessary for its survival. The tension between administrative management and entrepreneurial management creates a conflict potentially fatal to the organization. The techniques of administrative management, such as listening to the customer, coordinating activities across the value chain, and investing in areas with the most promising financial return, will weaken and possibly destroy the entrepreneurial management (and its implied innovation potential) necessary to survive in the face of technological change. Since all organizations are facing such change today, the separation of entrepreneurial from administrative management has never been so critical for organizations.

In summary, better administration will not be the key to competitive advantage in the new competitive landscape. The companies that survive will be joined by new companies that practice entrepreneurial management.

Notes

1   Interestingly for our purposes, in the preface to the 1985 edition Drucker claims that the first title of this book was *Business Strategies*, but the publisher strongly advised him to change the title.
2   Entrepreneurial management is similar to "corporate entrepreneurship." This chapter's intended contribution is to explore the relationship between entrepreneurial and administrative management, not to add to the literature on corporate entrepreneurship. But, to briefly contrast the two constructs, using the definition of Covin and Miles (1999) of corporate entrepreneurship as innovation, our concept of entrepreneurial management differs slightly by emphasizing the process of discovery rather than the outcome of innovation.
3   The development of mainland China may be a partial exception to this.
4   Current research in economics is moving beyond this limitation, but the topics and skills likely to be available to most strategic management researchers and doctoral students are primarily static.

References

Amit, R. H., Brigham, K., and Markman, G. D. 2000. Entrepreneurial management as strategy. In G. D. Meyer and K. A. Heppard (eds), *Entrepreneurship as strategy: Competing on the entrepreneurial edge*. Thousand Oaks, CA: Sage Publications, 83–100.

Amit, R., Glosten, L. and Muller, E. 1990. Entrepreneurial ability, venture investments, and risk sharing. *Management Science*, 36(10): 1232–45.

Andrews, K. A. 1971. *The concept of corporate strategy*. Homewood, IL: Dow Jones-Irwin.

Arrow, K. 1975. Vertical integration and communication. *Bell Journal of Economics*, 6(1): 173–83.

Baker, G., Gibbs, M., and Holmstrom, B. 1994. The wage policy of a firm. *Quarterly Journal of Economics*, 109(4): 881–919.

Barney, J. 1991. Firm resources and sustained competitive advantage. *Journal of Management*, 17(1): 99–120.

Barney, J. B. 1986. Strategic factor markets: expectations, luck and business strategy. *Manage-*

ment Science, 32(10): 1231–41.

Baumol, W. J. 1968. Entrepreneurship in economic theory. *American Economic Review*, 58(2): 64–71.

Baumol, W. J. 1990. Entrepreneurship: productive, unproductive, and destructive. *Journal of Political Economy*, 98(5): 893–921.

Bettis, R. A., and Hitt, M. A. 1995. The new competitive landscape. *Strategic Management Journal*, 16 (special summer issue): 7–16.

Bhide, A. 1994. How entrepreneurs craft strategies that work. *Harvard Business Review*, 72(2): 150–61.

Bruderl, J., Preisendorfer, P., and Ziegler, R. 1992. Survival chances of newly founded business organizations. *American Sociological Review*, 57 (April): 227–42.

Brynjolfsson, E., Malone, T. W., Gurbaxani, V. and Kambil, A. 1994. Does information technology lead to smaller firms? *Management Science*, 40(12): 1628–44.

Burns, T. and Stalker, G. M. 1961. *The management of innovation*. London: Tavistock.

Chandler, A. D. 1990. The enduring logic of industrial success. *Harvard Business Review*, 68(2): 130–40.

Chandler, A. D. 1994. The functions of the HQ unit in the Multibusiness firm. In R. P. Rumelt, D. E. Schendel, D. J. Teece (eds), *Fundamental issues in strategy*. Boston: Harvard Business School Press, 323–60.

Chandler, A. D., Jr. 1962. *Strategy and structure: Chapters in the history of the American industrial enterprise*. Cambridge, MA: MIT Press.

Christensen, C. M. 1997. *The innovator's dilemma*. Boston: Harvard Business School Press.

Clark, K. B., and Baldwin, C. Y. 1997. Managing in an age of modularity. *Harvard Business Review*, 75(5): 84–93.

Clemons, E. K. 1993. Information technology and the boundary of the firm: who wins, who loses, who has to change. In S. P. Bradley, J. A. Hausmann, and R. L. Nolan (eds), *Globalization, technology, and competition: The fusion of computers and telecommunications in the 1990s*. Boston: Harvard Business School Press, 219–42.

Cooper, A. C. and Smith, C. G. 1992. How established firms respond to threatening technologies. *Academy of Management Executive*, 6(2): 55–70.

Covin, J. G. and Miles, M. P. 1999. Corporate entrepreneurship and the pursuit of competitive advantage. *Entrepreneurship: Theory and Practice*, 23(3): 47–63.

Darr, E. D., Argote, L., and Epple, D. 1995. The acquisition, transfer, and depreciation of knowledge in service organizations: productivity in franchises. *Management Science*, 41(11): 1750–62.

Deeds, D. L., De Carolis, D., and Coombs, J. 2000. Dynamic capabilities and new product development in high technology ventures: an empirical analysis of new biotechnology firms. *Journal of Business Venturing*, 15(3): 211–29.

Drucker, P. F. 1964. *Managing for results*. New York: Harper Collins.

Dyer, J. H., and Singh, H. 1998. The relational view: Cooperative strategy and sources of interorganizational competitive advantage. *Academy of Management Review*, 23(4): 660–79.

Eisenhardt, K. M. 1989. Agency theory: an assessment and review. *Academy of Management Review*, 14(1): 57–74.

Eisenhardt, K. M., Brown, S. L., and Neck, H. M. 2000. Competing on the entrepreneurial edge. In G. D. Meyer and K. A. Heppard (eds), *Entrepreneurship as strategy: Competing on the entrepreneurial edge*. Thousand Oaks, CA: Sage Publications, 49–62.

Evans, D. S., and Jovanovic, B. 1989. An estimated model of entrepreneurial choice under liquidity constraints. *Journal of Political Economy*, 97(4): 808–27.

Fama, E. F., and Jensen, M. C. 1983. Separation of ownership and control. *Journal of Law and Economics*, 26(2): 301–25.

Fornell, C. 1995. The quality of economic output: empirical generalizations about its distribution and relationship to market share. *Marketing Science*, 14(3 (Part 2)): G203–G211.

Gartner, W. B. 1985. A conceptual framework for describing the phenomenon of new venture creation. *Academy of Management Review*, 10(4): 696–706.

Ghemawat, P. and Ricart i Costa, J. E. 1993. The organizational tension between static and dynamic efficiency. *Strategic Management Journal*, 14 (special issue): 59–73.

Goold, M., and Campbell, A. 1987. Many best ways to make strategy. *Harvard Business Review* 65(6): 70–6.

Govindarajan, V. and Gupta, A. K. 1985. Linking control systems to business unit strategy: impact on performance. *Accounting, Organizations & Society*, 10(1): 51–66.

Haeckel, S. H. and Nolan, R. L. 1993. Managing by wire. *Harvard Business Review*, 71(5): 74–82.

Hamel, G. and Prahalad, C. K. 1994. *Competing for the future*. Boston: Harvard Business School Press.

Hax, A. C. and Majiluf, N. S. 1984. *Strategic management: An integrated perspective*. Englewood Cliffs, NJ: Prentice-Hall.

Hill, C. W. L. 1988. Internal capital market controls and financial performance in multivisional firms. *Journal of Industrial Economics*, 37(1): 67–83.

Hill, C. W. L., and Hoskisson, R. E. 1987. Strategy and structure in the multiproduct firm. *Academy of Management Review*, 12(2): 331–41.

Hitt, M. A., and Ireland, R. D. 2000. The intersection of entrepreneurship and strategic management research. In D. L. Sexton and H. Landstrom (eds), *The Blackwell handbook of entrepreneurship*. Oxford, UK: Blackwell, 45–63.

Holmstrom, B. 1989. Agency costs and innovation. *Journal of Economic Behavior and Organization*, 12(3): 305–27.

Hopkins, W. E. and Hopkins, S. A. 1997. Strategic planning – financial performance relationships in banks: a causal examination. *Strategic Management Journal*, 18(8): 635–52.

Hoskisson, R. E. and Hitt, M. A. 1994. *Downscoping: How to tame the diversified firm*. New York: Oxford University Press.

Hoskisson, R. E. Hitt, M. A., and Hill, C. W. L. 1993. Managerial incentives and investment in R&D in large multiproduct firms. *Organization Science*, 4(2): 325–41.

Johnson, R. A. 1996. Antecedents and outcomes of corporate refocusing. *Journal of Management*, 22: 437–81.

Kogut, B. 1991. Joint ventures and the option to expand and acquire. *Management Science*, 37(1): 19–33.

Labich, K. 1994. Class in America, *Fortune*, April: 114–26.

Levitt, B. and March, J. G. 1988. Organizational learning. *Annual Review of Sociology*, vol. 14. Greenwich, CT: JAI Press.

Lieberman, M. B. 1984. The learning curve and pricing in the chemical processing industries. *RAND Journal of Economics*, 15(2): 213–28.

Mahoney, J. T. and Pandian, J. R. 1992. The resource-based view within the conversation of strategic management. *Strategic Management Journal*, 13(5): 559–84.

Malone, T. W. and Rockart, J. F. 1993. How will information technology reshape organizations? Computers as coordination technology. In S. P. Bradley, J. A. Hausman and R. L. Nolan (eds), *Globalization, technology, and competition: The fusion of computers and telecommunications in the 1990s*. Boston: Harvard Business School Press.

March, J. G. 1991. Exploration and exploitation in organizational learning. *Organization Science*, 2(1): 71–87.

Miles, R. E., Snow, C. C., Mathews, J. A., Miles, G., and Coleman, H. J., Jr. 1997. Organizing in the knowledge age: anticipating the cellular form. *Academy of Management Executive*,

11(4): 7–20.

Miller, D. 1996. A preliminary typology of organizational learning: Synthesizing the literature. *Journal of Management*, 22(3): 485–505.

Mintzberg, H. 1987. Crafting Strategy. *Harvard Business Review*, 65(4): 66–75.

Mintzberg, H. 1994. *The Rise and Fall of Strategic Planning*. New York: Free Press.

Nelson, R. R. and Winter, S. G. 1982. *An evolutionary theory of economic change*. Cambridge, MA: Harvard University Press.

Nolan, R. L. 1999. Information technology management from 1960–2000, *Harvard Business School Working Paper*. Boston.

Penrose, E. 1995. *The theory of the growth of the firm*. Cambridge, MA: Blackwell. Originally published 1959, New York: John Wiley.

Pettigrew, A. M. 1985. *The awakening giant: Continuity and change in Imperial Chemical Industries*. New York: Blackwell.

Pindyck, R. 1990. Irreversibility, uncertainty, and investment. *National Bureau of Economic Research*, Working Paper 3307.

Porac, J. F., Thomas, H., Wilson, F., Paton, D., and Kanfer, A. 1995. Rivalry and the industry model of Scottish knitwear producers. *Administrative Science Quarterly*, 40(2): 203–27.

Porter, M. E. 1980. *Competitive strategy*. New York: Free Press.

Porter, M. E. 1985. *Competitive advantage*. New York: Free Press.

Prusa, T. J. and Schmitz, J. A., Jr. 1994. Can companies maintain their initial innovative thrust? A study of the PC software industry. *Review of Economics and Statistics*, 76(3): 523–40.

Sahlman, W. A. 1990. The Structure and governance of venture-capital organizations. *Journal of Financial Economics*, 27(2): 473–521.

Simon, H. A. 1964. On the concept of organizational goal. *Administrative Science Quarterly*, 9: 1–22.

Snow, C. C., Miles, R. E., and Coleman, H. J., Jr. 1992. Managing 21st century network organizations. *Organizational Dynamics*, 20(3): 5–20.

Swedberg, R. (ed.) 1991. *Joseph A. Schumpeter: The economics and sociology of capitalism*. Princeton, NJ: Princeton University Press.

Teece, D. J., Pisano, G., and Shuen, A. 1997. Dynamic capabilities and strategic management. *Strategic Management Journal*, 18: 509–33.

Wernerfelt, B. 1984. A resource-based view of the firm. *Strategic Management Journal*, 5(2): 171–80.

Westhead, P. and Storey, D. 1996. Management training and small firm performance: why is the link so weak? *International Small Business Journal*, 14(4): 13–24.

Williamson, O. E. 1985. *The economic institutions of capitalism*. New York: Free Press.

Zenger, T. R. and Hesterly, W. S. 1997. The disaggregation of corporations: selective intervention, high-powered incentives, and molecular units. *Organization Science*, 8(3): 209–22.

CHAPTER FOUR

A Framework For Entrepreneurial Strategy

Scott Johnson, Andrew H. Van de Ven

What differentiates successful from unsuccessful entrepreneurial firms as they create new businesses that transform the basis of competition in an industry? To address this question we focus on the process of industry emergence and examine the sources of competitive advantage among entrepreneurial firms engaged in the creation of a new product technology. The period of industry emergence is the temporal setting in which this question of entrepreneurial strategy is important for both the fields of strategy and entrepreneurship (Van de Ven and Garud, 1993). For strategy scholars, study of industry-level processes is needed to make comparative performance assessments among firms and to identify the new technologies and products that change the basis of industrial competition. The by-products of industry emergence are often the factors that are used to explain performance differences when an industry reaches maturity. Barriers to entry, technological competence, market power, consumer markets, and reputations (to name just a few) may all be forged during the period of industry emergence.

Many entrepreneurial ventures do not represent new businesses that create new industries. As the chapter by Kazanjian, Drazin, and Glynn in this book indicates, most entrepreneurial ventures are either product line extensions (variations of baseline products for an existing market) or new platform developments (that either introduce an advanced technology to existing customers, or target new customers with an existing product technology). New businesses transform the basis of industrial competition by creating new product technologies for new markets. Seldom are new businesses successfully commercialized by individual entrepreneurs; instead they depend upon the actions of numerous entrepreneurs who collectively build a new industrial infrastructure that supplants or replaces existing populations or industries. Thus, new industries can be seen as the aggregated results of numerous entrepreneurial firms that create new population niches of commercial enterprises. Our question deals with the performance variations often observed among the population of entrepreneurs who interact during the emergence of a new industry to commercialize their new product technologies. This focus on industry emergence represents an intermediate (or meso) level of analysis between the micro characteristics and activities of individual entrepreneurs (Cooper and Gasco, 1992) and macro national innovation systems (Nelson, 1982).

Industry emergence is a complex process that can be modeled in various ways. We will present four different models of industry emergence, each of which is based on a different perspective from organizational theory: population ecology, new institutionalism, organization evolution, or industrial communities. Each model describes the strategic actions that firms can take as a new industry emerges and explains how these actions affect other firms in the industry. The models vary in the extent to which they simplify firm effects on each other and their interactions with their environment. For each model we will identify the potential strategies of entrepreneurial firms that are consistent with the model. Then we will examine some empirical research that fits the model and points to potential areas of fruitful research.

We rely on the resource-based perspective to develop our explanation of what entrepreneurial actions create relative competitive advantage. This perspective asserts that resources are the main source of firm competitive advantage. These resources may be tangible (e.g., technology, financing, or patents) or intangible (e.g., reputation, competence, trade secrets). Overall, the resource-based view argues that firms can generate long-lasting profits when they possess resources that are valuable, rare, nonsubstitutable, and imperfectly imitable (Barney, 1996; Peteraf, 1993; Wernerfelt, 1984). In particular, we rely on the "cornerstones of competitive advantage" developed by Peteraf (1993). These cornerstones are four logically necessary conditions that must be present in order for a firm to enjoy competitive advantage.

Four Cornerstones of Competitive Advantage

A basic conclusion of Neoclassical microeconomics is that, in equilibrium, all firms in an industry with free entry earn normal returns. Earning normal returns is the same as earning zero profit, which means that after the firm pays all of its bills it has just enough left over to compensate its owners for the investment they have made. The reason for the claim that all firms should have zero profits is that a firm earning profits will attract other firms to enter the industry and the resulting competition will drive the profits to zero. Note that sometimes firms do earn positive profits but this is a temporary situation until other firms enter the industry and the equilibrium situation of zero profits is achieved. What if other firms cannot enter the industry? In this case, it is possible for firms to earn profits in equilibrium. The classic example of this is a farmer with a valuable plot of scarce land. The farmer can earn positive profits because there is no other land available to allow new competitors to begin farming. These sustained profits are called rents and indicate the market value of the farmer's land (Varian, 1999). In the framework of microeconomics, excess returns that will soon be competed away are called *profits* while sustainable excess returns are called *rents*.

As we analyze the four different models of industry emergence, there will be different predictions about the relative performance of different firms. When an action taken by a firm during industry emergence creates superior performance but, according to the model, the performance difference can be expected to diminish over time, we will say that firm has created entrepreneurial profits. When an action taken by a firm during industry emergence can be expected to create long-term superior performance, we will say that firm has created entrepreneurial rents. It should be clear that rent creation is more difficult than profit creation. A firm can earn a profit when it has some advantage over other firms. A firm can only create a rent if it has some advantage that no other firm is able to mimic. Since we are exploring the possibilities for firms to create future competitive advantage through entrepreneurial activity, we need a logical framework for assessing whether an action can create an advantage that other firms will not be able to mimic. The four cornerstones of competitive advantage proposed by Peteraf (1993) provide a set of four necessary conditions that must be met in order for a firm to create a rent.

We will call any advantage that meets these four conditions a *resource*. Our use of the term resource is related to the way resources are conceptualized in the resource-based view of the firm, but there is an important difference. Our use of the term resource will apply to any firm attribute that allows a firm to earn a rent. So, for example, we will show that firm size and industry entry barriers allow firms to gain competitive advantage in some of the industry models and so we will talk about these as rent-earning resources even though these would not be considered resources in the resource-based view of the firm. In this chapter, a resource is anything (attribute, object, capability) that meets the four conditions and allows the firm with the resource to outperform the firm without the resource.

The first requirement for the existence of a rent-earning resource is that there must be firm heterogeneity. If all firms are basically the same, there is no reason to expect one firm to consistently perform better than other firms. This will become an important point later when we explore the assumptions of the four organizational theory perspectives and find that some of these perspectives presume that firms are essentially homogeneous.

Second, there must be ex ante limits to competition. If something, for example a good reputation, gives a firm the ability to earn rents then firms would compete vigorously for reputation. In fact, if there were perfect competition for reputation, the cost of achieving a valuable reputation would exactly offset the value of the future rents it creates. However, the point made by the resource-based view is that sometimes the price paid for a resource is much less than its actual value. Importantly for the study of entrepreneurship, the period of industry emergence is a time of imperfect competition for resources. Since the future of the industry is uncertain, the value of things like patents, market position, and qualified staff are not clear. This time of uncertainty in the development of a new industry creates what Barney calls an imperfect factor market for strategic resources. Entrepreneurs with foresight or "luck" have the opportunity to acquire resources at bargain prices.

The third necessary condition for a resource to create rents is ex post limits to competition. While the second condition implied an imperfection in the factor market at the time the resource is acquired, the third condition implies that imperfect competition for the resource continues for a sustained period of time. In practical terms this means that there must not be close substitutes for the resource and it must not be easily imitated. A patent for a drug exemplifies this condition. Patent laws preclude imitation of the drug and the slow pace of scientific discovery and medical testing limits the possibility of substitution.

A final condition that must be present in order for a resource to create rents is that the resource must be imperfectly mobile; it must be firmly attached to a specific firm. Return again to the example of reputation. If corporate reputations could be easily transferred from one firm to another then reputations would be a commodity or input for production, not a rent-creating resource. When the four conditions are met – firm heterogeneity, ex ante and ex post limits to competition for the resource, and imperfect immobility – a resource can create sustained, above-normal profits for a firm.

Alvarez and Barney (2000), in assessing how the resource-based view can provide insight into entrepreneurship, note that the clearest conception of entrepreneurship in economics comes from Schumpeter and other Austrian-school economists who view the marketplace as in constant disequilibrium. The resource-based view of rents, on the other hand, is a concept that only applies in equilibrium. We take the middle ground between these two extremes by approximating the Schumpeterian process of creative destruction as a continuing cycle of industry emergence (disequilibrium) where a new industry emerges to replace the old. The strategic resources acquired in this stage earn rents in the period of industry maturity (equilibrium) until the whole industry is upset by the emergence of a new industry. So, while we have presented a clear distinction between rents and profits, it should be noted that it is really a matter of degree. Strategic resources allow a firm to earn rents (relative to other firms in the same industry) not into perpetuity but only as long as the industry remains undisturbed by the emergence of another industry.

Models from Organizational Theory

In most strategy research it is natural to compare performance of firms that operate in the same industry. By controlling for industry, a researcher controls for a wide variety of different opportunities faced by fundamentally different firms. For example, a steel firm and a semiconductor firm have different strategic options, different competitors and are affected differently by macroeconomic conditions. It would be difficult to attribute performance differences between a steel firm and a semiconductor firm to differences in strategic choices. But, when comparing firms within an industry, the effects of strategic choices come into clearer focus. A model of an industry provides both a model of the environment in which a firm operates and model of the population with which a firm competes. Competitive advantage depends on the nature of competition within an industry.

In the entrepreneurship literature, the industry is not a static model of the environment; it is an emergent construct. Entrepreneurial activity takes place before industry boundaries are clear. Shane and Venkataraman (2000) emphasize that study of entrepreneurship must be broader than the study of *firm* performance. They point out that entrepreneurship includes the formation of new organizations as well as the entrepreneurial actions taken by existing firms. Furthermore, they note that traditionally the study of entrepreneurship has focused on individuals or firms but needs to expand to include the study of population-level factors. Consequently they define entrepreneurship as the study "of how, by whom, and with what effects opportunities to create future goods and services are discovered, evaluated and exploited" (Shane and

Venkataraman, 2000: 218). Examining the financial performance implications of entrepreneurial actions, then, requires clarifying a model of industry emergence and entrepreneurial action. In order to do this we need a richer understanding of what firms are and how they interact. To add this depth to the cornerstones of competitive advantage, we turn to organizational theory.

Organizational theory provides a rich variety of perspectives to understand organizations in the context of their industrial environment. Four perspectives are particularly relevant for examining entrepreneurial strategy: *population ecology, institutional theory, organizational evolution*, and *industrial communities*. The four perspectives differ on two basic questions. The first question is whether or not firms within an industry can significantly alter the environment in which they operate. The second question is whether or not firms can significantly change themselves. Of course, these simplifying distinctions sacrifice a degree of realism in some areas in order to create clarity in other areas. By presenting four different models, we have the opportunity to select a model that is parsimonious without being over-simplified.

Population ecology

In their seminal article, Hannan and Freeman (1977) departed from previous research on organization environment relationships in two directions. First, they claimed that the population should be the unit of analysis rather than the organization. They defined a population as a collection of essentially homogeneous firms. Second, although recognizing that adaptation sometimes occurs inside of organizations, they claimed that strong inertial pressures constrained organizational change. These assumptions led to the conclusion that the organization–environment relationship should be observed most strongly in the patterns of births and deaths of organizations within a population. Both of these distinctions were later relaxed as the population ecology grew to embrace neoinstitutional and evolution perspectives (Amburgey and Rao, 1996). However, for the purpose of this analysis, we will characterize the perspective with these two foundational assumptions.

In this perspective, organizations – all with similar forms, or blueprints for transforming inputs into outputs – compete within an ecological niche. The quantity of inputs[1] in the niche, which is fixed and finite, determines the optimal number of organizations, or carrying capacity, of the niche. In population ecology, carrying capacity is defined as the maximum number of firms that can be sustained in an ecological niche. When the population of the niche is below the carrying capacity, the population grows at a natural rate. If the population increases to above the carrying capacity, competition for resources increases organizational mortality until the population level is reduced to the carrying capacity.

In this view an industry is an ecological niche. The origin of new industries is not explicitly included in population ecology because there is no explanation for where new ecological niches come from. There may be numerous unpopulated niches at any given time simply waiting to be noticed or some external process may create new ecological niches. Whatever the source of a new ecological niche, the population ecology model describes industry emergence as starting when the first firm enters the industry and continuing until the number of firms in the industry reaches carrying capacity. This model of organizations competing for scarce inputs where excess inputs attract new entrants is similar to the industrial organizations (IO) economic view of competition within an industry. However, IO economics concentrates on the potential for larger firms to attain competitive advantage through market power, while the population ecology perspective assumes firm homogeneity.

With this understanding of industry emergence, the relevant firm decisions are limited to the timing of the entry into an industry. The main task of entrepreneurs is to find unpopulated or underpopulated niches. These niches are analogous to what Shane and Venkataraman call entrepreneurial opportunities. They claim that a requirement for entrepreneurship is that perceptions of opportunities vary, either because of differing access to information or differing abilities to process this information. Entrepreneurship, in this view, is recognizing an underpopulated niche and founding an organization there.

Traditionally, the population ecology perspective does not explicitly study organizational performance separate from survival rates, but the view of competition within a niche suggests that the first firms to enter a niche will perform well until new entrants increase the competition for inputs. This suggests that the performance of entrepreneurial firms will be higher than the performance of firms entering a niche that is already populated. Early entering firms earn excess profits as an industry emerges but there are very limited opportunities for entrepreneurial activity to earn rents in this perspective, as we can see by going through the four requirements for rent-earning resources. First there is firm heterogeneity in only one variable – order of entry into the industry. To the extent that there are differences in abilities to recognize opportunities, there are ex ante limits to competition but the only possibility of ex post limits to competition is the natural growth rate. A niche with a high carrying capacity and a low natural growth rate would allow a first mover to earn a profit for longer but ultimately, when the population reaches carrying capacity, there will be no heterogeneity (since order entry is irrelevant when the industry reaches maturity) and thus no competitive advantage.

There are at least two situations where new firm entrance into an industry will be limited in such a way as to allow the population of the niche to remain below carrying capacity. The first is the situation of monopoly or oligopoly where a very small number of firms is sufficient to supply the industry demand.[2] New firms will not enter the industry because, while there are excess inputs in the niche, this excess is not sufficient to support a whole firm. The other situation, as shown by Lippman and Rumelt (1982), is when new entrants are uncertain of their ability to imitate incumbent firms. Although excess inputs are available in the niche, the expected value of these inputs may not be positive if there is a high possibility of failure for a new firm. In both of these cases the incumbent firms in the industry earn rents. The strategic resource that enables these rents is market position achieved through early opportunity recognition. Entrepreneurial strategy in the population ecology model can be summarized as follows:

In the population ecology model, entrepreneurial strategies rely on early entry through opportunity recognition.

- *Firms earn profits in the period of time before an industry reaches carrying capacity.*
- *Firms can only earn rents if new entrants are barred.*

An interesting extension to the population ecology model is the idea that opportunity recognition can be a strategic resource (Alverez and Barney, 2000). In this view, profits are expected to dissipate for incumbent firms as an ecological niche reaches carrying capacity; however, a firm that has the ability to repeatedly identify and enter new niches will sustain above-normal profits. Later, we will discuss another extension of the basic population ecology model that combines the idea of legitimacy from the institutional perspective with the concept of competition for scarce inputs. However, the simplified version of population ecology just presented is at least a part of any theory that focuses on the importance of opportunity recognition and organizational founding. In applying population ecology to entrepreneurial strategy, a basic assumption that must be tested is that firm performance is directly related to mortality rate within an industry.

New institutionalism

While population ecology sees organizational survival as fundamentally dependent upon access to scarce inputs, the new institutionalism perspective proposes that the survival of organizations ultimately depends on following socially constructed norms and rules. This perspective builds on the idea of organizational inertia introduced by population ecologists suggesting that the constraints limiting organizational options can be separated into what W. Richard Scott calls the three pillars of institutions: the regulative pillar encoded in the law; the normative pillar maintained through social obligation; and the cognitive pillar of things simply taken for granted. Organizations conform to these institutional pillars in order to be viewed as legitimate. These isomorphic pressures create industries of homogeneous firms as in population ecology. An industry has cognitive legitimacy when there is a high level of public knowledge and socio-political legitimacy when there is a high level of public acceptance (Aldrich and Fiol, 1994). If these isomorphic pressures do not change then there is little room for entrepreneurial activity, so the key to understanding entrepreneurship in this perspective is understanding how institutions change over time and more specifically understanding how new organizational forms become legitimate.

The fundamental distinction between population ecology and the new institutional perspective is the idea that populations of firms have the ability to change the environment by influencing what society views as legitimate. In this perspective industry emergence is an endogenous part of the model. Firms create a viable industry by establishing legitimacy in order to have access to customers, investors, regulators, and suppliers. There is no competition for scarce inputs that limits firm survival, instead legitimacy, once established, will ensure firm survival. Legitimacy for a new industry is not simply granted by society, it is embedded in institutions. For example, the legitimacy of the automobile industry is institutionalized by the road system, parking lots, drivers' licenses, pollution standards, name recognition of car companies, etc. The struggle for legitimacy can take a long time. Aldrich and Fiol (1994) cite work that shows some industries take several years or even decades before reaching a stable number of firms and attribute this time lag to the process of creating legitimacy for a new industry.

To institutionalists, the concept of entrepreneurial activity is broader than simply the decision of whether or when to enter an industry. As firms enter an industry they must act to establish legitimacy, and they do so by adopting socially approved conventions. Without firm heterogeneity there can be no rent-earning resources for firms. However, legitimacy may be a rent-creating resource for the industry as a whole. In other words, all firms within the industry would be expected to earn above-normal profits. Ex ante limits to competition exist if the requirements are obtained through a mechanism other than purchase on the open market. Ex post limits to competition exist if there is no substitute for legitimacy, an assumption that fits this model well since legitimacy is the only factor that influences performance. Finally, limited mobility exists if there are high transaction costs for transferring industry membership from one firm to another. An example of an industry that fits this description would be state lotteries. Only state governments have the necessary legitimacy to run lotteries. This legitimacy cannot be purchased, at any price, by other types of organizations. The resource of legitimacy allows state governments to earn a substantial rent, relative to other types of organizations, but the concept of legitimacy alone is not enough to explain relative performance of different state lotteries. Entrepreneurial strategy in the institutional perspective can be summarized as follows:

In the new institutionalism model, entrepreneurial strategies rely on achieving legitimacy.

- *All firms earn negative profits until legitimacy is established for the industry.*
- *To the extent that legitimacy creates rents, all firms within the industry earn these rents.*

While in the population ecology model industry emergence is seen as a process where early entrants earn extra profits until the industry reaches carrying capacity, in the institutional model industry emergence is seen as a process that requires extra effort from early entrants that is only rewarded after the industry has established legitimacy. In this model, entrepreneurs are pioneers who open up a new territory. Aldrich and Fiol develop a set of propositions about what characteristics of founders and founding firms are likely to lead to industry legitimacy. Aldrich and Baker (2001) extend this work to the context of Internet retailers and derive a set of strategies that firms, individually and collectively, can take to establish legitimacy. Swaminathan and Wade (2001) take a slightly different tack, making the case that the strategies of new populations of firms are very similar to the strategies of social movements.

All of this work focuses on legitimacy as an industry-level construct but does little to explain whether individual firms are able to reap the benefits of legitimacy. Two research questions that would help to flesh out the firm-level strategies of legitimacy creation are: (1) Can firms create firm-specific legitimacy separate from industry legitimacy? (2) What can incumbent firms do to inhibit more new entrants from entering an industry? Fombrun and Stanley (1990) address the first question by examining the antecedents and consequences of firm reputation. In a related manner, Rao (2001) examines certification contests in the automobile industry. These contests helped to establish legitimacy for the industry by educating the public on the relevant criteria for comparing automobiles. Furthermore, the winners of these contests were able to attain firm-specific legitimacy. The second question is important for explaining why entrepreneurial firms would ever bear the expense of establishing legitimacy for an industry if later entrants can achieve this legitimacy by mimicking incumbent firms. The industrial communities perspective discussed below may be a more appropriate model for addressing this question.

Organizational evolution

Like population ecology, the organizational evolution perspective emphasizes the struggle between organizations for limited inputs. However, unlike the ecological view, firms are not homogeneous within a population nor are they unchangeable over time. Instead firms are seen as a stable collection of routines (Nelson and Winter, 1982) or attributes into which variations are occasionally introduced. In this perspective, industry emergence remains exogenous as it is in population ecology. Firms can change but have no power to change the environment in which they operate. Astley's (1985) idea of punctuated equilibrium producing quantum speciation is one way of describing the process of new industry creation. In times of stability, selection pressures allow only small changes to occur. However, accidents, exogenous shocks, or fundamental breakthroughs in technology can create rich, untapped niches. When this happens, selection pressures are diminished, allowing mutant organizational forms (new species) to thrive. A given set of firm attributes creates a certain level of fitness for a given environment. This fitness level relative to other firms in the industry determines firm performance. Whenever one firm in an industry achieves a higher level of fitness, all other firms in the industry are negatively affected. The essence of entrepreneurial strategy in this perspective is making choices that improve the chances of attaining superior fitness. This adds a level of complexity to entrepreneurial strategy. Instead of simply making entry decisions based on the performance for a given population density and perhaps anticipating the likelihood of future entrants, an entrepreneurial firm in the evolutionary perspective must aim to achieve greater fitness while anticipating that all rivals are also attempting to achieve greater fitness.

There are various ways of modeling the competition of multiple firms simultaneously working to achieve greater fitness than the competition. A very simple model is contained in Hannan and Freeman's (1977) introduction to population ecology. They suggest that the ability of a firm to change is itself an attribute of the firm. A firm can be characterized as either a specialist tuned to perform well in a particular environment, or a generalist that is able to adapt to a wider variety of conditions. They predict that the generalist firm will have superior performance if the environmental conditions fluctuate regularly within a wide range, while the specialist firm that matches the current environment will have superior performance until the environment changes. The best strategy depends on whether or not the environment changes significantly. This model of firms achieving fitness is not a true evolutionary model because there is no room for progressive change of a firm over time, only the one-time decision of whether to be a specialist or generalist.

A more complex model is developed by Nelson and Winter (1982) who model progressive change in organizations along one dimension – efficient production. The basic choice that firms must make is the amount of spending on innovation of new technology versus imitation of competitors' technology. In this model, firm heterogeneity is caused first by differences in the basic choice between imitation and innovation and second by different levels of production efficiency achieved by firms. The rent-producing resources that entrepreneurial firms can acquire at the time of industry emergence can be classified into either size advantages or learning advantages. Larger firms in the models have the advantage of being able to commit greater resources to research (either imitation or innovation). An even greater advantage of larger firms is their ability to bring new ideas up to a very large scale. When a small firm makes a technological innovation it does not have a large effect on the relative fitness of other firms since it affects a small percentage of the sales in the industry. The small firm will grow, due to its enhanced fitness, but in the time it takes to scale up production other firms in the industry have ample opportunity to either imitate the innovation or make a competing discovery of their own. Large firms, however, can immediately bring an innovation to scale and negatively affect the fitness of competing firms. Size then (in terms of market share) becomes a rent-earning resource. There are not substitutes for size, nor can size be transferred from one firm to another. The other resource that can be acquired by entrepreneurial firms is knowledge. If knowledge is cumulative – that is if firms must acquire a certain level of knowledge before the next level is accessible – then knowledge becomes a resource. An example of this is the conventional wisdom of the microprocessor industry. Microprocessors evolve in generations with each generation operating at faster speeds and having more dense electronics. Because of the tacit process knowledge required in the industry, a firm must achieve production in one generation before progressing to the next generation. Because of this, early, successful entry can put a firm ahead in the knowledge race. Again, this knowledge is a resource to the extent that there are not substitutes for it and to the extent that it is not transferable between firms (because it is tacit knowledge, for example). Size and knowledge are rent-producing resources if the evolutionary mechanisms described above hold. They are specifically entrepreneurial resources if size and knowledge are more easily or more cheaply attained in the period of industry emergence. This finding from the evolutionary perspective nuances the prediction from population ecology where early entry was seen as a way to earn extra profits. The evolutionary perspective highlights the importance, not just of early entry, but also of concentrating on achieving scale and acquiring tacit knowledge. Concentrating on growth and technological innovation might mean sacrificing short-term performance (as the industry is emerging) in order to create long-term competitive advantage.

A third way of analyzing entrepreneurial strategies is to examine the multiple attributes on which firms can change. The fitness level of a firm depends on how all of the firm attributes correspond to environmental conditions. The fitness of a given combination of attributes cannot be anticipated but must be experienced by a firm. The evolution of a firm is modeled either as a repeating process of variation–selection–retention (Miner, 1993) or more mathematically as an NK complexity model (Kauffman, 1995). In NK models, N is the number of elements that can vary in the system and K is the degree of interdependence between these elements. The combination of these two parameters determines whether a firm faces a smooth landscape where small changes in form will produce small changes in fitness or a rugged landscape where there are multiple local optima. A basic conclusion of these models is that it is possible to "tune" an organization's evolution to match the environment. McKelvey (1999) suggests that organizations can achieve better fitness by choosing the correct level of coevolutionary complexity in the value chain. Levinthal and Warglien (1999) advocate designing organizational configurations to match the environment. To the extent that a superior ability to adapt is obtainable through early entry into an industry, tuned adaptability is a strategic resource that entrepreneurial firms can acquire. Entrepreneurial strategy in the evolutionary perspective can be summarized as follows:

In the evolution model, entrepreneurial strategies depend on achieving fitness.

- *Improvements in fitness produce profits until they are matched by competitors.*
- *Advantages in size, knowledge, or "tuned adaptability" can produce rents.*

The institutional perspective emphasized entrepreneurial actions that create legitimacy in the environment. The evolutionary perspective emphasizes entrepreneurial actions that create adaptability within the firm. Burton (2001) explores one aspect of new organizations – the founder's model of employment relationships – and finds significant variation within and across industries. These models were often chosen for strategic reasons as founders realized that initial relationships with employees would affect the firm long into the future. While this research does not directly address firm performance implications of these initial entrepreneurial choices, this work is an interesting first step toward fleshing out an evolutionary framework of entrepreneurial strategy by exploring at least one variable that affects the future adaptability of entrepreneurial firms.

Industrial communities

A fundamental limitation of the three perspectives discussed so far is that each views an industry as a collection of essentially similar firms. This is a simplifying assumption that has allowed each model to provide insight into important elements of entrepreneurial strategy – opportunity recognition, legitimacy, or fitness. However, in most cases the assumption that new industries are created by essentially similar firms is not warranted. A fourth perspective advanced by Van de Ven and Garud (1989), Van de Ven (1993), Van de Ven et al. (1999) relaxes this assumption by adopting an augmented view of an industry and by examining the emergence of an industrial infrastructure that an entrepreneurial community needs to sustain its members. It emphasizes that the creation of an industry is a collective achievement requiring numerous roles from a diverse set of entrepreneurs and organizations in both the public and private sectors.

This perspective, illustrated in figure 4.1, adopts the industrial community or the interorganizational field as the unit of analysis, and focuses on the issues and actors involved in constructing an industrial infrastructure that facilitates and constrains entrepreneurship. This infrastructure includes (1) institutional arrangements to legitimate, regulate, and standardize a new technology, (2) public resource endowments of

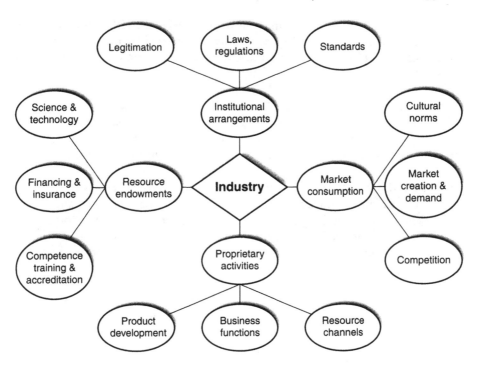

Figure 4.1   Augmented view of an industry in industrial community perspective
Source: Adapted from A. H. Van De Ven and R. Garud, "A Framework for Understanding the Emergence of New Industries," *Research on Technological Innovation, Management and Policy*, 4: 295–325, 1989.

basic scientific knowledge, financing mechanisms, and a pool of competent labor, (3) the creation of a market of consumers who are informed about and motivated to purchase the new product technology, as well as (4) proprietary R&D, manufacturing, marketing, and distribution functions by private entrepreneurial firms who commercialize products for generating profits and rents. Although extensive historical studies substantiate the importance of these infrastructure components for many industries, they have been treated as externalities to entrepreneurship. By incorporating these social, economic, and political components into a single framework, Van de Ven (1993) argues that we can systematically examine how various actors and functions interact to facilitate and constrain entrepreneurship.

This industrial community perspective takes a very different approach to our question of how entrepreneurial firms can acquire rents as a new industry emerges. It argues that entrepreneurial firms can generate rents in any of the four component arenas of an emergent industrial infrastructure. Implicitly or explicitly entrepreneurial firms make strategic decisions about how and in which of the four arenas they will participate. Moreover, if they choose not to play a role in some of the arenas, they are at the mercy of the decisions and actions taken by other firms and actors. Thus, entrepreneurial firms are seen as entities that require many things from the environment (acceptance from regulators, knowledge from research institutions, trained workers from universities, etc.), and the environment is made up of many different types of entities. In this view the industry is endogenous; it is constructed by the actors in the model and so this view is much better able to answer the question of what causes industry emergence.

The industrial communities perspective simplifies by segmenting this complexity into four arenas of activity in which firms must work simultaneously.

The first arena of activity is proprietary. This includes most commercial activities that are required to bring a firm into existence – forming an organization, developing a product, establishing relationships or alliances upstream and downstream in the supply chain.

The second arena of activity is where the raw materials are developed that firms depend on – scientific and technical knowledge, competent workers, and investment capital. These are all public goods which firms appropriate and transform into commercial products for profit. The development of this raw material that will become essential to an industry can happen without the direct involvement of firms but eventually firms will need to gain access to these things.

The third arena of activity is the institutional arrangements – laws, standards, and legitimacy. This is the arena that is the focus of the new institutional perspective.

The final arena of activity is the consumer market where the products from the industry are purchased. A market of knowledgeable consumers demanding a product typically does not exist for new businesses; this market must be constructed during industry emergence. The dimensions of this market provide the most direct analogy to the limited inputs available in an ecological niche. Ultimately the survival of every firm depends upon its ability to sell its products to consumers.

In this final perspective, the limiting assumptions of the population ecology perspective are completely relaxed. The population of competing firms is not homogeneous and the view of the industry includes all organizations that have any connection with the central product or service. In this view, industry emergence is a much longer process than just the time between when the first firms enter an industry and the time that the industry reaches some sort of equilibrium. In fact, the process of industry emergence may start years, or even decades, before firms take any significant action. In this view entrepreneurial activity is defined much more broadly; firms now have the opportunity to act in four separate arenas. For example, the emergence of the cochlear implants industry (Van de Ven and Garud, 1993) did not begin with the actions of private sector firms in the late 1970s; it began some 20 years earlier with basic research performed in public universities and research institutes. Furthermore, entrepreneurial activities by private firms did not simply consist of bringing a new product to market, as implied by the other three perspectives. Instead, entrepreneurial activity consisted of initiating formal relationships with research universities and investing in FDA-mandated clinical trials. These activities by firms took place long before any firms earned profits from cochlear implants.

There is potential to acquire rent-earning resources by engaging in activities in each of the four arenas. Recall the four requirements for a rent-earning resource. First, there must be firm heterogeneity, which is a basic assumption of this augmented view of an industry. Next, there must be ex ante limits to competition. That is, firms that acquire a resource through entrepreneurial activity must be able to acquire the re-

Table 4.1 Examples of rent-generating resources in industrial community perspective

	Institutional arrangements	Resource endowments	Market consumption
Example	*Patent on a medical device*	*Relationship with a research university*	*Reputation*
Ex ante limits to competition	If differing abilities to anticipate potential value	If differing abilities to anticipate potential value	If differing abilities to anticipate consumer reaction
Limited mobility	Transaction costs	Firm specific	Firm specific
Ex post limits to competition	FDA approval	Limited number of universities	Work to set standards

source at a less-than-market price. This condition can be met if there are differing abilities to anticipate the future value of resources. This is opportunity recognition again but here the opportunity to be recognized is not simply a potential industry but the potential value of a resource in a new industry. The entrepreneurial firm must not only recognize the growth potential of the industry but also anticipate how a specific resource will create competitive advantage in the future. Third, there will be limited mobility of the resources acquired through entrepreneurial activity to the extent that resources are firm specific. Finally, ex post limits to competition can be secured, in some cases through actions in the institutional arena. In other cases ex post limits to competition are created by limited supply of the resource. Three examples of resources that could potentially be acquired in three different arenas of activity illustrate how the conditions for rent-earning resources can be met. Table 4.1 outlines these examples.

First, consider the potential value of a patent on a medical device. There will be ex ante limits to competition if most firms underestimate, or even fail to consider, the potential size of the market for a medical device. The firm with the correct forecast will be able to develop the technology at a cost less than the value of the patent. Mobility of this resource will be limited because it is likely that the research process leading up to acquiring the patent will create many firm-specific resources – knowledge about the full potential of the technology or experience producing prototypes of the device, for example. Finally, ex post limits to competition can be achieved through appropriate actions in the legitimacy arena that make imitations illegal and substitutions unacceptable.

Second, a relationship between a firm and a research university could be a strategic resource in the resources endowment arena. If competing firms do not anticipate the value of aligning with a research university there will not be open competition for the relationship, thus creating ex ante limits to competition. Once the relationship is established, mobility of this resource would be limited because personal connections and a history of working closely together make it unlikely that the relationship could be easily transferred to another firm. Finally, the very limited population of research universities creates ex post limits to competition for this resource.

Third, a reputation earned in the time of industry emergence could be a resource in the market consumption arena. If firms have differing expectations of what kind of reputation will be valuable, there will be ex ante limits to competition. For example, some firms may assume that a reputation for technological breakthroughs will be valuable in the product market, while other firms concentrate on safety or quality. Once a valuable reputation is established, there will be limited mobility because of the difficulty of transferring a reputation from one firm to another. Finally, the firm that has a good reputation can limit ex post competition for this resource by working in the institutional arena to establish standards that are advantageous for the firm.

In the industrial communities model, entrepreneurial strategies rely on achieving competitive advantage in any of four arenas of activity: resource endowments, institutional arrangements, proprietary activities, and market consumption. In this model, firm survival is threatened by poor performance in any one of these areas.

Discussion

As a new industry emerges, how do entrepreneurial firms gain future competitive advantage? The four perspectives discussed in this paper provide four answers. In a nutshell, the answers can be distilled into one-line claims about what determines the performance of entrepreneurial firms:

- *Population Ecology – Population density determines performance.*
- *Institutional Theory – Legitimacy determines performance.*
- *Organizational Evolution – Fitness level determines performance.*
- *Industrial Community – Roles in creating infrastructure determine performance.*

Clearly each of these models of firm performance and industry emergence is a simplification of reality. Combining the four perspectives into a single framework creates a tool for analyzing specific situations in order to see which model fits.

The first distinction to be made among the four models is whether or not firms can significantly affect the environment in which they operate. In other words, is the environment exogenous or endogenous to the model? The critical components of the environment in the context of industry emergence are the origin of the industry, the potential size of the industry, and the basis of competition within the industry. In two perspectives – population ecology and organizational evolution – the environment is exogenous to the firm so the creation and size of a new industry is left unexplained and outside of the control of firms. Furthermore, firms do not have any control over the basis of competition. In these models, performance differences can only be explained by how firms react to the environment. In the remaining two perspectives – new institutionalism and industrial communities – the environment is endogenous. In these perspectives, the individual and collective actions of firms create new industries and determine their ultimate size. Firms do not simply react to the environment; they participate in changing the environment. The next distinction to be made among the four models is whether or not firms have the power to change themselves. The per-

		Can firms change themselves?	
		No	Yes
Can firms affect their environment?	No	Population ecology	Organizational evolution
	Yes	New institutional	Industrial community

Figure 4.2 A framework of the four perspectives

spectives of population ecology and new institutionalism emphasize organizational inertia. Essential firm characteristics are imprinted at the time of their founding. Consequently, in these perspectives, firms are seen as essentially homogeneous. In these perspectives relevant actions of firms are limited to entry into a new market and cooperating to create legitimacy. The potential for firms to change is included in the other two perspectives – organizational evolution and industrial communities. In these perspectives, firms are heterogeneous. They differ not only in the immediate strategic options available but also in their ability to acquire new abilities over time. While organizations are simply born or founded in the first two perspectives, the later two perspectives see organization development as an essential entrepreneurial task.

The two by two matrix in figure 4.2 illustrates the essential differences between the four perspectives. In the upper left-hand cell is population ecology, the simplest perspective. In this view homogeneous firms maintain a commensalistic relationship by competing within an environmental niche for the same scarce resources. The niche of population ecology is very similar to the concept of industry in industrial organization economics, defined as the set of firms that produce similar or substitute products (Porter, 1985). In this view firms have few real choices, the only significant choice being whether or when to enter an industry. Also in this perspective is the idea that industry emergence is exogenous to the model. Firms can only respond to the existence of ecological niches; there is not room in this perspective for firms to change the environment.

The other perspectives augment the population ecology view by either allowing firms to change and thus differ or by allowing firms to act proactively to affect the environment. The evolution perspective expands along the first dimension by allowing firms to change over time. In the evolution perspective, the environment is still essentially fixed but within a population of firms there is much more freedom to experiment with new ideas and practices. The new institutional perspective expands along the second dimension. In this perspective firms do not change significantly over time but they can work proactively to change the environment in which they operate. They do this most significantly by working to create legitimacy. The most complex view is the industrial community perspective. In this view, firms have a much wider spectrum of choices. They can work to change themselves as in the evolutionary view but they can also work to construct their collective environment.

		Can firms change themselves?	
		No	No
Can firms affect their environment?	No	**Population ecology** Rewards – early exploitation Risk – none Image – opportunist Question – how are opportunities recognized?	**Organizational evolution** Rewards – fast learning Risk – uncertain evolution Image – risk taker Question – do entrepreneurial firms learn faster?
	Yes	**New institutional** Rewards – none Risk – no legitimacy Image – pioneer Question – why be first?	**Industrial community** Rewards – writing the rules Risk – being out-maneuvered Image – industry architect Question – what strategies work?

Figure 4.3   Summary of entrepreneurial strategy in four perspectives

Of course, very little research can be completely contained in any of these four boxes. We have drawn sharp distinctions between the perspectives in order to clarify how differing conceptualizations of firms and their environments lead to differing conclusions about the results of entrepreneurial activity. Also, it should be noted that the perspectives we are describing were not originally created to answer questions of performance and entrepreneurship. However, each perspective is a coherent and fruitful framework and thus has something to offer to the question of entrepreneurial strategy.

Taking the perspectives together gives a comprehensive view of the rewards and risks inherent in entrepreneurial activity. On the positive side there are three potential rewards for entrepreneurship. First, entrepreneurs may face less competition for inputs in the early stages of an industry. Second, entrepreneurial firms may take an early and decisive lead in the race for knowledge and scale. Third, entrepreneurs get an opportunity to write the rules that will control competition and create profit opportunities in the future. On the negative side, there are three potential risks of entrepreneurship. First, any new kind of activity lacks legitimacy and faces many obstacles before earning a profit. Second, the process of learning may be uncontrollable and unpredictable. Third, in negotiating the rules of the industry, there is always the chance of being outmaneuvered by other organizations involved in the process. When analyzing a specific context one can determine the degree to which the environment is affected by firm actions and the degree to which firms can proactively take actions to change themselves. The answer to these two questions will point to one of the four perspectives, which will highlight the relevant risks and rewards of entrepreneurial activity. The important risks and rewards of each perspective are summarized in figure 4.3.

Although the answers provided by each perspective are different, each perspective is related to a popular conceptualization of entrepreneurship, and each perspective highlights one question about entrepreneurship. According to the population ecology perspective, successful entrepreneurship is related to the ability to recognize opportunity. The important question not answered by this perspective is how some individuals or organizations are able to recognize opportunity more quickly than others. In the evolution perspective, on the other hand, risk taking is the essence of entrepreneurship. Being successful in a new industry requires developing the right competencies quicker than anyone else; there are no guarantees of success but high potential payoffs. The important question from this perspective is how can firms learn quicker than other firms? In the neo-institutional perspective, the entrepreneur is seen as a pioneer, blazing a new trail for others to follow. However, in this perspective it seems that higher profits are only possible later, after legitimacy has been established. The important question for this perspective is what motivates entrepreneurship if not profits? Finally, the industrial community perspective sees entrepreneurship as an extended game of negotiation in the industry infrastructure that emerges for an inter-organizational field of numerous different actors in the public and private sectors. Entrepreneurial activity creates the rules and resources that will define the industry. The important question is what roles in this infrastructure should an entrepreneurial firm perform that may lead to entrepreneurial rents in the process of industry creation? The image of entrepreneurship and the unanswered question in each perspective are summarized in figure 4.3.

Conclusion

The industry is an uncommon level of analysis in the study of entrepreneurship. The firm and the entrepreneur are more frequently studied. At the same time, industry emergence is an uncommon context in the study of strategy. The study of firms in well-established industries is the norm. We believe that the study of industry emergence can synthesize the learning in these two disciplines. More importantly, industry emergence may be a key to unlock further discoveries in both fields. In strategy, where the debate often centers on whether industry characteristics or firm attributes are the source of competitive advantage, we wonder if a better understanding of industry emergence can answer a more fundamental question – where do these advantages (whether at the firm level or industry level) come from in the first place? In entrepreneurship, we echo the sentiments of Mezias and Kuperman (2000) who argue that successful entrepreneurship is not the result of solitary individuals acting in isolation; entrepreneurs are members of larger collectives.

One way of linking the study of industry emergence with a lower level of analysis may be through the study of entrepreneurial mindsets. The different predictions of each model and, more importantly, the different image of what it means to be entrepreneurial in each model raise the question of whether there might be four entrepreneurial mindsets that correspond to the four models of industry emergence. The mindsets of the opportunist, the risk taker, the pioneer, and the negotiator are quite different but at the same time they are all entrepreneurial. Perhaps this framework can be used to better understand how entrepreneurs succeed in different contexts. The final perspective, the industrial community model, is the most complicated and may be the most widely applicable. We suggest extending this model of entrepreneurial activity taking place in four distinct arenas of activity to include cognitive models. Porac et al. (1995) have shown that the cognitive models of managers determine patterns of rivalry. It is reasonable to suggest that there are similarly powerful cognitive models in the institutional arena, the resource endowment arena, the proprietary activities arena, and the market consumption arena. Four related cognitive models may be at work defining the competitive dynamics of an industry and ultimately the performance firms. One powerful tool that entrepreneurs have for shaping cognitive models is storytelling, an idea developed by Lounsbury and Glynn (2000) in their work on the idea of cultural entrepreneurship. To the extent that cognitive models are formed as the industry emerges, industry emergence becomes an even more important context of study for both strategy and entrepreneurship scholars.

Notes

1   Note that we are using the term "inputs" instead of "resources" as Hannan and Freeman did. We do this to make clear the distinction between the idea of resources contained in the resource-based view of the firm, where resources are items contained within the firm that enable competitive advantage, and the idea of resources in population ecology, where resources are scarce goods in the environment for which firms compete.
2   Oligopoly may also be created by other means, such as government regulation that limits new entrants; however, the population ecology model is simply a model of firms and inputs. The issue of government regulation can be better modeled in the new institutional perspective.

References

Aldrich, H. E. and Baker, T. 2001. All or nothing at all: Entrepreneurial responses to constraints of new populations of organizations. In C. B. Schoonhoven and E. Romanelli (eds), *The entrepreneurship dynamic*. Stanford, CA: Stanford University Press.

Aldrich, H. E. and Fiol, C. M. 1994. Fools rush in? The institutional context of industry creation. *Academy of Management Review*, 19(4): 645–70.

Alvarez, S. and Barney, J. (2000). Entrepreneurial capabilities: A resource-based view. In G. D. Meyer and K. A. Heppard (eds), *Entrepreneurship as strategy: Competing on the entrepreneurial edge*. Thousand Oaks, CA: Sage Publications, 63–81.

Amburgey, T. L. and Rao, H. 1996. Organizational ecology: Past, present, and future directions. *Academy of Management Journal*, 39(5): 1265:86.

Astley, W. G. 1985. The two ecologies: Population and community perspectives on organizational evolution. *Administrative Science Quarterly*, 30: 224–41.

Barney, J. B. 1986. Strategic factor markets: Expectations, luck, and business strategy. *Management Science*, 32(10): 1231–41.

Barney, J. B. 1996. The resource-based theory of the firm. *Organization Science*, 7: 469.

Burton, M. D. 2001. The company they keep: Founders' models for organizing high-technology firms. In C. B. Schoonhoven and E. Romanelli (eds), *The entrepreneurship dynamic*. Stanford, CA: Stanford University Press, 13–39.

Cooper, A. C. and Gasco, F. J. G. (1992). Entrepreneurs, processes of founding, and new-firm performance. In D. Sexton and J. Kasarda (eds), *The state of the art of entrepreneurship*. Boston: PWS-Kent Publishers, 301–40.

Fombrun, C. and Stanley, M. 1990. What's in a name? Reputation building and corporate strategy. *Academy of Management Journal*, 33(2): 233–58.

Hannan, M. T. and Freeman, J. 1977. The population ecology of organizations. *American Journal of Sociology*, 82(5): 929–64.

Kauffman, S. 1995. *At home in the universe: the search for the laws of self-organization and complexity*. New York: Oxford University Press.

Levinthal, D. A. and Warglien, M. 1999. Landscape design: Designing for local action in complex worlds. *Organization Science*, 10(3): 342:57.

Lippman, S. A. and Rumelt, R. P. 1982. Uncertain imitability: An analysis of interfirm differences in efficiency under competition. *The Bell Journal of Economics*, 13: 418–38.

Lounsbury, M. and Glynn M. A. 2000. Cultural entrepreneurship: stories, legitimacy and the acquisition of resources. *Strategic Management Journal*, 22 (special issue): 545–64.

McKelvey, B. 1999. Avoiding complexity catastrophe in coevolutionary pockets: Strategies for rugged landscapes. *Organization Science*, 10(3): 294–321.

Mezias, S. J. and Kuperman, J. C. 2000. The community dynamics of entrepreneurship: The birth of the American film industry. 1895–1929. *Journal of Business Venturing*, 16: 209:33.

Miner, A. S. 1993. Seeking adaptive advantage: Evolutionary theory and managerial action. In J. Baum and J. Singh (eds), *Evolutionary dynamics of organizations*. New York, Oxford, 76–89.

Nelson, R. N. 1982. *Government and technical progress: A cross-industry analysis*. New York: Pergamon Press.

Nelson, R. R. and Winter, S. G. 1982. *An evolutionary theory of economic change*. Cambridge, MA: The Belknap Press of Harvard University Press.

Peteraf, M. A. 1993. The cornerstones of competitive advantage: A resource-based view. *Strategic Management Journal*, 14: 179–91.

Porac, J. F., Thomas, H., Wilson, F., Paton, D., and Kanfer, A. 1995. Rivalry and industry model of Scottish knitwear producers. *Administrative Science Quarterly*, 40: 203:27.

Porter, M. E. 1985. *Competitive advantage: Creating and sustaining superior performance*. New York: Free Press.

Rao, H. 2001. Certification contests and organizational foundings in new industries: A study of the early automobile industry. In C. B. Schoonhoven and E. Romanelli (eds), *The entrepreneurship dynamic*. Stanford, CA: Stanford University Press, 262–85.

Scott, W. R. 1995. *Institutions and organizations*. Thousand Oaks, CA: Sage Publications.

Shane, S. and Venkataraman, S. 2000. The promise of entrepreneurship as a field of research. *Academy of Management Review*, 25(1): 217–26.

Swaminathan, A. and Wade, J. 2001. Social movement theory and the evolution of new organizational forms. In C. B. Schoonhoven and E. Romanelli (eds), *The entrepreneurship dynamic*. Stanford, CA: Stanford University Press, 286–313.

Van de Ven, A. 1993. The development of an infrastructure for entrepreneurship. *Journal of Business Venturing*, 8: 211–30.

Van de Ven, A. H. and Garud, R. 1989. A framework for understanding the emergence of new industries. *Research on Technological Innovation, Management and Policy*, 4: 195–225.

Van de Ven, A. H. and Garud, R. 1993. Innovation and industry development: The case of cochlear implants. *Research on Technical Innovation, Management and Policy*, 5: 1–46.

Van de Ven, A. H., Polley, D., Garud, R., and Venkataraman, S. 1999. *The innovation journey*. New York: Oxford University Press.

Varian, H. R. 1999. *Intermediate microeconomics: A modern approach*. New York: W. W. Norton & Company.

Wernerfelt, B. (1984). A resource-based view of the firm. *Strategic Management Journal*, 5: 171–80.

Entrepreneurial Resources

CHAPTER FIVE

Resource-Based Theory and the Entrepreneurial Firm

Sharon A. Alvarez, Jay B. Barney

> *The term "entrepreneur" is used to describe those who direct resources in the firm. I use this term to refer to the person or persons who, in a competitive system, take the place of the price mechanism in the direction of resources.*
>
> Coase, *The nature of the firm*

Presently the field of entrepreneurship, despite calls for the development of a unique theory, continues to lack a unifying theoretical base that can be used to explain, predict, and empirically examine entrepreneurial phenomena. Within the field of entrepreneurship much of entrepreneurship scholarship is still in the "describing the phenomena" stage, including empirical studies, and using ad hoc theories already in existence from several other fields. The result is that scholars from other disciplines use entrepreneurship as the setting to extend their own theoretical frameworks, but leave little behind that extends entrepreneurship theory. Unless the field of entrepreneurship moves beyond these studies, and entrepreneurship journals require that multidisciplinary work from other areas contributes to the unique conceptual domain of entrepreneurship, the field's legitimacy and distinctive contribution will be at stake.

Currently resource-based theory lacks the insights provided by creativity and the entrepreneurial act (Barney, 2001). The addition of entrepreneurial actions to resource-based theory can augment this view by suggesting alternative uses of resources that have not been previously discovered leading to heterogeneous assets and thus firm advantages. Indeed, entrepreneurial actions are about creating new resources or combining existing resources in new ways that result in wealth creation benefits through the mechanism of the sustainable competitive firm (Ireland et al., 2001).

Indeed, it may be by examining the intersection between entrepreneurship and the resource-based view (RBV) that clarity may be achieved with regard to the larger impact of entrepreneurship on strategic management. Ireland et al. (2001: 6) define entrepreneurship "as a context-dependent social process through which individuals and teams create wealth by bringing together unique packages of resources to exploit marketplace opportunities." However, this chapter extends this definition by extending the constructs examined when analyzing the comprehensiveness of entrepreneurial actions. Entrepreneurial actions refer to individual-level actions in the creation of the firm, firm-level actions in the pursuit of innovations, and market-level actions in the exploitation of opportunities presented.

Application of the RBV shifts the emphasis in entrepreneurship research from opportunity recognition (Kirzner, 1973) to an emphasis on the entrepreneurial firm as the means of transforming homogeneous inputs into heterogeneous outputs. These heterogeneous outputs, in turn, can become sources of wealth creation (Barney, 1986). Similar to Coase (1937) and Schumpeter (1934), the RBV suggests that entrepreneurial knowledge manifests itself through the firm. The purpose of this chapter is to describe the relationship between entrepreneurial actions, on the one hand, and the creation of firms, on the other, by applying resource-based logic to the study of entrepreneurship.

Entrepreneurship scholars agree that entrepreneurial opportunities exist primarily because different actors have different beliefs about the relative value of resources and the potential future value of these resources when they are converted from inputs into outputs (Schumpeter, 1934; Kirzner, 1973; Shane and Venkataraman, 2000). Resource heterogeneity is the cornerstone of resource-based theory. Indeed resource-based theory may be the unifying theory that the field of entrepreneurship has lacked. Unlike theories from other disciplines that reduce entrepreneurial firms to a "database," the RBV can potentially extend entrepreneurship theory by focusing on the unique entrepreneurial actions needed to create sustainable heterogeneous firms that create wealth long-term.

The goal of this chapter is to examine the four conditions of RBV that must be present for the existence of sustained above-normal returns or entrepreneurial returns; resource heterogeneity, ex post limits to competition, imperfect factor mobility, and ex ante limits to competition (Peteraf, 1993) within the context of existing theory on entrepreneurship. By examining RBV together with existing entrepreneurship theory this chapter makes the case that RBV can theoretically inform and extend current research on entrepreneurship theory.

Resource Heterogeneity

Resource heterogeneity is the most basic condition of resource-based theory and it assumes that resource bundles and capabilities underlying production are heterogeneous across firms (Barney, 1991). Resource-based theory suggests that heterogeneity is necessary for a sustainable advantage, but not sufficient. For example, a firm can have heterogeneous assets, but not the other conditions suggested by resource-based theory, and those assets will only generate a short-term advantage until they are imitated.

Similar to RBV, heterogeneous resources and the transformation of resources are also a basic condition of entrepreneurship (Kirzner, 1997). Some scholars (Kirzner, 1973; Casson, 1982) suggest that entrepreneurial opportunities exist when different actors have insight into the value of resources that other actors do not, and the actors with the insight act upon these unexploited opportunities. If these actors are correct an entrepreneurial rent will be earned, if not an entrepreneurial loss will occur (Rumelt; 1987; Alvarez and Barney, 2000). Wealth creation and the ability to produce wealth over time result when actors through the mechanism of the firm can sustain the above-normal economic rents that are derived from entrepreneurial activity.

The *Journal of Management* issue on the resource-based theory in 1991 contributed special insights as to the role played by heterogeneous assets in achieving a firm sustainable competitive advantage. There has also been further refinement to the resource-based theory concept of assets to include tacit socially complex resources (Barney, 1991). Paradoxically, while the importance of resource heterogeneity has been acknowledged, strategists have given scant attention to the process by which these resources are discovered, turned from inputs into outputs, and exploited to extract greater profits. What the authors of this chapter suggest is that it is through the entrepreneurial process of cognition, alertness, understanding market opportunities, and coordinated knowledge that inputs become heterogeneous outputs.

Cognition

There is probably no group of individuals that has received more discussion and has been assumed to be more heterogeneous from the rest of the population than entrepreneurs. The notion that entrepreneurs were somehow different from the rest of the population provided the impetus for substantial research on the subject in the 1960s and 1970s. Unfortunately, most of this research focused on a host of traits such as risk taking and need for achievement, but overall, the findings were disappointing (see Low and MacMillan, 1988 for a review). Recently, the emergence of cognitive approaches to understanding how entrepreneurs think and make strategic decisions is showing much promise (Busenitz and Barney, 1997; Baron, 1998). If entrepreneurs do indeed have a unique mindset, the right cognitive approach in the right context may represent a source of sustained competitive advantage (Barney, 1991).

Entrepreneurial mindset is used here in reference to cognitive abilities that utilize heuristics to impart meaning to an ambiguous and fragmented situation.[1] The term "heuristics" refers to simplifying strategies that individuals (entrepreneurs in this case) use to make strategic decisions (Tversky and Kahneman, 1974), especially in complex situations where less complete or uncertain information is available. The ability to impose heuristic-based logic onto decisions in a complex and fragmented situation may be the most efficient way to navigate through decisions involving new business opportunities. Indeed, entrepreneurs have been found to use heuristics more extensively than managers of larger organizations (Busenitz and Barney, 1997). The managerial mindset is referred to as more systematic decision making where management uses accountability and compensation schemes, the structural coordination of business activities across various units, and justifies future developments using quantifiable budgets.

Given the cognitive differences between entrepreneurial and managerial mindsets, researchers have begun to explore the competitive implications of such differences (Busenitz and Barney, 1997) and how these mindsets may be appropriate for different contexts. For example, Wright et al. (2000) argued that entrepreneurial buyouts need leaders with an entrepreneurial cognition makeup while efficiency-oriented buyouts needed more of a managerial cognition. Thus, given that individuals differ in their cognitive orientation and assuming that these differences are relatively stable over time, they may be a source of competitive advantage.

Most of the cognition literature has assumed that issues with heuristics are of concern to virtually all decision makers. Entrepreneurial cognition indicates that decisions are significantly influenced by individual heuristics (Baron, 1998; Forbes, 1999; Busenitz and Lau, 1996) and an understanding of entrepreneurs is significantly limited without attention to these cognitive processes (Hitt and Tyler, 1991). This has particular implications for entrepreneurs because they regularly find themselves in situations that tend to maximize the potential impact of various heuristics (Baron, 1998).

In probing these cognitive processes, it is important to first understand the utility of such decision making. Given the level of uncertainty entrepreneurs face, they frequently use heuristics to piece together limited information to make convincing decisions in the face of much turbulence (Busenitz and Barney, 1997). Without heuristic-based logic, the pursuit of new opportunities becomes too overwhelming and costly for those decision makers who seek a more factual base. The decision-making contexts facing entrepreneurs also tend to be more complex. Without the elaborate policies, procedural routines, and structural mechanisms common to established organizations, heuristics may have a great deal of utility in enabling entrepreneurs to make decisions that exploit brief windows of opportunity (Tversky and Kahneman, 1974).

Central to most models of learning is the issue of achieving new understandings, interpretations, and insights (Daft and Weick, 1984). Learning in the context of entrepreneurship may also have some important links to the use of heuristics in decision making. Sources of competitive advantage are thought to potentially evolve around knowledge-creation and decision-making capabilities (Barney, 1991). Lower-level learning tends to follow the more rational model by focusing on repetitious observations and routinized learning. Such learning tends to be short-term and temporary (Fiol and Lyles, 1985). Consistent with the notion of single-loop learning, there are few changes in underlying policies or values (Argyris and Lauderdale, 1983). Such learning modes tend to be slower and more imitable (Lei, Hitt, and Bettis, 1996), in part because decision makers usually wait on results from repeated outcomes of success or failure to reach their decisions.

Higher-level learning involves the formation and use of heuristics to generate new insights into solving ambiguous problems (Lei et al., 1996). Such learning tends to create new insights and direction for emerging paths to solve specific problems that are chaotic, fragmented, and unfocused (Zahra, Ireland and Hitt, 2000). While the heuristic-based logic may use less information and be less accurate, using heuristics embedded in individual-specific clusters of knowledge facilitates quick adjustments to emerging trends (Krabuanrat and Phelps, 1998; Autio, Sapienza and Almeida, 2000). For example, decision makers can integrate new information with their heuristic-based logic to make inferences and adjust developing innovations (Daft and Weick, 1984; Lei et al., 1996). We suggest that faster learning is enhanced by the more extensive use of heuristic-based decision making. Such higher-level learning also tends to produce specialization (Levitt and March, 1988) and sometimes a unique understanding of an entrepreneurial situation that may be a source of competitive advantage because high specialization is more likely to result in successful outcomes in rapidly changing environments (Lei et al., 1996).

Taken together, the more frequent presence of heuristic-based logic in decision making by entrepreneurs (Busenitz and Barney, 1997) suggests that they make decisions in fundamentally different ways and that these decision mechanisms enable them to more quickly make sense out of uncertain and complex situations. Such decision approaches can lead to forward-looking approaches (Gavetti and Levinthal, 2000) perceiving new opportunities, faster learning, and unorthodox interpretations (innovations). The more extensive use of heuristics by entrepreneurs allows them to more readily navigate through a wide array of problems and irregularities inherent in the development of new opportunities. The attainment of knowledge in this way is an intangible asset that, given its rareness among business leaders, may be a source of competitive advantage for entrepreneurs.

Entrepreneurial alertness

Entrepreneurial alertness is the ability to see where products (or services) do not exist or have become unsuspectedly valuable to consumers and where new methods of production have, unknown to others, become feasible. This alertness exists when different actors have insight into the value of resources that other actors do not. Kirzner (1997) terms entrepreneurial alertness "flashes of superior insight."

An important feature in entrepreneurship theory is that entrepreneurial alertness and the possession of knowledge are distinct. Entrepreneurial alertness is necessary but not sufficient for entrepreneurial actions to work effectively. Alertness is the recognition of the opportunity and knowledge is the coordination of obtaining inputs at below market value and converting inputs into outputs for a profit. Knowledge flows across space and time and can be either stored in memory or communicated. Organizational knowledge is individual knowledge that collectively resides within the organization and may even be contained within an individual or group that specializes in the cataloging of organizational knowledge. However, coordinating knowledge in different ways that change the allocation of resources in order to obtain profits is an entrepreneurial action (Casson, 1999). The possession of knowledge is passive, the coordination of knowledge for profit is proactive and entrepreneurial and is often associated with firm size.[2] It is the distinction between entrepreneurial alertness and the possession and coordination of knowledge that is key to understanding how the entrepreneur systematically detects and helps eliminate error when determining the ex post value of resources.

Entrepreneurial alertness is a subject that has long eluded entrepreneurship scholars. We do not understand precisely how entrepreneurs experience superior foresight; however, we do know that this alertness is stimulated by the lure of profits, the generation of cash flows greater than their expected returns. In an entrepreneurial context, information asymmetries create unexploited opportunities. Alertness depends on the attractiveness of an opportunity and its ability to be grasped once it is perceived (Kirzner, 1979). This alertness is motivated by the incentive of future opportunities and not by present opportunities available through the comparison of currently known alternatives.

Market opportunities

An unanswered question by entrepreneurship scholars that directly impacts the field is: Where are the boundaries between firms (Schumpeter, 1934) and markets (Kirzner, 1997)? The market versus firm debate remains currently blurred and ambiguous in the study of entrepreneurship, in large part due to the obsession of trying to distinguish equilibrium and disequilibrium. The roots of this controversy stem primarily from the Austrian view of entrepreneurship and Kirzner's (1973) work which distinguishes the market process from market equilibrium.

It is outside of the scope of this chapter to explicitly address the debate between equilibrium models and disequilibrium models, therefore we will give a simplified version of this debate. The market equilibrium referred to in Kirzner's (1973, 1979, 1997) work is price theory and the model of perfect competition. Kirzner's view is that perfect competition models fail to understand the market process, and that newer models of imperfect competition continue to fail to recognize the shortcomings of the perfect competition model. In short, Kirzner criticizes these models because they do not include entrepreneurship or the entrepreneurial act of discovery.

The market process as described by Kirzner is a disequilibrium process in which the entrepreneur recognizes market disequilibrium opportunities and exploits these opportunities. The entrepreneur in this model is alert to unnoticed market changes that may make it possible to get far more in exchange than had been previously possible. In this scenario the entrepreneur is able to sell something at a price higher than its buy price. Anyone can be an entrepreneur since it presupposes no initial good fortune in the form of valuable assets (Kirzner, 1973).

The shortcomings of price theory and the perfect competitive model also have long ago been uncovered by Knight (1921) and Coase (1937). Both Knight and Coase made important contributions by suggesting that markets are imperfect, that there are costs associated with market transactions, and that the entrepreneurial function is missing from these models.

Continuing to focus on price theory and perfect competition models will not move the field of entrepreneurship closer to a theoretical base. The reason is that the price model was developed over 200 years ago in England and Central Europe to answer the question, is central economic planning necessary to avoid chaotic economic conditions? As the model was developed what it actually models is not perfect competition, but instead extreme decentralization. The model assumes full and free knowledge, information at low to zero cost, no decision making, and most importantly no central authority that coordinates the allocation of resources. In this model entrepreneurship is assumed to be limited, costly, and exogenous. The weakness of this model is its inability to analyze entrepreneurial coordinated knowledge and the entrepreneur's ability to coordinate knowledge as a scarce resource. Instead of the perfect competition model, Demsetz (1991) suggests it should be named the perfect decentralization model.

In the field of entrepreneurship the distinction between the discovery of market opportunities (Kirzner, 1979) and the exploitation of these opportunities (Schumpeter, 1934) is a crucial element in entrepreneurship theory not yet addressed. The important question to ask is not whether price theory models or the perfect competition model addresses the role of entrepreneurship, either through equilibrium or disequilibrium, because several scholars have already answered this question (Knight, 1921, Schumpeter, 1934; Coase, 1937; Kirzner, 1973). Instead we argue that the important question is, "When is it less costly for the entrepreneur via the firm to coordinate resources and disparate knowledge and when is it less costly for the market to coordinate resources?"

At the core of this controversy is the treatment of knowledge (Hayek, 1949; Kirzner, 1997). Schumpeter (1934) distinguished between invention and innovation, with invention being the discovery of an opportunity and innovation the exploitation of a profitable opportunity. The importance of the distinction between invention and innovation is that it takes the preoccupation away from price theory and its shortcomings and instead focuses on the firm as a problem-solving institution (Demsetz, 1991). Instead of concentrating on the market, the focus is on the role of entrepreneurship as the integration of disparate specialized knowledge (as suggested by Schumpeter).

Hayek (1945) further expands on the importance of learning and knowledge incorporated within entrepreneurial actions. In this view the entrepreneur experiences both partial ignorance and learning at the same time. The ignorance is a result of uncertainty about the future. The learning, however, is a result of buyers and sellers learning to adjust their behavior over time in order to conduct their transactions at the optimal level. The entrepreneurial process in this sense is about information discovery of the market and the coordination of knowledge. What distinguishes this view of the entrepreneur as a pure buyer and seller (markets) and the entrepreneur as the exploiter of opportunities (firms) is the incorporation of learning and knowledge. If the application of knowledge requires coordinating many types of specialized knowledge then the firm is required for the integration of knowledge.

This section suggests that entrepreneurship theory should move beyond markets because the entrepreneur exploring the buy or sell system of the market does not necessarily create wealth. However, through the market process actors learn through an evolving decision-making process how to identify opportunities, thus it is through the market process that entrepreneurs learn to be alert to potentially profitable situations. However, once the entrepreneur learns to identify opportunities, it is through the firm that the entrepreneur tests his or her knowledge by obtaining and redeploying inputs into heterogeneous outputs. If the entrepreneur is successful his or her tacit knowledge will enable the entrepreneur to rebundle resources without producing waste, redeploying these now heterogeneous resources and generating entrepreneurial rents. Thus it is through the firm that entrepreneurs create wealth.

Coordinated knowledge and the firm

Entrepreneurial knowledge is a conceptual, abstract knowledge of where to obtain undervalued resources, explicit and tacit, and how to deploy these resources. Both Kirzner (1973) and Schumpeter (1934) describe the entrepreneurial role as the decision to direct inputs into certain processes rather than into other processes. Entrepreneurship involves what Schumpeter termed "new combinations" of resources. Schumpeter (1934) described the entrepreneur as the one who combined productive factors in some new way, a product, production method, or a market. He further maintained that innovation was driven by the entrepreneur (who is at the heart of the firm) and not consumer driven (markets). Schumpeter suggested five situations where the phenomenon of bundling resources by entrepreneurs to produce new resources occurs. The entrepreneur "reforms or revolutionizes the pattern of production by exploiting an invention or an untried technology for producing a new commodity or producing an old one in a new way, by opening up a new source of supply of materials, or a new outlet for products, or by reorganizing a market" (Schumpeter, 1934; 132).

The focus of most current entrepreneurship research into opportunities has been on markets (Kirzner, 1997). This is true whether the market is a product market or a factor market (Shane and Venkataraman, 2000). However, once the discussion turns to factor markets and thus production (the creation of value through the transformation of inputs into outputs), there becomes a need for the coordination of numerous types of specialized knowledge (Grant and Baden-Fuller, 1995).

Knowledge comprises information, technology, know-how, and skills (Grant and Baden-Fuller, 1995) and can either be explicit such as in technology or tacit which is personal and more difficult to communicate (Polanyi, 1962) or imitate (Barney, 1991). Individuals acquire knowledge and individuals store tacit knowledge. However, until it is coordinated, knowledge is often dispersed, fragmented, and sometimes even contradictory. The entrepreneurial problem is how to secure the best use of resources in order to obtain a profit. Thus entrepreneurial knowledge is an abstract knowledge of where and how to obtain these resources. When the market is unable to organize distributed knowledge, the entrepreneur understands this and capitalizes upon the opportunity resulting in a new firm. Therefore it is not the market that organizes tacit knowledge, in fact it is often the case that markets are inefficient at knowledge transfer and integration, it is the firm that efficiently organizes knowledge. The primary role of the firm is the integration of specialized knowledge (Demsetz, 1991; Conner and Prahalad, 1996).

If we assume that the primary role of the firm is the integration of specialized knowledge, we then go back to our question, "When are markets more efficient at organizing knowledge and when are entrepreneurial firms more efficient at organizing knowledge?" Since individuals have cognitive limitations, the acquisition of knowledge is often specialized. Specialized knowledge is usually achieved at the expense of breadth of knowledge. However, in order to apply knowledge the need is for breadth of knowledge and not necessarily specialized knowledge. The integration of knowledge is achieved through each knowledge specialist establishing guidelines in order to codify tacit knowledge into explicit knowledge. Then the entrepreneur, who has knowledge breadth, transfers and applies the specialized knowledge through the transformation of inputs into outputs. The entrepreneur's knowledge in this case is the knowledge of where the knowledge specialist has imperfections that keep the specialist from obtaining an entrepreneurial profit or generating wealth (Kirzner, 1973). Therefore, if efficiency is the acquisition of specialized knowledge, the application of knowledge requires knowledge breadth and a means for the integration of knowledge.

Markets are inefficient at integrating knowledge because explicit knowledge can be easily imitated and tacit knowledge cannot be articulated (Grant and Baden-Fuller, 1995). Explicit knowledge has the character of a public good: it can be transferred at low cost. Once explicit knowledge is made known, it is easily imitated and it becomes incapable of creating wealth for the original knowledge producer. Tacit knowledge by definition cannot be articulated and thus cannot be transferred at arm's length.

Kirzner (1973) distinguishes between entrepreneurial knowledge and the knowledge expert, suggesting that it is the entrepreneur that hires the latter. The knowledge specialist does not fully recognize the value of his or her knowledge or how to turn that knowledge into a profit or else the expert would act as an entrepreneur. The entrepreneur may not have the specialized knowledge of the expert (such as technology expertise) but it is the entrepreneur who recognizes the value and the opportunity of specialized knowledge. The ability to recognize how to exploit specialized knowledge and create wealth is knowledge breadth. Thus the knowledge expert has specialized knowledge and the entrepreneur has knowledge breadth and it is through the firm that the two types of knowledge are joined to create wealth.

Ex Post Limits to Competition

Regardless of the nature of the firm heterogeneity, sustained competitive advantage requires that heterogeneity be preserved. If heterogeneity is not durable it will not add value, and real wealth creation will not be realized. This is the case when there are ex post limits to competition. What this means is that subsequent to a firm's gaining a superior position there must be forces which limit competition (Peteraf, 1993). Competition may dissipate heterogeneous advantages enjoyed by firms by increasing the supply of scarce resources. Indeed, it is at this junction where entrepreneurial knowledge becomes the crucial core knowledge of the firm.

Schumpeter theorized that innovation proceeded in a jerky fashion rather than an even fashion because after the initial entrepreneurs introduced an innovation other less capable entrepreneurs would "swarm" and new enterprises would appear en masse. The appearance of the first (more qualified) entrepreneurs facilitates the appearance of others by making innovation easier for less qualified entrepreneurs; in essence innovation becomes increasingly familiar and we now have "new processes" of innovation. The innovative success of the leader entrepreneurs results in an increase in the price of the means of production. Physical units of production are produced under conditions of constant returns to scale, characterized by falling average cost but constant marginal cost. Resources that were once scarce are now profitable and becoming less scarce and heterogeneous advantages held by the leader entrepreneurs will dissipate.

Schumpeter suggests that new combinations of resources are new ways of competing and that these new ways of competing do not as a rule come from existing firms but rather from new firms that develop alongside established firms. This is consistent with the notion of strategic complementarity[3] which suggests that when quantities of capital goods that are complements go up, the marginal productivity of the good is raised and the demand goes up. If a firm exists it increases its output; this is also the time when new firms enter markets. Strategic complementarity is also consistent with Schumpeter's work in that he suggests that the early entrepreneur appears alongside existing firms and then the swarm-like appearance of other entrepreneurs leads to many small firms forming en masse in a concentrated area. A familiar form of monopolistic competition characterizes the resulting equilibrium, though now instead of one large firm there are a large number of small firms. What has occurred is that total profits have likely minimized at the lowest level of uncertainty and we now have firms functioning efficiently whereas before there might have been waste which occurred as a result of reorganizing resources. The more imitative entrepreneurs that enter during the monopoly stage, the more uncertainty is minimized and profits are redistributed, possibly diluting total wealth. During this stage of the innovative process endogenous innovation motivated by the leader entrepreneurs is sufficient to generate robust, endogenous fluctuations in aggregate investment in new innovations (Evans, Honkapohja, and Romer, 1996). In other words, the innovative entrepreneurial act of once again recombining new resources starts a new cycle (Schumpeter, 1934). The entrepreneur's ability to continuously innovate is the primary competitive advantage of the entrepreneurial firm, leading to sustainable entrepreneurial firms and sustainable wealth creation.

However, as firms get larger the costs of organizing additional transactions within the firm may rise and the returns to the entrepreneurial function decrease (Coase, 1937). Once a firm reaches the point where the cost of organizing an extra transaction becomes equal to the market costs, either the market will organize the transaction or a new entrepreneur will enter and organize the new knowledge. The entrepreneurial knowledge of resource reorganization that is critical to the transformation of inputs into heterogeneous outputs becomes lost as the firm grows (Coase, 1937) and the now large firm begins to resemble the market. If the explanation of entrepreneurship stops at this point, we have nothing more than a transaction cost story of entrepreneurship. What stops the cycle is the isolating mechanism of causal ambiguity (Lippman and Rumelt, 1982).

Causal ambiguity is the uncertainty regarding the causes of efficiency differences among firms. It prevents potential imitators from knowing exactly what to imitate and how to imitate. If, as Schumpeter assumed, firms must incur a fixed research and development cost before they can produce a new type of good, then these sunk costs along with the uncertainty of how to imitate may limit competition and preserve heterogeneity.

Uncertainty

If we assume that entrepreneurship is, as Schumpeter suggested, new production functions, then firm heterogeneity is an outcome rather than a given (Rumelt, 1987). If we assume that causal ambiguity is necessary in order to maintain heterogeneity and keep competitors from imitating the existing entrepreneurial firm then the theory of uncertain imitability may provide insight into the potential sustainability of entrepreneurial heterogeneity (Lippman and Rumelt, 1982).

In Schumpeter's business cycle theory firms disrupting the cycle select new production functions from a known bundle of current production functions. In other words, the new discoveries are path dependent. The imitative attempts of the "swarms" equilibrate firm efficiencies, and long-term differences in profitability are assumed to be inefficiencies in factor markets. While this scenario might be true most of the time, there are entrepreneurial firms that produce new combinations with ambiguous factors of production and uncertainty as to how these factors interact, thus the condition of uncertainty is present and we have causal ambiguity – preserving heterogeneity (Rumelt, 1987). Causal ambiguity is a barrier to entry for potential competitors because it is almost impossible to imitate a product that has ambiguous factors.

An important argument of the RBV is that a firm can obtain unusual returns only when other firms are unable to imitate its resources, otherwise these resources are less rare or valuable (Barney, 1991; Lippman and Rumelt, 1982). There are two broad groups of resources, property-based and knowledge-based resources (Miller and Shamsie; 1996). Knowledge-based resources are difficult to understand, are illusive, and their connection to firm performance is often not clear. Knowledge-based resources can be the creative expertise that entrepreneurs use in entrepreneurial firms to develop new product combinations. In this way entrepreneurial firms create barriers to entry not by precluding competition but through causal ambiguity. Therefore, entrepreneurial firms create wealth because their competitors are ignorant as to the cause of the entrepreneurial firm's competitive advantage. Competitors may eventually understand the knowledge resources of the entrepreneurial firm, but it is usually time consuming.

Information asymmetries

Kogut and Zander (1992) divide knowledge into two categories, knowledge as information and knowledge as know-how. By information they mean knowledge which can be transmitted without loss of integrity. An example is shareholder reports that convey information about the firm in a common format. Know-how is the knowledge of how to do something. Know-how is an accumulated practical skill or expertise that allows one to do something smoothly and efficiently (von Hippel, 1986) and it is learned and acquired (Kogut and Zander, 1992).

Know-how is a description of what defines current practice in the firm, including how to organize factors of production. Know-how in a firm becomes interesting when it differs across firms and has persistent effects on performance outcomes. These persistent effects are a result of the difficulty of transferring and imitating knowledge and result in information asymmetries among firms.

During the process of rebundling resources waste occurs through knowledge imperfections. In a market view, throughout the process of resource rebundling information asymmetries are removed and "no perceived opportunity for improving the allocation of resources is left ungrasped" (Kirzner, 1973: 235). Resource-based theory suggests that firms wishing to obtain expected above normal returns from implementing product market strategies must be consistently better informed about the future value of those strategies than other firms in the same market (Barney, 1986).

What the entrepreneur does during the rebundling of resources is to use currently best-known information to make decisions to produce a product that utilizes those same resources in a superior and more efficient manner than in the past. This information and its application, know-how, is available to the entrepreneur through previous learning. The information owned by the entrepreneur is deeply imbedded, socially complex know-how of how to recombine resources and this know-how combined with entrepreneurial decision making is a source of firm heterogeneity.

In order for the entrepreneur to appropriate the returns from her or his recognition of a market opportunity there are two possibilities: to take a speculative position or to implement the strategy for the recombination of resources; implementing the strategy is the most promising since speculation has limited potential (Casson, 2000). The difference between the entrepreneur and the non-entrepreneur is the combination of the recognition of opportunities and the knowledge to exploit these opportunities through the recombination of resources.

Imperfect Factor Mobility

Dierickx and Cool (1989) focus on the conditions that prevent the imitation of valuable but non-tradable asset stocks. They suggest that how imitable an asset is depends on the process by which it was accumulated. They identify the following conditions under which imitation may be limited: time compression diseconomies, asset mass efficiencies, interconnectedness of asset stocks, asset erosion, and causal ambiguity. The importance to resource-based theory is that these assets are inimitable because they have a strong tacit dimension and are socially complex.

Socially complex assets are more difficult to understand and imitate; these assets are often intangible resources that are more likely to lead to a competitive advantage than are tangible resources (Barney, 1991). Because of the nature of these assets they are often asset specific to the firm in which they are deployed. These are idiosyncratic assets that are more valuable when used in the firm than outside of the firm. These often intangible assets are difficult to observe, describe, and value but have a significant impact on a firm's competitive advantage (Itami, 1987). For example, some of these assets are cooperation among managers, brand awareness, trust, and entrepreneurial decision making and the entrepreneurial ability to integrate factors of production. In general when a firm's resources and capabilities are socially complex they are likely to be sources of sustained heterogeneity (Barney, 1995). Entrepreneurial knowledge is a socially complex asset that is difficult to imitate and thus can lead to sustained heterogeneity.

Path dependent

The resource-based distinctive assets may also be evolutionary. In this view heterogeneous assets may depend upon past entrepreneurial decisions and these decisions made by founders and entrepreneurs may be the DNA composition of the firm. Sustainable advantage is thus a history (path) dependent process (Barney, 1991; Nelson and Winter, 1982). Because of the role of chance and luck (Barney, 1986) in the firm, firms will develop different knowledge bases for coordinating their stocks of distributed knowledge. It is the different paths that firms take that account for differential capabilities and thus firm heterogeneity.

In firms different people have different habits, thoughts, and models of the world that present obstacles to the efficient coordination of their actions (Foss, 1999). Therefore, a collective knowledge base is required for coordination (Penrose, 1959). This collective knowledge base coordinates existing distributed knowledge but also coordinates intra-firm learning processes. Indeed, coordinated knowledge bases help the firm organize a localized discovery process.

Certainly there is a possibility that path-dependent resources might inhibit entrepreneurship since investments in resources, particularly intangible resources that take longer to develop, have already been made. Additionally, as Coase (1937) posits, there may be decreasing returns to the entrepreneurial function as a firm gets larger and has more transactions to organize. These insights might indicate that there is a point where the path-dependent resources are a determent to the entrepreneurial process. However, if we assume a Schumpeterian view (which this chapter builds upon), entrepreneurship occurs when there are already resources in place. If resources are exploited through the entrepreneurial activity of recombining these resources, then entrepreneurship is path dependent. We also refer to Ireland et al. (2001) who suggest that gaining access to a variety of resources and knowing how to leverage them creatively are two core entrepreneurial functions. Therefore, having resources, at least some resources, is critical to effective entrepreneurial actions.

Ex Ante Limits to Competition

The last condition that must be met in order to have a sustainable advantage is that there must be ex ante limits to competition. In other words, for a firm to enjoy a sustainable advantageous position there must be limits to competition. As we have discussed earlier in this chapter, Schumpeter's business cycles start with equilibrium and then the entrepreneur disrupts the cycle through innovation. This is followed by other less capable entrepreneurs imitating the innovation and dissipating the competitive advantage of the first firm. Schumpeter (1934) called the downtime a time of depression.

However, if the entrepreneurial firm has resources that are causally ambiguous these resources will be costly and difficult to imitate and the advantage enjoyed by this first firm will not be dissipated. Causal ambiguity is a barrier to entry for potential competitors because it is almost impossible to imitate a product that has ambiguous factors.

Conclusion

Within the field of entrepreneurship, prominent entrepreneurship scholars (Shane and Venkataraman, 2000) have criticized the work on small and new businesses and their focus on either the performance of individuals or the firm. These scholars argue that since strategic management focuses on firm performance it is not unique to entrepreneurship. More important, these scholars suggest that performance approaches do not adequately test entrepreneurship because "entrepreneurship is about the discovery and exploitation of profitable opportunities" (Shane and Venkataraman, 2000: 217).

Within these debates there are two additional assumptions that hinder the incorporation of entrepreneurial insight into the resource-based view and the advancement of entrepreneurship theory. The first is what is meant by firm performance, and the second is that resource-based theory is about equilibrium and entrepreneurship research is about disequilibrium (Shane and Venkataraman, 2000). Both arguments are addressed in this chapter using a Schumpeterian view of entrepreneurship.

Shane and Venkataraman (2000) suggest that examining firm performance is not unique to entrepreneurship. In addition, they suggest that by examining firm performance we do not contribute to entrepreneurship theory since firm performance is measured by differences between firms and their sustainability. Certainly firm performance is more than firm differences and sustainability. However, if we only address these two parts of firm performance this chapter suggests that at the heart of firm heterogeneity and sustainability is entrepreneurial insight and knowledge. Schumpeter (1934) described innovation as originating in the firm, where the heart is the entrepreneur. In order for the recombination of resources by the entrepreneur to create wealth, firms need to be sustainable.

A theory of entrepreneurship should be concerned with the sustainability of the firm, because when entrepreneurial firms fail the benefits such as knowledge creation and innovation from entrepreneurial activities that may be firm specific are often lost. Entrepreneurial firm failure causes investors to not realize the returns on their investments, investments that could have generated a profit elsewhere, i.e., lost opportunities. In addition, other stakeholders such as employees who have made firm-specific investments will lose the value of these investments because these tacit investments, such as entrepreneurial insight, cannot be traded on competitive markets.

As to the second issue on equilibrium, Schumpeter theorized that entrepreneurship is about disrupting the equilibrium through business cycle fluctuations – neither a Pareto optimal equilibrium nor a constant disequilibrium story (Schumpeter, 1934). Schumpeter has often been mis-classified as a disequilibrium economist. In fact Shane and Venkataraman (2000) incorrectly cite Schumpeter as constantly viewing the economy in a state of disequilibrium. Schumpeter was not concerned with disproving Neoclassical economists or their view of the perfect competition model. Schumpeter was, however, interested in explaining the role of entrepreneurship in development. Thus Schumpeter did not overly concentrate on equilibrium debates, but instead focused on entrepreneurship and the recombination of resources. Schumpeter's approach should be an example to entrepreneurship scholars who continue to debate equilibrium notions within an entrepreneurship context. Even if entrepreneurship scholars could contribute to this debate, we would be contributing to a theory of economics, not entrepreneurship.

The contribution of entrepreneurship to RBV is an understanding that heterogeneous factor outputs are likely to occur in entrepreneurial small firms. Past understanding of the RBV would suggest that entrepreneurship can occur in large firms as they transform inputs into heterogeneous outputs. However, Coase (1937) suggested that as a firm gets larger, there may be decreasing returns to the entrepreneurial function. Coase further suggests that as the firm's transactions that are organized increase, the entrepreneur fails to place the factors of production in the uses where their value is greatest. Thus, in order for firms to exploit resources in heterogeneous ways, there appears to be a significant link to firm size.

Resource-based theory contributes to entrepreneurship theory an understanding of the importance of the firm in the entrepreneurial action of transforming inputs into heterogeneous outputs that others had not previously recognized. In addition, the RBV recommends that entrepreneurship scholars be aware of the wealth creation implications when considering entrepreneurial firms and the long-term sustainability of these firms.

Notes

The first author would like to thank Dale Meyer for introducing me to the works of Schumpeter and Kirzner. Both authors would like to thank Lowell Busenitz who contributed the section on cognition.

1   McGrath and MacMillan (2000) use the same term in their book *The Entrepreneurial Mindset*. While their use of this term overlaps with ours, their primary interest is concerned with helping managers of established companies become more entrepreneurial. Hence, their definition incorporates the concepts of discipline and execution.
2   We apply Coase's theory of the firm whereby Coase suggests that entrepreneurial benefits accrue to smaller firms and that larger firms lose their entrepreneurial advantages.
3   Strategic complementarities arise when the optimal strategy of an agent depends positively upon the strategies of the other agents. Multiple equilibria and a multiplier process may arise when strategic complementarities are present. Strategic complementarities arise from production functions, matching technologies, and commodity demand functions in a multisector, imperfectly competitive economy (Cooper and John, 1988).

References

Alvarez, S. A. and Barney, J. B. 2000. Entrepreneurial capabilities: A resource-based view. In G. D. Meyer and K. A. Heppard (eds), *Entrepreneurship as strategy: Competing on the entrepreneurial edge*. Thousand Oaks, CA: Sage Publications.
Argyris, Chris and Lauderdale, M. L. 1983. Action Science and Intervention/Comments/Reply. *The Journal of Applied Behavioral Science*, 19(2): 115–40.
Autio, E., Sapienza, H. J., and Almeida, J. G. 2000. Effects of age at entry, knowledge intensity, and imitability on international growth. *Academy of Management Journal*, 43: 909–24.
Barney, J. B. 1986. Strategic factor markets: Expectations, luck and business strategy. *Management Science*, 42: 1231–41.
Barney, J. B. 1991. Firm resources and sustained competitive advantage. *Journal of Management*, 17: 99–120.
Barney, J. B. 1995. Looking inside for competitive advantage. *Academy of Management Executive*, 9: 49–61.
Barney J. B. 2001. Is the resource-based view a useful perspective for strategic management research? Yes. *Academy of Management Review*, 26: 41–56.
Baron, R. 1998. Cognitive mechanisms in entrepreneurship: Why and when entrepreneurs think differently than other people. *Journal of Business Venturing*, 13: 275–94.
Busenitz, L. and Barney, J. 1997. Differences between entrepreneurs and managers in large organizations: Biases and heuristics in strategic decision-making. *Journal of Business Venturing*, 12: 9–30.
Busenitz, L. and Lau, C. 1996. A cross-cultural cognitive model of new venture creation, *Entrepreneurship Theory and Practice*, 20(4): 25–39.
Casson, M. 1982. *The entrepreneur*. Totowa, NJ: Barnes and Noble Books.
Casson, M. 1999. An entrepreneurial theory of the firm. Department of Economics University of Reading. Working paper.
Casson, M. 2000. An entrepreneurial theory of the firm. In N. Foss and V. Mahnke (eds), *Competence, governance, and entrepreneurship: Advances in economic strategy research*. Oxford, UK: Oxford University Press, 116–45.
Coase, R. H. 1937. The nature of the firm. *Economica*, 4: 386–405.

Conner, K. R. and Prahalad, C. K. 1996. A resource-based theory of the firm: Knowledge versus opportunism. *Organization Science*, 7: 477–501.

Cooper, R. and John, A. 1988. Coordinating coordination failures in Keynesian models, *Quarterly Journal of Economics*, 103: 441–63.

Daft, R. and Weick, K. 1984. Toward a model of organizations as interpretation systems. *Academy of Management Review*, 9: 284–95.

Demsetz, H. 1991. The theory of the firm revisited. In O. Williamson and R. Winter (eds), *The nature of the firm*. New York: Oxford University Press, 159–78.

Dierickx, I. and Cool, K. 1989. Asset stock accumulation and sustainability of competitive advantage, *Management Science*, 35: 1504–11.

Evans, G., Honkapohja, S. and Romer, P. 1996. Growth Cycles. National Bureau of Economic Research, Working Paper 5659.

Fiol, C. M. and Lyles, M. A. 1985. Organizational learning. *Academy of Management Review*, 10: 803–13.

Forbes, D. 1999. Cognitive approaches to new venture creation. *International Journal of Management Review*, 1: 415–39.

Foss, N. 1999. Edith Penrose, economics and strategic management, *Contributions to Political Economy*, 18: 87–104.

Gavetti, G. and Levinthal, D. 2000. Looking forward and looking backward: Cognitive and experimental search. *Administrative Science Quarterly*, 45: 113–37.

Grant, R. M. and Baden-Fuller, C. 1995. A knowledge-based theory of inter-firm collaboration. Academy of Management, Best Papers Proceedings, 17–21.

Hayek, F. A. 1945. The use of knowledge in society. *American Economic Review*, 35: 519–30.

Hitt, M. A. and Tyler, B. B. 1991. Strategic decision models: Integrating different perspectives. *Strategic Management Journal*, 12: 327–51.

Ireland, R. D., Hitt, M. A., Camp, S. M., and Sexton, D. L. 2001. Integrating entrepreneurship and strategic management thinking to create firm wealth. *Academy of Management Executive*, 15(1): 49–63.

Itami, H. 1987. *Mobilizing invisible assets*. Cambridge, MA: Harvard University Press.

Kirzner, I. 1973. *Competition and entrepreneurship*. Chicago: The University of Chicago Press.

Kirzner, I. 1979. *Perception, opportunity, and profit*. Chicago: University of Chicago Press.

Kirzner, I. 1997. *How markets work: Disequilibrium, entrepreneurship and discovery*. Great Britain: The Institute of Economic Affairs.

Knight, R. H. 1921. Cost of production and price over long and short periods. *Journal of Political Economy*, 29: 332.

Kogut, B. and Zander, U. 1992. Knowledge of the firm, combinative capabilities, and the replication of technology. *Organization Science*, 3: 383–97.

Krabuanrat, K. and Phelps, R. 1998. Heuristic and rationality in strategic decision making: An exploratory study. *Journal of Business Research*, 41: 83–93.

Lei, D., Hitt, M. A., and Bettis, R. 1996. Dynamic core competences through meta-learning and strategic context. *Journal of Management*, 22(4): 549–69.

Levitt, B. and March, J. G. 1988. Organizational learning. *Annual Review of Sociology*, 14: 319–40.

Lippman, S. and Rumelt, R. 1982. Uncertain imitability: An analysis of interfirm differences in efficiency under competition. *Bell Journal of Economics*, 13: 418–38.

Low, M. B. and Macmillan, I. C. 1988. Entrepreneurship: Past research and future challenges. *Journal of Management*, 14, 138–61.

McGrath, R. G. and MacMillan, I. 2000. *The entrepreneurial mindset: Strategies for continuously creating opportunity in an age of uncertainty*. Boston: Harvard Business School Press.

Miller, D. and Shamsie, J. 1996. The resource-based view of the firm in two environments: The

Hollywood film studios from 1936 to 1965. *Academy of Management Journal*, 39: 519–43.

Nelson, R. R. and Winter, S. G. 1982. *An evolutionary theory of economic change*. Cambridge, MA: Harvard University Press.

Penrose, E. T. 1959. *The theory of the growth of the firm*. New York: Wiley.

Peteraf, M. 1993. The cornerstones of competitive advantage: A resource-based view. *Strategic Management Journal*, 13: 363–80.

Polanyi, M. 1962. *Personal knowledge: Towards a post-critical philosophy*. Chicago: University of Chicago Press.

Rumelt, R. P. 1987. Theory, strategy, and entrepreneurship. In D. Teece (ed.), *The competitive challenge*. Cambridge: Ballinger, 137–58.

Schumpeter, J. 1934. *The theory of economic development*. Cambridge, MA: Harvard University Press.

Shane, S. and Venkataraman, S. 2000. The promise of entrepreneurship as a field of research. *Academy of Management Review*, 25(1): 217–26.

Tversky, A. and Kahneman, D. 1974. Judgment under uncertainty: Heuristics and biases. *Science*, 185: 1124–31.

Von Hippel, E. 1986. Lead users: A source of novel product concepts. *Management Science*, 32: 791–805.

Wright, M., Hoskisson, R. E., Busenitz, L. W., and Dial, J. 2000. Entrepreneurial growth through privatizations: The upside of management buyouts. *Academy of Management Review*, 25(3): 591–601.

Zahra, S. A., Ireland, R. D., and Hitt, M. A. 2000. International expansion by new venture firms: International diversity, mode of market entry, technological learning, and performance. *Academy of Management Journal*, 43: 925–50.

CHAPTER SIX

Overcoming Resource Disadvantages in Entrepreneurial Firms: When Less Is More

Elaine Mosakowski

Introduction

New ventures almost by definition possess fewer resources than do established firms. Even in well-funded entrepreneurial companies, many resources associated with the organizational infrastructure, such as organizational practices, policies, and routines, are not in place. Yet academic research emphasizes a firm's resources for their ability to generate economic rents. Does this imply that an entrepreneurial firm must necessarily be at a performance disadvantage *vis-à-vis* established firms? And is this performance disadvantage likely to be sustained in the long run if the entrepreneurial firm remains in the undesirable position of continually playing resource "catch-up" to established firms? How can we explain entrepreneurial firms that surpass large firms endowed with substantial resources?

Some scholars working within the resource-based view of strategy have highlighted the entrepreneur's role in firm strategy (Alvarez and Barney, 2000; Conner, 1991; Mosakowski, 1998a; Rumelt, 1987). Other scholars interested in entrepreneurial phenomena have drawn from the resource-based view of strategy to understand outcomes associated with new ventures (Brush and Chaganti, 1999; Deeds, DeCarolis, and Coombs, 2000; Guillen, 2000; Majumdar, 2000; McGrath, Venkataraman, and Macmillan, 1994; McGrath, 1995; Thornhill and Amit, 2001). In some cases, work bridging the entrepreneurship and resource-based view literatures has wrestled with the appropriateness of integrating these distinct perspectives.

While they propose that a resource-based view may incorporate entrepreneurship within its scope, Alvarez and Barney (2000) indicate that an Austrian view – which assumes that disequilibrium is a natural state of affairs – may be the most suitable perspective for studying entrepreneurship.[1]

Traditional research on the resource-based view of strategy has generally ignored the wide range of human choices and behaviors involved in identifying, leveraging, and creating resources. Penrose's work (1959: 54) is perhaps most sensitive to the importance of managerial choices and behaviors by suggesting that a firm's resources alone do not matter, but how a firm uses its resources is also important. Barney (1986a, 1986b), however, argued for limited managerial discretion by proposing that factor markets price existing rent-generating resources or inputs into a process for creating rent-generating resources such that the manager cannot expect, ex ante, above-normal returns from activities directed toward resource acquisition or creation. This logic suggests that whether a manager decides to acquire or create a resource cannot be expected to have a significant impact on his or her firm's performance. Thus, instead of looking to human choices and behaviors for explanations of which firms succeed, the resource-based view of strategy has emphasized disembodied assets – especially knowledge-based assets that are described as virtually unconnected to the people possessing them – to which property rights can be assigned.

The greater stability of large, established firms, in which most of the critical resources are already established and embedded in a firm's organizational context, may be better suited to the focus on enduring resources – a focus characteristic of the resource-based view of strategy. The dynamic conditions within the entrepreneurial firm naturally highlight individuals' choices and decisions. In fact, Majumdar's (2000) interesting analysis of transformational processes within the US telecommunications industry suggests that a dynamic perspective on resources is also necessary within the resource-rich firm. His findings indicate that large resource pools were not a source of inertia, but instead facilitated dynamic learning processes, which generated valuable knowledge that could be more efficiently diffused and exploited within the large firm.

While an individual's choices and behaviors within the firm may be tied to the individual's or firm's enduring resources and capabilities, these choices and behaviors are not linked to resources and capabilities with a simple one-to-one mapping. In other words, not all managers in firms with a certain type of resource or capability will behave in a specific way, and not all individuals behaving in a certain way will be associated with a specific type of resource or capability. This chapter develops an explanation of success or failure that looks not only to resources but also considers the entrepreneur, the entrepreneurial process, and entrepreneurial decisions as important factors that influence individuals' choices and behaviors. I distinguish among three steps in the entrepreneurial process (see Stevenson and Gumpert, 1985): the identification of a business opportunity, the development of a business model and strategy for capitalizing on this opportunity, and the acquisition or development of resources to implement this business model and strategy.

Flowing from this discussion is a consideration of how a firm's resource endowments may impair its ability to identify new business opportunities and develop business models and strategies for capitalizing on these opportunities. I identify four costs associated with large resource endowments that result when resources impinge upon the entrepreneurial process: core rigidities, reduced experimentation, reduced incentive intensity, and increased strategic transparency. These four costs are often unacknowledged and should be considered when examining the relative merits or demerits associated with holding any individual resource or combination of firm resources within the boundaries of the firm. I also discuss the common argument that the entrepreneurial firm is more flexible than the established firm is.

In the next section, I draw upon extant work on the resource-based view of strategy to offer key distinctions, such as rent-generating versus value-destroying resources and isolated resources versus combinatorial competences. The third section of this chapter distinguishes among different types of rents and argues that entrepreneurial rents allow for the possibility of value destruction. As a result, I focus on the entrepreneurial process and examine this process from the perspective of the resource-based view of strategy. The fourth section focuses on when fewer resources are preferred over more resources. The discussion in this section builds upon the previous discussion of the entrepreneurial process to consider how resource endowments may impair this process. The final section concludes this discussion by considering how the chapter falls within some broader debates within and outside of the resource-based view of strategy.

The Resource-Based View of Strategy

A central premise of the resource-based view of strategy is that, to understand the success or failure of firms, one must examine the tangible and intangible assets of the firm. Particular attention has been directed toward detailing characteristics that describe rent-generating resources. Barney (1991), for example, emphasizes resources that are valuable, unique or rare, inimitable, and nonsubstitutable. Taking a slightly different approach, Peteraf (1993) points to superior resources, ex ante and ex post limits to competition, and imperfect resource mobility. Collis and Montgomery (1995) highlight resource scarcity, appropriability, and demand as determinants of the economic rents generated by a resource.

In addition, individual or isolated resources, such as a patent or manufacturing process, are distinguished from the more systemic capabilities or competences that combine or span isolated resources (Hitt and Ireland, 1985; Sanchez, Heene, and Thomas, 1996). The core competence idea promoted by Prahalad and Hamel (1990: 81) refers to "the collective learning in the organization." The arguments about the necessary and sufficient conditions for rent generation developed for isolated resources have also been applied to more systemic competences, such as Barney's (1986b) work on organizational culture, Barney and Hansen's (1994) work on trustworthiness, or Castanias and Helfat's (1991) work on general managerial resources (1991).

Previous discussion of resource characteristics has focused almost exclusively on characteristics of rent-generating resources, and generally ignored value-destroying resources. Drawing from Daft (1983), Barney (1991: 101) clearly defines resources in a way to indicate that they have only positive consequences. He defines resources as "all assets, capabilities, organizational processes, firm attributes, information, knowledge, etc. controlled by a firm that enable the firm to conceive of and implement strategies that improve its efficiency and effectiveness." In a less explicit fashion, Caves's (1980) definition of resources as all tangible and intangible assets that are tied in a relatively permanent fashion to a firm emphasizes the positive side of resources by equating them with assets. Montgomery (1995: 261), however, takes the opposite position by arguing that special attention should be given to "those resources and capabilities that, *in toto*, have a negative impact on the firm." Instead of basing the definition of resources on "assets" as Caves did, this chapter will employ the definition of resources as all tangible and intangible inputs that are tied in a relatively permanent fashion to the firm. The word "input" includes inputs that destroy value, inputs with no influence on firm value, and inputs that create firm value.

There has been no discussion that the author knows of to date of the necessary and sufficient conditions for resources to destroy rents. Resources or competences that do not meet the necessary and sufficient conditions for rent generation – that is, those that are commonplace, substitutable, imitable, and not valuable – could be either neutral or negative with regard to their impact on a firm's value added.

While there are plentiful examples of incompetences and firm resources that destroy values, such as neurotic organizational cultures (Kets de Vries, 1995) and company founders unable to help their growing firms make the transition to professional management (Flamholtz and Randle, 2000), the current discussion focuses on how value is destroyed by an increase in total resource endowments. Attention is directed to the marginal effects of incorporating additional resources into a firm's resource pool. It is useful to examine a firm's total rent stream as the sum of the three types of rents: Ricardian rents generated because of the scarcity of inputs, quasi-rents associated with the value of an input in its first best use and its value in the next best use (Klein, Crawford, and Alchian, 1978), and entrepreneurial rents. Rumelt (1987) defines the latter as the difference between a new venture's ex post value and the ex ante cost of the resources.

Ricardian rents will be unaffected by the total size of a firm's resource endowments. If the scarcity of inputs is the only factor determining the rents associated with a firm's resources, the rents generated by resource X will not depend upon the presence of resource Y. In other words, the scarcity of X does not depend upon the presence of Y. The rents generated by a firm's resources will not depend upon the firm's total resource endowments.

The situation where the firm's total resource endowments matter may appear as quasi-rents. When the best use of resource X requires the presence of resource Y, and resource Y is not available to other firms that can instead use resource X only in its second best use, quasi-rents will be generated by the interdependence of these two resources.[2] In this way, quasi-rents will be influenced by the firm's total resource endowment pool. A comparison of the first and second best use of the resource, however, does not identify a path toward value destruction: the best use of the resource is definitionally superior to the next best use and quasi-rents highlight the value created by the presence of a second scarce resource.

The definition of entrepreneurial rents suggests the potential for value destruction. A new venture's ex post value can be less than the cost of the inputs. Because of this, the current paper directs its attention to the entrepreneurial process to consider how a firm's total resource endowment affects this process and the entrepreneurial rents generated by it.

The next section focuses on this process and uses this discussion to consider potential value-destroying aspects of firm resources and competences in the following section.

The Entrepreneurial Process

There has been a long-standing tradition of distinguishing entrepreneurial resources or services from other types (Menger, 1963; Kirzner, 1973, 1979; Rumelt, 1987). This chapter argues that the decisions and choices made during the entrepreneurial process – in particular, the identification of business opportunities and the development of business models and strategies for exploiting these opportunities – should not be classified as resources at all.

Stevenson and Gumpert (1985) discuss the entrepreneurial process, and raise five critical questions: (1) Where is the opportunity? (2) How do I capitalize on it? (3) What resources do I need? (4) How do I gain control over them? (5) What structure is best? While questions 3 through 5 address concerns with resources and their organization, how questions 1 and 2 relate to the resource-based view of strategy is unclear. In the following discussion, I address these two questions in the following forms: Is the business opportunity identified by the entrepreneur a firm resource? Do the business models and strategies developed by the entrepreneur to capitalize on this opportunity represent firm resources?

The process of identifying a business opportunity revolves around the entrepreneur being alerted to a business opportunity. Can this state of alertness solely be explained by an intangible input that is tied in a relatively permanent fashion to a firm? The answer is clearly no. Kirzner (1973, 1979) emphasizes transient or momentary alertness to opportunities that wax and wane as individuals engage in market processes. Given its transient nature, Demsetz (1983) equates Kirzner's concept of alertness with luck because it is not attributable to a firm's resources. Therefore, Kirzner's discussion of the identification of an entrepreneurial opportunity points to an extremely transitory phenomenon which the firm might not be able to repeat with any consistency, and which would not qualify under the definition of a resource. Others have defined alertness as a behavioral tendency to spend significant amounts of time engaging the environment with a search for profit opportunities (Kaish and Gilad, 1991; Mosakowski, 1998a). This alternative view of alertness is consistent with it as an individual- and/or firm-level resource. The position taken in this chapter is that, while alertness in a Kirznerian sense is not a firm resource, it may be facilitated or impaired by the existence of firm resources, including behavioral tendencies to engage the environment searching for profit opportunities.

Do the business model and strategy that the entrepreneur develops to capitalize on the business opportunity qualify as firm resources? By business model, I refer to the definition of the value chain that will be employed to fulfill the business opportunity. For example, which marriage of technology, manufacturing processes, distribution channels, etc. will be used to serve the business opportunity identified by the entrepreneur? By strategy, I emphasize the firm's plan for interacting with competitors and complementors in its environment (Brandenburger and Nalebuff, 1995).[3] For example, does the firm intend to enter the market niche at a capacity level sufficient to preempt subsequent entry? In this case, the firm's success depends not on its resources endowments, but instead on its strategy to deter entry and create market power.

One must take care not to imply that, in this example of a preemptive strategy, the firm's strategy leads to a first mover position, which subsequently becomes a firm resource since it is permanently tied to the firm. A slightly different form of ex post logic can be found in the backward deduction underlying Barney's (1991) suggestion that a first mover position must necessarily be ascribed to heterogeneous resources, such as differences in information sets. In either case, ex post logic necessarily leads to the conclusion that each and every managerial decision or action that had the net result of producing a sustainable competitive advantage must be associated with firm resources. Obviously, this ex post approach would suffer from tautological problems: one could not refute the assertion that firm resources produce sustainable competitive advantage. Instead, an ex ante approach to firm resources – looking at resource endowments at the time strategic choices are made – is required to disentangle the contribution of resources versus managerial decisions, processes, and behaviors that do not in themselves qualify as firm resources. An ex ante approach will facilitate our ability to attribute outcomes to firm resources versus managerial choices as well as to describe the link between resources and choices.

Thus, I must apply the definition of resources to the business model and strategy developed by the entrepreneur without regard to what occurs after this model and strategy have been implemented. The definition of resource requires the consideration of whether the business model and strategy are inputs and, if they are, whether they are tied to the firm in some relatively permanent fashion.

My position is that the business model and strategy taken together define which inputs the entrepreneur will combine to serve the business opportunity identified, but they themselves are not inputs. An alternative perspective is that they define the production function with which the entrepreneur will operate, and in the economic sense of the word, they define the "technology" the entrepreneur will employ. This metalevel perspective would, however, if taken to the extreme, classify virtually every decision as an input even though the function of certain decisions is primarily the defining of input requirements. Thus, I suggest that the business model and strategy instead should be viewed not as inputs, and therefore, cannot be considered firm resources.

To summarize this discussion so far, I have argued that the key to understanding how resource endowments might destroy firm value lies in an examination of the entrepreneurial process and entrepreneurial rents. Yet the opportunity identified by the entrepreneur does not qualify as a firm resource because of its inherently transient nature. Also, the business model and strategy developed by the entrepreneur to capitalize on the opportunity also are not firm resources because they are not inputs. Having distinguished these steps in the entrepreneurial process from firm resources, I turn next to a consideration of the marginal effect of firm resources on the entrepreneurial process.

Marginal Effects of Firm Resources on the Entrepreneurial Process

The resource-based view has been relatively silent on value-destruction within the firm. Montgomery (1995: 261) notes that "existing theory not only fails to offer advice about [resources and capabilities that have a negative impact on the firm], it barely acknowledges that they exist." Highlighting the value-destroying possibilities of firm resources, Leonard-Barton (1992) offers one general rationale for when a firm's competences might destroy value. She identified core rigidities as the dysfunctional flip side to core capabilities that occur when a deeply embedded knowledge set inhibits innovation within the firm.

The marginal effects of adding resources to the firm might influence the entrepreneurial process by impairing the firm's ability to identify new business opportunities and/or to develop business models and strategies for capitalizing on these opportunities. I identify four costs associated with large resource endowments that hinder the entrepreneurial process: core rigidities, reduced experimentation, reduced incentive intensity, and increased strategic transparency. After discussing these four costs, I address the common argument celebrating the flexibility of the entrepreneurial firm.

Core rigidities

As Leonard-Barton (1992) noted, core competences may produce sufficient inertia that the established firm is unable to respond and adapt to its environment. While it is unclear from Leonard-Barton's (1992) discussion whether the inertia she associated with core competences might also exist in firms without core competences, one can explicate a tie between competences and rigidities with such behavioral phenomena as competence traps (Levinthal and March, 1993; Levitt and March, 1988). This occurs when successful individuals or firms are unable to look beyond trajectories created by past successes. As creativity research suggests (Amabile, 1996), the tunnel vision created by past successes may hamper the identification of radically new opportunities. In addition, business models and strategies developed to capitalize on opportunities identified may be limited to relatively familiar forms, thereby diminishing the potential for innovation in this stage of the entrepreneurial process.

Core rigidities are affiliated with large resource endowments because of associated routines (Nelson and Winter, 1982). Regardless of whether one includes routines as part of, or distinct from, a firm's resource endowments, ways of thinking and behaving are often tied to past successes and the resources responsible for these successes. Thus, the success associated with core competences could contribute to the development of routines that produce core rigidities. Even if resource endowments such as technological innovations or brand equity disappear from the firm – either due to catastrophic events or intentional choice – the associated routines may persist. Thus, the history of a firm's resource endowments as well as its current resource endowments may influence the core rigidities currently experienced.

Reduced experimentation

Even if firms do not suffer from the behavioral phenomenon described as core rigidities, they may nonetheless take fewer risks when identifying new business opportunities. Working with a large resource-endowment, an established firm may maximize its profits by focusing its attention on better exploiting and leveraging its existing resources (Winter, 1995; Dierickx and Cool, 1989). Because opportunities for exploiting and leveraging resources are limited in the resource-poor entrepreneurial firm, it is forced to seek out alternative ways to create a sustainable source of economic rents. The

primary avenue may involve frequent experimentation to pursue radical business opportunities, some of which will fail while others succeed (Mosakowski, 1997; 1998b).
While the chance of success may be quite small and unattractive to the resource-rich
established firm, this chance may be one of very few options available to the resource-
poor entrepreneurial firm. The rare entrepreneurial firms that succeed are more likely
to do so with radical, as opposed to incremental, innovations.

Thus, established firms may not, on average, be at a disadvantage *vis-à-vis* entrepreneurial firms for this reason; however, successful and surviving established firms may
be at a disadvantage relative to successful and surviving entrepreneurial firms. This
effect may be particularly pronounced when uncharted business opportunities are plentiful. When most business opportunities have been well identified, as in mature markets, the ability of entrepreneurial firms to identify radical new opportunities may be
limited by the coverage of incumbents' extant positions. Emerging markets offer one
context for observing greater benefits associated with the experimentation of entrepreneurial firms.

Reduced incentive intensity

Another way in which resource endowments may impair the entrepreneurial process is
through a diminution of incentives. When human-capital-based resources are widely
dispersed across many individuals in the resource-rich established firm, the use of high-
powered incentives might be impaired.[4] When a firm internalizes a large number of
transactions or, more importantly to the current argument, when it possesses a large
stock of human-capital resources, it may be forced to rely upon lower-powered incentives than relied upon by the resource-poor entrepreneurial firm where human-capital
resources are concentrated in one or a few key individuals. The reason for this is that
the intensity of the incentives is reduced when they are tied to the joint performance of
a large number of individuals possessing critical human-capital resources, relative to
the intensity of the incentives associated with the joint performance of only a few key
individuals.

As a result of reduced incentive intensity, shirking may occur within the firm. Less
intensive incentives may produce shirking in the resource-rich firm with respect to an
individual's utilization of his or her individual resources. Of particular relevance here is
shirking with regard to the use of creative resources within the firm, which may result
in less time and attention allocated to the identification of new business opportunities
(Mosakowski, 1998a). Thus, the overall ability of the established firm to identify new
business opportunities, develop a business model and strategy for capitalizing on these
opportunities, and implement the business model and strategy by acquiring and developing resources may be mitigated, relative to the entrepreneurial firm.

Increased strategic transparency

Finally, the large resource endowments of established firms may destroy value because
they make the firm's business model and strategy relatively transparent to its competitors, regardless of whether this is desirable for strategic reasons. Patent holdings, brand

equity, and other potentially valuable resources often indicate future strategic propensities of resource-rich firms. This is because "a firm's competitive position is defined by a bundle of unique resources and relationships" (Rumelt, 1984: 557), such that a firm's resources to some extent determine its strategy.

The definition of entrepreneurial rents highlights the entrepreneurial role of combining resources, and this role becomes less significant and the outcome becomes more certain when the inputs to the entrepreneurial combinatorial process are specified. In other words, the more resources possessed by a firm, the more complete the roadmap provided to the competitor for predicting what business model and strategy will be used by the resource-rich firm to capitalize on a business opportunity. When this occurs, certain strategic possibilities may be precluded because they are so transparent and competitors can anticipate them. As a result, the possible opportunities and business models and strategies that can be employed by the established firm are reduced.

This discussion does not intend to imply that the transparency of a firm's business model and strategy is outside of its control. When the firm chooses whether to patent technological know-how, for example, any increase in the appropriability of this resource is weighed against the increased transparency of future firm behaviors. Even if resource appropriability is sacrificed to obscure future strategic choices, observations of business models and strategies employed in the past may serve as information useful for predicting business models and strategies to be employed in the future. The relative lack of data on past behaviors of an entrepreneurial firm may diminish competitors' ability to predict its future behavior. This lack of transparency is valuable when the element of surprise is important to the successful execution of an entrepreneurial firm's strategy.[5]

Flexibility

Perhaps the most common argument about the disadvantages of the resource-rich established firm is its inflexibility. I suggest that the logic behind the argument that entrepreneurial firms are more flexible has not been fully developed, and this subsection delves into this argument based on the following approach.

First, the established firm that owns and controls a large resource endowment is explicitly compared with a collection of entrepreneurial firms that each owns and controls a small resource endowment. This comparison is illustrated in figure 6.1, with figure 6.1a representing the established firm with large resource holdings and figure 6.1b representing the collection of entrepreneurial firms, each of which owns only a small cache of resources. One assumption underlying figure 6.1 is that the business model and strategy are equivalent in both scenarios, so the resources employed in the value chain are identical. What differs is the extent of integration (either vertical or horizontal), with greater integration in the established firm than in the set of entrepreneurial firms, and this is reflected in different boundaries of the firms in the two scenarios.

Second, I equate each of a firm's resources with a real option. Real options logic has been the primary theoretical framework underpinning research on strategic flexibility (Kogut, 1991; Sanchez, 1993; Folta, 1998; McGrath, 1999), and the equating of certain types of resources, like R&D or knowledge, with real options has been estab-

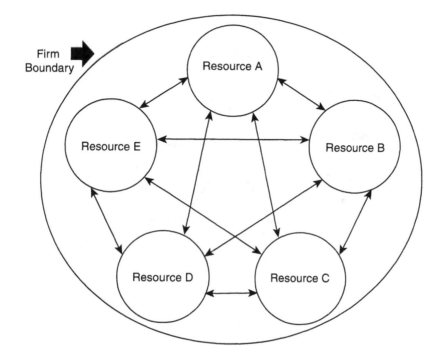

Figure 6.1a   Resource-rich firm with common ownership and control of resources

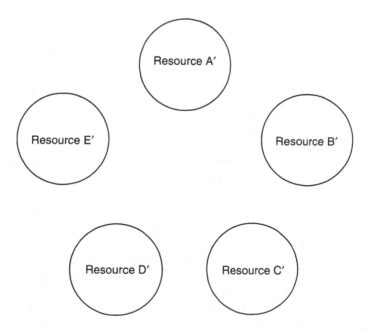

Figure 6.1b   Collection of entrepreneurial firms, no ownership or control ties

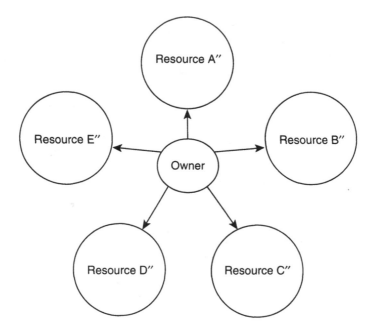

Figure 6.1c Collection of entrepreneurial firms linked by common ownership

lished in previous research (Childs and Triantis, 1999; McGrath and MacMillan, 2000). I begin with the extreme case in which all resources are considered real options, and later modify this argument.

Research on compound options is relevant to the comparison in figure 6.1. In the case of the resource-rich firm, compound options may create value for the firm's portfolio of resources. In particular, compounding options that are positively correlated increases the option value of a firm's portfolio, thereby increasing its flexibility (Geske, 1979; Vassolo, 2000). In this case, the established, resource-rich firm may be *more* flexible than the entrepreneurial firm. The opposite occurs when the options are negatively correlated, such that the value of a portfolio of negatively correlated options is lower than the total value of the options outside of the portfolio. Only with negatively correlated options will the flexibility of the entrepreneurial firms depicted in figure 6.1b exceed than that of the established firms depicted in figure 6.1a. Thus, it is likely that firms with large resource endowments will be more prevalent when options are positively correlated, and entrepreneurial firms will be more prevalent when options are negatively correlated.

It is important to note, however, that the disintegrated scenario consisting of several entrepreneurial firms does not preclude a compounding effect. A third party can invest in each of the entrepreneurial firms and enjoy the benefits of owning a portfolio of positively correlated options (see figure 6.1c). When this is achieved, the increase in this third party's portfolio value attributable to positively correlated options would be equivalent to the increase in the integrated firm's portfolio value. Common ownership

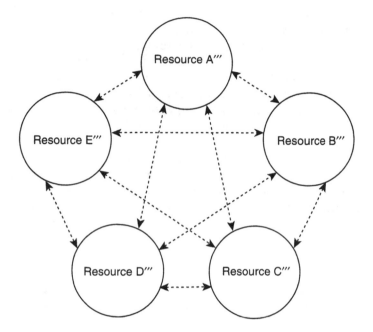

Figure 6.1d   Collection of entrepreneurial firms linked by credible commitments or other alignment mechanisms

of the options, which may occur without common control over their use, is sufficient to achieve the compounding effect that results from the correlation of the options.

The value of the portfolio in the resource-rich firm holding positively correlated options will be further enhanced when the uncertainty experienced by each of the options in the portfolio is reduced as a result of the common control over the resources.[6] The integrated firm may experience the benefits of reduced uncertainty that is endogenous to the portfolio of holdings (Folta, 1998). This might occur when, for example, the transactional uncertainty associated with the market exchange between subunits controlling resources A and B is reduced through the common control over the use of these resources (Williamson, 1985). These benefits would not be available to the disintegrated scenario with no ownership ties (figure 6.1b) or the disintegrated scenario with common ownership over the resources (figure 6.1c). Thus, the value of the portfolio of options in the established firm will be greater than or equal to the value of the portfolio of options in the entrepreneurial firm when endogenous uncertainty is reduced. In this case, the flexibility of the portfolio of options held by the established firm is not greater, but the value of this portfolio increases.

Is it possible for the collection of entrepreneurial firms depicted in figure 6.1b to experience the benefits of common control over the portfolio of options, without common ownership of the options? Entrepreneurial firms without ownership ties may be able to act in concert – to act as if centrally controlled – when their strategic goals are aligned to a significant degree. This collection of entrepreneurial firms may engage in credible commitments, such as bilateral investments in assets specific to the relationship (Williamson, 1985), or other types of mechanisms that align these firms' interests but do not involve the joint ownership of any resources. Figure 6.1d illustrates what might be described as a network of entrepreneurial firms, acting in concert without common ownership. When this occurs, the mechanisms that align the interests of the entrepreneurial firms serve to achieve the benefits associated with common control over resources. As a result, the network of entrepreneurial firms may benefit from the reduction in endogenous uncertainty, without the compound option effects associated with the common ownership of resources.

It is now useful to relax the assumption that all resources are real options and allow instead that the value chains represented in figure 6.1 consist of a combination of resources that are real options and those with little option value. Would one expect that the mix of these two types of resources would differ between the established firm shown in figure 6.1a and the collection of entrepreneurial firms shown in figures 6.1b, 6.1c, or 6.1d? In other words, would the established firm generally possess fewer or more resources with real option value than would the entrepreneurial firm?

A critical assumption implicit in many arguments that the entrepreneurial firm is more flexible than the established firm is that more of the resources illustrated in figure 6.1b, 6.1c, or 6.1d have option values than do the resources in figure 6.1a. Thus, resources A', A'', and A''' may be options, while resource A is not. Scholars have not adequately offered a rationale to support this assumption.

Fundamental to the comparisons illustrated in figure 6.1 is the idea that the uncertainty surrounding a resource's value may not influence a firm's decision to buy the resource or contract for the services of a resource. If it is expected that the productive life of a resource is ten years but this expectation is uncertain, a risk premium would influence the firm's decision to acquire the resource or would be factored into the charges for the resource's services from an outside firm that owns the resource. In either case, the firm cannot avoid the costs of the uncertainty surrounding the productive life of the resource. Clearly, this comparison must be evaluated with an options lens to determine if paying out for this uncertainty over time has more option value than paying for this uncertainty up front. Typically, deferred payments are associated with options. Nonetheless, the terms of the contract for the services of the resource will determine the option value of this contract, relative to an outright purchase. For example, if a contract specifies a substantial penalty for the premature termination of the contract, it may have limited option value because this penalty in effect commits the firm to at least this minimum payment, regardless of future states of nature. One example of this type of discussion can be found in Chi's (2000) analysis of whether an acquisition/divestiture price is specified ex ante or ex post in a joint venture agreement.

Beyond this fundamental comparison, are the types of resources that entrepreneurial and established firms can acquire different? If the resources available to entrepreneurial firms are superior to the resources available to the established firm, one must explain why the established firm cannot produce the same combination of resources, some of which might have option value, as the entrepreneurial firms. This has not been adequately addressed in the literature on the flexibility of entrepreneurial firms.

The four costs associated with large resource endowments may serve as starting points for this discussion. Both core rigidities and reduced experimentation limit the resource-rich firm's ability to explore radically new opportunities, which are related to investments in resources that represent options on new business arenas or new technologies. Reduced incentive intensity and the resulting shirking may limit the established firm's use of creative resources within the firm and reduce the established firm's attention to new business opportunities. Thus, the option value of these creative resources may be diminished in the resource-rich firm. When core rigidities, reduced experimentation, and reduced incentive intensity occur, fewer of the established firms' resources will have significant option value.

How strategic transparency influences the reliance of a firm on resources with significant option value is complex. Strategic transparency associated with large resource endowments may reduce the uncertainty associated with an established firm's future strategic possibilities, restricting which options can be acquired. For example, high levels of transparency may preclude investment in certain types of resources with option value because competitors could easily anticipate and preempt the strategies associated with these resources. Yet strategic transparency also influences the uncertainty experienced by a firm's competitors, such that greater transparency may reduce the value of the options held by the transparent firm's competitors. When this occurs, however, the value of competitors' portfolios may generally increase because of the diminished uncertainty they experience.

In conclusion, the argument that increased flexibility is the primary advantage of entrepreneurial firms over established ones is not straightforward. Comparative static logic highlights many instances in which established firms are more flexible than entrepreneurial firms. I suggest that the critical assumption implicit in most arguments about the greater flexibility of entrepreneurial firms is that entrepreneurial firms possess more resources that have significant option value than do established firms. Why established firms cannot construct resource portfolios similar to those of entrepreneurial firms has not been widely discussed. This chapter briefly considered how the four costs associated with large resource endowments may act as barriers to the acquisition of resources with high option values, which may influence the flexibility of established versus entrepreneurial firms.

Concluding Discussion

The chapter has examined the resource-based view of strategy from the perspective of entrepreneurial firms, with a focus on understanding if entrepreneurial firms will always be at a competitive disadvantage to resource-rich firms. The primary conclusions are twofold. First, an understanding of a firm's resource base is insufficient for predicting its ultimate success or failure. The business opportunities identified by the firm and the business models and strategies developed by the firm to capitalize upon these opportunities must be considered in addition to a firm's resources. I have advocated that the identification of business opportunities and the development of business models and strategies fall outside of the definition of firm resources, and must be considered separately.

Second, even though firm resources may serve as important sources of economic rents, the resource-rich firm is not always at a competitive advantage *vis-à-vis* the resource-poor firm. A consideration of different types of economic rents highlights the idea that value-destruction is likely associated with entrepreneurial rents and the entrepreneurial process. Resource-rich established firms may experience disadvantages attributable to (1) core rigidities; (2) reduced experimentation; (3) reduced incentive intensity; and (4) increased transparency of the strategy and business models employed. The arguments advanced suggest that the entrepreneurial firm may not always prefer a larger resource base. Under certain circumstances, it may be better for the entrepreneurial firm to continue to beg, borrow, or scavenge its resources (Starr and MacMillan, 1990), instead of accumulate them.

In advancing these arguments, this chapter has implicitly taken a stand on several points of debate within and outside of the resource-based view of strategy. These points include: (1) the acceptability of combining equilibrium-based arguments with disequilibrium ones; (2) the importance of human action over disembodied assets; and (3) the sufficiency of luck and firm resources for explaining firm performance. As part of this discussion, I also highlight possibilities for future research.

Combining equilibrium-based and disequilibrium-based arguments

In a critique of the resource-based view of strategy, Bromiley and Fleming (in press) argue against the theoretical legitimacy of combining equilibrium- and disequilibrium-based arguments. They criticize the expansion of the resource-based view outside of the narrow bounds of a foundation of equilibrium assumptions on which the theory was originally developed to embrace such disequilibrium concepts as dynamic capabilities (Teece, Pisano, and Shuen, 1997).

This chapter draws upon equilibrium-based arguments because of its acknowledgment that resources demonstrate long-run effects on a firm's rent stream. The primary contribution of this chapter lies in the marriage of these equilibrium arguments with disequilibrium arguments represented by its discussion of the entrepreneurial process. By separating resources from entrepreneurial choices, I have advocated clear distinctions between arguments of these two forms such that the long-run arguments associated with the resource-based view of strategy must clearly be distinguished from the dynamic arguments involving entrepreneurial processes.

It is my position that theoretical value is created, not destroyed, by bringing together these two types of arguments. One metaphor is a system in motion toward some long-run stable point. To understand where the phenomenon is at any point in time, one needs to understand both the long-run stable point and the trajectory or dynamics leading up to this point. Without the equilibrium arguments, the dynamics can be studied only in relative terms (position today compared to yesterday) because nothing would anchor the movements in absolute space. Yet without the disequilibrium arguments, only information about the anticipated ending point is available. It is possible that the phenomenon may not even converge to its equilibrium point, but instead oscillate around some central tendency. Absent disequilibrium arguments, this would remain unknown.

This marriage of disequilibrium and equilibrium approaches can be seen in other theoretical frames. Cybernetic views of human action (Simon, 1957; Cyert and March, 1963) represent an organizational theory that approximates the dynamic system metaphor described in the previous paragraph. This theory predicts individuals' or firms' actions based on their progress toward some goal or aspiration. These goals or aspirations are related to equilibrium arguments in the sense that they represent a steady-state tendency. This organizational theory's primary emphasis lies in understanding the short-run dynamics influencing movements or adjustments between periods as individuals or firms approach this goal. In this way, both equilibrium and disequilibrium arguments are employed in the cybernetic view of behavior, with a clear delineation of the two types of arguments. It is this approach I advocate for future research in the resource-based view of strategy.

Human actor versus disembodied asset

There has been a tendency in the resource-based view of strategy to ignore the human actor behind a firm's resources. While a focus on human capital remains in vogue, this discussion seldom considers the motivations, emotions, habits, and other characteristics of the human actor in which this capital is embedded. Describing what is in someone's head as capital draws upon an overly simplistic metaphor that ignores the behavioral, cognitive, and emotional complexities surrounding knowledge-based resources. And these complexities also spill over to tangible resources, such as physical plant and equipment, which would not exist without someone deciding to invest in them, someone building them, and someone using them.

The stance taken in this chapter is to incorporate human choice in terms of what business opportunities will be identified by the entrepreneur and what business models and strategies he or she will develop to exploit these opportunities. While these choices are clearly a circumscribed view of the myriad of decisions available to, and behaviors exhibited by, individuals within the firm, the current focus on entrepreneurial choices was dictated by the interest in the value-destroying aspects of large resource endowments. What is arguably the most important aspect of this focus is its intentional separation of human choice from a firm's resources and the argument that choices and resources cannot be studied in identical ways.

For example, this chapter does not advocate applying the criteria of unique, valuable, inimitable, and nonsubstitutable developed by Barney (1986a) to characterize rent-generating resources to the business opportunity identified by the entrepreneur. While thousands of entrepreneurs may have identified the same business opportunity – thereby violating the uniqueness criterion – one of these entrepreneurs may generate economic rents. The entrepreneur whose choices and actions serve to develop a business model and strategy appropriate for capitalizing on this opportunity as well as to deploy the resources necessary for implementing this business model and strategy will succeed. Thus, uniqueness may not be a necessary condition for a business opportunity to generate economic rents.

The criteria for entrepreneurial-rent generation associated with the entrepreneurial process differ from the criteria for Ricardian-rent and quasi-rent generation associated with a firm's resources. A fruitful avenue for future research involves an examination of the criteria for rent generation associated with the business opportunity, business model, and firm strategy and how these criteria may interrelate with the criteria for rent-generation associated with firm resources.

This chapter's emphasis on human choice has been foreshadowed by similar calls to incorporate human discretion into the resource-based view of strategy. Amit and Schoemaker (1993), for example, discuss rents stemming from individuals' discretionary choices about which resources and competences to develop and deploy. They see discretion as influenced by decision biases exhibited by boundedly rational managers experiencing uncertainty, complexity, and conflict within the firm. While Amit and Schoemaker's focus on human discretion revolves around biases and mistakes, particularly as they relate to the management of a firm's resources, this chapter instead emphasizes the entrepreneurial process that identifies and develops opportunities.

More than luck and resources

The resource-based view of strategy has relied almost exclusively upon resources and competences, on one hand, and luck on the other hand, as explanators of firm performance. In evaluating whether entrepreneurship is something unique, Demsetz (1983) equates it with luck because he argues it is not a resource and must, therefore, be luck.

But as stories of mishaps during the inventive process illustrate, is not luck the source of virtually every resource? Winter (1987: 165) describes the principle of "full imputation" to mean that "a proper economic valuation of a collection of resources is one that precisely accounts for the returns the resources make possible." This principle underlies the backward deduction employed in the resource-based view of strategy. As Winter notes (1987: 166), every rent stream would be imputed to luck under the full imputation principle. Yet it is not terribly useful or illuminating to attribute the rents earned by Microsoft to the random confluence of events that brought together Bill Gates's parents or grandparents. Looking down to spy a $20 bill on the street should be distinguished from an entrepreneur's or manager's systematic efforts to maximize his or her firm's profits.

The approach that underlies this chapter's arguments is that an ex ante view of a firm's current situation is more useful than backward deduction. An ex ante approach is suited to the scientific goal of forward-looking prediction instead of backward-looking explanation (McKelvey, 1997; Mosakowski and McKelvey, 1997). It encourages the application of a broad range of theories of human behaviors and choices that assist in making predictions and influencing the likelihood of certain types of results. Another way to view an ex ante approach is that while luck, resources, and human behavior may interact to determine a firm's success or failure, drawing upon existing knowledge of human behavior offers considerably greater prospects for influencing firm outcomes (Hendrickx, 2001) and increasing the firm's chances of positive outcomes.

By building a triad of human choice, resources, and luck, future research can incorporate what might seem to be transient phenomena without equating them with luck. Who would dispute that behaviors, decisions, and choices that might be viewed at the time as transitory – impulsive decisions, fleeting emotions, moments of organizational skepticism – often have significant and lasting influence on firms? For example, whistle blowers within certain firms and industries have forever changed the future of these firms and industries, even though the decision to reveal internal company information may not be carefully considered (Near and Miceli, 1996). Yet it seems inappropriate to refer to these decisions as luck since they are influenced by individual, organizational, and environmental factors. Without incorporating human choice in some fashion within the resource-based view of strategy, by attributing every outcome to either luck or extant firm resources, the strategy field is in danger of ignoring free will and human discretion.

Notes

The author would like to thank Arnie Cooper and Tim Folta for their suggestions and guidance.

1 Alvarez and Barney (2000) also note that the Austrian view's inherent inability to model disequilibrium phenomena limits the Austrian view's ability to generate predictions.

2 Conner (1991) notes that the concept of the firm as an input combiner is at the heart of the resource-based view of strategy.

3 A different view of strategy is reflected in Rumelt (1984: 557–8): "In essence, the [strategy] concept is that a firm's competitive position is defined by a bundle of unique resources and relationships and that the task of general management is to adjust and renew these resources and relationships as time, competition, and change erode their value."

4 This argument is similar to that proposed by Williamson (1985) concerning the limits to the firm.

5 For some strategies, competitors' ability to anticipate a firm's future moves may facilitate the execution of a firm's strategy. For example, in advocating a colonial approach to exporting strategies across cultures, Mosakowski (2000) indicates that competitors' abilities to anticipate these unfamiliar strategies may be useful to some extent.

6 I am indebted to Tim Folta for this discussion of how a firm's portfolio of options may affect its endogenous uncertainty.

References

Alvarez, S. A. and Barney, J. B., 2000. Entrepreneurial capabilities: A resource-based view. In G. D. Meyer and K. Heppard (eds), *Entrepreneurship as strategy: Competing on the entrepreneurial edge*. Thousand Oaks: Sage Publications, 63–81.

Amabile, T. M. 1996. *Creativity in context*. Boulder, CO: Westview Press.

Amit, R. and Schoemaker, P. J. H. 1993. Strategic assets and organizational rent. *Strategic Management Journal*, 14: 33–46.

Barney, J. B. 1986a. Strategic factor markets: Expectations, luck, and business strategy. *Management Science*, 32: 1230–41.

Barney, J. B. 1986b. Organizational culture: Can it be a source of sustained competitive advantage? *Academy of Management Review*, 11: 656–65.

Barney, J. B. 1991. Firm resource and competitive advantage. *Journal of Management*, 17: 99–120.

Barney, J. B. and Hansen, M. H. 1994. Trustworthiness as a source of competitive advantage. *Strategic Management Journal*, 15 (special winter issue): 175–90.

Brandenburger, A. and Nalebuff, B. 1995. The right game: Using game theory to shape strategy. *Harvard Business Review*, 73(4): 57–71.

Bromiley, P. and Fleming, L. in press. The resource based view of strategy: an evolutionist's critique. In M. Augier and J. G. March (eds) *The economics of choice, change, and organizations: Essays in memory of Richard M. Cyert*. Cheltenham, UK: Edward Elgar Publishing Limited.

Brush, C. G. and Chaganti, R. 1999. Businesses without glamour? An analysis of resources on performance by size and age in small service and retail firms. *Journal of Business Venturing*, 14(3): 233–57.

Castanias, R. P. and Helfat, C. E. 1991. Managerial resources and rents. *Journal of Management*, 17: 155–71.

Caves, R. E. 1980. Industrial organization, corporate strategy and structure. *Journal of Economic Literature*, 58: 64–92.

Chi, T. 2000. Option to acquire or divest a joint venture. *Strategic Management Journal*, 21: 665–87.

Childs, P. D. and Triantis, A. J. 1999. Dynamic R&D investment policies. *Management Science*, 45: 1359–77.

Collis, D. and Montgomery, C. 1995. Competing on Resources. *Harvard Business Review*, 74(5): 118–28.

Conner, K. C. 1991. A historical comparison of resource-based theory and five schools of thought within industrial organization economics. *Journal of Management*, 17: 121–54.

Cyert, R. M. and March, J. G. 1963. *A behavioral theory of the firm*. Englewood Cliffs, NJ: Prentice-Hall.

Daft, R. 1983. *Organization theory and design*. New York: West.

Deeds D. L., Decarolis, D., and Coombs, J. 2000. Dynamic capabilities and new product development in high technology ventures: An empirical analysis of new biotechnology firms. *Journal of Business Venturing*, 15(3): 211–29.

Demsetz, H. 1983. The neglect of the entrepreneur. In J. Ronen (ed.), *Entrepreneurship*. Lexington, MA: Lexington Books 271–80.

Dierickx, I. and Cool, K. 1989. Asset stock accumulation and sustainability of competitive advantage. *Management Science*, 35: 1504–11.

Flamholtz, E. G. and Randle, Y. 2000. *Growing pains*. San Francisco: Jossey-Bass.

Folta, T. B. 1998. Governance and uncertainty: The tradeoff between administrative control and commitment. *Strategic Management Journal*, 19: 1007–28.

Geske, R. 1979. The valuation of compound options. *Journal of Financial Economics*, 7: 63–81.

Guillen, M. F. 2000. Business groups in emerging economies: a resource-based view. *Academy of Management Journal*, 43: 362–80.

Hendrickx, M. 2001. *Viewing the resource-based view literature as a collection of metaphors: Implications for the study of core competences*. Unpublished doctoral dissertation, Purdue University, Krannert School.

Hitt, M. A. and Ireland, R. D. 1985. Corporate distinctive competence, strategy, industry, and performance. *Strategic Management Journal*, 6: 273–93.

Kaish, S. and Gilad, B. 1991. Characteristics of opportunities search of entrepreneurs versus executives: Resources, interests, general alertness. *Journal of Business Venturing*, 6: 45–61.

Kets de Vries, M. F. R. 1995. *Life and death in the executive fast lane*. San Francisco: Jossey-Bass.

Kirzner, I. M. 1973. *Competition and entrepreneurship*. Chicago, IL: University of Chicago Press.

Kirzner, I. M. 1979. *Perception, opportunity, and entrepreneurship*. Chicago, IL: University of Chicago Press.

Klein, B., Crawford, R. G., and Alchian, A. 1978. Vertical integration, appropriable rents, and the competitive contracting process. *Journal of Law and Economics*, 21: 257–85.

Kogut, B. 1991. Joint ventures and the option to acquire. *Management Science*, 37: 19–33.

Leonard-Barton, D. 1992. Core capabilities and core rigidities. *Strategic Management Journal*, 13 (special summer issue): 111–25.

Levinthal, D. A. and March, J. G. 1993. Myopia of learning. *Strategic Management Journal*, 14:

95–112.

Levitt, B. and March, James G. 1988. Organizational learning. *Annual Review of Sociology*, 14: 319–40.

Majumdar, S. K. 2000. Sluggish giants, sticky cultures, and dynamic capability transformation. *Journal of Business Venturing*, 15(1): 59–78.

McGrath, R. G. 1995. Advantage from adversity – Learning from disappointment in internal corporate ventures. *Journal of Business Venturing*, 10: 121–42.

McGrath, R. G. 1999. Falling forward: Real options reasoning and entrepreneurial failure. *Academy of Management Review*, 24: 13–30.

McGrath, R. G. and MacMillan, I. 2000. Assessing technology projects using real options reasoning. *Research in Technology Management*, 43: 35–49.

McGrath, R. G., Venkataraman, S., and Macmillan, I. C. 1994. The advantage chain – antecedents to rents from internal corporate ventures. *Journal of Business Venturing*, 9: 351–69.

McKelvey, B. 1997. Quasi-natural organization science. *Organization Science*, 8: 352–80.

Menger, C. 1963. *Problems of economics and society*, translated by F. J. Nock. Urbana, IL: University of Illinois.

Montgomery, C. A. 1995. Of diamonds and rust: A new look at resources. In C. A. Montgomery (ed.), *Resource-based and evolutionary theories of the firm: A synthesis*. Boston, MA: Kluwer, 251–68.

Mosakowski, E. 1997. Strategy making under causal ambiguity: Conceptual issues and empirical evidence.*Organization Science*, 8: 414–42.

Mosakowski, E. 1998a. Entrepreneurial resources, organizational choices, and competitive outcomes. *Organization Science*, 9: 625–43.

Mosakowski, E. 1998b. Managerial prescriptions under the resource-based view of strategy: The example of motivational techniques. *Strategic Management Journal*, 19: 1169–82.

Mosakowski, E. 2000. Strategic colonialism in unfamiliar cultures. In P. C. Earley and H. Singh (eds), *Innovations in international and cross-cultural management*. Thousand Oaks, CA: Sage Publications, 311–37.

Mosakowski, E. and McKelvey, B. 1997. Predicting rent generation in competence-based competition. In A. Heene and R. Sanchez (eds), *Competence-based strategic management*. Chichester, UK: John Wiley.

Near, J. P. and Miceli, M. P. 1996. Whistle-blowing: Myth and reality. *Journal of Management*, 22: 507–26.

Nelson, R. R. and Winter, S. G. 1982. *An evolutionary theory of economic change*. Cambridge, MA: Harvard:

Penrose, E. 1959. *The theory of growth of the firm*. New York: John Wiley.

Peteraf, M. A. 1993. The cornerstones of competitive advantage: a resource-based view. *Strategic Management Journal*, 14: 179–91.

Prahalad, C. K. and Hamel, G. 1990. The core competence of the corporation. *Harvard Business Review*, 70(3): 79–90.

Rumelt, R. P. 1984. Towards a strategic theory of the firm. In R. B. Lamb (ed.), *Competitive strategic management*. Englewood Cliffs, NJ: Prentice Hall.

Rumelt, R. P. 1987. Theory, strategy, and entrepreneurship. In D. J. Teece (ed.), *The competitive challenge*. Cambridge, MA: Ballinger, 137–58.

Sanchez, R. 1993. Strategic flexibility, firm organization, and managerial work in dynamic markets, *Advances in Strategic Management*, 9: 251–93.

Sanchez, R., Heene, A., and Thomas, H. 1996. *Dynamics of competence-based competition*. Oxford, UK: Elsevier.

Simon, H. A. 1957. *Administrative behavior*, 2nd edn. New York: Free Press.

Starr, J. A. and MacMillan, I. C. 1990. Resource cooptation via social contracting: Resource acquisition strategies for new ventures. *Strategic Management Journal,* 11 (special summer issue): 79–92.

Stevenson, H. H. and Gumpert, D. E. 1985. The heart of entrepreneurship. *Harvard Business Review,* 63(2): 2–11.

Teece, D. J., Pisano, G., and Schuen, A. 1997. Dynamic capabilities and strategic management. *Strategic Management Journal,* 18: 509–33.

Thornhill S. and Amit, R. 2001. A dynamic perspective of internal fit in corporate venturing. *Journal of Business Venturing,* 16: 25–50.

Vassolo, R. 2000. Strategic alliances as tools of exploration: An exotic options approach. Working paper, Purdue University, Krannert School.

Williamson, O. E. 1985. *The economic institutions of capitalism.* New York: Free Press.

Winter, S. G. 1987. Knowledge and competence as strategic assets. In D. J. Teece (ed.), *The competitive challenge.* Cambridge, MA: Ballinger, 159–84.

Winter, S. G. 1995. The four R's of profitability. In C. A. Montgomery (ed.), *Resource-based and evolutionary theories of the firm: A synthesis.* Boston, MA: Kluwer, 147–78.

PART III

Innovation

CHAPTER SEVEN

Bisociation, Discovery, and the Role of Entrepreneurial Action

Ken G. Smith, Dante Di Gregorio

> [I]t is by means of new combinations of existing factors of produc-
> tion, embodied in new combinations of existing factors of produc-
> tion, embodied in new plants and, typically, new firms producing
> either new commodities, or by a new, i.e. as yet untried, method, or
> for a new market, or by buying means of production in a new
> market. What we, unscientifically, call economic progress means
> essentially putting productive resources to uses hitherto untried in
> practice, and withdrawing them from the uses they have served so
> far. This is what we call "innovation."
> Schumpeter, The instability of capitalism, emphasis in original

> The creative act is not an act of creation in the sense of the Old
> Testament. It does not create something out of nothing; it uncov-
> ers, selects, re-shuffles, combines, synthesizes already existing facts,
> ideas, faculties, skills. The more familiar the parts, the more strik-
> ing the new whole. Man's knowledge of the changes of the tides and
> the phases of the moon is as old as his observation that apples fall to
> earth in the ripeness of time. Yet the combination of these and other
> equally familiar data in Newton's theory of gravity changed man-
> kind's outlook on the world.
> Koestler, The act of creation

The competitive dynamics literature, which reflects the market process movements of firms in pursuit of profits, has begun to identify the alternative actions firms can under-take to build, defend, and sustain superior profits (Grimm and Smith, 1997). One class of action that is prominent in this literature is entrepreneurial actions. For exam-ple, Grimm and Smith (1997) use entrepreneurial action to characterize how firms move to exploit new opportunities that rivals have yet to perceive. Schumpeter (1934, 1942) was perhaps the first to describe entrepreneurial action. He used the expression to depict the actions firms employ to break away from the everyday status quo compe-tition in pursuit of entrepreneurial rents. Kirzner (1973) employed the idiom to clarify how markets resolve information problems and move toward equilibrium.

This chapter examines the processes by which entrepreneurial actions come about, as well as how and why they vary in their market effect. This focus is important for at least two reasons. First, we contend that entrepreneurial actions are a fundamental behavior of firms by which they *move* into new markets, *seize* new customers, *introduce* new resources, and/or *combine* markets, customers, and resources in new ways. As such, the study of entrepreneurial action may advance our understanding of how firms build and develop new competitive advantages and earn superior profits. The study of entrepreneurial action is also important because, as we shall show, entrepreneurial actions are the fundamental element of the competitive market process. In Schumpeter's (1942) theory of creative destruction it is the entrepreneurial actions of firms that threaten rival firms, forcing them to attempt to respond. Indeed, the actions and profits of leaders prompt rivals to respond in an ever-escalating game of competition that can be both disruptive and encouraging. The study of entrepreneurial actions thus also has the potential to advance our understanding of how markets change and evolve.

In an effort to explain entrepreneurial actions, we integrate and combine ideas from two ostensibly unrelated schools of thought. First, Austrian economics provides a mechanism to understand entrepreneurial action as the result of a decision process (entrepreneurial discovery) and to explain the consequences of action in terms of a market process. Concerning the market process, we contend that entrepreneurial actions form the key element of the competitive market process, whereby equilibrating actions generate and diffuse new knowledge in the marketplace, while disequilibrating actions upset the trend toward equilibrium by calling into question means–ends relations that had previously been taken for granted. Second, research on creativity also depicts innovative actions as resulting from a decision process. For example, Koestler (1964) described this process as essentially involving *bisociation*, whereby a deliberate action entails the combination of two previously unrelated "matrices" of information and resources, resulting in a creative action. The literature on creativity thus provides a decision framework to explain variation in entrepreneurial action. The process of bisociation is a prominent feature of this decision framework. The common element from both of these literatures is the focus on combination of resources and information that is reflected in the two opening quotations.

We define entrepreneurial actions as *any newly fashioned behavior by which firms exploit opportunities others have not noticed or exploited*. The defining characteristic of entrepreneurial action is "*newness.*" Entrepreneurial actions are original along at least one of the following four dimensions: they entail new resources, new customers, new markets, and/or new combinations of existing resources, customers, and markets. Treating these actions as a variable, our goal is to predict why firms diverge in their entrepreneurial behavior. We first characterize the firm's environment as varying in levels of buyer and seller knowledge held by all industry participants about what are the ideal products, customers, and markets. We contend that variation in knowledge serves as a basis of profit opportunity for alert entrepreneurs and when such opportunities are discovered, entrepreneurial actions follow. Drawing from the decision literature on creativity, we develop a set of propositions that explain variation in entrepreneurial action.

In presenting our theory of discovery and entrepreneurial action we must make a number of assumptions and boundary conditions. First, our theory is constructed at the individual level of analysis. This condition follows from the central assumption of

Austrian economics (Kirzner, 1973) and is consistent with the majority of the creativity literature (Amabile, 1996). As a result of this simplification, we predict firm action based on the decisions of individuals within the firm, an assumption that is consistent with research on top management (Finkelstein and Hambrick, 1996). Second, and also consistent with the Austrian literature, we adopt a subjective "bounded rationality" viewpoint of human action and knowledge. This supposition permits us to conceive of the environment and economic opportunity in terms of the information/ knowledge problem to be solved through effective search and action. Finally, we treat action based on technological innovation to be a subset of a larger class of entrepreneurial action, primarily because the current technology literature suggests this as a viable way of furthering our understanding of innovation (Henderson and Clark, 1990; Christensen, 1997; Tushman and Anderson, 1986). Therefore, we view technological innovation as a special case of a more general class of innovative actions, which we refer to as entrepreneurial actions.

Variations in Market and Resource Knowledge as a Source of Opportunity

The environment of information and knowledge

Equilibrium models have traditionally been used to explain competitive markets. Most of these models start with the assumption of complete knowledge or that sellers and buyers know the lowest cost or price at which a product can be produced and sold – for example, that individual buyers will have the knowledge that when they buy a product they will be able to secure this product at the lowest price (e.g., price Y). Likewise, it assumes that individual sellers know that customers are willing to pay a certain price (e.g., price Y). With this assumption, economists and management scientists have not needed to pay attention to the process by which markets reach the equilibrium whereby all buyers and sellers have the same information and expectations about pricing. For the most part, they assume that forces for equilibrium, and this price agreement, are swift and efficient (Kirzner, 1973).

Recently, however, there has been more attention to the process of competition and especially how markets move toward and away from equilibrium (D'Aveni, 1994; Grimm and Smith, 1997). Of particular interest have been the information or knowledge problems associated with this competitive equilibrium process (Hayek, 1945, 1949; Grimm and Smith, 1997). Hayek (1945, 1949) was one of the first to question the assumptions of perfect information associated with equilibrium models. He documented that market knowledge cannot be held by sellers and buyers before the process of competition starts (1949: 96). Hayek argued that the knowledge of the alternatives before them is a result of what happens in the market. Thus, Hayek conceived of the environment as containing varying levels of information on what are the best product features and prices that sellers can offer and buyers are willing to pay.

Importantly, Hayek (1945, 1949) argued that the correct knowledge is only discovered through the process of competition – e.g., the entrepreneurial actions of firms in the process of competition. Moreover, he contended that the function of competition is to educate buyers and sellers of what is available and possible (1949: 101). He concluded: "Competition is essentially a process of the formation of opinion: by spreading information, it creates that unity and coherence of the economic system which we presuppose when we think of it as one market" (Hayek, 1949: 106).

Only through the introduction of varying levels of knowledge in the environment can we begin to understand the process of competition and the forces driving for and against equilibrium. Kirzner (1973) captured this idea more formally with his concept of market ignorance:

> Market participants are unaware of the real opportunities for beneficial exchanges which are available to them in the market. The result of this state of ignorance is that countless opportunities are passed up. . . . The potential sellers are unaware that sufficiently eager buyers are waiting, who might make it worth their while to sell. Potential buyers are unaware that sufficiently eager sellers are waiting, who might make it attractive for them to buy. Resources are being used to produce products which consumers value less urgently, because producers are not aware that these resources can produce more urgently needed products. Products are being produced with resources badly needed for other products because producers are not aware that alternative, less critically needed resources can be used to achieve the same result (1973: 69–70).

According to Kirzner (1973), market ignorance creates potential opportunities for the entrepreneur who can spot these knowledge problems and correct them with new action. He argued that it is only through the introduction of these knowledge problems that the potential for an opportunity emerges and the possibility that the first one to discover this opportunity can "capture the associated profits by innovating, changing and creating" (1973: 67). As he noted:

> The discovery during the course of yesterday's market experiences, that the other market participants were not making these expected decisions can be seen as generating changes in the corresponding price expectations with which market participants enter the market today (1973: 71).

Consistent with the above arguments, we conceive of markets as varying substantially with regard to the knowledge, and the accuracy of this knowledge, that all market participants (buyers and sellers) hold regarding the appropriate products (resource combinations), types of customers or customer preferences (e.g., high and low price customers), and market locations (where customers can be found). In other words, each potential seller and each potential buyer will have their own theory or mental map (Walsh, 1995) of the ideal product, customer, and market, as well as the manner in which these are believed to relate to each other. These mental maps are conceived of in terms of three information matrices that are related according to the underlying causal relations that are believed to exist: a matrix of viewpoints on the ideal product features, a matrix of the best customer types, and a matrix of the best market locations. If all buyers and sellers were to possess identical opinions and expectations, the market would reach equilibrium, but such a scenario is unlikely. At the *extreme*, we can imagine every buyer and every seller having a different view of the ideal product, customer, and market, as well as having a unique image of how these matrices can be combined. Figure 7.1 captures this variation.

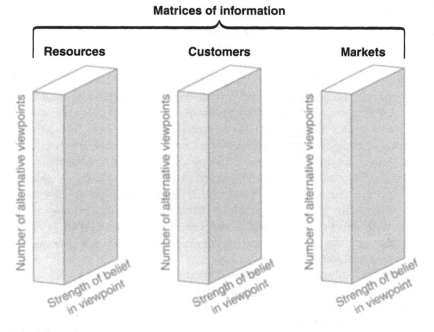

Figure 7.1   The information environment: knowledge problems as a basis of economic opportunity

We also contend that the current viewpoints that market participants hold will be in a constant state of flux. These viewpoints can be moving toward a state whereby all participants have the same position or that there is movement toward a consensus and little confusion about the ideal product types, customers, and markets (e.g., the market may be approaching "perfect" information); however, it can also be moving in the opposite direction so that the viewpoints are becoming more dispersed or a case whereby there is increased disagreement and a great deal of confusion about the ideal product types, customers, and markets.[1] We contend that it is the entrepreneurial actions that move this knowledge problem in both directions. Hayek captured this possibility when he described the process of competition and equilibrium:

> It creates the views people have about what is best and cheapest, and it is because of it that people know at least as much about the possibilities and opportunities as they in fact do. It is thus a process which involves a continuous change in the data and whose significance must therefore be completely missed by any theory which treats these data as constant (1949: 106).

The entrepreneur and the discovery/decision process

Conceiving the environment as varying in terms of viewpoints or knowledge problems allows us to insert the entrepreneur.[2] The entrepreneur is fundamental to our model for it is the entrepreneur or team of entrepreneurs that discovers opportunities to correct misperceptions in the environment. We now introduce the concepts of alertness, discovery, and decision, which explain how action comes about and allows us to connect the information/knowledge environment described above with entrepreneurial action.[3]

According to Mises, before there can be action, there must be thinking: "Man is in a position to act because he has the ability to discover causal relations which determine change. . . . Acting requires and presupposes the category of causality. Only a man who sees the world in light of causality is fitted to act. . ." (1949: 22). Mises argued that thinking is to deliberate beforehand over future action and to reflect afterwards upon past action. He noted that every action is always based on a definite idea about causal relations, for example, the ideal product, price, and location with which a buyer will buy. Thus, the entrepreneur creates a causal mental map of the information environment prior to any plan of action. Note that this causal mental map need not be entirely accurate but merely plausible in order to enable action (Weick, 1995). Thus, action is taken and the result of such action allows entrepreneurs to adjust/correct their information leading to further action.

Kirzner contended that the key aspect of knowledge that is so relevant to entrepreneurship is "not so much substantive knowledge of market data as alertness, the 'knowledge' of where to find market data. Once one imagines knowledge of market data to be already possessed with absolute certainty, one has . . . imagined away the opportunity." He further clarified, "I view the entrepreneur not as a source of innovative ideas ex nihilo, but as being alert to the opportunities that exist *already* and are waiting to be noticed" (1973: 74). In this context, the innovation that is often seen as a product of entrepreneurship is perhaps best examined as a consequence of an individual's process of opportunity search and discovery.

In describing the preconditions of action, Mises (1949) contended that for action to occur, the entrepreneur must: (1) have a dissatisfaction with the current condition (this is referred to as the stimulus in our model); (2) have an image of a more satisfactory state or outcome (this is developed from the search and decision process); and (3) hold an expectation that his/her actions have the power to remove the dissatisfaction and achieve the satisfactory state. Absent these conditions, according to Mises, no action is feasible.

Mises also contended that dissatisfaction often is created by past actions that are no longer capable of achieving their desired end. This forces the entrepreneur to begin the conscious but open-ended search and decision process to identify new potential opportunities or causal relationships. We contend that these mental models of causal relationships include the discovery of an opportunity (based on our decision model) *and* a conceived action that the entrepreneur believes will seize the opportunity (to produce a more desirable state). In essence, it is a belief that the entrepreneur can divert the future course of events with his or her entrepreneurial action from the way it would go in the absence of this action. Mises noted, "He searches for the regularity and the 'law,' because he wants to interfere" (1949: 22). Mises declared that the entrepreneur "imagines conditions which suit him better, and his action aims at bringing about this desired state" (1949: 13). The resultant opportunity will be the identification of knowledge problems or misperceptions that can be corrected through action.

Kirzner contends, "The entrepreneur, in my view, brings into mutual adjustment those discordant elements which result from prior market ignorance" (1973: 73). Thus, although we see entrepreneurial actions as firm behaviors, they are motivated by individual perceptions of opportunity.

In this section we have highlighted the discovery process, particularly with regard to entrepreneurial alertness and discovery of opportunity. We will more formally describe this process in the proposition section of this chapter. We now turn to explaining entrepreneurial action.

Entrepreneurial action

As noted, in this chapter we focus on newly invented behaviors or actions, which we refer to as entrepreneurial actions. Entrepreneurial actions are behaviors designed to exploit the discovery of unnoticed opportunities. According to Mises (1949), prior actions that have less positive benefit over time are abandoned in favor of newly created actions that are designed to provide a more positive benefit. Entrepreneurial actions are thus always directed toward the future; their aim is to render future conditions more satisfactory than they would be without the action. It is the uneasiness with the present that impels the entrepreneur to search for opportunities and to act to improve the future.

We therefore see entrepreneurial action expressed in the kinds and qualities of new goods, new promotions, and new services being produced and offered for sale in the marketplace. Schumpeter (1942) argued that the most important type of competition in the market process was that created by the new commodity, product, technology, source of supply, and type of organization. Such actions allow the firm to break away from status quo, to break down the forces of inertia, to destroy existing structure, and to move the system away from the circular flow of equilibrium. According to Schumpeter's theory of market process and creative destruction, it is the entrepreneurial actions of the leaders – the innovators or "trailblazers" – which are contrasted with the activity of the imitators who follow the leaders. In this theory, it is entrepreneurs that break away from the equilibrium with their actions and it is the imitators that bring the economy back to rest and to a new level of equilibrium. Thus, Schumpeter distinguished entrepreneurs whose actions break away – to cause disequilibrium – from imitators that bring the system back to equilibrium. In Schumpeter's theory, the imitators were not entrepreneurs.

Kirzner (1973) had a different perspective on entrepreneurial actions. Although similar to Schumpeter with the emphasis on the entrepreneurial action and discovery, the crucial element from Kirzner's perspective is that entrepreneurial actions stem from the perception of entrepreneurs that there are some "unexploited opportunities" whose prior existence meant that the appearance of equilibrium was illusory. That, far from being a state of equilibrium, it represents a situation of disequilibrium inevitably destined to be disrupted by new action. Kirzner argued, "We see the process whereby an above-equilibrium price is beaten down toward equilibrium as an entrepreneurial process; it requires entrepreneurial alertness to the realities of the situation to adjust to the true eagerness of prospective buyers" (1973: 128). He further noted, "In fact, it is precisely the short run market processes, which are responsible for the ever present agitation tending toward market equilibrium positions, that we wish to illumine by our emphasis on entrepreneurship" (1973: 128). For Kirzner, entrepreneurial action serves the purpose of exploiting the variation in knowledge in the environment and only when this knowledge is completely exploited will action end. Thus, any action, even only slightly new actions, relative to prior historical actions, may be considered entrepreneurial.

There are important differences between Schumpeter's position and that of Kirzner. For Schumpeter, entrepreneurial action disrupted the status quo equilibrium. For Kirzner, entrepreneurial actions were responsible for bringing the system back to equilibrium once all the profits were "squeezed" out. These two perspectives emphasize two different forms of entrepreneurial actions: disequilibrating actions move the market away from equilibrium (Schumpeter), and equilibrating actions move the market toward equilibrium (Kirzner). Since markets are neither eroding into sheer chaos nor stabilizing to a final equilibrium, it is logical that both types of action coexist and are mutually dependent. Therefore, it is possible to evaluate entrepreneurial actions by the extent to which they are disequilibrating or equilibrating in nature. The common element of both types of action is that they are newly designed behaviors to seize opportunities that others have not noticed or exploited.

As is apparent in the terminology we have employed, equilibrating actions move the market toward equilibrium. More specifically, entrepreneurs correct market knowledge about what is possible through equilibrating actions by exploiting opportunities that previously existed but had not yet been perceived and acted upon by others. These actions build upon, refine, diffuse, and correct existing knowledge held by market participants. For instance, when an American company replicates a strategic innovation first introduced in Europe or vice versa, as happened when alternative mobile communications technologies crossed the Atlantic, both producers and consumers became more capable of making sound resource allocation decisions. Equilibrating actions build upon and diffuse existing knowledge through the combination of resources, markets, and customers. It is only through these entrepreneurial actions that the market can be said to approach equilibrium, and opportunities for short-lived entrepreneurial rents will persist until all opportunities for equilibrating action have been discovered and exploited.

But equilibrium is an elusive state, and competitive markets are never accurately described as resting at a state of equilibrium. While equilibrating actions increase the body of knowledge of means–ends relations among market participants, disequilibrating actions actually increase the variation in viewpoints of what is appropriate by calling into question means–ends relations that were previously taken for granted and by extending the scope of what is believed to be knowable. As long as Europeans believed the end of the world lay to the west, no additional knowledge was perceived to be needed. More importantly than introducing new knowledge, Columbus' voyage to the Americas demonstrated that countless discoveries were yet to be made. In the commercial domain, it is easy to think of successful and unsuccessful product innovations that have had a disequilibrating impact on the market, such as the Sony Walkman, the Apple Newton, and the Iridium global communication system. For instance, although Iridium was a complete failure, its introduction signaled the expansion of the set of potentially profitable opportunities in communications.[4] These technology-intensive innovations are merely a special, albeit highly visible, type of disequilibrating entrepreneurial action, and such action need not entail technological novelty. For instance, the recent introduction of milk packaged in sports bottles and distributed through convenience stores forced consumers to reconsider their image of milk as a beverage, dairy producers to reconsider their image of milk as a commodity, and marketers to reconsider how goods are packaged and marketed. Also, disequilibrating actions need not entail the introduction of new or even revised products. By allowing an established service to be provided via a novel channel, recent innovations in online financial services have upset the status quo and brought to light the need for additional discoveries to be made.

The bold contention that disequilibrating actions create additional knowledge problems in the market merits further explanation. By stating that disequilibrating actions increase knowledge problems, we mean that the knowledge discovered by one market participant is incompatible with preexisting and widely diffused knowledge. This may occur for two reasons. First, disequilibrating actions may destroy existing knowledge. For instance, when Columbus landed in the Americas he disproved the validity of existing maps. More recently, insurance companies such as Geico and Progressive that sell policies via telephone and the Internet have disproved the validity of the industry's prevailing causal map, which had indicated that personal contact with sales agents was necessary to gain new customers. In such cases, the action serves to correct causal maps which the entrepreneurial action has proved incorrect or not accurate. Second, disequilibrating actions may broaden the range of what is deemed to be knowable. In this case, means–ends relations that were previously unthinkable suddenly become plausible. Early efforts to link computer technology with communications may be classified as such actions, as may efforts to sell basic groceries online. With the benefit of hindsight, the link between computers and communications is obvious, and this innovation has unleashed seemingly endless opportunities for additional innovations. In the future, the link (or lack thereof) between groceries and e-commerce may appear just as "obvious," and will have spurred the acquisition of additional knowledge and additional innovations. Whether or not a disequilibrating action ultimately enhances the focal firm's performance, the immediate result of such action will be market confusion: rivals may choose to disregard the action because they fail to see its relevance, certain customers may be positively surprised by the action while others react negatively because it diverges from their expectations, and the company's own employees may even question whether or not the action is appropriate. Eventually, market participants will settle on a more coherent judgment of the action's appropriateness, but the immediate reactions will vary widely between judges.

Together, equilibrating and disequilibrating actions are co-dependent elements of a single market process. The circular flow of the market relies upon individual entrepreneurs seizing previously unexploited opportunities by extending existing strategies to new domains. Just as importantly, the circular flow is disrupted by new combinations of preexisting but seemingly unrelated resources, dethroning market incumbents and disrupting the commonly held beliefs of market participants.

Identifying equilibrating and disequilibrating actions

In order to demonstrate how to empirically identify and distinguish between equilibrating and disequilibrating actions, we build upon existing research methods used to assess creativity. Research on creativity commonly utilizes two criteria to assess the creativity of a particular action: novelty and appropriateness. An action is deemed creative to the extent that "appropriate observers" independently reach a momentary consensus judgment that the action is appropriate (Amabile, 1996). These criteria are useful indicators by which to identify and distinguish equilibrating and disequilibrating entrepreneurial actions and are illustrated in table 7.1.

Table 7.1   Criteria to identify and distinguish equilibrating and disequilibrating entrepreneurial actions

	Equilibrating action	Disequilibrating action
Combination of matrices	New combinations of seemingly *related* resources, customers, and markets	New combinations of seemingly *unrelated* resources, customers, and markets
Novelty and impact on opportunity set	Novel, relative to traditional resource combinations, customers and markets. Decrease confusion about the potential set of available opportunities	Novel, unseen or untried in past relative to traditional resource combinations, customers, and markets. Increase confusion about the potential set of available opportunities
Appropriateness	Greater consensus judgment of appropriateness at the time of the action	No consensus judgment exists; more likely to be viewed as inappropriate by some customers and markets
Consequences	Solves knowledge problems	Adds to the knowledge problem
Examples	Amtrak's Acela	Southwest Airlines, Gobi's free PCs

Whereas creativity researchers evaluate the novelty and appropriateness of action jointly in order to assess creativity, we believe that evaluating novelty and appropriateness independently can help us distinguish equilibrating from disequilibrating actions, and it also has implications for the market process. As we have noted, both types of actions will be judged innovative, to varying degrees. They may be original along one or more of four dimensions: they may entail new resources, new customers, new markets, and/or new combinations of existing resources, customers, and markets.

However, equilibrating actions will be also novel in the way they provide *new information* that reduces confusion about what is potentially an opportunity. They will do this by combining *existing information* on resource combinations, customers, and markets in new ways. As such, equilibrating action will reduce marketplace confusion about the set of potential opportunities available from existing resources, customers, and markets. The novelty of disequilibrating actions, in contrast, will increase confusion about what is potentially an opportunity. They will do so by combining previously unheard sets of resources, customers, and markets in new and unconventional ways. The effect will be to increase the level of confusion and information about what is the ideal combination of resources, customers, and markets.

Although both types of action will vary in terms of the types of novelty and their impact on refining or expanding the set of potentially profitable opportunities, they will also vary to the extent they are deemed appropriate. Appropriateness concerns a viewpoint by market participants as to a new action's value in solving knowledge problems. Specifically, we contend that market participants will independently and almost immediately reach a momentary consensus judgment of an equilibrating action's appropriateness[5]. We see this even in the case when there are significant asymmetries in viewpoint among market participants. In such a case, equilibrating actions will provide the necessary information to help market participants form a momentary consensus judgment (mental maps will converge). Equilibrating actions thus build upon and diffuse existing knowledge and expectations, thereby moving the market toward equilibrium. As such, by resolving confusion about what is an opportunity, equilibrating actions will be perceived as appropriate extensions of past actions to new domains (i.e., customers, market locations, or resources). Via their role in diffusing information, equilibrating actions work to resolve the knowledge problem in the market. This is often seen when managers creatively extend successful strategies to new geographic or demographic markets, when rivals find innovative ways to imitate the successful strategies of market leaders, and when managers or entrepreneurs introduce incrementally improved versions of their previous products and strategies.

Disequilibrating actions, in contrast, are distinguished by the manner in which they create dissonance by challenging the established mental models of market actors. This dissonance will be reflected by observing wide variation in the initial reaction of customers, competitors, and other judges to the action's ability to solve knowledge problems. Because they are incompatible with established mental models, disequilibrating actions are likely to be viewed as being inappropriate by some, and a momentary consensus judgment of the action's appropriateness will not be reached in the short term. Eventually, as the action's impact on the market becomes apparent and forces the revision of established mental models, the ultimate appropriateness of a disequilibrating action will become evident, but appropriateness will be difficult to assess initially.

By upsetting the status quo by increasing the level of confusion of what is an opportunity and increasing the different viewpoints of whether the action is appropriate, disequilibrating actions actually add to the market's knowledge problem. Actions that are more likely to be disequilibrating in nature include the introduction of radically innovative products based on new combinations of resources, the creation of new markets, and first movers into new segments of existing markets.

The differences between equilibrating and disequilibrating actions can be further illustrated by use of examples. For instance, consider the difference between Amtrak's recent introduction of the Acela train, versus Southwest Airline's short-haul, no-frills strategy. Introduction of the Acela train, which is a high-speed service operating along the Eastern seaboard of the United States and employs technologies that have been in use in Europe and Japan for over a decade, represents an equilibrating action because it "logically" (i.e., in congruence with the industry recipe) extends existing resources (in this case, rail technologies) into a new market domain (the northeastern US). Although Amtrak has received criticism for the inefficient and costly manner in which it has implemented the Acela service, the combination of European and Japanese rail technologies with the northeastern US transport market has generally been perceived as appropriate and reduced confusion about how rail travel should proceed in the future. In contrast, Southwest Airline's initial introduction of a no-frills, short-haul system was initially incompatible with the prevailing industry recipe, which entailed a hub-and-spoke system and full service. The appropriateness of Southwest's strategy did not become apparent to all market actors until Southwest effectively demonstrated that a distinct business model could succeed in the airline industry. Similarly, Gobi and Free-PC entered the personal computer market by challenging current industry leaders Compaq and Dell by creatively acting to *give away* PCs to customers who committed to a three-year Internet service contract or to give up 20 percent of their computer screen for ad space. To traditional PC manufacturers, Compaq and Dell, these actions, which reflect an attempt to promote free PCs to sell online services (a combination of two previously unconnected resource/markets), were initially judged as foolhardy. Subsequently, the incumbents responded aggressively with their own Internet innovations, further disrupting competition and viewpoints about what is the product, who are the customers, and where is the market.

Again, while both equilibrating and disequilibrating actions are creative entrepreneurial actions, disequilibrating actions are often more radically novel, and are certain to elicit a more varied initial judgment of appropriateness from market actors than are equilibrating actions, since they entail the combination of seemingly unrelated or even incompatible resources, customers, and markets. In the next section, we present a formal model predicting variation in entrepreneurial action.

Predicting Variation in Entrepreneurial Action

As noted, we used the creativity literature to explain the search and decision process leading to entrepreneurial action. The focus is on the individual search and decision process that identifies opportunity and precedes action. Four important characteristics will explain this process: the stimulus for action, the level and breadth of the entrepreneur's domain knowledge, the creativity/search skills of the entrepreneur, and the process of bisociation.

Stimulus

Amabile (1996) contends that task motivation is one of the most important predictors of creative actions. More specifically, empirical research supports the idea that intrinsically motivated decision processes and analysis will lead to different decision outcomes, than will extrinsically motivated analysis.[6] The premise is that unconstrained analysis associated with intrinsic motivation is most conducive to creativity (Wallach and Kogan,

1965). The intrinsic motivation hypothesis is based on social-psychology theories of motivation that suggest that extrinsic motivation constrains search and analysis behavior. Lepper and Greene (1978) suggest that entrepreneurs will pay attention to those aspects of the task that are necessary to attain the extrinsic goals. Creativity would suffer under these conditions because of constrained search and analysis activity. Amabile (1996) defines intrinsic motivation as an impulse that arises from the entrepreneur's positive reaction to qualities of the task itself, including self-interest, involvement, curiosity, satisfaction, and a positive challenge. In contrast, extrinsically motivated behavior is motivation that arises from sources peripheral to the task itself. Extrinsic motivation could result from sources related to evaluation, reward, power, and external directives. We contend that whether an entrepreneur is extrinsically or intrinsically motivated will impact the kind of information that is brought to the decision process.

Domain knowledge

Domain knowledge[7] comprises the decision maker's complete set of information and understanding of the world against which alternative new entrepreneurial actions would be judged (Amabile, 1996). More specifically, domain knowledge consists of the cognitive pathways for solving a given problem (Simon, 1945). Domain knowledge includes the factual knowledge and technical understanding of the various domains in question as well as current causal maps about means–end relationships. We conceive of domain knowledge as varying in terms of the extensiveness within a particular domain and in terms of the scope of knowledge across domains. Thus, a decision maker/ entrepreneur can have extensive knowledge across a variety of domains or have extensive knowledge only within one domain. Alternatively, the decision maker may have limited knowledge within a domain and also a very narrow scope of knowledge. It is our contention that domain knowledge will affect the amount and structure of knowledge brought to the search and decision process.

Creativity skills

Amabile (1996) suggests that the entrepreneur's creativity skills will determine the extent to which entrepreneurial actions depart from previous behaviors. Creativity skills include the ability of the entrepreneur to break away from previous entrepreneurial actions and routines, to manage and manipulate diverse matrices of information, to suspend judgment as complexity increases, to consider extensive and broad categories of domain information, to remember accurately, and to notice and recognize patterns or opportunities from alternative matrices of information (Amabile, 1996). She notes that, assuming an adequate level of motivation and domain skills, it will be the level of creativity skills that determines the extent to which entrepreneurial actions depart from prior actions.

Bisociation

For Schumpeter, innovation entailed the novel combination of existing resources. Likewise, research conducted by psychologists and sociologists emphasizes that creative

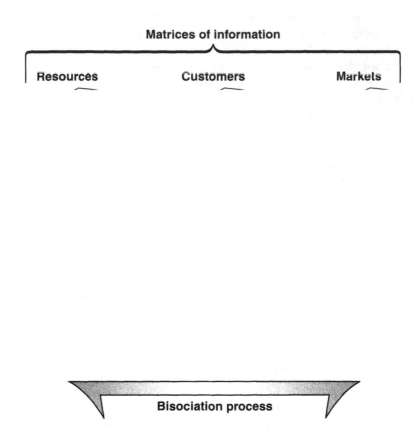

Figure 7.2   The bisociation process: relating matrices to one another to identify opportunities

action results when an individual combines two or more previously unrelated matrices of information. Arthur Koestler (1964) referred to this process as "bisociation," which he defined as "the sudden interlocking of two previously unrelated skills, or matrices of thought" (Koestler, 1964: 121). For both Schumpeter and Koestler, creative acts do not arise ex nihilo, but rather creative actions occur when an entrepreneur actively integrates preexisting skills or resources to identify an opportunity and to seize the opportunity with action.

Consider three historical examples of creative genius provided by Koestler (1964): Gutenberg, Kepler, and Darwin. Gutenberg invented the movable-type printing press by combining the techniques of the wine press and the seal. Kepler demonstrated that physics and astronomy could be combined to explain the orbit of the planets. Darwin, in turn, combined the existing idea of biological evolution with an organism's struggle for survival. Their ideas were revolutionary, yet at the same time, their innovations entailed nothing more (and nothing less) than the bisociation of existing matrices of thought. For this reason, innovations such as these are often written off as resulting from "ripe" social conditions, and revisionists take pleasure in noting that others arrived at the same innovations independently. Nonetheless, the ripeness and self-evident nature of such innovations is only intuitive once the innovations have been discovered. Even then, incompatibility with preexisting "knowledge" may inhibit the identification of appropriate innovations. For instance, Darwin presented his theory of natural selection with Alfred Wallace to the Linnean Society in 1848, prior to publishing *The Origin of Species*. At the end of that year, the President of the Society announced in his annual report that "The year which has passed . . . has not, indeed, been marked by any of those striking discoveries which at once revolutionize, so to speak, the department of science on which they bear" (cited in Koestler, 1964: 142).

In the commercial arena, bisociation is the process of combining matrices of information that allows the entrepreneur to identify an opportunity and seize it through action. This process is outlined in figure 7.2. Matrices may be combined in a flash of insight which interrupts a period of mental incubation; bisociation may also occur following a conscious and sequential process of logical reasoning and experimentation (Wallas, 1926; Storr, 1972). In either case, the bisociative thought process that leads to entrepreneurial action is dependent upon the existence of an appropriate stimulus, domain knowledge, and creativity skills (Amabile, 1996).

Propositions

Figure 7.3 portrays how the stimulus for action, and the domain and creativity skills of the entrepreneur, affect the bisociation process (the kinds of information matrices that are combined and examined), and in turn, how the bisociation process will impact the type of entrepreneurial action undertaken. We now explain the different connections of the model with a set of formal propositions.

The individual entrepreneur is the key actor in this process, given that creative actions stem from the purposive action of individuals. Mises (1949) explained that entrepreneurial action is preceded by the conscious identification of an opportunity and the purposeful decision to exploit the opportunity. Moreover, he identified the entrepreneur's uneasiness with the current state of the world and self-driven desire to seek improvement as a crucial stimulus behind entrepreneurial action. Along the same lines, psychologists studying creativity have demonstrated that intrinsic motivation facilitates creative thinking, while extrinsic motivation may have a detrimental impact on creativity. We therefore propose that the bisociative thought process of an individual entrepreneur will depend upon the existence of an appropriate stimulus (i.e., intrinsic vs. extrinsic motivation):

> *P1: Intrinsically motivated entrepreneurs will be more likely to develop, combine and examine more advanced and complex combinations of previously unrelated matrices of information than will extrinsically motivated entrepreneurs.*

The nature of the entrepreneur's knowledge structure is also likely to influence bisociation. Entrepreneurs possess knowledge pertaining to various domains, and their knowledge will vary in magnitude between domains. The pool of domain-specific knowledge that can be integrated via bisociation is dependent upon both the breadth and depth of the entrepreneur's knowledge structure. In this case, breadth refers to the

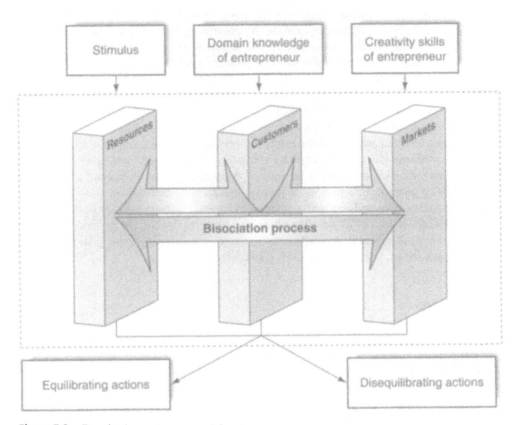

Figure 7.3 Developing entrepreneurial actions

number and diversity of distinct domains (i.e., matrices) in which the entrepreneur possesses expertise, while the depth of knowledge refers to the entrepreneur's magnitude of expertise in any given domain. Breadth and depth are conceptually independent.

Just as creative artists typically learn prevailing techniques and styles prior to creating their own innovative style, the depth of an entrepreneur's domain-specific knowledge will impact the entrepreneur's ability to engage in creative bisociation. Extensive knowledge of a given domain is often essential in order to identify which needs are being met and which remain unfulfilled, as well as to ascertain how to meet any unfulfilled needs that are identified. We contend that the greater an entrepreneur's knowledge in any given domain, the more likely the entrepreneur will be able to generate a unique combination that includes the given domain. More formally,

P2: Entrepreneurs possessing deep knowledge in any given domain will develop, combine and examine more advanced and complex combinations of related matrices of information than will entrepreneurs whose domain knowledge is less extensive.

The breadth of domain knowledge possessed by the entrepreneur will determine the number of matrices that can potentially be combined, as well as the likelihood of generating a novel combination. We contend that entrepreneurs who have experience in a wide range of industry and market contexts are more likely to engage in creative bisociation, particularly when those contexts are perceived by others to be unrelated.

P3: Entrepreneurs possessing domain knowledge of broad scope will develop, combine and examine more advanced and complex combinations of previously unrelated matrices of information than will entrepreneurs whose domain knowledge is relatively narrow in scope.

In addition to requiring a stimulus (i.e., the proper motivation) and domain knowledge, bisociation requires creativity skills in order to result in a truly novel combination. Just as Koestler (1964) explained that the creative artist or scientist is able to perceive opportunities for combination that are meaningless to others, Kirzner (1973) and Schumpeter (1942) explained that unique entrepreneurial combinations follow from the alertness or awareness of the entrepreneur, and that this alertness is an indispensable input to the discovery process. Alertness (or, more generally, creativity skills) enables the perception of opportunities that others have overlooked.

P4: Entrepreneurs possessing creativity skills will develop, combine and examine more advanced and complex combinations of previously unrelated matrices of information than will entrepreneurs whose creativity skills are relatively lower.

To describe the bisociative thought processes that enable entrepreneurial action, we have drawn analogies to creative acts in the arts and sciences. The bisociation of milk and sports drinks may appear mundane relative to Kepler's bisociation of physics and astronomy, but the implications of these associations are similar: bisociation enables creative action, and the nature of the matrices or resources that are combined as well as the manner in which they are combined determine the novelty and appropriateness of the resulting action. In this section, we elaborate on the bisociative thought process that enables creative entrepreneurial action and present propositions linking bisociation to equilibrating and disequilibrating entrepreneurial action.

We have argued that entrepreneurial action follows directly from the bisociative thought process of the entrepreneur, which in turn is contingent upon the existence of an appropriate stimulus, domain knowledge, and creativity skills. Variation in entrepreneurial action can therefore be predicted from analysis of difference in the bisociative thought process of entrepreneurs. Previously, we explained that entrepreneurial actions vary to the degree that they are equilibrating and/or disequilibrating in nature, and that these types of action can be identified and distinguished by subjectively assessing their novelty and appropriateness (see table 7.1).

We contend that the novelty of an entrepreneurial action follows from the nature of the information that is analyzed and integrated in the bisociative thought process of the entrepreneur. As outlined in the above propositions, when the proper stimulus, domain knowledge, and creativity skills are present, the bisociation of complex and varied information matrices is likely to occur. The greater the diversity of information that enters into the bisociative process, the more likely the resultant entrepreneurial action's novelty will increase confusion about the potential set of available opportunities primarily because the action will be presenting new information.

With regard to the action's appropriateness, again the nature, complexity, and newness of the information on resource combinations, customers, and markets that is brought to the bisociation process will affect resultant action and impact market participants' evaluation of this action. In particular, the greater the complexity of unrelated information that is combined in the bisociation process, the greater the likelihood that the resultant action will be judged inappropriate by some market participants. Referring to his theory of untidy elliptical orbits that displaced the commonly held belief in uniform, circular cycles and epicycles, Kepler declared that "I have cleared the Augean stables of astronomy of cycles and spirals, and left behind me only a single cartful of dung" (cited in Koestler, 1964: 129). Eventually, Kepler's ideas were diffused and expanded, and are now perceived to eloquently and accurately depict planetary motion. Similarly, disequilibrating entrepreneurial actions not only introduce new knowledge into the market, but also displace commonly held beliefs and may be dissonant with prevailing mental models. Eventually, such disequilibrating actions may be deemed appropriate, and are thereafter subjected to imitation, replication, extension, and possibly substitution. But stakeholders' initial reaction to such actions will be quite different from their reaction to equilibrating actions.

We contend that the greater the extent to which an entrepreneur's bisociative thought process entails unprecedented combinations of previously unrelated resources, customers, and markets that are incompatible with prevailing mental models of customers, suppliers, employees, and competitors, the more likely these stakeholders are to initially disagree as to the appropriateness of the entrepreneurial action.

> *P5: The more advanced and complex combinations of previously unrelated matrices of information that are incorporated into the bisociative thought process, the more likely subsequent entrepreneurial actions will be judged disequilibrating.*

Alternatively:

> *P6: The greater the extent to which preexisting and related information matrices are incorporated into the bisociative thought process, the more likely subsequent entrepreneurial action will be judged equilibrating.*

Discussion and Conclusion

We have written this chapter to explain the concept of entrepreneurial action and to present a model depicting its variation. First, we discussed the knowledge environment surrounding the market process and the important role of discovery and entrepreneurial action in this process. Second, we applied concepts from research on creativity to produce a model explaining entrepreneurial action. Among entrepreneurial actions, there will be variation in the extent to which these actions resolve the knowledge problem in the market or create new knowledge problems. Equilibrating actions resolve the knowledge problem by refining and diffusing existing knowledge via the logical combination of related resources, customers and markets. In the case of equilibrating actions, resolution of the knowledge problem will be signaled by a momentary consensus judgment among market participants as to the action's appropriateness and such action will reduce confusion about the potential set of available opportunities. Disequilibrating actions, in contrast, create new problems by demonstrating incongruence with prevailing mental models, challenging means–end relations that were previously taken for granted; these actions are identified by the lack of consensus among market participants as to the actions' perceived appropriateness and they increase the level of confusion about the set of available market opportunities. Variation in entrepreneurial action can be explained by investigating the bisociation process, which is influenced by the nature of the stimulus, domain knowledge, and creativity skills possessed by the entrepreneur.

By linking two or more previously unrelated matrices in a fashion that often appears obvious with the benefit of hindsight, bisociation may result in the creation of new entrepreneurial action, and may also expose incorrect information by indicating seemingly endless avenues for additional possibilities for action. We have introduced equilibrating and disequilibrating actions as two distinct types of actions. Although it entails adding another layer of complexity, it may be more appropriate to view them as two dimensions along which entrepreneurial actions may vary. Entrepreneurial actions often entail complex combinations of resources, customers, and markets, and it is conceivable that certain actions will both solve knowledge problems and create new problems. Such actions confirm portions of the mental models of market actors while disconfirming other portions, and hence contain both equilibrating and disequilibrating elements. We have chosen to introduce these types of action as mutually exclusive for ease of exposition, while recognizing the possibility that certain actions may contain elements of both. Indeed, it may be that the same action, while reducing knowledge problems for some, increases it for others with no net gain in the market process.

Our analysis has important implications for the long-standing emphasis within strategic management on isolating mechanisms and other defensive actions that are employed to sustain competitive advantages. As D'Aveni (1994), Grimm and Smith (1997), and others have indicated, defensive strategies that are based in either product markets or resource markets are futile in dynamic competitive environments, and managers should instead emphasize the creation of new advantages. Our analysis indicates one way managers can obtain a longer-lasting competitive advantage without resorting to defensive tactics. Disequilibrating actions may yield lasting competitive advantage when competitors notice the actions but fail to perceive their ultimate appropriateness and become confused by the nature of the opportunity. These actions go a step beyond those that exploit competitors' blind spots (Grimm and Smith, 1997; Zahra and Chaples, 1993; Zajac and Bazerman, 1991). Whereas actions targeted at blind spots can be compared to an unexpected attack, rivals of firms that undertake disequilibrating actions may not even notice that the attack occurred. In this era of hypercompetition, the best defensive strategy may actually be a good offensive strategy composed of actions that create knowledge problems among important stakeholders and constituencies.

Although we have borrowed from creativity research to produce a model of entrepreneurial action, we can also demonstrate how our analysis may be applied to improve future research on creativity. Researchers have relied upon consensus judgments of novelty and appropriateness to assess creative actions. While the subjective nature of this assessment is essential, the reliance upon consensus may be detrimental, and may be masking important phenomena. We have explained why certain creative actions, which we refer to as equilibrating actions, will be amenable to a consensus judgment of appropriateness, while disequilibrating actions will invoke disparate reactions from market judges. We contend that novelty and appropriateness are distinct dimensions of creativity, actions will vary along these dimensions, and variation along these dimensions will have important implications on the impact of creative action.

Although we have argued that the bisociative search and decision process occurs at the individual level and therefore that entrepreneurial action stems from the purposive thought processes of individuals, organizational variables are certain to impact this process. For example, attributes that provide direct incentives for performance will increase extrinsic motivation for action, while other attributes, such as opportunities for self-actualization, may foster intrinsic motivation. Primary among these extrinsic attributes is the nature of the administrative controls and compensation schemes utilized to motivate employees (Eisenhardt, 1989). Another factor that is likely to enable intrinsic motivation is organizational slack (Cyert and March, 1963). Firms that possess greater slack can be more loosely coupled with their immediate environment (Thompson, 1967), and their employees should have greater resources to pursue activities that do not directly and unambiguously impact the bottom line. Additionally, firms that possess a corporate culture that encourages exploration and discovery are more likely to engage in intrinsically motivated action than will firms in which efficiency and compliance with norms are emphasized.

Another set of firm-level attributes will affect the nature of the information matrices that individuals may integrate to yield creative combinations. Factors that influence a firm's access to information regarding diverse resources, customers, and markets, such as the level of diversification and the social networks and the experience of top managers, will increase the likelihood of disequilibrating action, while factors associated with specialization within a single domain will foster equilibrating action. Finally, organizational attributes may impact the nature of the creativity skills possessed by the individuals that propagate entrepreneurial action. One manner in which this will likely occur is through the adoption of particular decision-making processes and practices. For example, fast decision-making processes may hasten the bisociation process, impeding the novelty of action and confining such actions to an equilibrating nature. In contrast, comprehensive decision making may, in fact, facilitate a complete search and evaluation process leading to more novel actions of a disequilibrating nature. Organizational culture may also serve to facilitate or impede the creativity process (Schein, 1985).

In this chapter we have attempted to provide a more complete understanding of the role of entrepreneurial actions. As we argue, entrepreneurial actions play a fundamental role in leading markets both toward and away from equilibrium. In doing so, entrepreneurial action can both correct and contribute to the knowledge problems that serve as the basis of economic opportunity. A better understanding of the drivers of this market process will improve our theories of how competitive advantage is created and our knowledge of how markets and industries evolve.

In presenting our theory we have had to make a number of simplifications, including limiting the chapter to the individual unit of analysis, taking a subjectivist "bounded rationality" perspective, and maintaining a broad technology-inclusive definition of entrepreneurial action. Even with these boundary assumptions we have perhaps raised more questions about the role of entrepreneurial action than we have answered. Nonetheless, we are hopeful that the ideas presented here will inspire more work on the role of entrepreneurial action.

Notes

The authors thank Mike Hitt, Duane Ireland, Harry Sapienza, Scott Shane, Daniel Simon, and Greg Young for their very useful comments on earlier drafts of this paper.

1   The problem is that participants may be both unaware of the full set of options available and/or mistaken in their own viewpoints.

2   We must distinguish our use of the term entrepreneur from the traditional viewpoint of the person who creates a business. Consistent with Schumpeter (1942), Hayek (1949), and Kirzner (1973), we will use the term entrepreneur to refer to any person who goes through the entrepreneurial discovery process and subsequently takes new action to seize the opportunity. As such, the entrepreneur may be an owner, a manager, or even a team of managers acting as one. Kirzner explains that entrepreneurship is expressed whenever a market participant recognizes that doing something even a little different from what is currently being done may more accurately anticipate the actual opportunities available. Mises (1949) also captures this entrepreneur: "those who have more initiative, more venturesomeness, and a quicker eye than the crowd, the pushing and promoting pioneers of economic improvement" (1949: 255). Entrepreneurship researchers are increasingly utilizing a similar conceptualization of the entrepreneur (Shane and Venkataraman, 2000).

3   Although we distinguish discovery of an opportunity from action, in our viewpoint both discovery and action are two necessary parts of the market process. As such, we only consider opportunities that are acted upon. Moreover we assume that the individual responsible for discovery is also the actor.

4   Note that it is not necessary for an action to be successful in terms of profits for it to be important for the market process. Indeed, all actions carry information that can clarify the direction of the market towards and away from equilibrium.

5   We use the term momentary consensus to reflect the fact that future action (which could be virtually instantaneous) may change the level of consensus, due to changing perceptions of the current action's appropriateness.

6   Although the entrepreneurship literature generally assumes that entrepreneurs are intrinsically motivated (see Timmons, 1985), our broader definition of the entrepreneur as "any person who goes through the entrepreneurial discovery process and subsequently takes new action" makes the focus on intrinsic motivation especially relevant. In other words, managers of logistics, marketing, manufacturing, and service departments may all engage in attempts to improve their respective positions by undertaking new entrepreneurial actions.

7   Recall that entrepreneurial actions can represent new combinations of existing knowledge and resources found in a single domain, such as in the case of equilibrating actions, or they may represent new combinations of new resources found in new and multiple domains, such as in the case of disequilibrating actions.

References

Amabile, T. M. 1996. *Creativity in context* (update to *The social psychology of creativity*). Boulder: Westview Press.

Christensen, C. M. 1997. *The innovator's dilemma*. Boston: Harvard Business School Press.

Cyert, R. and March, J. 1963. *A behavioral theory of the firm*. Englewood Cliffs, NJ: Prentice Hall.

D'Aveni, R. 1994. *Hypercompetition*. New York: Free Press.

Eisenhardt, K. 1989. Agency theory: an assessment and review. *Academy of Management Review*, 14: 57–75.

Finkelstein, S. and Hambrick, D. 1996. *Strategic leadership*. Cincinnati: South Western College Publishing.

Grimm, C. and Smith, K. G. 1997. *Strategy as action*. Cincinnati: South Western College Publishing.

Hayek, F. A. 1945. The use of knowledge in society. *American Economic Review*, 35: 529–30.

Hayek, F. A. 1949. *Individualism and economic order*. London: Routledge and Kegan Paul.

Henderson, R. and Clark, K. 1990. Architectural innovation: the reconfiguration of existing product technologies and the failure of established firms. *Administrative Science Quarterly*, 35: 9–30.

Kirzner, I. M. 1973. *Competition and entrepreneurship*. Chicago: University of Chicago Press.

Koestler, A. 1964. *The act of creation*. New York: Dell.

Lepper, M. and Greene, D. 1978. Overjustification research and beyond: Toward a means-end analysis of intrinsic and extrinsic motivation. In M. Lepper and D. Greene (eds), *The hidden costs of reward*. Hillsdale, NJ: Lawrence Erlbaum, 109–48.

Mises, L. von. 1949. *Human action*. New Haven: Yale University Press.

Schein, E. 1985. *Organizational culture and leadership*, San Francisco: Jossey-Bass.

Schumpeter, J. A. 1928. The instability of capitalism. *Economic Journal*, Sept.: 361–86, reprinted in J. A. Schumpeter. 1989. *Essays*. New Brunswick, NJ: Transaction Publishers.

Schumpeter, J. A. 1934. *The theory of economic development*. Cambridge, MA: Harvard University Press.

Schumpeter, J. A. 1942. *Capitalism, socialism, and democracy*. New York: Harper & Row.

Shane, S. and Venkataraman, S. 2000. The promise of entrepreneurship as a field of research. *Academy of Management Review*, 25: 217–26.

Simon, H. A. 1945. *Administrative behavior: A study of decision-making processes in administrative organizations*. Englewood Cliffs, NJ: Prentice-Hall.

Storr, A. 1972. *The dynamics of creation*. New York: Atheneum.

Thompson, J. D. 1967. *Organizations in action*. New York: McGraw-Hill.

Timmons, J. A. 1985. *New venture creation*, 2nd edn. Homewood, IL: Richard D. Irwin.

Tushman, M. and Anderson, P. 1986. Technological discontinuities and organizational environments. *Administrative Science Quarterly*, 31: 439–66.

Wallach, M. A. and Kogan, N. 1965. *Modes of thinking in young children*. New York: Holt, Rinehart & Winston.

Wallas, G. 1926. *The art of thought*. New York: Harcourt, Brace and Company.

Walsh, J. P. 1995. Managerial and organizational cognition: Notes from a trip down memory lane. *Organization Science*, 6: 280–321.

Weick, K. 1995. *Sensemaking in organizations*. Thousand Oaks, CA: Sage Publications.

Zahra, S. A. and Chaples, S. S. 1993. Blind spots in competitive analysis. *Academy of Management Executive*, 7: 7–28.

Zajac, E. J. and Bazerman, M. H. 1991. Blind spots in industry and competitor analysis. *Academy of Management Review*, 16: 37–56.

CHAPTER EIGHT

Market Uncertainty and Learning Distance in Corporate Entrepreneurship Entry Mode Choice

Robert E. Hoskisson, Lowell W. Busenitz

Company experiences and research results suggest that small businesses and independent entrepreneurial ventures may have superior product invention skills while larger corporations may have superior innovation management skills (i.e., the skills required to maximize the marketplace return of product innovations). Although 80 percent of the world's R&D activity in developed nations is concentrated in firms with 10,000 or more employees, these large firms account for under half of the world's technological activity, as measured by US patenting (Stringer, 2000; Yin and Zuscovitch, 1998). These data suggest that while large firms are important for technological advances, small businesses, entrepreneurial ventures, and individual entrepreneurs account for a significant share of today's entrepreneurial activity and the technological progress resulting from it (Acs, 1992; Aronson, 1991).

Of course, entrepreneurial market entry is not the exclusive domain of the founding entrepreneurs and the firms they create. In response to performance and competitive problems, many corporations have restructured in an attempt to become more entrepreneurial (Hitt et al., 1999; Markides, 1998; Stringer, 2000). Increasingly, large firms are seeking the benefits of entrepreneurial initiatives. We refer to entrepreneurial initiatives in large firms as corporate entrepreneurship, explicitly defined here as a "process whereby an individual or a group of individuals, in association with an existing organization, create a new organization or instigate renewal or innovation within that organization" (Sharma and Chrisman, 1999). Furthermore, we define innovation as bringing something into new use, whereas an invention brings something new into being (Rogers, 1962; Sharma and Chrisman, 1999). The criteria for innovations regards commercialization activities whereas inventions are usually technical in nature

(Burgelman and Sayles, 1986). Many established firms have redeployed new, innovative combinations of resources in order to maintain market leadership and promote new revenue streams (Markides, 1998; Stopford and Baden-Fuller, 1994; Zahra, 1991). There are various ways to pursue entrepreneurial activity in an established organization. These sources of entrepreneurial entry can be viewed as internal or external to the established firm. Internal activity involves the establishment of extensive research and development capabilities as well as the organizational structure and social characteristics that will capitalize on the new, internally introduced inventions (Kogut and Zander, 1996; Cheng and Van de Ven, 1996). Externally, firms can pursue entrepreneurial activities through cooperative strategy (e.g., strategic alliances) and acquisitions (Gulati, 1999; Hitt et al., 2000; Hitt, Hoskisson, and Johnson, 1996). This chapter seeks to add value to the corporate entrepreneurship literature (Zahra, Nielsen, and Bogner, 1999) by examining when internal corporate ventures and external approaches, strategic alliances and acquisitions are best suited to accomplish entrepreneurial entry and overcome inherent difficulties associated with each approach.

The Challenges of Corporate Entrepreneurship

It is increasingly apparent in today's economy that earlier success has little to do with a corporation's longevity. Furthermore, entrepreneurial startup firms often seriously challenge once-powerful large organizations. As a result, many established firms are attempting to build on their existing knowledge base to create and capture new opportunities. Corporate managers have often concluded that they must adjust and sometimes transform themselves to keep pace with environmental changes and increasing competition. However, entrepreneurial activity, defined as attempts to exploit opportunities others have not identified or exploited (see Ireland et al. (2001) for a parallel definition of entrepreneurial actions), presents a significant challenge for larger corporations because their core competencies do not always extend into the areas of new development and management and incentive systems frequently stifle entrepreneurial initiatives. This presents a significant dilemma for most organizations. On the one hand, established core competencies and inertia can be persistent forces that lead to core rigidities (Leonard-Barton, 1992) making change difficult, particularly in larger organizations (Barkema and Vermeulen, 1998). On the other hand, change is imperative for keeping pace with the competitive environment. Sometimes established core competencies can provide a foundation from which to build new advantages while other times very different skills and capabilities need to be obtained to engage in the desired entrepreneurial activity. To deal with these dilemmas, numerous organizational arrangements and new hybrids have evolved to address these needs. The most common organizational arrangements or modes of entry include internal new ventures, joint ventures, and acquisitions.

This chapter develops a framework for understanding when these various organizational entry mode choices are most likely to be appropriate (and inappropriate), given different entrepreneurial settings. In recognition of the growing importance of entrepreneurial activity within today's rapidly changing environment, we attempt to bring further understanding to the different types of entry strategies seeking to foster entrepreneurship. We contend that the entry strategies chosen in the pursuit of various

forms of corporate entrepreneurship can be better understood by examining the linkages between the requirements to pursue uncertain market opportunities with the
capabilities and learning needs necessary to achieve the opportunity visualized. Stated
differently, for various entrepreneurial strategies to be successfully implemented at the
corporate level, there needs to be a fundamental understanding of the market context
in which the potential invention or innovation resides and the learning capabilities and
needs of the focal organization when entrepreneurial entry is contemplated. We now
define the two dimensions that we consider central to entrepreneurial entry, market
uncertainty and firm capabilities and learning distance.

Market uncertainty

Uncertainty is often described as a perceptual phenomenon derived from the inability
to assign probabilities to future events, a lack of information about the cause and effect
relationship, and the inability to predict the outcome of a decision (Milliken, 1987;
Miller and Shamsie, 1999). More specifically, we define market uncertainty as the state
of not knowing or a lack of knowledge about the future direction of a given market. As
strategic managers contemplate the future, they often face many complexities, making
it very difficult to know in advance what the appropriate response should be in regard
to entering a given market (Leifer and Mills, 1996). Furthermore, markets are often
unstable as entrepreneurial startup firms enter the market and as competitors become
more aggressive. As new products or services are being developed, unanticipated anoma-
lies invariably emerge. The receptivity of a new invention or innovation once it is
released to the market is extremely difficult to predict. Often intended markets reject a
new alternative while unanticipated markets can emerge to adopt it. The market environment can be very turbulent in regard to the acceptance and implementation of
entrepreneurial endeavors.

These issues suggest that market uncertainty has a substantial impact on the development, introduction, and commercialization of entrepreneurial opportunities. More
specifically, market uncertainty is characterized as an interaction between complexity
(simple /complex) and stability (stable/unstable) (Duncan, 1972; Daft, 1995). Complexity addresses the number of market elements a venture faces, the extent of their
dissimilarity along with the frequency and unpredictability of change. With many inventions and innovations, there is great heterogeneity in the elements and components that are potentially relevant to the business venture and there may be numerous
unknown interactions between the components as well.

The degree of stability in the market also influences uncertainty. Stability addresses
the dynamic nature of the elements in the environment. If technology has remained
largely unchanged over time along with the way competitors respond to one another,
the market environment is usually characterized as fairly stable. However, when new
technology such as the World Wide Web develops, the emergence of new competitors
and aggressive actions of existing competitors tend to create unstable markets. In the
context of a complex and unstable environment, managers must reconcile differing
opinions, cope with irrational decision making, and struggle with imperfect attempts
to implement decisions regarding entrepreneurial activity. Thus, market uncertainty
increases the probability of failure.

To deal with varying amounts of uncertainty associated with entrepreneurial pursuits, real options reasoning has recently been introduced. Entrepreneurial initiatives
have been characterized as *real options*, where the value of the initiative is fundamentally influenced by the level of uncertainty involved (McGrath, 1999). In the financial
markets, the purchase of an option contract gives one the right but not the obligation
to purchase specific assets. This allows for the staging of investments in a way that
allows for the truncation of further investments under poor conditions and enhance-
ment if the prospects remain positive. Furthermore, a limited downside investment is
a way of providing access to future opportunities before the window of opportunity
closes. As with financial options, the greater the uncertainty, the more the option is
worth because the cost of acquiring the option remains constant while the maximum
potential for upside benefit increases (McGrath, 1999). Because the very nature of
entrepreneurial initiatives is characterized by large amounts of uncertainty and substantial variations in their potential returns (Shane and Venkataraman, 2000), real
options reasoning is used below to shed light on the differences between entrepreneurial entry modes.

Firm capabilities and learning distance

Organizational learning theorists are interested in how and when organizations learn
because it is assumed that better knowledge and understanding will improve actions
(Fiol and Lyles, 1985). Strategy scholars have become increasingly interested in a better understanding of the learning process and how it may be a source of competitive
advantage (Conner and Prahalad, 1996), particularly as a firm pursues entrepreneurial
activities in the context of rapidly changing environments and hyper competition
(Hagedoorn, 1995; Mezias and Glynn, 1993). The key assumption is that learning
specifically, and gaining access to resources more generally, are key sources of competitive advantage (Stuart, 2000). Faster learning that builds on firm-specific knowledge and causal beliefs can lead to a unique understanding of an entrepreneurial
situation. Stated differently, a competency-based view of the firm is at least partially
linked to a firm's learning ability that has evolved from earlier learning opportunities.

Stuart (2000) refers to a type of learning where two or more partners contribute
complementary skills and knowledge to a new application. From this perspective, learning primarily occurs for participating firms because knowledge from their core competencies is being applied and extended in new ways. Learning occurs not so much from
the participating partner(s) current capabilities within their own firm environments
but by extending their capabilities into a new context or setting. In particular, this
chapter focuses on learning related to the extension of existing capabilities. This is
important because firms that are pursuing entrepreneurial entry and such complementary or combined capabilities (Amit and Schoemaker, 1993) are needed to realize the
opportunity perceived.

To further articulate the framework in this chapter and the learning needs associated
with pursuit of innovative activities, we address the idea of learning distance. Learning
distance has reference to the proximity of a firm's knowledge base and causal beliefs
stemming from previous business activities (March and Simon, 1958). Stated differently, this issue addresses the extent to which a firm's current capabilities are adjacent

to the capabilities needed to create the desired inventions and innovations. Entrepreneurial opportunities that are in the immediate neighborhood of existing capabilities face fewer risks and are unlikely to significantly alter current performance (Gavetti and Levinthal, 2000). Close-in neighborhood innovations would usually attempt to further exploit current capabilities whereas more distant learning is likely to substantially stretch existing capabilities as a means to exploiting greater but currently undeveloped opportunities.

Partial capabilities that become complete only in combination with a partner, such as through acquisitions or joint ventures, are complementary capabilities (Dyer and Singh, 1998). Entrepreneurial entry often requires firms to seek partnership arrangements in order to complete partial capabilities needed to realize the perceived opportunity. This co-specialization brings together the skills and firm-specific resources of two or more firms (Doz and Hamel, 1998). Many markets, for example, are converging due to market opportunities on the Internet which combines telecommunication (networks), computers, and media content. To realize more complete capabilities in emerging Internet market opportunities, acquisitions and joint ventures are pursued. When a firm has capabilities that represent only part of the total capabilities needed to realize an emerging market opportunity, learning distance exists.

Strategic Approaches to Entrepreneurial Entry

Three widely used approaches for facilitating corporate diversification, expansion, and internationalization include internal corporate venturing, acquisitions, and joint ventures (e.g., Porter, 1987; Barkema and Vermeulen, 1998; Inkpen and Li, 1999).[1] In this chapter, we examine these three modes of entry as they relate to entrepreneurial entry. The literature on strategic entry does not have a well-defined and accepted theory of determinants of choice between modes of entry. The three approaches mentioned above have varying levels of ownership possibilities. Both acquisition and greenfield startups (Hennart and Park, 1993; Barkema and Vermeulen, 1998) are alternative ways of full ownership to enter new markets and especially foreign markets, while joint ventures represent partial ownership.

This research is directed at entrepreneurial entry by larger, existing firms. More specifically, in line with Madhok (1997), our work emphasizes capability development versus exploitation of capabilities. Because so little research focuses on entrepreneurial entry, this chapter develops a matrix (see table 8.1) with the intent of enhancing our understanding of corporate entry into entrepreneurial ventures. By doing so, we hope to enhance our knowledge of when different entry modes are most likely to be successful. More research is needed here because of the frequently disappointing outcomes associated with corporate entrepreneurship via new entry, corporate acquisitions, and joint ventures (Christensen, 1997; Inkpen and Li, 1999; Park and Russo, 1996; Sirower, 1997). Entrepreneurial entry is viewed from the point of view of both perceived market uncertainty (an external orientation) and firm capabilities and learning distance (an internal orientation). Table 8.1 illustrates the aspects of each mode of entry strategy. The following section will discuss learning issues, real options reasoning, and implementation issues as they relate to each entry mode. We will first address internal

Table 8.1   Matching market uncertainty and learning needs associated with different modes of corporate innovation

	Firm capabilities and learning distance	
	Low learning distance	**High learning distance**
Market uncertainty	**Quadrant 4: no entrepreneurial entry**	**Quadrant 3: acquisitions**
Low uncertainty	*Learning*: incremental learning seeking efficiency gains	*Learning*: incremental learning seeking complementary capabilities to pursue innovation
	Real options reasoning: no bets are made on future opportunities	*Real options reasoning*: the opportunity for options has passed
	Implementation: keep refining current operations	*Implementation*: must be able to overcome adverse selection and moral hazard problems
	Quadrant 1: internal venture	**Quadrant 2: joint venture**
High uncertainty	*Learning*: further development of existing knowledge in a new context in anticipation of new inventions	*Learning* significant learning seeking complementary capabilities with partner firm(s) in pursuit of new inventions
	Real options reasoning: make modest investments in evolving but unproven technologies	*Real options reasoning*: by co-investing, an option is purchased on a future entrepreneurial opportunity while risk is diversified
	Implementation: development standalone unit within the parent organization with customized structure and accountability	*Implementation*: develop a standalone unit. Must be able to overcome adverse selection and moral hazard problems

corporate venturing, which will be followed by subsections on acquisitions and joint ventures.

Invention through internal venture (quadrant 1)

Internal venturing is associated here with a set of activities used to create inventions through internal means (Burgelman, 1995). Large firms encounter substantial problems in attempting to engage in inventive-type activities. Control systems and mindsets appropriate for the activities that most large organizations typically engage in tend to be incongruent with inventive activity. Thus, when large firms choose to engage in inventive activities, it is usually best for them to develop a standalone unit with a small team of individuals with the skills appropriate and necessary for the inventive activities to be pursued. Such an arrangement allows the unit to act in an entrepreneurial manner appropriate for the pursuit of new innovations without being subject to the bureaucratic constraints common to the core businesses of the corporation.

A central issue in determining whether or not a corporation should pursue an internal venture should evolve around its internal skills and abilities. If it has a strong set of skills and capabilities that largely provide the foundation for the development of a new invention, then the pursuit of the targeted innovation should largely remain internal. In this regard, Barkema and Vermeulen (1998) and Davis, Desai, and Francis (2000) suggest that firms with strong centralized approaches to entrepreneurial activity will generally pursue a wholly owned approach (startup or acquisition) versus a joint venture. Such centralized organizations often have strong technological capabilities and centralized R&D units. Organizations that have developed strong intangible capabilities conducive for inventive activity may be able to more readily leverage these entreprencurial capabilities through wholly owned startups. The pursuit of inventive activity also has the possibility of invigorating further learning in a way that may benefit other parts of the parent organization. Finally, this wholly owned approach allows protection of their strategic assets and reduces risk of diffusion of the first-to-market ideas that emerge from these technologically capable firms.

We assume that with each situation in table 8.1, there may be market opportunity that might be achieved if the right invention can be formulated. Quadrant 1 focuses on the conditions of high market uncertainty and low learning distance. The presence of high uncertainty suggests that substantial change is occurring or is about to occur. High market uncertainty tends to obviate current products and strategic approaches to the market, but it also provides fertile ground for the emergence of new technologies and new ways of conducting business (Schumpeter, 1942). Consequently, substantial and often disruptive-type invention is usually necessary to penetrate the perceived emerging market opportunity. While entrepreneurial activity is usually necessary to take advantage of opportunities created by market uncertainty, the specific invention that will be suitable to the evolving market remains largely unknown and tends to evolve over time.

Learning   An internal venture is suggested when the invention to be pursued is largely within the knowledge base related to the focal firm's current resources and capabilities. This is therefore a situation of low learning distance. Firms that have developed strong, intangible capabilities in a specific domain are often in an excellent position to leverage these capabilities through a new, internal venture when a related opportunity is perceived to be arising (Brouthers and Brouthers, 2000).

Assuming that a potential invention is closely aligned with the firm's core competencies, this should allow the venture team to draw on their own skills and experience stemming from earlier firm-specific experiences. This would also increase the chances that the venture team could draw on some very specific skills and expertise of personnel functioning within the main firm. In short, inventions via an internal venture should generally be pursued only if the inventive activity and market opportunity are attainable using existing learning capabilities associated with the firm's current set of core competencies.

Real options reasoning   As already noted, real options reasoning is fundamentally influenced by the level of uncertainty involved. More specifically, the pursuit of real options makes the most sense in the context of much uncertainty. When internal venturing is pursued, the parent firm shoulders all of the risk associated with the pursuits of invention. It becomes imperative then that large firms find ways to create options to protect their downside risk. Making modest investments in internal startups is a way of creating some options for the future even though specific directions of the evolving technology remain largely unknown. Developing technologies that facilitate and coordinate change with suppliers of components, equipment, and material as new opportunities are considered, as well as listening to ideas from market sources (buyers), will better prepare them for future opportunities (Granstrand, Patel, and Pavitt, 1997). If information from the initial investment results in positive signals, a firm could proceed with further investments, especially if one has developing technologies that facilitate absorption. Doing so opens the door for substantial learning and staging for the evolving changes while other competitors will be under-prepared for the changes when they do indeed become clearer.

Organizational arrangements and implementation   Given the radical nature of inventions targeted towards an uncertain market, it seems best to set a small team of individuals apart in a separate unit to start an internal venture. A smaller team of people, with capabilities consistent with the parent's specific resources and capabilities associated with their firm, should be set apart from the normal corporate bureaucracies and operations to develop new market ideas. Building from the firm's resources and capabilities, entrepreneurial insights can be initially developed on a limited scale to begin to test their market potential.

As has been noted by Christensen (1997) and others, large firms typically have difficulty coping with radical or disruptive invention. To maintain industry leadership, these firms are heavily invested in sustaining their current technologies and core capabilities. Such industry leaders find it hard to embrace emerging, non-traditional technologies because the cost is too great, in terms of both capital and entrepreneurial energy. Often it is a matter of vision because the current leaders have a difficulty in "visioning" the potential of the new technology because it usually changes the base of competition and competence of the incumbent leader. Even if the strategic leadership of the incumbent firm recognizes the fundamental shift, it is often too difficult for the company to reallocate resources fast enough to capitalize on the entrepreneurial opportunity. Accordingly, the cultures of most large companies act as powerful stabilizing influences, which unfortunately lead to strategic inertia in the face of innovative opportunities (Leonard-Barton, 1992).

To deal with this dilemma, large firms have R&D budgets which seek to keep them abreast of major breakthrough ideas. However, the major problem is that most R&D budgets have little money invested in searching breakthrough ideas and are more committed to incremental innovation in their existing products and services. Many large firms have responded to pressure to innovate by decentralizing R&D budgets, such that divisions have control. However, division managers are often reluctant to suggest to the corporate headquarters significant frame-breaking inventions because it may disrupt not just their own power structure, but the power structure of the whole organization. For this reason, Eisenmann and Bower (2000) have suggested that an entrepreneurial M-form with the CEO leading entrepreneurial change from the top down is necessary. However, this is likely to be a rare event in inventions, especially where technological distance is apparent. It's more likely in firms such as media integration where the learning distance is not great among media content firms. Eisenmann and Bower (2000) suggest that Summer Red Stone's integration of Nickelodeon, MTC, and Paramount at Viacom required such a top-down strategy. Frank Biondi, Viacom's former CEO, was reluctant to pursue this opportunity because of the presence in Viacom of decentralization of operating decisions and the use of high-powered incentives to foster divisional entrepreneurial venturing. Thus, such an approach is a rare event in large decentralized corporations.

Of course, this centralized approach also flies in the face of logic suggesting that the evaluation and funding of breakthrough R&D should be separate from a large company's normal R&D decision-making processes. Also, the logic that decentralized R&D budgets will lead to breakthrough inventions seems flawed. Divisional managers are not likely to suggest such breakthrough inventions; rather, this approach is more likely to lead to incremental thinking. Such breakthrough inventions, in general, need to be fostered in organizations separate from the traditional managerial mindset and associated control system. Assigning managers with an entrepreneurial mindset and setting the internal venture at some distance from the main organization will give it some freedom to act in a way that is more consistent with an entrepreneurial venture while also maintaining connections with the corporate parent for critical resources (Burgelman, 1995).

There are a number of other strategic approaches that large firms have used to foster corporate entrepreneurship (Stringer, 2000). One approach is to publicly highlight the importance to organizational members that entrepreneurial activity is a strategic and cultural priority. The essence of this idea is to create a sense of urgency that stimulates increased entrepreneurial activity in conservative companies. However, peer rhetoric is usually not enough to consistently create new ideas and requires other approaches in support of this approach. Another approach is to hire creative people from the outside in order to invigorate old lines of business. This has worked fairly well in IBM in hiring an outside CEO to help the internal managers to challenge or break the rule of the former culture that may be hindering inventive activity. Granting inventors free time to invent by building flexibility and slack into R&D budgets and modifying the performance management system so that creative ideas can emerge is another approach which has been exemplified with invention stories at 3M Corporation. However, managers have found that reducing rigorous evaluation criteria often resulted in little commercial or market ideas that realized significant results.

Creating an internal market for ideas or knowledge markets to help identify and commercialize radical inventions has been tried by a number of companies such as Royal Dutch/Shell, Nortel, and Procter & Gamble. Nortel uses "phantom stock" to compensate those who seek to be part of a team that is seeking to realize a high-risk product in a development project. Although this approach is useful in creating good ideas, it is less useful as a vehicle for commercializing inventions. Once the idea is established and accepted, most companies pass off the responsibility for implementing the idea to an established business, with little success.

Organizationally, we argue here that an internal venture generally needs to be set aside from the rest of the corporation. Without this separation, most attempts at invention ultimately lead to incremental innovation at best. The established structures, rules, and compensation system appropriate for established firms and divisions tend to be largely incompatible with the pursuit of inventive activity (Burgelman, 1995; Williamson, 1985). Evaluating the experimentation and development of new products is simply very different from what is needed in managing the business activities of various corporate divisions. As mentioned earlier, the new internal venture with substantial autonomy provides more flexibility to foster innovation while still maintaining necessary links to the corporate parent.

Another reason inventions often fail at the large firm level is because the learning distance between the current knowledge capabilities and the targeted invention is simply too great. If large firms are trying to deal with an emerging invention which is substantially beyond their capabilities, it is very difficult and time consuming to create such inventions when it requires capabilities too far removed from the current competencies. Other outside approaches such as acquisitions or joint ventures are necessary to realize the emerging technological opportunity. Next we will discuss acquisitions as a mode of entrepreneurial entry.

Innovation through acquisitions (quadrant 3)

Acquisitions are another common entry mode, especially when a firm finds learning distance between its current capabilities and those needed to pursue the perceived entrepreneurial opportunity. However, such acquisitions are intended to pursue capabilities that are *dissimilar* from the current capabilities of the firms, and, as such, go counter to that which is usually normally pursued through an acquisition. One of the most commonly cited reasons for acquisitions is to achieve operational synergy by combining activities to gain efficiencies that could not have been gained otherwise (Chatterjee, 1986; Singh and Montgomery, 1987). The word synergy is often used synonymously with economies of scope, which describes the concept of utilizing resources (e.g., slack) from the production of one product in manufacturing another (Teece, 1980; Panzar and Willig, 1981).

The concept of economies of scope includes both tangible interrelationships such as the sharing of common machinery or marketing channels among divisions and intangible interrelationships such as the application of a skill to several of a firm's businesses (Porter, 1985). Among the most frequently mentioned are operational synergistic opportunities: utilization of the same marketing channels to sell multiple products, employing previously unused production capacity, allocating capital more efficiently (economies of scale), and sharing technology. Two firms that are both primarily engaged in the same stage of the supply chain are likely to have opportunities to take advantage of some types of operating synergies, in addition to enjoying the potential corporate-level benefits explained above.

Conventional thought holds that related acquisitions are likely to outperform other (unrelated) acquisitions (Singh and Montgomery, 1987). This usually implies that similarities are sought in regard to resources as implied by the review above regarding operational synergies. In fact, related acquisitions have been found to pursue resource similarities in R&D intensity (MacDonald, 1985) and in advertising intensity (Stewart, Harris, and Carleton, 1984). Galbraith and Kazanjian (1986) demonstrated that firms that are at the same stages of the supply chain have similar objectives and orientations. Thus, their executives would be expected to have similar dominant logics (Grant, 1988). According to Prahalad and Bettis (1986), the dominant logic of an organization consists of a knowledge structure and a set of management processes that are developed by corporate managers through their experiences in the organizations in which they work. They explain that "the characteristics of the core business, often the source of top managers in diversified firms, tend to cause managers to define problems in certain ways and develop familiarity with and facility in the use of those administrative tools that are particularly useful in accomplishing the critical tasks of the core business" (1986: 491). Thus, an emphasis on similarities can cause learning to be curtailed.

However, in our framework learning distance or technological *dissimilarities* are emphasized. Thus, this research adds value to the strategy literature by examining how firms seek complementarities in regard to technological distance (dissimilarities) to achieve new entrepreneurial opportunities. Thus, acquisitions attempt to create value through uniting the complementary innovative resources or capabilities of the acquirer and the target or acquired firm in order to create whole capabilities that did not exist previously. Companies that seek to enhance their technical capabilities with speed and efficiency often target innovative firms with expertise in targeted complementary research and development fields (Folta, 1998). Since R&D activities are difficult to transfer across firm boundaries and often highly proprietary, an acquisition may be necessary. Due to the size of the investment and the risk associated with such actions, acquiring firms pursue such strategies when they are more assured that such actions will result in success. Accordingly, we argue that they represent lower market uncertainty levels than do internal ventures or joint ventures when an innovative market opportunity is perceived. In other words, the opportunity has evolved more fully and clearly so that the capabilities necessary to commercialize the venture are coming into view.

Learning   From an innovation perspective, acquisitions are sought because a parent firm sees the need to expand or move into a given area but they do not have the capabilities and resources to be effective in the targeted domain. The low uncertainty characteristic of quadrant 3 also suggests that substantial progress has been made with the innovations, often by entrepreneurial startup firms. The emerging industry or technology has survived the critical early development stage and its acceptance by the marketplace has become relatively certain. However, when the larger incumbent firms have not participated in the innovation, they are likely to be at a competitive disadvantage with the technological emergence and are unlikely to have the learning capabilities to quickly catch up with the emerging technology.

Since it has become largely certain that the commercial potential of an invention is imminent in the marketplace, an incumbent firm essentially has two alternatives. It can rely on its own learning capabilities and start from ground zero to develop its own version of the innovation or it can purchase the needed technology via an acquisition. We argue that when the learning distance between the capabilities of the incumbent (acquiring) firm and the emerging invention or innovation is too great, then an acquisition becomes a viable alternative. Furthermore, the amount of time it would take to learn the necessary capabilities to take advantage of the emerging entrepreneurial opportunity or technology will usually be much too long.

Real options reasoning   In the context of increased clarification of technological and marketplace advances, the opportunity for modest investments as a means of betting on evolving technologies has largely passed. The purchase of options pending the evolution of the technology and marketplace changes is no longer available. Confirmation is readily apparent that the technological advances are becoming accepted by the marketplace. The decision now is whether or not to play in this new area. Without the placement of earlier options, the choice now essentially involves purchasing the technology (usually an entrepreneurial firm) at the market price.

An acquiring firm may be able to place options on the future development of subsequent technologies that are likely to emerge if it is able to absorb and integrate the target firm's learning capabilities and skills. This capability is often known as "absorption capacity" (Cohen and Levinthal, 1900). If a firm has such a capacity to learn quickly, it may be able to overcome some of the problems and risks associated with an acquisition mode of entry. However, it is difficult to develop this uncommon characteristic. When a firm has a strong learning capability, it is likely to have placed some options with earlier internal ventures rather than taking the acquisition approach. Of course, it is possible that a "learning firm" did place options on changes in an emerging industry but those bets were not rewarded. Often a firm might miss the right opportunity because it was betting on a technology closely associated with its current capabilities. When learning distance is an issue and past bets did not work out, an acquisition to catch up with the accepted technologies and practices may be required. Uncertainty may be reduced also because the technological standard may have emerged and thus the acquisition is required because the technological direction has become clear.

Organizational arrangements and implementation   In regard to entrepreneurial entry through an acquisition mode, there are a number of implementation issues that deserve consideration. Our consideration of the pertinent issues builds on logic from transaction cost theory (Williamson, 1985) and the resource-based view of the firm and knowledge transfer (Tsang, 2000). We will first address the logic associated with transaction cost theory followed by that associated with the resource- and knowledge-based views of the firm.

When there are issues of moral hazard, adverse selection, and asset specificity, transaction cost theory suggests that these issues should be internalized through a hierarchical arrangement. When there is no acquisition involved, these issues are solved using an internal venturing approach because all the issues originate from the same organization and there are no transactions involved because they are created internal to the organization. However, when an acquisition involving high technology capability is sought, possible transaction costs become an issue.

More specifically, adverse selection and moral hazard are an issue because of the greater learning distance inherent in this quadrant. In the negotiation process for the target, the acquiring firm may not know whether the target firm has accurately represented its complementing capability due to the acquiring firm's unfamiliarity with the technology and the learning distance involved. Thus, adverse selection becomes a potential problem if members of the target firm misrepresent their background or capabilities in an attempt to gain more favorable terms in an exchange. Moral hazard can become an issue if members of the target firm fail to carry through its innovations and further develop their capabilities in the post-acquisition era. Some members of the target firm may even leave to start another business after the acquisition has occurred. Sirower (1997) suggests that this is a significant "trap" that many large firms fall into because the actual innovation sought does not materialize. Again, this is especially pertinent when there is great learning distance between the capability sought in the acquisition and the current capabilities of the acquiring firm.

The specialized nature of the assets sought in the acquisition may also be problematic. If the assets are embedded in the target firm's organizational structure and are socially complex, it may be difficult for the acquiring firm to understand how the capability functions. The less uncertainty associated with the capability (that is, the more codified the knowledge), the more likely it is that an acquisition will be successful. This suggests that the target firm sought should be in the growth stage because lower market uncertainty exists at this stage rather than in the earlier emerging stage of technology to provide an acquiring firm with more of an opportunity of successful entry. Also, if the capability sought in the acquisition is dependent on a few key innovators, this puts the appropriability of the assets at risk by the acquiring firm. If these key individuals leave the firm subsequent to the acquisition, the capabilities sought may not be realized. Accordingly, making sure that the acquiring firm understands the nature of the assets being acquired is important. However, when the assets are distant from the capabilities of the acquiring firm, then this tends to create more risk for the acquiring firm.

Although the acquisition approach has the advantage of speed of entry and control (similar to internal venture), it creates risks in an R&D intensive environment because it may be over-committing to a technology that is unrelated to its current capabilities and may find it hard to understand. Accordingly, an acquisition fits better when market uncertainty is reduced relative to other types of entrepreneurial situations. Thus, as we argue next, the joint venture fits well where there is both learning distance and high uncertainty.

Invention through joint ventures (quadrant 2)

The popularity of joint ventures and strategic alliances is widely thought to be an important way to increase entrepreneurial activities and organizational learning. However, the failure rate of strategic alliances is commonly estimated to be 50 percent or higher (Bleeke and Ernst, 1995; Whipple, 2000). For example, problems emerge with transferring skills. Some skills end up being non-transferable due to social complexity or causal ambiguity (Barney, 1991) and other skills and capabilities that are transferable end up diluting a parent firm's core competencies through the learning of the partner.

Much of the research of joint ventures and collaborations has focused on similarities and relatedness of partners. However, our conceptualization again focuses on dissimi-larities versus similarities, in particular, in regard to technological distance to create a potential invention. While cultural distance (Johanson and Vahlne, 1977) and organi-zational distance (Simonin, 1999) have been found to hinder knowledge transfer in international joint ventures, we argue that technological distance is necessary to facili-tate invention to realize an entrepreneurial opportunity. We suggest that a joint ven-ture is the appropriate mode of entry choice to facilitate transfer when technological distance and market uncertainty are high. If the knowledge is tacit, the partner firm gets the opportunity to examine it first hand before possible transfer attempts take place as in an acquisition.

Accordingly, when both market uncertainty and learning distance are high, we pro-pose that joint ventures provide the best alternative for the pursuit of new inventions. As already noted, uncertain environments indicate that major changes are likely to occur but the specifics of such changes typically remain ambiguous for some time. Perhaps the parent firm's historical market is becoming dated or the capabilities devel-oped in its historical industry appear to be substantially distant from a newly emerging area. This distancing occurred in the watch industry in the 1980s as it moved from a mechanical technical base to an electronic base. When a new and different industry segment emerges, invention and restructuring are often necessitated. An acquisition is not an option because the desired invention does not exist or the new standard has not emerged. An acquisition in these situations is either impossible or too risky. Internal venturing is very difficult because of the substantial learning distance that exists. To complicate matters, although change is on the horizon, the direction of the newly emerging industry segment remains largely uncertain.

Learning   Because a firm desires to pursue the newly emerging technologies and in-ventions, alliances are often formed (Shilling and Hill, 1998). Many inventions and the emergence of new industries often lie at the crossroads of two or more industries. Consequently, a firm as a standalone entity is rarely in a position to capitalize on a business opportunity because it is too far removed from the firm's core competencies. There will generally be substantial distance between what a firm knows and what it needs to learn for such an endeavor to be successful. A joint venture provides a viable solution for the pursuit of such inventions. Under such an arrangement, the parent organizations send resources to the joint venture that best represent the strengths of each parent. Because joint ventures are faced with a high degree of market uncertainty in terms of developing inventions, the new organization necessitates greater discretion to respond to market variations. Accordingly, similar to internal ventures, autonomy is needed to deal with high uncertainty along with the freedom to be entrepreneurial with minimal bureaucratic constraints (Harrigan, 1985). Simultaneously, firms in the alliance use experimentation and creativity to extend their respective learning capabili-ties and develop the intended invention for an emerging market.

Much has been written about the learning potential that resides in joint ventures. While part of this literature has discussed the possibility of learning from alliance part-ners and how they do things (Dussauge, Garrette, and Mitchell, 2000), we emphasize a different perspective here. The learning incentive associated with inventive joint ven-tures should be seen as an extension of firm-specific resources that, when coupled with firm-specific resources of other firms, greatly enriches the development of co-special-ized firm-specific knowledge (Madhok and Tallman, 1998). The dissimilarity of capa-bilities to create new entrepreneurial capabilities facilitates a level of inventive activity that would have been impossible apart from the joint venture. From this perspective, joint ventures provide a context in which a firm's existing knowledge base becomes stretched beyond its normal bounds and further enhances the firm's core competen-cies.

Real options reasoning   The advantage of a joint venture relative to an acquisition when confronting an uncertain opportunity is that a joint venture provides a way for a firm to essentially purchase an option on an entrepreneurial opportunity. Further-more, it gives the partners the flexibility to internalize the capability or to dissolve the venture at less cost than an acquisition if the entrepreneurial opportunity is discovered to be minimal. It may also be that an invention could successfully emerge from a joint venture different from what was anticipated but the potential learning and the result-ing product do not mesh with the core competencies of a parent, allowing the firm to truncate further investments. Stated differently, a joint venture reduces the risk associ-ated with a highly uncertain technological advance and where learning distance is quite high. Because learning occurs more efficiently inside an organization (Kogut and Zander, 1992), a joint venture is appropriate. At the same time, a joint venture allows a longer time before a decision is made to acquire if an acquisition is the ultimate strategic intent. This time, therefore, allows fuller evaluation of the entrepreneurial opportunity to make sure that it will emerge into a viable venture.

Joint ventures also help lessen the problem of adverse selection (the lemon's prob-lem) discussed by Akerlof (1970). Joint ventures accordingly provide the parties to collaboration the opportunity to learn and gather information and facilitate better pricing of target firms' technology assets for future acquisition (Balakrishnan and Koza, 1993). There are fewer problems also in regard to moral hazard because of the signifi-cant relationship development which is necessary to create a successful joint venture collaboration or ultimate acquisition. More time is taken in the negotiation and more trust is developed before the partnership is undertaken relative to that of an outright acquisition.

From a strategic point of view, joint ventures allow the right of first refusal (Chi, 1994). Joint ventures discourage third parties from entering bidding for the target. Accordingly, the risk of preemption by rivals in a close technological subfield is de-creased because the collaborating firms have an opportunity for exercising the option to pursue an internal development strategy (because of the learning from the joint venture) or to pursue an outright acquisition. Thus, joint ventures can be initiated to preempt rivals in uncertain technological areas where emerging entrepreneurial entry seems feasible.

Organizational arrangements and implementation   In regard to asset specificity, high uncertainty and high learning distance are facilitated by a joint venture as well. This is due to the fact that in a joint venture, one has the opportunity to watch the sequence of learning take place without total commitment to a single hierarchy. Furthermore, one can also see whether there is a higher degree of asset specificity in regard to the technology, which is not marketable external to the collaboration. Accordingly, a commitment by both firms allows better management of asset specificity (Folta, 1998).

Although joint ventures are facilitative of controlling for problems of adverse selection and moral hazard in regard to technological evolution, there are problems of moral hazard in regard to the shared control of assets inherent in joint ventures. Yoshino and Rangan (1995) suggest that it's hard to anticipate partner expectations from a joint venture. Empirical work by Bleeke and Ernst (1995) reports that in two-thirds of cases studied "management difficulties" were encountered, which frequently required renegotiations between the parents involved in the joint venture. The complexity of governance issues in joint ventures is pointed to as a reason that termination is usually due to acquisition of one partner by another. Joint ventures, therefore, are argued to be used in situations where the firm cannot determine whether a target is digestible at the time it is considered as an entrepreneurial opportunity. Thus, Hennart and Reddy (1997) found that in situations where the corporation was not sure as to whether the technology or learning was possible (i.e., whether the target was digestible) the use of joint ventures increased.

Again, however, the use of joint ventures will increase only when there is a large enough benefit to compensate for the additional alliance cost. Such benefits are likely to be higher in high-tech industries and where knowledge is available to be absorbed. Furthermore, these benefits are likely to be higher when knowledge is complementary to a firm's current capabilities in pursuing an entrepreneurial entry opportunity.

No innovation (quadrant 4)

Companies that are in a position of low uncertainty and low learning distance are likely to be in a position to pursue only incremental product innovations and process innovations associated with current technology. These organizations momentarily enjoy a clear and well-defined environment in which management is seeking few if any new answers. Cost reduction or process innovations often motivate firms in this situation, as long as the change does not radically affect the established norms and routines of the firms involved.

Just because firms in this quadrant are unlikely to directly or indirectly encounter many entrepreneurial opportunities does not imply that they will experience a lack of success or even failure in the long term. Rather, it suggests that their opportunities are likely to be associated with strategic moves to increase efficiency and incremental improvements in operations. As long as the environmental context remains relatively stable, there are substantial long-term benefits to be had from these incremental improvements. However, because our focus here is on invention and innovation, the further development of these ideas is beyond the scope of this chapter.

Implications and Conclusion

This chapter has implications for theory and practice in regard to mode of entry when considering significant entrepreneurial opportunities. For firms that have low levels of uncertainty and higher levels of learning distance, acquisitions may be considered more prominently than either internal corporate venturing or joint ventures. Alternatively, internal corporate ventures may be given more serious consideration when uncertainty exists but the entrepreneurial opportunity is likely to emerge in a technology that's closely related to the firm's current set of capabilities. Finally, joint ventures are most likely to be appropriate when the entrepreneurial market opportunity is found in situations of high learning distance as well as high uncertainty.

Although the criteria used are broad, firms may improve success of entrepreneurial entry by paying closer attention to the contingencies and implementation issues raised in this chapter. It is hoped that managers can make better decisions concerning entrepreneurial entry using this conceptualization. We have introduced real options reasoning and governance aspects of the transaction, including moral hazard, adverse selection, and asset specificity. Furthermore, we have discussed possible preemption regarding the entry of rivals. We have also discussed the implications of short or substantial learning distance in the consideration of entrepreneurial opportunities. This should affect the type of entrepreneurial entry decision, as we have described above. Seeking to learn the skills necessary to realize an entrepreneurial opportunity when the capabilities are distant from the current set may not always be appropriate. Accordingly, a joint venture or an acquisition may be appropriate. An acquisition, however, may be more appropriate and more preemptive when uncertainty is lower and learning distance issues can be resolved administratively. Similarly, internal venturing may be useful in highly uncertain situations where a firm has significant knowledge capacity relevant to the inventions to be pursued. When the firm has strong absorptive capacity and the required capabilities to realize the entrepreneurial opportunity are not too distant from the current set of firm capabilities, the pursuit of new inventions through an internal venture approach has the potential to stretch an existing firm's capabilities in a positive manner.

Besides having significant implications for practice, our framework has implications for research on corporate entrepreneurship. Global competition, corporate downsizing, rapid technological progress, and numerous other factors have contributed to the decline of numerous corporations. Corporate entrepreneurship has become recognized as a potential solution for established corporations to become innovative as a means to survival and profitability (Miles and Snow, 1978; Hitt et al., 1999; Zahra, 1991). However, numerous difficulties such as managing the property rights and incentives (Williamson, 1985) emerge when established corporations attempt to engage in innovative activities. Small firms appear to be significantly more efficient at the entrepreneurial process than are larger firms. Yet, in the current market economy, many large firms have little choice but to engage in entrepreneurial activities as a means to maintaining their future vitality. Future research on corporate entrepreneurship should pay attention to the implications presented by our framework. In particular, we suggest that research regarding our framework should facilitate understanding regarding large firms' successful entry into entrepreneurial ventures. Future research may therefore help to decide how entry should take place and when firms should acquire or cooperate with others to realize opportunities. For example, large firms often acquire or create joint ventures with small firms who have developed emerging technologies (Granstrand and Sjolander, 1990). When this is appropriate and how the implementation problems mentioned above can be overcome should be addressed in future research.

Future research regarding our framework may also provide a contribution to the strategy literature examining entry strategies. Our framework emphasizes technological differences (dissimilarities) and future research should address how these differences facilitate or decrease value in the acquiring firm. For example, from the research above, it appears that firms that seek complementarities in regard to technological distance (dissimilarities) have the opportunity of creating private synergy (Barney, 1988), which is less likely to create a bidding war when melding assets that create the opportunity for entrepreneurial entry. However, such entry is difficult because the acquisition to create the entry may not be appropriable because the merged assets are too fully embedded in the managers or social or human capital of the acquisition target. If the important human assets choose to exit the firm either to start their own firm or work for a competitor, the premium paid for the target may be lost (Coff, 1997). Also, it might be difficult to transfer the assets into a combined firm because transferring assets that are socially complex can be extremely difficult (Ranft and Lord, 1998). Our framework would suggest that acquisitions would a better mode of entry choice if market uncertainty is lower. As such, this choice should reduce problems due to overpayment. However, codification of information might also increase the number of bidders who also conceptualize the entrepreneurial opportunity. Therefore, future research is needed to show whether entrepreneurial acquisitions create value as implied by our framework or whether the implementation difficulties that are confronted will dissipate potential value creation.

In regard to joint ventures, because failure rates are high, firms would profit from knowing if failure comes from selecting the wrong entry model or from implementation difficulties. Implementation issues are pertinent for the framework itself because implementation could facilitate and hinder possible knowledge transfer and the creation of complementary capabilities. Understanding how such capabilities are best created would facilitate research in corporate strategy and corporate entrepreneurship. Understanding how such capabilities are sought when there are partner differences regarding size differences or industry background could add value to understanding the framework. Understanding how network externalities influence collaborative entrepreneurial ventures such as in the biotechnology industry (Stuart, Ha, and Hybels, 1999) might also be helpful to shed light on our framework.

Notes

1   Our approach focuses on corporate level capabilities because it regards making the entry mode choice. Although business unit-level capabilities may be necessary to implement the innovation, consideration of the utimate costs of entry would still be a corporate-level decision.

References

Acs, Z. J. 1992. Small business economics: A global perspective. *Challenge*, 35(6): 38–44.
Akerlof, G. A. 1970. The market for lemons: Quality uncertainty and the market mechanism. *Quarterly Journal of Economics*, 84: 488–500.

Amit, R. and Schoemaker, P. J. H. 1993. Strategic assets and organizational rent. *Strategic Management Journal*, 14: 33–46.

Aronson, R. L. 1991. *Self-employment: A labor market perspective*. Ithaca, NY: ILR Press.

Balakrishnan, S. and Koza, M. P. 1993. Information asymmetry, adverse selection and joint ventures. *Journal of Economic Behavior and Organization*, 20: 99–117.

Barkema, H. G. and Vermeulen, F. 1998. International expansion through start-up or acquisition: A learning perspective. *Academy of Management Journal*, 41: 7–20.

Barney, J. 1988. Returns to bidding firms in mergers and acquisitions: Reconsidering the relatedness hypothesis. *Strategic Management Journal*, 9: 71–8.

Barney, J. B. 1991. Firm resources and sustained competitive advantage. *Journal of Management*, 17: 99–120.

Bleeke, J. and Ernst, D. 1995. Is your alliance really a sale? *Harvard Business Review*, 73 (1): 97–105.

Brouthers, K. D. and Brouthers, L. E. 2000. Acquisition or greenfield start-up? Institutional, cultural and transaction cost influences. *Strategic Management Journal*, 21: 89–97.

Burgelman, R. 1995. *Strategic management of technology and innovation*. Boston: Irwin.

Burgelman, R. and Sayles, L. R. 1986. *Inside corporate innovation: Strategy, structure, and managerial skills*. New York: Free Press.

Chatterjee, S. 1986. Types of synergy and economic value: The impact of acquisitions on merging firms. *Strategic Management Journal*, 7: 119–39.

Cheng, Yu-Ting and Van De Ven, A. 1996. Learning the innovation journey: Order out of chaos. *Organization Science*, 7: 593–614.

Chi, T. 1994. Trading in strategic resources: Necessary conditions, transaction cost problems, and choice of exchange structure. *Strategic Management Journal*, 15: 271–90.

Christensen, C. 1997. *The innovator's dilemma*. Boston: Harvard Business School Press.

Coff, R. 1997. Human assets and management dilemmas: Coping with hazards on the road to resource-based theory. *Academy of Management Review*, 22: 374–402.

Cohen, W. M. and Levinthal, D. A. 1990. Absorptive capacity: A new perspective on learning and innovation. *Administrative Science Quarterly*, 35: 128–152.

Conner, K. R. and Prahalad, C. K. 1996. A resource-based theory of the firm: Knowledge versus opportunism. *Organization Science*, 7: 477–501.

Daft, R. L. 1995. *Organization theory and design*, 5th edn. New York: West.

Davis, P. S., Desai, A. B., and Francis, J. D. 2000. Mode of international entry: An isomorphism perspective. *Journal of International Business Studies*, 31: 239–258.

Doz, Y. L. and Hamel, G. 1998. *Alliance advantage: The art of creating value through partnering*. Boston: Harvard Business School Press.

Duncan, R. B. 1972. Characteristics of perceived environments and perceived environmental uncertainty. *Administrative Science Quarterly*, 17: 313–27.

Dussauge, P., Garrette, B., and Mitchell, W. 2000. Learning from competing partners: Outcomes and durations of scale and link alliances in Europe, North America and Asia. *Strategic Management Journal*, 21: 99–126.

Dyer, J. and Singh, H. 1998. The relational view: Cooperative strategy and sources of interorganizational competitive advantage. *Academy of Management Review*, 23: 660–79.

Eisenmann, T. R. and Bower, J. L. 2000. The entrepreneurial M-form: Strategic integration in global media firms. *Organization Science*, 11: 348–55.

Fiol, C. M. and Lyles, M. A. 1985. Organizational learning. *Academy of Management Review*, 10: 803–13.

Folta, T. 1998. Governance and uncertainty: The trade-off between administrative control and commitment. *Strategic Management Journal*, 19: 1007–28.

Galbraith, J. R. and Kazanjian, R. K. 1986. *Strategy implementation: Structure, systems, and process*. St. Paul: West Publishing Company.

Gavetti, G. and Levinthal, D. 2000. Looking forward and looking backward: Cognitive and experimental search. *Administrative Science Quarterly*, 45: 113–37.

Granstrand, O., Patel, P., and Pavitt, K. 1997. Multi-technology corporations: Why they have "distributed" rather than "distinctive core" competencies. *California Management Review*, 39(4): 8–25.

Granstrand, O. and Sjolander, S. 1990. The acquisition of technology and small firms by large firms. *Journal of Economic Behavior and Organization*, 13: 367–87.

Grant, R. 1988. On "Dominant Logic", relatedness and the link between diversity and performance. *Strategic Management Journal*, 9: 639–42.

Gulati, R. 1999. Network location and learning: The influence of network resources and firm capabilities on alliance formation. *Strategic Management Journal*, 20: 397–420.

Hagedoorn, J. 1995. A note on international market leaders and networks of strategic technology partnering. *Strategic Management Journal*, 16: 241–50.

Harrigan, K. R. 1985. Vertical integration and corporate strategy. *Academy of Management Journal*, 28: 397–425.

Hennart, J.-F. and Park, Y. 1993. Greenfield vs. acquisition: The strategy of Japanese investors. *Management Science*, 39: 1054–71.

Hennart, J.-F. and Reddy, S. 1997. The choice between mergers/acquisitions and joint venture: The case of Japanese investors in the United States. *Strategic Management Journal*, 18: 1–12.

Hitt, M., Dacin, M. T., Levitas, E., Arregle, J.-L., and Borza, A. 2000. Partner selection in emerging and developed market contexts: Resource-based and organizational learning perspectives. *Academy of Management Journal*, 43: 449–67.

Hitt, M. A., Hoskisson R. E., and Johnson, R. A. 1996. The market for corporate control and firm innovation. *Academy of Management Journal*, 39: 1084–110.

Hitt, M. A., Nixon, R. D., Hoskisson, R. E., and Kochhar, R. 1999. Corporate entrepreneurship and cross-functional fertilization: Activation, process and disintegration of a new product design team. *Entrepreneurship: Theory and Practice*, 23(3): 145–67.

Inkpen, A. C. and Li, K. Q. 1999. Joint venture formation: Planning and knowledge-gathering for success. *Organizational Dynamics*, 27(4): 33–47.

Ireland, R. D., Hitt, M. A., Camp, S. M., and Sexton, D. L. 2001. Integrating entrepreneurship actions and strategic management actions to create firm wealth. *Academy of Management Executive*, 15(1): 49–63.

Johanson, J. and Vahlne, J. E. 1977. The internationalization process of the firm: A model of knowledge development and increasing foreign market commitments. *Journal of International Business Studies*, 8(1): 23–32.

Kogut, B. and Zander, U. 1992. Knowledge of the firm, combinative capabilities, and the replication of technology. *Organization Science*, 3: 383–97.

Kogut, B. and Zander, U. 1996. What firms do? Coordination, identity, and learning. *Organization Science*, 7: 502–18.

Leifer, R. and Mills, P. K. 1996. An information processing approach for deciding upon control strategies and reducing control loss in emerging organizations. *Journal of Management*, 22: 113–37.

Leonard-Barton, D. 1992. Core capabilities and core rigidities: A paradox in managing new product development. *Strategic Management Journal*, 13(Summer): 363–80.

MacDonald, J. M. 1985. R&D and the directions of diversification. *Review of Economics and Statistics*, 67: 583–90.

Madhok, A. 1997. Cost, value and foreign market entry mode: The transaction and the firm. *Strategic Management Journal*, 18: 39–61.

Madhok, A. and Tallman, S. B. 1998. Resources, transactions and rents: Managing value through interfirm collaborative relationships. *Organization Science*, 9: 326–39.

March, J. G. and Simon, H. A. 1958. *Organizations.* New York: Wiley.

Markides, C. C. 1998. Strategic innovation in established companies. *Sloan Management Review*, 39(3): 31–42.

McGrath, R. G. 1999. Falling forward: Real options reasoning and entrepreneurial failure. *Academy of Management Review*, 24: 13–30.

Mezias, S. J. and Glynn, M. A. 1993. The three faces of corporate renewal: Institution, revolution, and evolution. *Strategic Management Journal*, 14: 77–101.

Miles, R. E. and Snow, C. C. 1978. *Organizational strategy, structure, and process.* New York: McGraw-Hill.

Miller, D. and Shamsie, J. 1999. Strategic response to three kinds of uncertainty: Product line simplicity at the Hollywood studios. *Journal of Management*, 25: 97–116.

Milliken, F. J. 1987. Three types of perceived uncertainty about the environment: State, effect and response uncertainty. *Academy of Management Review*, 12: 133–43.

Panzar, J. C. and Willig, R. D. 1981. Economies of scope. *American Economic Review*, 71: 268–72.

Park, S. H. and Russo, M. V. 1996. When competition eclipses cooperation: An event history analysis of joint venture failure. *Management Science*, 43: 875–89.

Porter, M. E. 1985. *Competitive advantage.* New York: Free Press.

Porter, M. E. 1987. From competitive advantage to corporate strategy. *Harvard Business Review*, 65(3): 43–59.

Prahalad, C. K. and Bettis, R. A. 1986. The dominant logic: A new linkage between diversity and performance. *Strategic Management Journal*, 7: 485–501.

Ranft, A. and Lord, M. 1998. Acquiring knowledge-based resources through the retention of human capital: Evidence from high-tech acquisitions. *Academy of Management Best Paper Proceedings*.

Rogers, E. M. 1962. *Diffusion of innovation.* New York: Free Press.

Schumpeter, J. 1942. *Capitalism, socialism and democracy.* New York: Harper.

Shane, S. and Venkataraman, S. 2000. The promise of entrepreneurship as a field of research. *Academy of Management Review*, 25: 217–26.

Sharma, P. and Chrisman, J. J. 1999. Toward a reconciliation of the definitional issues in the field of corporate entrepreneurship. *Entrepreneurship: Theory and Practice*, 23(3): 11–27.

Shilling, M. and Hill, C. W. L. 1998. Managing the new product development process: Strategic imperatives. *Academy of Management Executive*, 12(3): 67–81.

Simonin, B. L. 1999. Transfer of marketing know-how in international strategic alliances: An empirical investigation of the role and antecedents of knowledge ambiguity. *Journal of International Business Studies*, 30: 463–90.

Singh, H. and Montgomery, C. A. 1987. Corporate acquisition strategies and economic performance. *Strategic Management Journal*, 8: 377–86.

Sirower, M. 1997. *The synergy trap: How companies lose the acquisition game.* New York: Free Press.

Stewart, J. F., Harris, R. S., and Carleton, W. T. 1984. The role of market structure in merger behavior. *Journal of Industrial Economics*, 32: 293–312.

Stopford, J. M. and Baden-Fuller, C. W. F. 1994. Creating corporate entrepreneurship. *Strategic Management Journal*, 15: 521–36.

Stringer, R. 2000. How to manage radical innovation. *California Management Review*, 42(4): 70–88.

Stuart, T. E. 2000. Interorganizational alliances and the performance of firms: A study of growth and innovation rates in a high technology industry. *Strategic Management Journal*, 21: 791–811.

Stuart, T. E., Ha, H., and Hybels, R. C. 1999. Interorganizational endorsements and the performance of entrepreneurial ventures. *Administrative Science Quarterly*, 44: 315–49.

Teece, D. J. 1980. Economies of scope and the scope of the enterprise. *Journal of Economic Behavior and Organization*, 1: 223–47.

Tsang, E. W. K. 2000. Transaction cost and resource-based explanations of joint ventures. A comparison and synthesis. *Organization Studies*, 21: 215–42.

Whipple, J. M. 2000. Strategic alliance success factors. *Journal of Supply Chain Management*, 36(3): 21–8.

Williamson, O. E. 1985. *The economic institutions of capitalism*. New York: Free Press.

Yin, X. and Zuscovitch, E. 1998. Is firm size conducive to R&D choice? A strategic analysis of product and process innovations. *Journal of Economic Behavior and Organization*, 35: 243–62.

Yoshino, M. Y. and Rangan, U. S. 1995. *Strategic alliances: An entrepreneurial approach to globalization*. Boston: Harvard Business School Press.

Zahra, S. A. 1991. Predictors and financial outcomes of corporate entrepreneurship: An exploratory study. *Journal of Business Venturing*, 6: 259–85.

Zahra, S. A., Nielsen, A. P., and Bogner, W. C. 1999. Corporate entrepreneurship, knowledge, and competence development. *Entrepreneurship: Theory and Practice*, 23(3): 169–89.

CHAPTER NINE

Implementing Strategies For Corporate Entrepreneurship: A Knowledge-Based Perspective

Robert K. Kazanjian, Robert Drazin, Mary Ann Glynn

Although the field of entrepreneurship originated in the study of those individuals who created new ventures (e.g., Schumpeter, 1936), it has expanded to embrace entrepreneurship as a firm-level phenomenon (e.g., Covin and Slevin, 1991; Miller, 1983; Stevenson and Jarillo, 1990; see Special Issue on Corporate Entrepreneurship, *Strategic Management Journal*, Summer 1990). Building on the basic notion of entrepreneurship as "the identification of market opportunity and the creation of combinations of resources to pursue it" (Guth and Ginsberg, 1990: 5), a firm-level perspective focuses on those organizational characteristics and behaviors aimed at innovation and strategic renewal (Zahra and Covin, 1995). The need for such study lies in findings that demonstrate that corporate entrepreneurship has significant consequences for firm survival, performance, and growth (e.g., Barringer and Bluedorn, 1999; Zahra, 1993). However, as Zahra and Covin (1995) note, these consequences of corporate entrepreneurship are usually seen in intermediate to longer-term results.

The link between strategic management and corporate entrepreneurship is a fundamental one (Schendel, 1990) well supported by empirical research. For instance, Barringer and Bluedorn (1999) demonstrate the relationship between corporate entrepreneurship and strategic management practices of scanning, planning, and control in their study of 169 US manufacturing firms. In his examination of 127 Fortune 500 companies, Zahra (1996) found a link between corporate entrepreneurship and corporate governance and ownership. Consistent with this strategic view is that corporate entrepreneurship requires "changes in the pattern of resource deployment and the creation of new capabilities to add new possibilities for positioning markets" (Stopford and Baden-Fuller, 1994: 522). In other words, an essential aspect of corporate entrepreneurship is developing and configuring organizational resource and capabilities, an idea that resonates with strategic theories taking a resource-based view of the firm.

In contrast to the industrial organization paradigm which exalts industry structure and market power as the determinants of firm performance (Bain, 1956; Porter, 1991), the resource-based perspective asserts that heterogeneous endowments of resources and capabilities shape organizations' fortunes (Selznick, 1957; Penrose, 1959; Snow and Hrebeniak, 1980; Wernerfelt, 1984; Barney, 1986; Rumelt, 1984; Prahalad and Hamel, 1990; Teece, Pisano, and Shuen, 1990). The resource-based view defines resources as inputs into the production process and depicts capabilities as capacities to coordinate and deploy resources to perform tasks. Resources may be tangible (e.g., equipment, finance) or intangible (e.g., brand name, trade secrets) and capabilities may consist of sub-routines and master routines (e.g., product development, distribution) that integrate sub-routines into performance. Thus, resources underlie firm capabilities and capabilities are the main source of competitive advantage (Nelson and Winter, 1982; Grant, 1991). The resource-based perspective holds that firms secure high profits when they possess resources and capabilities that are firm-specific, rare, durable, and difficult to imitate or substitute (Lippman and Rumelt, 1982; Barney, 1990; Peteraf, 1993; Amit and Schoemaker, 1993).

A recent extension of the resource-based view of the firm (Kogut and Zander, 1996) is that of the knowledge-based view (KBV), which models organizations as knowledge-bearing entities (Nonaka and Takeuchi, 1995) that leverage knowledge for competitive advantage (Barney, 1996; Conner and Prahalad, 1996; Foss, 1996; Grant, 1996). According to KBV researchers, knowledge can be uniquely retained by an organization and thereby yield sustainable profit (Liebeskind, 1996). A core premise of this perspective is that growth within companies occurs through entrepreneurial activities that exploit and create knowledge (March, 1991; Foss, 1996; Kogut and Zander, 1996; Grant, 1996; Spender and Grant, 1996; Spender, 1996a, 1996b). As Grant (1996: 112) succinctly noted, ". . . the primary role of firms is the application of existing knowledge to the production of [new] goods and services."

Building on both the resource- and knowledge-based views, we examine strategies for corporate entrepreneurship (CE) to knowledge management processes. Consistent with extant theorizing, we view knowledge as a critical resource and organizational design as a capability that leverages knowledge in the service of innovation and venturing that is the hallmark of corporate entrepreneurship.

A rather broad literature has developed around the study of entrepreneurial activities within the bounds of established, mature corporations. For example, Covin and Miles (1999) identify several forms of CE including: *sustained regeneration* which relates to the organization's ability to regularly introduce new products or enter new markets and *domain redefinition* which relates to the firm's creation and exploitation of new product-market arenas. Based upon a careful and thorough review of this literature, Sharma and Chrisman (1999) identified ten definitions of corporate entrepreneurship and another fifteen similar definitions under labels such as internal corporate venturing and strategic or organizational renewal. The two common themes that cut across all these definitions are a focus on innovation, and a reference to the relatedness of the innovative activity to the core activities of the firm. Representative of this widely employed definitional approach is the work of Venkataraman, MacMillan, and McGrath (1992: 488), who define CE as a process whereby "members of an existing firm bring into existence products and markets which do not currently exist within the repertoire of the firm."

Given our interest in the *implementation* activities central to corporate entrepreneurship, we focus our approach to CE in a more fine-grained fashion on three different types of product innovation strategies that represent differences in the degree to which firms stretch and leverage their existing resources (Hamel and Prahalad, 1993). These are: product line extensions, new product platforms, and new business creation. We begin with the assertion that the particular product strategy chosen by management determines task requirements for search and idea generation, decision making, and institutionalization. The chosen CE strategy thus defines a target domain of entrepreneurial projects with some degree of relatedness to existing knowledge base(s) of the existing organization; in our framework, degree of relatedness is defined relative to a firm's extant knowledge bases rather than as a business-level construct (e.g., Rumelt, 1974). In turn, the contingencies that determine the design of the organizational elements to support these task and knowledge requirements are defined by the relatedness of the strategy to existing firm resources.

In this chapter, we outline how the knowledge-based view of the firm can form the basis for an integrative model for corporate entrepreneurship. To anticipate our arguments, we propose that different CE strategies create different contingencies for knowledge management; in turn, these contingencies have implications for the structuration of both knowledge domains and workflows. Our objectives are twofold: *first*, in response to recent calls (e.g., Schendel, 1990; Guth and Ginsberg, 1990), we seek to articulate a more integrative framework that relates corporate entrepreneurship to underlying theories of strategic management, and *second*, we seek to redress an existing gap in the literature concerning the implementation of strategies for knowledge-based growth. We begin by applying the knowledge-based view to the study of corporate entrepreneurship.

A Knowledge-Based View of Corporate Entrepreneurship

A central tenet of the knowledge-based view is that organizations create, maintain, and apply knowledge bases as a means of competing through entrepreneurship and innovation (Kazanjian and Drazin, 1987; Kogut and Zander, 1992; Cohen and Levinthal, 1990). Knowledge bases in organizations are built up through processes of creativity and exploration; in turn, they are implemented through processes of product-line extension and organizational exploitation (March, 1991; Grant, 1996; Grant and Baden-Fuller, 1995).

Organizations consist of multiple bases of knowledge (Kogut and Zander, 1996; Ciborra, 1996; Kogut and Kulatilaka, 1994; McGrath, 1997, 1999), each of which can intersect with an organizational set of products or services to yield innovations and product extensions for a variety of market opportunities (Sanchez and Mahoney, 1996; Grant, 1996; Grant and Baden-Fuller, 1995; Prahalad and Hamel, 1990). It is knowledge that allows an organization to compete in product areas (Kim and Kogut, 1996). For instance, Hewlett-Packard developed substantial knowledge of inkjet printing that it used to create product-line extensions to fit the needs of different market niches. More generally, knowledge bases have been shown to operate in a diverse range of contexts and industries, including automobiles, consumer electronics, consulting, computers, software, power tools, and financial services (Meyer and Lehnerd, 1997; McGrath, 1994; Sanchez and Mahoney, 1996).

Strategies of knowledge-based growth have been described under an umbrella of terms, including natural paths of growth (Penrose, 1959), repeated replication (Normann, 1977), growth trajectories (Dosi, 1982), stepping stones (Wernerfelt, 1984), and sequential product introduction (Aaker and Keller, 1990). Researchers have examined the viability of these strategies using the related lenses of real options (McGrath, 1997, 1999) and product platforms (Aaker, 1996; McGrath, 1997; Sawhney, 1998). In general, this work tends to focus on the viability of the strategy of knowledge extension rather than on the organizational issues of strategic implementation. In the latter effort, relatedness is the central construct that maps task requirements onto appropriate organizational designs.

In the literature on attained diversification, the prevalent approach is to operationalize relatedness as a business-level construct using business units as the construct of comparison. Categorical schemes are a common measurement approach. In his much-cited work, Rumelt (1974) offered a typology that placed firms into four primary categories; single businesses, dominant business, related business, and unrelated business (see Montgomery, 1982 for a discussion of other relatedness measures). Although such a categorization scheme can depict effectively the firm's achieved business strategy, it is based on aggregate business-level assessments which provide little detail at the operational or functional level. Other business-level measures of relatedness include the use of a herfindahl index, entropy measures, or industry count measures. [For a recent review and analysis of the diversification-performance literature, see Palich, Cardinal, and Miller (2000).]

More recently, Collis and Montgomery (1998) have argued that resources, not businesses, are the appropriate construct and measure of relatedness. Consistent with this view, we argue that a detailed understanding of the existing resource and knowledge base of the firm is necessary to frame the learning process associated with innovation and corporate entrepreneurship. CE strategy targets a domain of new products or services that creates a shared vision of some new business idea (Galbraith, 1982; Normann, 1977) among key actors. Inherent in this vision are certain attributes, including the market to be pursued, the design and characteristics of the product or service, and the administrative and production mechanisms required. Each of these attributes of the new business idea represents a potential requirement to develop knowledge that goes beyond that currently in the firm. Then, the organization must develop competencies beyond those associated with current products and markets to compete in the new businesses.

Corporate entrepreneurship can be understood as an organizational learning process directed at developing the knowledge necessary to compete in a targeted new product-market domain (Normann, 1977; Kazanjian and Drazin, 1987; Pennings, Barkema, and Douma, 1994). When an organization targets its CE efforts at new product development, it necessarily defines the knowledge requirements for implementing that product. The implementation task facing the organization is to learn the knowledge necessary to introduce the targeted product(s). If a targeted product is related to an existing knowledge base, the extent of knowledge development is incremental or small (Normann, 1977; Henderson and Clark, 1990). Alternatively, if the targeted product does not use any of the organization's existing bases of knowledge, then the learning task is more substantial or radical. In effect, the introduction of unrelated products is a process of establishing a new knowledge base that can be exploited in the future (March, 1991; Henderson and Clark, 1990; Kim and Kogut, 1996; McGrath, 1997).

Following this line of argument, we propose that CE activity should be assessed relative to a firm's current bases of knowledge (Kazanjian and Drazin, 1987; Kogut and Zander, 1992). Organizations differ widely in past investments in knowledge or their absorptive capacity (Cohen and Levinthal, 1990); thus relatedness, when it is defined relative to an organization's bases of current knowledge, is firm-specific and target-oriented, determined jointly by the knowledge base and the nature of the new products to be introduced.

Strategies for corporate entrepreneurship

By viewing corporate entrepreneurship (CE) through the KBV lens, we establish the foundation for a contingency approach to implementing CE strategies. Figure 9.1 portrays our view of three archetype CE strategies and the types of knowledge development necessary for each. For the sake of parsimony, the figure depicts only two dimensions (marketing and technology) and we limit our discussion to these two. However, the framework can easily be extended to other dimensions, such as manufacturing, finance, or branding. Additionally, we focus on product development, but acknowledge that the framework readily applies to service innovations as well.

The point of origin in the graph represents the firm's current knowledge base. Any position within the graph represents an area for new product development targeted by the organizational CE strategy. The horizontal axis indicates the extent of knowledge development needs in the technological arena, including domains such as research, design, and product engineering. The vertical axis indicates the extent of knowledge development needed in the marketing arena, including domains such as marketing research, sales, promotion, and customer service.

Three types of corporate entrepreneurial activities are displayed in figure 9.1: product line extension, new platform development, and new business creation. Each of the three archetypes reflects a different diversification intent and implies a different level of knowledge to be developed. The auto industry provides a widely observed and easily understood example of these archetypes. The first archetype, product line extension, is prevalent; established models of existing brands are introduced routinely as variations of a baseline product. These variations typically require little new technology development and are typically directed at existing customers. For example, the K car, critical to the survival of Chrysler during the 1980s, was introduced initially as a fuel-efficient, mid-sized sedan and quickly found market acceptance. From the sedan model, the car was reconfigured as a coupe and as a convertible, in order to target different market segments. Each model was sold with both four- and six-cylinder engines. Naturally, annual model changes within each of the K-car offerings also evidenced product line extensions. Additionally, however, the K-car subsequently became the basis for Chrysler's very popular mini-van, which effectively created a whole new market segment that the company has continued to dominate.

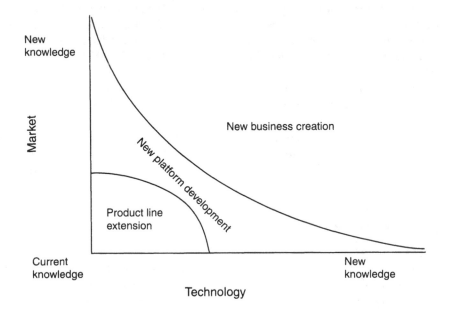

Figure 9.1   Knowledge management and strategies for corporate entrepreneurship

The second archetype, new product platform, is introduced periodically when companies target a new market and/or technology domain. Here, a firm is either developing some new or more advanced technology to take to existing customers, or is targeting new customers with its own advanced technologies. Two recent examples evidence new platform development strategies in the auto industry. Ford, in an effort to attract younger, more affluent consumers who traditionally favor European or Japanese cars, developed a high-end automotive platform which could be configured differently for different niches. Targeting younger, affluent buyers, one version of the car emphasizing performance-handling features was introduced as a Lincoln. Another version with a more luxurious feel was introduced as a Jaguar. The development of alternative drive system designs is another example of a new platform. Ford, General Motors, and other manufacturers have invested in the development of electric drive capability that will emerge soon as a platform from which a range of electric cars and hybrid (gasoline and electric combined) vehicles will be offered over time.

Finally, with regard to the third archetype, some firms may decide to create entirely new businesses that place them in new markets with new technologies. The development of the "On Star" system by General Motors is one such example. Initially offered on luxury models only, the service combines an onboard wireless communications module developed by Motorola with a Global Positioning System satellite capacity and a service center staffed by customer service representatives. Eventually, the service will be extended to all models of the manufacturer's cars. Early services concentrated on automotive-related services only such as providing driving directions and roadside service. However, a range of other services are also planned such as concierge services for restaurant and hotel reservations, cellular services for voice and data for both telephony and Internet access, as well as an expanded entrée to insurance services and financing. These services, termed "telematics," place General Motors into a new business providing new services to a new market and relying on unrelated technologies and new knowledge bases.

Central tasks of knowledge management

We propose three tasks of knowledge management that are central to implementing these three CE strategies: *leveraging* existing knowledge bases; *recombining* and extending existing knowledge bases; and *importing* or acquiring new knowledge bases. Each of these central tasks entails extending knowledge in some way. And, although all are fundamental to CE strategies, these knowledge management tasks differ in their primacy and focus in the different CE strategies we identify.

Leveraging existing knowledge embedded in products, technologies, and customer relationships presents clear and distinct strategic advantages (Kekre and Srinivasan, 1990). Leveraging utilizes an existing knowledge base directly in new applications (Hamel and Prahalad, 1993). This might take the form of applying components from existing products to new products (Clark and Fujimoto, 1991), or the use of specialists, such as consultants, who have specific knowledge of a class of problems, to apply their services to customers in different markets. Additionally, companies might leverage existing knowledge by creating ad hoc teams of individual specialists drawn from different parts of the organization to solve a particular technology- or market-related problem associated with the entrepreneurial initiative. Once the problem is solved, team members would then return to their ongoing assignments (Kazanjian and Nayyar, 1994). Leveraging is evident when the skills of individual employees, as well as the knowledge embedded in physical resources such as products or equipment, are applied to new applications (Leonard, 1998).

Recombining and extending existing knowledge presents opportunities to compete in new domains. Major innovations are often the product of the integration of existing technologies or even the integration of existing products. For example, the first CT scanner was developed by EMI (Teece, 1986), a company with a small presence in medical products, and a larger position in consumer electronics and aerospace. The CT scanner was developed from known technologies associated with data processing, X-ray, and display. Kodama (1992) has discussed Fanuc as a company that created a strong presence in computerized numerical controllers for machine tools by combining skills in mechanics, electronics, and materials development. Similarly, 3M developed non-rusting, non-scratching plastic soap pads from capabilities in abrasives, adhesives, coatings, and non-wovens (Leonard, 1998).

Importing knowledge entails a net new addition to the stock of knowledge in the organization. It is driven either by observed gaps in the knowledge base of the firm or by an emergent strategic intent (Hamel and Prahalad, 1989) of senior management to target a new domain. Imported knowledge can take multiple forms, including new employees, purchased equipment, licensed technologies, or acquisitions of other companies. Sources of imported knowledge include customers (Von Hippel, 1988), suppliers (Leonard, 1998), alliance partners (Gomes-Casseres, 1989; Kogut, 1988), universities, government laboratories, and consultants.

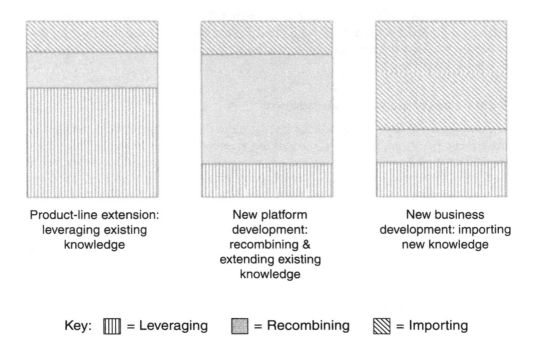

Product-line extension:
leveraging existing
knowledge

New platform
development:
recombining &
extending existing
knowledge

New business
development: importing
new knowledge

Key: ▯▯▯ = Leveraging   ▢ = Recombining   ▨ = Importing

Figure 9.2   Strategies for corporate entrepreneurship

We argue that different CE strategies require different knowledge management tasks. Building on our re-framing of relatedness as a construct referencing the underlying resources of the firm (Collis and Montgomery, 1998), we propose that a detailed understanding of the existing resource and knowledge base of the firm is necessary to frame the knowledge management process associated with innovation and corporate entrepreneurship. CE strategies that target related domains (e.g., product-line extensions) exploit existing knowledge, while strategies that target less related domains (e.g., new business creation) develop knowledge competencies beyond those associated with current products and markets. We summarize our arguments in figure 9.2.

As depicted in figure 9.2, although each strategy is predicated on one of the central knowledge management tasks, each strategy contains elements of the other two central tasks of knowledge management. Therefore, none of the three knowledge management tasks is effectively utilized in isolation, but must be viewed as building blocks deployed to maximally manage the exploitation of existing knowledge or the development of new knowledge. The difference is in the emphasis or primacy of the knowledge management tasks to the CE strategy. Finally, in all three instances, new knowledge is being created, but the amount and type depends on the relatedness of the targeted domain. In other words, exploitation of existing knowledge typically involves developing new knowledge in the process and vice versa. Next, we turn to an elaboration of this linkage between the knowledge management requirements of these three CE strategies and their implications for organizational design.

Knowledge Management Designs that Implement CE Strategies

The relationship of organization design to CE has typically been discussed in conceptual terms. For example, Dess, Lumpkin, and McGee (1999) offer an interesting analysis of the suitability of modular, virtual, and barrier-free organization designs to the reduction of boundaries which they see as central to innovation-related tasks. One contribution of the knowledge management literature is in the movement toward a more problem-based, normative perspective (Leonard, 1998; Christensen, 1997). Consistent with this approach, we propose that three distinct CE strategies, each embedding differing needs for new knowledge development, must be implemented differently. In the following sections, we propose specific knowledge management structures required for implementation in each case.

Product-line extensions: leveraging existing knowledge

One of the major sources of organizational growth is the extension of existing product lines. Growing companies follow a path of least resistance – that is, they use established products as a base for attempts to grow over larger, but highly related product-market areas. Normann (1977: 52) labels this process as growth through "repeated replication," characterizing it as the sequential introduction of new products that are variations or modifications of current products or brands (Keller and Aaker, 1992; Kekre and Srinivasan, 1990; Kotler, 1996). Such a strategy of product-line extension can be viewed as knowledge exploitation – a process of expansion around an underlying core technology or brand knowledge base (Sawhney, 1998; Kim and Kogut, 1996; Kogut and Zander, 1992; McGrath, 1994; Meyer and Lehnerd, 1997).

The implementation of product-line extensions depends highly on the sharing of knowledge between existing and new products. For example, Chandler (1996) discussed how product-line extension occurred at Allison-Chalmers and International Harvester. Both firms exploited economies of scope in production and technology knowledge to allow them to introduce a set of closely related products.

One of the major contributions of the literature on attained diversification has been the development of a conceptual framework that links organizational performance to the economies of scope that arise from the sharing of organizational resources across related products. The primary attributes of the framework are twofold. First, senior managers choose to diversify into product-market areas that are related to the current organization on some basis such as customers, technologies, manufacturing, or brand. Second, this strategy is implemented through an organization design that promotes the sharing of resources. This framework has been successfully applied to the study of several practical and theoretical issues. Historians (Chandler, 1962, 1992, 1996) and economists (Panzar and Willig, 1981; Teece, 1980, 1982) have used these concepts to explain the rise of the multi-product firm. Strategy researchers have found that product diversification enhances performance when firms are able to exploit common resources and realize economies of scope (Rumelt, 1974; Pitts, 1977; Vancil, 1980; Porter, 1985; Gimeno and Woo, 1999). Others argue that related diversification improves performance only when implemented through organization designs that promote the sharing of resources (Nayyar and Kazanjian, 1993; Nayyar, 1993; Gupta and Govindarajan, 1986; Govindarajan and Fisher, 1990, Hill, Hitt, and Hoskisson, 1992; Markides and Williamson, 1996; Porter, 1985).

A wide spectrum of resources can be shared across business units (Porter, 1985). Researchers have focused on the sharing of functional areas, such as manufacturing, marketing, distribution, or research and development (Govindarajan and Fisher, 1990; Montgomery and Hariharan, 1991; Davis and Thomas, 1993; Chandler, 1996; Klette, 1996: Brush, 1996) as well as intangible resources, such as brand reputation (Sawhney, 1998). Despite the utility of understanding the mechanisms of sharing functional departments and intangible resources, the literature is deficient in two ways: (1) it has not fully addressed the sharing of managerial and professional resources; (2) it has not addressed resource sharing as knowledge leveraging in the context of corporate entrepreneurship. Given the importance of managers in implementing product diversification, such a deficiency is curious. Teece (1982) wrote that the tacit knowledge embodied in managers was critical for achieving economies of scope. Both Penrose (1995) and Nelson and Winter (1982) proposed that under-utilized management and professional talent was the incentive for pursuing related product diversification. Chandler (1996: 36) identified managerial skills as the engine for growth and diversification, arguing: "The combined capabilities of top and middle management can be considered the organization itself. The skills were the most valuable of all those that made up the organizational capabilities of the new modern enterprise."

Managerial roles subject to resource sharing across old and new products would include all forms of knowledge workers, including, but not limited to, product and project managers, brand managers, and account and relationship managers. Early writers suggested that managerial resources were more important than physical resources in implementing growth through product extensions (Chandler, 1962; Ansoff, 1965; Teece, 1982; Penrose, 1995). Penrose (1995) argued that firms develop specialized knowledge that is embodied in managers. The use of that knowledge in the production of existing products may create indivisibilities wherein a specialized expert is under-utilized. This provides an inducement for the firm to share that resource across existing and new products to fully utilize its services.

According to Panzar and Willig (1981), economies of scope exist when it is less costly to combine two or more products under the responsibility of one organizational entity (here, a manager) than to produce them separately. They argue (1981: 286) that ". . . when there are economies of scope, there exists some input which is shared by two or more product lines. . ." And, that ". . .whenever the costs of providing the services of the sharable input to two or more product lines are subadditive (i.e., less than the costs of proving these services for each product line separately), the multi-product cost function exhibits economies of scope." In the case of our argument, the shared resource possesses extensive knowledge about an existing product line. The resource being shared is this knowledge as most of it can be applied to the new product. At least a small amount of knowledge needs to be developed that applies to the new market or technological features of the new product. But, for the most part, the organization is leveraging its existing knowledge by applying a great deal of it towards implementing the new product line. Therefore, there are economies of scope of knowledge sharing.

When implementing a product-line extension, senior managers have several design

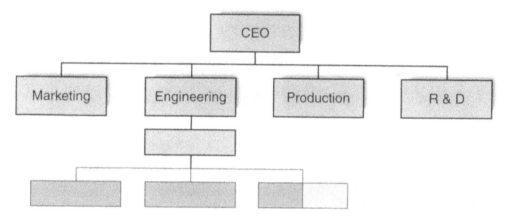

Figure 9.3   Within-job differentiation

options available to them to share and leverage knowledge. All of these options involve sharing knowledgeable managerial resources across old and new products. The first two design options are shown in figures 9.3 and 9.4. In both cases a manager or knowledge worker (for example, an engineer or a marketer) who works on current products is assigned to work on new products. The design option in figure 9.3 is called within-job differentiation. It implies that a shared manager or knowledge worker has responsibility for a previously existing product and a new product. In essence, a manager is assigned two jobs simultaneously. Brand managers in a consumer product company are an example (Choi, 1998). A new product may be assigned to a brand manager already responsible for one or more products, or may be assigned to a dedicated manager responsible only for that product. By definition, a new product extension consists of mostly well-known facts about technology and marketing. The primary advantage of this design is that the manager already has an extended base of knowledge in the existing product and can efficiently transfer that knowledge to the new product extension. In effect, this is the most direct example of leveraging knowledge because an individual is applying his or her knowledge to a new application. However, by differentiating the manager's job into two responsibilities, the manager now also has time to develop the incremental knowledge necessary to launch the new product. The new product or service therefore consists of a high percentage of old knowledge, plus some smaller amount of knowledge necessary to position the new product. For example, a camera company may have a strategy of creating new cameras that appeal to new market segments. But, the underlying technology stays the same while some feature set is added to an existing camera to modify it to handle new customers.

The second design option we propose still involves product-line extension but this design is intended to incrementally increase the organization's capacity to generate new knowledge. That is, this design is intended to serve extensions that mostly leverage old bases of knowledge, but where the mix of new knowledge required increases. Figure 9.4 shows the job differentiation design, where a manager or knowledge worker is assigned full time to a product-line extension, but still remains within the depart-

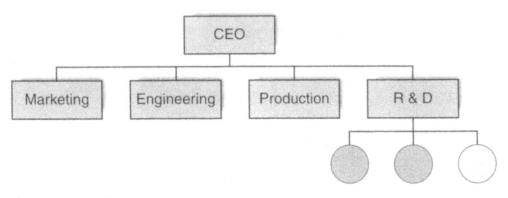

Figure 9.4   Job differentiation

ment responsible for managing current product lines. In effect the individual is as-signed full time to develop the extension, thereby yielding a higher level of knowledge generation capacity. However, the assigned individual comes from, and remains, in the department responsible for the old knowledge base. In this fashion the person is simultaneously freed to engage in creative behavior, but also remains physically and organizationally close to a well-established base of knowledge. An example might be the development of a camera that still uses core organizational technologies, but that has to invent new and unknown technology in order to appeal to a market segment.

The final design option we propose as a mechanism for product-line extension is the creation of an intra-functional task team. As seen in figure 9. 5, an ad hoc team may be created within engineering to investigate new technologies which could make existing products cheaper or more responsive to customer needs. The same design of an ad hoc team might be used within marketing to investigate new product features desired by existing customers. Individuals assigned to such a team may be part time or full time, depending on the task. By drawing individuals from the existing functional organiza-tion, the company is tapping into several sub-elements of the existing knowledge base. Individuals bring that knowledge with them to the team directly. Part-time individuals are simultaneously supporting existing products and product extension providing a direct opportunity for leverage. When the assignment is completed, the task team is disbanded. Although such assignments could be as short as a few weeks, some may be extended over months or even years when associated with complex product line exten-sions for industries such as aerospace.

Each of the three design options (shown in figures 9.3, 9.4, and 9.5) for knowledge leveraging for product-line extension is intended to facilitate the application of exist-ing knowledge to new applications. By having individuals who support existing prod-ucts and services contribute to the development of new products, they will of course apply what they already know. Further, given that the design builds off a close associa-tion with the existing functional organizations (which are the knowledge structures for existing products), those individuals can easily access databases, equipment, and colleagues to leverage that knowledge as well. Note, however, that in all three designs, the degree of differentiation for each individual involved will directly affect the level of

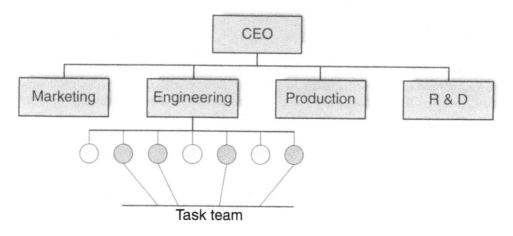

Figure 9.5   Intra-functional task team

knowledge-generating capacity. All three options also demonstrate tight linkages to the existing organization, minimizing the barriers to leveraging existing knowledge.

New product platforms: recombining and extending existing knowledge

We view diversified organizations as consisting of multiple bases of knowledge that can be developed as product platforms (Kogut and Zander, 1996; Ciborra, 1996; Kogut and Kulatilaka, 1994; McGrath, 1997, 1999). We define a product platform as a collection of common elements related to technology and market segments. Product platforms present the opportunity to innovate in a new domain, yet are firmly anchored in existing knowledge related to either technology or the market. Therefore, the development of a new platform represents the ability to leverage some existing knowledge on at least one dimension, while also combining and extending knowledge in new areas. Most importantly, a new product platform is carefully designed to provide the foundation for a number of product-line extensions and the associated benefits of economies of scope and resource sharing. Thus, the development of a new product platform positions the organization to then pursue a strategy of product-line extension within this new class of products, thereby gaining additional economies of scale and resource-sharing benefits.

McGrath (1995) has identified product platform strategies in a number of industries. In personal computing, platforms are composed of a microprocessor combined with an operating system. In application software products, platforms are composed of the hardware architecture (mainframe, client/server) and the interfaces (database drivers, user interfaces). In pharmaceuticals, a platform might be the delivery vehicle for a class of drugs; in specialty chemicals, perhaps a core compound itself. In all of these examples, the "product platform is the foundation for a number of related products . . . all . . . unique in some way but related by the common characteristics of the product platform" (McGrath, 1995: 40).

Meyer and Lehnerd (1997) provide an early but dramatic example of a strategy of new platform development. In the early 1970s, Black and Decker, a consumer power tool company, faced major competitive threats in the form of new global competition and an impending regulatory change which would require substantially increased insulation around power tool motors. Rather than simply redesign each product to meet new insulation requirements, Black and Decker chose to redesign all tools at the same time, redesign all manufacturing processes simultaneously, incorporating the new designs without a price increase to customers. The platform development effort had five objectives: (1) develop a common or "family" look across all products; (2) simplify offerings with standardized parts, interfaces, couplings, and connections; (3) reduce per unit manufacturing costs; (4) improve performance while allowing for the ability to subsequently add new features which could be sold as product-line extensions with minimal cost to the firm; and (5) design global products that meet worldwide customer needs and regulatory requirements (opening many new potential markets).

The financial and strategic results were positive and substantial. Labor and development costs dropped markedly, allowing Black and Decker to reduce price to gain market share. At the same time, given that the platform was designed to facilitate product-line extension, new product development cycles were dramatically reduced. For several years, Black and Decker averaged introducing one new product *per week*. Black and Decker's strategy of new platform development led to a dramatic competitive advantage. Many of the new designs were patented and most competitors were slow to respond. In fact, the Black and Decker strategy of platform development led to a shakeout with several firms exiting the industry.

When developing a new platform, several design options are available to recombine knowledge across disciplines. As we noted in figure 9.1, new platform development can occupy a range of space relative to the firm's existing market and technology knowledge bases. Some platforms may emanate from bringing a dramatically new technology to an existing market, such as the case of emerging biotechnologies in the pharmaceutical industry. In this instance, the platform being developed requires new technological knowledge, but the market for application is the same. This requires a new and separate group within the technology function dedicated solely to the development of a new class of technologies; such a structure is shown in figure 9.6. Given the unit's task of developing knowledge, it must be large enough to attain critical mass; at the same time, though, given its focus on new knowledge, it should be removed from the ongoing technical operations of the organization and perhaps located in a different physical space or off-site. Ultimately, this new technical knowledge must be integrated with the existing market knowledge of the organization to bring the platform and subsequent product extension offerings to market. That integration should be implemented through a matrix organization, with characteristics suggested in the next design proposal.

A second type of platform would be one that requires the combination and extension of knowledge in an integrated fashion more evenly across functions. The example of 3M's development of non-rusting, non-scratching plastic soap pads presents an interesting context for recombining and extending. Existing soap pads were made of steel wool and rusted after several uses. Additionally, steel wool damaged some of the popular cookware coatings like Teflon. 3M created a platform for a range of new

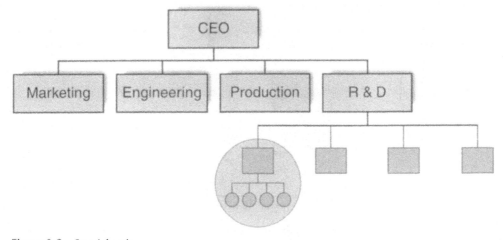

Figure 9.6 Special unit

products by identifying individuals or small groups from existing divisions and expertise in abrasives, adhesives, coatings, and non-wovens (Leonard, 1998). Combining and extending known technologies already existing within the firm and applying them to an existing market allowed 3M to develop the platform. It was so successful that it ultimately claimed 30 percent of the market for soap pads. Note that the innovation here is in the combination of technologies not previously applied in this way.

Such initiatives are typically implemented with multi-functional matrix structures, such as that depicted in figure 9.7. Teams are designed around the requirement for tapping into the knowledge bases to be combined in some new product, service, or market application. Members are drawn from technical functions as well as representatives of the organizations such as marketing and manufacturing, which serve the existing customers. Some individuals might be assigned part time, others full time, depending upon their potential to contribute and the extent to which existing knowledge is being leveraged. The combination of these individuals and groups allows for experimentation on how unorthodox ideas might succeed in a new context.

The deployment of multi-functional matrix teams (Clark and Fujimoto, 1991; Takeuchi and Nonaka, 1986) have been widely discussed in the literature. Clark, Chew, and Fujimoto (1987), Gupta and Wilema (1990), and Womack, Jones, and Roos (1990) have all argued that the use of multi-functional teams creates clear benefits. Clark and Fujimoto (1991), in their global study of product development practices in the auto industry, found that the use of multi-functional teams was a critical factor influencing success. Similarly, Eisenhardt and Tabrizi (1995) also found that the use of such teams shortened development cycles in their study of new product development in the global computer industry. Although the advantages of using multi-functional matrix teams appears well established, Hitt et al. (1999) found that contextual factors such as cross-functional politics and the role of institutional leadership may be more important than internal team processes and activities. While recognizing the

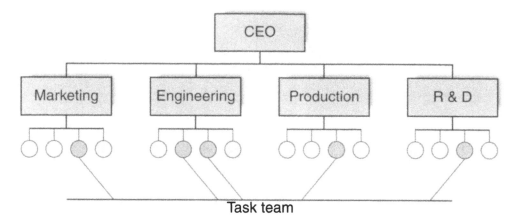

Figure 9.7   Multi-functional matrix team

scope and contribution of this work, we note that the design of multi-functional ma-trix teams has not been explicitly related to the knowledge management requirements of an innovation context.

In the case of new platform development, multi-functional teams integrate the com-bination of knowledge by allowing all team members to consider their contribution to the platform relative to the objectives of the project and the possible contributions of other team members (Gerwin and Moffat, 1997). In the case of particularly complex platform assignments (automobiles, aircraft, computers), this process may be facili-tated through the extensive use of information technology tools such as computer-aided design and computer-aided manufacturing (Argyres, 1999; Cordero, 1991). Associated benefits include reduced time to market, reduced development costs, and the development of more competitive products (Imai, Nonaka, and Takeuchi, 1985; Liker and Hull, 1993).

Combining and extending knowledge for a new platform development requires con-siderable individual-level creativity. In the case of Black and Decker (cited earlier), it is likely that product design engineers deconstructed the product into subsystems and then into individual components. Similarly, manufacturing process engineers may have been presented with specifications which call for faster manufacturing cycles for a product that may be more complex than previous products. In both cases, existing knowledge had to be extended to satisfy the new specifications. The interaction of these groups, combining their understanding of the state of the art in each of their specialties, searching for insights from seemingly unrelated contexts, and experimenting with emerging but unproven approaches, generates the new knowledge necessary for the new platform to become a reality. Note that much of the innovation required to successfully imple-ment this strategy may emerge from the recombination of knowledge from previously unconnected disciplines, or from the recombination of functionally based knowledge. This recombination constitutes new knowledge, but the process of development un-doubtedly leverages and extends existing knowledge.

New business creation: importing new knowledge

Firms that create new businesses internally diversify their position through market developments or by undertaking technological innovations (Zahra, 1993). A strategy of creating new businesses therefore places a firm in the upper right corner of figure 9.1. Although this move initially may be from a base of existing knowledge, it nonetheless requires considerable new knowledge about the market and technology. We define a strategy of new business creation as the pursuit of a new business opportunity that is: new to the firm; implemented internally (not via acquisition); and places the firm into an unrelated domain (Block and MacMillan, 1995; Zahra, 1991).

New business creation strategies have been attempted by a number of companies in different industries. Allied-Signal, Colgate, 3M, and Kodak have all, at various times, engaged in new business creation (Block and MacMillan, 1995). Some of these companies went so far as to create a new venture division (Fast, 1978). More recently, companies such as Intel, Microsoft, McKinsey, and others have engaged in related activities to position themselves into businesses related to the Internet and e-commerce.

One detailed example of new business creation completely unrelated to the existing knowledge of the firm is offered by Sykes (1986), through his analysis of the establishment of Exxon Enterprises. Exxon was a large oil and petro-chemical company that was vertically integrated from exploration and production through to retailing. The oil embargoes of the 1970s created windfall profits for much of the industry. Exxon decided to pursue diversification into unrelated markets with products new to the market based on new electronic technologies. The company acquired very early stage ventures, then internally funded development and commercialization of a range of businesses including a microprocessor, an early text editor, and a fax machine directed at the consumer market, as well as some voice recognition technologies. Overall, approximately 40 new businesses were created, most by acquiring very early stage firms, then developing them internal to Exxon. Over one billion dollars was invested in these ventures. Many of these businesses later were grouped into a division called Exxon Information Systems. In this example, neither the new technology nor the market related to any of Exxon's existing knowledge in any way. Ultimately, Exxon exited these unrelated businesses to concentrate on their core operations. More recently, Hamel (1999) has described a new business creation initiative at Royal Dutch Shell that appears to rely much more fundamentally on the existing knowledge of the company, at least for the original source for the idea. He cites one new business focused on renewable geothermal energy sources. Although the idea originated within the firm, it involves unrelated technology and new markets.

The creation of a new business within the bounds of an established firm requires developing or adopting new organizational structures that spur innovation and new knowledge development (Zahra, 1993). As we argued earlier, the creation of a new business that is not reliant on the existing knowledge of the firm will be implemented largely through importing new knowledge into the firm. Such businesses are typically unrelated to existing businesses and therefore require no coordination or sharing of resources. Further, the task of the new business entity early in the process relies extensively on innovation processes that benefit from a degree of differentiation from

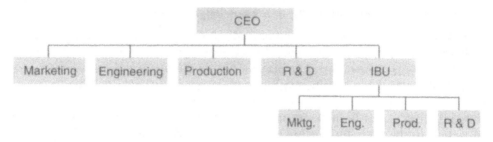

Figure 9.8   Independent business units

existing operations. Therefore, many new businesses that are being created by existing firms are structured as independent business units. As depicted in figure 9.8, the new business is structured as a standalone entity reporting to senior management directly and not through managers of the existing business.

A new and separate unit established to create the new business serves as a vehicle to amass resources, both capital and human, and by extension, to build new knowledge. As defined above, importing knowledge entails a net new addition to the stock of knowledge in the organization, taking multiple forms. With a clear focus on establishing a knowledge base related to the new market and technology, an independent business unit becomes the vehicle for knowledge building: new employees can be hired, specialized equipment can be purchased, and license agreements or alliances can be negotiated (Leonard, 1998).

The building block of this knowledge-importing process is the primary functional groups of the firm such as marketing, engineering, or R&D. A number of authors have argued that knowledge manifests itself as the ability to perform the basic functional activities of the firm more efficiently and effectively than the competition (Collis, 1994; Amit and Schoemaker, 1993). Grant (1991) and Kogut and Zander (1992) have also discussed how routines established within functional groups facilitate the institutionalization of functional-based knowledge. By establishing an independent business unit, each of the functions can be created from scratch, importing (and also extending) knowledge relevant to the new business opportunity.

In addition to each function serving as a base for imported knowledge, they also might search out additional knowledge to import from their natural constituency. For example, the marketing function, or sub-elements within it, might scan the customer base for relevant new knowledge. Research indicates that certain customers may be a source for knowledge about emerging market trends, user preferences, and possible products. Many commercially important products are conceived and sometimes even prototyped by customers (von Hippel, 1988). Von Hippel, Thomke, and Sonnack (1999) describe 3M's Medical Surgical Markets Division development of low-cost, infection-resistant surgical drapes through close cooperation with leading customers. In such cases, the marketing function can then import knowledge in the form of new product ideas, designs, prototypes, and sometimes new employees who might be attracted to join the company. Engineering and production functions within the technical core of the company might also work closely and cooperatively with suppliers,

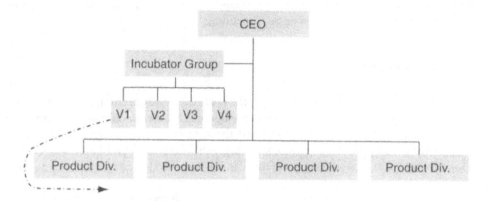

Figure 9.9   Corporate incubators

again to identify solutions to technical problems or suggestions for product improvements. HP was able to offer more reliable and cheaper keyboards for PCs because of the adoption of new injection modeling equipment from a plastics supplier which was modified to HP's needs (Leonard, 1998). In this way, these newly created functions can search for and import new knowledge relevant to their domain.

Some companies have outlined a strategy to create multiple new businesses each of which might be established as an independent new business unit. The oversight of these new businesses requires dedicated managerial resources. Earlier these units were called new venture divisions (Fast, 1978) and in the past few years have been called corporate incubators (Hansen et al., 2000). As an example of the number of new businesses within such an incubator, Hansen et al. (2000) cite Lucent, which has created more than 20 new businesses from technologies originated within the firm, but that do not fit with the company's existing businesses. Another example is Ford which also created an incubator to create Internet businesses with some tie to the automotive industry. The head of Ford's incubator reports directly to the CEO of Ford. In describing the Ford incubator, Hansen et al. (2000) noted that Ford staffed these new businesses partly with managers and knowledge workers from inside Ford, but also with new employees from outside of both Ford and the auto industry. The corporate incubator, depicted in figure 9.9, suggests that over time some of the new businesses may be integrated into the portfolio of existing businesses. In fact, three businesses originally established by Lucent in their incubator were subsequently integrated into their existing operations, based on their increasing relevance to Lucent's overall business strategy as seemingly unrelated technologies converged with existing businesses.

In this section, we have proposed a series of organizational designs that meet the knowledge management tasks demanded by different strategies for corporate entrepreneurship. More specifically, we suggest that the different tasks of knowledge leveraging, recombining, and importing – present to varying degrees in different types of CE strategies – created contingencies for different forms of organizational structure. Designing appropriate organizational forms to address these critical contingencies enhances the management of knowledge, and, ultimately, the effectiveness of any strategy for corporate entrepreneurship.

Discussion and Conclusions

In this chapter, we defined three strategies for corporate entrepreneurship and related them to their requisite tasks of knowledge management. More specifically, we propose that: product-line extension is implemented through leveraging existing knowledge; new platform development is implemented through recombining and extending existing knowledge; and new business creation is implemented through importing new knowledge.

We proposed that a detailed understanding of the existing resource and knowledge base of the firm is necessary to frame the knowledge management process associated with innovation and corporate entrepreneurship. In contrast to much of the strategic growth literature, we argue that relatedness is not a business-level construct but rather a construct defined by links between a specific CE strategy and the underlying knowledge of the firm. Therefore, a detailed understanding of the existing resource and knowledge base of the firm is necessary to frame the knowledge management process associated with innovation and corporate entrepreneurship. Strategies for corporate entrepreneurship that target related domains must exploit existing knowledge, while strategies that target less-related domains must develop knowledge competencies beyond those associated with current products and markets.

In order for strategies for corporate entrepreneurship to be effective, organizations must design structures and processes that support the associated degree of knowledge development required. In considering organization design options for knowledge management, the major challenges center on questions of differentiation and integration of knowledge management structures. In general, we have argued that the degree of structural differentiation should match the amount of new knowledge to be developed. The more existing knowledge is being exploited, the less differentiated the structure of knowledge management units should be; the more that new knowledge needs to be imported and explored, the more differentiated organizational structures need to be. Finally, matrix designs are recommended to integrate the activities of multiple knowledge management structures.

Our framework suggests several potentially fruitful areas for further research. Because we sought to forge the initial link between knowledge-based views of the firm and ways of implementing strategies for corporate entrepreneurship, our formulation sought parsimony and simplicity over generalizability (Thorndike, cited in Weick, 1979). As Weick (1979) urges, we hope that strategy researchers will "complicate" the current state of our thinking and theorizing. We suggest a number of ways in which such complications can occur.

First, there is a need to build more dynamic models that examine how the knowledge creation and development processes involved in implementing CE strategies replenish and change the existing bases of knowledge in form. This calls for more recursive models that map knowledge flows as bi-directional and recognize how innovations may, in and of themselves, affect organizational configurations and bases of knowledge. Certainly, the new knowledge created through the process of corporate entrepreneurship returns to existing stocks, increasing and changing a firm's absorptive capacity (Cohen and Levinthal, 1990) and affecting organizational value creation. And, because new business creation involves a redefinition of the business domain (Hoskisson and Hitt, 1994) by changing the scope of business, its competitive approach, or both (Stopford and Baden-Fuller, 1994; Zahra, 1993), the firm's definition of a "relatedness" will commensurately change. Such redefinition will, in turn, impact subsequent strategic thinking. Thus, as much as CE strategies affect knowledge management, knowledge management, in turn, can reshape and redefine CE strategies.

How those shifts in knowledge content and structure affect corporate entrepreneurship over time needs to be addressed through longitudinal research, in the spirit of those crafted by Hitt and colleagues (e.g., Hitt et al., 1999). Moreover, allowing for more emergent or evolutionary strategic change, as a result of historical trends, would be a welcome addition to our model. Our focus was on more intentional or planned strategies that pursue challenging competitive goals by using entrepreneurial activities to overcome resource limitations (Hamel and Prahalad, 1989). Incorporating experiential and evolutionary learning to inform strategic direction would capitalize on variations that can result from innovation (Mezias and Glynn, 1993).

In addition, we have focused on the critical contingencies of the knowledge management–innovation interface without consideration of factors that may moderate this relationship. Certainly, environmental factors, which signal opportunities as well as threats, and corporate characteristics, including reward structures, reporting relationships, and cultural values, may affect this relationship. Features of the external environment as well as the internal organizational systems have been proposed to affect corporate entrepreneurship, which in turn affects organizational learning (Zahra, Nielsen, and Bogner, 1999). Future researchers might attend to how environmental uncertainty or munificence may affect the direction, deployment, and implementation of CE strategies, as well as the role of new strategic leadership.

Finally, while we have emphasized the *formal* elements of organizational design that enable knowledge management, there is work to be done in extending our model to encompass the role of *informal* elements of structuration in organizations. Social structures, networks of information, and cultural norms about information sharing have all been identified as important sources of learning in organizations (e.g., Nonaka, 1991). In addition, knowledge bases and flows are affected not only by individual employees' education, expertise, experience, and intelligence, but also by the social capital (Nahapiet and Ghoshal, 1998) and the status, legitimacy, and reputation that such knowledge and skills may cue. Thus, incorporating the politics of influence and attention to the power dynamics that leverage, change, and create knowledge will be an important aspect of theorizing for future research examining corporate entrepreneurship. We hope that future academic entrepreneurs will embrace such work.

Notes

We would like to thank Jeff Covin, Mike Hitt, Duane Ireland, and Shaker Zahra for their helpful comments on the initial draft of this chapter.

References

Aaker, D. A. 1996. *Building strong brands.* New York: Free Press.

Aaker, D. A. and Keller, K. L. 1990. Consumer evaluation of brand extensions. *Journal of Marketing,* 54: 27–41.

Amit, R. and Schoemaker, P. J. H. 1993. Strategic assets and organizational rent. *Strategic Management Journal,* 14(1): 33–46.

Ansoff, H. I. 1965. *Corporate strategy: An analytic approach to business policy for growth and expansion.* New York: McGraw Hill.

Argyres, N. S. 1999. The impact of information technology on coordination evidence from the B-2 stealth bomber. *Organization Science,* 10: 162–80.

Bain, J. 1956. *Barriers to entry.* New York: Free Press.

Barney, J. B. 1986. Strategic factor markets: Expectations, luck, and business strategy. *Management Science,* 32(10): 1231–41.

Barney, J. B. 1990. Employee stock ownership and the cost of equity in Japanese electronics firms. *Organization Studies,* 11(3): 353–73.

Barney, J. B. 1996. The resource-based theory of the firm. *Organization Science,* 7: 469.

Barringer, B. R. and Bluedorn, A. C. 1999. The relationship between corporate entrepreneurship and strategic management. *Strategic Management Journal,* 20: 421–44.

Block, Z. and MacMillan, I. C. 1995. *Corporate venturing: Creating new businesses within the firm.* Boston: Harvard Business School Press.

Brush, T. H. 1996. Predicted change in operational synergy and post-acquisition performance of acquired businesses. *Strategic Management Journal,* 17: 1–24.

Chandler, A. D. 1992. Organizational capabilities and the economic history of the industrial enterprise. *Journal of Economic Perspectives,* 6: 79–100.

Chandler, A. D. 1996. *Scale and scope: The dynamics of industrial capitalism.* Cambridge, MA: Belknap.

Chandler, A. I. 1962. *Strategy and structure.* Cambridge, MA: MIT Press.

Choi, J. P. 1998. Brand extension as informational leverage. *The Review of Economic Studies,* 65: 655–69.

Christensen, C. M. 1997. *The innovator's dilemma: When new technologies cause great firms to fail.* Boston: Harvard Business School Press.

Ciborra, C. U. 1996. The platform organization: Recombining strategies, structures, and surprises. *Organization Science,* 7(2): 103–18.

Clark, K. B., Chew, W. B., and Fujimoto, T. 1987. Product development in the world auto industry. *Brookings Papers on Economic Activity,* 3: 729–81.

Clark, K. B. and Fujimoto, T. 1991. *Product development performance: Strategy, organization, and management in the world auto industry.* Boston: Harvard Business School Press.

Cohen, W. M. and Levinthal, D. A. 1990. Absorptive capacity: A new perspective on learning and innovation. *Administrative Science Quarterly,* 35(1): 128–53.

Collis, D. 1994. How valuable are organizational capabilities? *Strategic Management Journal,* 15: 143–52

Collis, D. J. and Montgomery, C. A. 1998. Creating corporate advantage. *Harvard Business Review,* 76(3): 70–83.

Conner, K. R. and Prahalad, C. K. 1996. A resource-based view of the firm: Knowledge versus opportunism. *Organization Science,* 7 477–501.

Cordero, R. 1991. Managing for speed to avoid product obsolescence: A survey of techniques. *The Journal of Product Innovation Management,* 8(4): 283–94.

Covin, J. G. and Miles, M. P. 1999. Corporate entrepreneurship and the pursuit of competitive advantage. *Entrepreneurship Theory and Practice,* 23(3): 47–63.

Covin, J. G. and Slevin, D. P. 1991. A conceptual model of entrepreneurship as firm behavior. *Entrepreneurship Theory and Practice,* 16: 7–25.

Davis, R. and Thomas, L. G. 1993. Direct estimation of synergy: A new approach to the diversity-synergy debate. *Management Science,* 39: 1334–46.

Dess, G. G., Lumpkin, G. T., and McGee, J. E. 1999. Linking corporate entrepreneurship to strategy, structure, and process: Suggested research directions. *Entrepreneurship Theory and Practice,* 23(3): 85–102.

Dosi, G. 1982. Technological paradigms and technological trajectories. *Research Policy,* 11: 147–62.

Eisenhardt, K. M. and Tabrizi, B. N. 1995. Accelerating adaptive processes: Product innovation in the global computer industry. *Administrative Science Quarterly,* 40: 84–110.

Fast, N. D. 1978. New venture departments: Organizing for innovation. *Industrial Marketing Management,* 7(2): 77.

Foss, N. J. 1996. Knowledge-based approaches to the theory of the firm: Some critical comments. *Organization Science,* 7(5): 470–76.

Galbraith, J. R. 1982. Designing the innovating organization. *Organizational Dynamics,* 11: 5–25.

Gerwin, D. and Moffat, L. 1997. Authorizing processes changing team autonomy during new product development. *Journal of Engineering and Technology Management,* 14: 291–313.

Gimeno, J. and Woo, C. Y. 1999. Multimarket contact, economies of scope, and firm performance. *Academy of Management Journal,* 42: 239–59.

Gomes-Casseres, B. 1989. Joint ventures in the face of global competition. *Sloan Management Review,* 30(3): 17–27.

Govindarajan, V. and Fisher, J. 1990. Strategy, control systems, and resource sharing: Effects on business unit performance. *Academy of Management Journal,* 33: 259–85.

Grant, R. M. 1991. Resource-based theory of competitive advantage: implications for strategy formulation. *California Management Review,* 33(3): 114–36.

Grant, R. M. 1996. Knowledge, strategy, and the theory of the firm. *Strategic Management Journal,* 17: 109–22.

Grant, R. M. and Baden-Fuller, C. 1995. A knowledge based theory of inter-firm collaboration. *Academy of Management Journal,* Best Paper Proceedings: 17–25.

Gupta, A. and Govindarajan, V. 1986. Resource sharing among SBUs: Strategic antecedent and administrative implications. *Academy of Management Journal,* 29: 695–714.

Gupta, A. K. and Wilema, D. L. 1990. Accelerating the development of technology-based new products. *California Management Review,* 32: 24–44.

Guth, W. D. and Ginsberg, A. 1990. Guest editors' introduction: Corporate entrepreneurship. *Strategic Management Journal,* 11: 5–15.

Hamel, G. 1999. Bringing Silicon Valley inside. *Harvard Business Review,* 77(5): 70–84.

Hamel, G. and Prahalad, C. K. 1989. Strategic intent. *Harvard Business Review,* 67(3): 63–76.

Hamel, G. and Prahalad, C. K. 1993. Strategy as stretch and leverage. *Harvard Business Review,* 71: 75–84.

Hansen, M. T., Chesbrough, H. W., Nohria, N., and Sull, D. 2000. Networked incubators: Hothouses of the new economy. *Harvard Business Review,* 78(5): 74–84.

Henderson, R. and Clark, K. 1990. Architectural innovation: The reconfiguration of existing product technologies and the failure of established firms. *Administrative Science Quarterly,* 35: 9–30.

Hill, C. W. L., Hitt, M. A., and Hoskisson, R. E. 1992. Cooperative versus competitive structures in related and unrelated diversified firms. *Organization Science,* 3: 501–21.

Hitt, M. A., Nixon, R. D., Hoskisson, R. E., and Kochhar, R. 1999. Corporate entrepreneurship and cross-functional fertilization: Activation, process and disintegration of a new product design team. *Entrepreneurship Theory and Practice*, 23(3): 145–67.

Hoskisson, R. E. and Hitt, M. A. 1994. *Downscoping: How to tame the diversified firm*. New York: Oxford University Press.

Imai, K., Nonaka, I., and Takeuchi, H. 1985. Managing product development: How Japanese companies learn and unlearn. In K. Clark, R. Hayes, and C. Lorenz (eds), *The uneasy alliance: Managing the productivity–technology dilemma*. Boston: Harvard Business School, 337–76.

Kazanjian, R. K. and Drazin, R. 1987. Implementing internal diversification: Contingency factors for organization design choices. *Academy of Management Review*, 12(2): 342–54.

Kazanjian, R. K. and Nayyar, P. R. 1994. Attaining technological synergies in diversified firms. In M. W. Lawless and L. R. Gomez-Mejia (eds), *Advances in global high technology management*, vol. 4 : Greenwich, CT: JAI Press, 121–38.

Kekre, S. and Srinivasan, K. 1990. Broader product lines: A necessity to achieve success? *Management Science*, 36: 1216–31.

Keller, K. L. and Aaker, D. A. 1992. The effects of sequential introduction of brand extensions. *Journal of Marketing Research*, 29(1): 35–51.

Kim, D.-J. and Kogut, B. 1996. Technological platforms and diversification. *Organization Science*, 7: 283–301.

Klette, T. J. 1996. R & D, scope economics, and plant performance. *The RAND Journal of Economics*, 27: 502–23.

Kodama, F. 1992. Technology fusion and the new R&D. *Harvard Business Review*, 70(4): 9.

Kogut, B. 1988. Joint ventures: Theoretical and empirical perspectives. *Strategic Management Journal*, 9(4): 319–32.

Kogut, B. and Kulatilaka, N. 1994. Options thinking and platform investments: Investing in opportunity. *California Management Review*, 36: 52–72.

Kogut, B. and Zander, U. 1992. Knowledge of the firm, combinative capabilities, and the replication of technology. *Organization Science*, 3: 383–97.

Kogut, B. and Zander, U. 1996. What do firms do? Coordination, identity, and learning. *Organization Science*, 7: 502–18.

Kotler, P. 1996. *Marketing management: Analysis, planning, implementation, and control* (9th edn). Englewood Cliffs, NJ: Prentice-Hall.

Leonard, D. 1998. *Wellsprings of knowledge: building and sustaining the sources of innovation*. Boston: Harvard Business School Press.

Liebeskind, J. P. 1996. Knowledge, strategy, and the theory of the firm. *Strategic Management Journal*, 17: 93–107.

Liker, J. K. and Hull, P. 1993. *What works in concurrent engineering?: Sorting through the barrage of practices*. Paper presented at the Academy of Management Conference, Atlanta, Georgia.

Lippman, S. A. and Rumelt, R. A. 1982. Uncertain imitability: An analysis of interfirm differences in efficiency under competition. *Bell Journal of Economics*, 13: 418–38.

March, J. G. 1991. Exploration and exploitation in organizational learning. *Organization Science*, 2: 71–87.

Markides, C. C. and Williamson, P. J. 1996. Corporate diversification and organizational structure: A resource-based view. *Academy of Management Journal*, 39(2): 340–67.

McGrath, M. E. 1994. *Product strategies for high-technology companies: How to achieve growth, competitive advantage, and increased profits*. New York: Irwin.

McGrath, R. G. 1997. A real options logic for initiating technology positioning investments. *Academy of Management Review*, 2: 974–96.

McGrath, R. G. 1999. Falling forward: Real options reasoning and entrepreneurial failure. *Academy of Management Review*, 24: 13–30.

Meyer, M. H. and Lehnerd, A. P. 1997. *The power of product platforms: Building value and cost leadership*. New York: Free Press.

Mezias, S. J. and Glynn, M. A. 1993. The three faces of corporate renewal: Institution, revolution, and evolution. *Strategic Management Journal*, 14: 77–101.

Miller, D. 1983. The correlates of entrepreneurship in three types of firms. *Management Science*, 29: 770–91.

Montgomery, C. A. 1982. The measurement of firm diversification: Some new empirical evidence. *Academy of Management Journal*, 25: 229–307.

Montgomery, C. and Harihran, S. 1991. Diversified entry by established firms. *Journal of Economic Behavior and Organization*, 15: 71–89.

Nahapiet, J. and Ghoshal, S. 1998. Social capital, intellectual capital, and the organizational advantage. *Academy of Management Review*, 23: 242–66.

Nayyar, P. R. 1993. On the measurement of competitive strategy: Evidence from a large U. S. multiproduct firm. *Academy of Management Journal*, 36(6): 1652–69.

Nayyar, P. R. and Kazanjian, R. K. 1993. Organizing to attain potential benefits from information asymmetries and economies of scope in related diversified firms. *Academy of Management Review*, 18(4): 735–59.

Nelson, R. R. and Winter, S. G. 1982. *An evolutionary theory of economic change*. Cambridge, MA: Belknap.

Nonaka, I. 1991. The knowledge-creating company. *Harvard Business Review*, 69(6): 96–105.

Nonaka, I. and Takeuchi, H. 1995. *The knowledge creating company*. New York: Oxford University Press.

Normann, R. 1977. *Management for growth*. New York: Wiley.

Palich, L. E., Cardinal, L. B., and Miller, C. C. 2000. Curvilinearity in the diversification-performance linkage: An examination of over three decades of research. *Strategic Management Journal*, 21(2): 155–75.

Panzar, J. C. and Willig, R. D. 1981. Economies of scope. *American Economic Review*, 71: 268–72.

Pennings, J. M., Barkema, H., and Douma, S. 1994. Organizational learning and diversification. *Academy of Management Journal*, 37(3): 608–41.

Penrose, E. 1959. *The theory of the growth of the firm*. New York: John Wiley.

Peteraf, M. A. 1993. The cornerstones of competitive advantage. *Strategic Management Journal*, 14(3): 179–92.

Pitts, R. A. 1977. Strategies and structures for diversification. *Academy of Management Journal*, 20: 197–208.

Porter, M. E. 1985. *Competitive advantage*. New York: Free Press.

Porter, M. E. 1991. Towards a dynamic theory of strategy. *Strategic Management Journal*, 12: 95–117.

Prahalad, C. K. and Hamel, G. 1990. The core competence of the corporation. *Harvard Business Review*, 68: 79–92.

Rumelt, R. P. 1974. *Strategy, structure, and economic performance*. Cambridge, MA: Harvard Business School Division of Research.

Rumelt, R. 1984. Towards a strategic theory of the firm. In R. B. Lamb (ed.), *Competitive strategic management*. Englewood Cliffs, NJ: Prentice-Hall, 556–70.

Sanchez, R. and Mahoney, J. T. 1996. Modularity, flexibility, and knowledge management in product and organization design. *Strategic Management Journal*, 17: 63–76.

Sawhney, M. 1998. Leveraged high-variety strategies: From portfolio thinking to platform thinking. *Journal of the Academy of Marketing Science*, 26: 54–61.

Schendel, D. 1990. Introduction to the special issue on corporate entrepreneurship. *Strategic Management Journal*, 11 (special issue): 1–3.

Schumpeter, J. A. 1936. *The theory of economic development*. Cambridge, MA: Harvard University Press.

Selznick, P. 1957. *Leadership in administration: A sociological interpretation*. Evanston, IL: Row, Peterson.

Sharma, P. and Chrisman, J. J. 1999. Toward a reconciliation of the definitional issues in the field of corporate entrepreneurship. *Entrepreneurship Theory and Practice*, 23(3): 11–27.

Snow, C. C. and Hrebiniak, L. G. 1980. Strategy, distinctive competence, and organizational performance. *Administrative Science Quarterly*, 25(2): 317.

Spender, J. C. 1996a. Making knowledge the basis of a dynamic theory of the firm. *Strategic Management Journal*, 17: 45–62.

Spender, J. C. 1996b. Organizational knowledge, learning, and memory: Three concepts in search of a theory. *Journal of Organizational Change Management*, 9: 67–79.

Spender, J. C. and Grant, R. M. 1996. Knowledge and the firm: overview. *Strategic Management Journal*, 17: 5–9.

Stevenson, H. H. and Jarillo, J. C. 1990. A paradigm of entrepreneurship: Entrepreneurial management. *Strategic Management Journal*, 11: 17–27.

Stopford, J. M. and Baden-Fuller, C. 1994. Creating corporate entrepreneurship. *Strategic Management Journal*, 15: 521–36.

Sykes, H. B. 1986. Lessons from a new ventures program. *Harvard Business Review*, 64(3): 69–75.

Takeuchi, H. and Nonaka, I. 1986. The new new product development game. *Harvard Business Review*, 64(1): 137–46.

Teece, D. J. 1980. Economies of scope and the scope of the enterprise. *Journal of Economic Behavior and Organization*, 1: 223–45.

Teece, D. J. 1982. Towards an economic theory of the multiproduct business. *Journal of Economic Behavior and Organization*, 3: 39–63.

Teece, D. J. 1986. Transactions cost economics and the multinational enterprise: An assessment. *Journal of Economic Behavior and Organization*, 7(1): 21–46.

Teece, D. J., Pisano, G., and Shuen, A. 1990. Dynamic capabilities and strategic management. *Strategic Management Journal*, 18(7): 509–33.

Vancil, R. F. 1980. Managing the decentralized firm. *Financial Executive*, 48: 34–43.

Venkataraman, S., MacMillan, I., and McGrath, R. 1992. Progress in research on corporate venturing. In D. L. Sexton and J. D. Kasarda (eds), *The state of the art of entrepreneurship*. Boston: PWS-Kent, 487–519.

Von Hippel, E. 1988. *The sources of innovation*. New York: Oxford University Press.

Von Hippel, E., Thomke, S., and Sonnack, M. 1999. Creating breakthroughs at 3M. *Harvard Business Review*, 77(5): 47–57.

Weick, K. E. 1979. *The social psychology of organizing*. New York: McGraw Hill.

Wernerfelt, B. 1984. A resource-based view of the firm. *Strategic Management Journal*, 5: 171–80.

Womack, J. P., Jones, D. T., and Roos, D. R. 1990. *The machine that changed the world: The story of lean production*. New York: Harper Perennial.

Zahra, S. A. 1991. Predictors and financial outcomes of corporate entrepreneurship: An exploratory study. *Journal of Business Venturing*, 6(4): 259–85.

Zahra, S. A. 1993. Environment, corporate entrepreneurship, and financial performance: A taxonomic approach. *Journal of Business Venturing*, 8(4): 319–40.

Zahra, S. A. 1996. Governance, ownership, and corporate entrepreneurship: The moderating impact of industry technological opportunities. *Academy of Management Journal*, 39: 1713–35.

Zahra, S. A. and Covin, J. 1995. Contextual influences on the corporate entrepreneurship-company performance relationship in established firms: A longitudinal analysis. *Journal of Business Venturing,* 10: 43–58.

Zahra, S. A., Nielsen, A. P., and Bogner, W. C. 1999. Corporate entrepreneurship, knowledge, and competence development. *Entrepreneurship Theory and Practice,* Spring: 169–89.

Alliances and Networks

CHAPTER TEN

Networks, Alliances, and Entrepreneurship

Arnold C. Cooper

This chapter examines the processes by which entrepreneurs, both independent and corporate, start and develop new ventures. It considers prior work on networks and alliances which add to our understanding of these processes. It then suggests opportunities for future research on entrepreneurship which build upon what has been done. As we shall see, networks and alliances can influence almost every aspect of new venture creation. Johannisson described the personal network of the entrepreneur as "the strategically most significant resource of the firm" (Johannisson, 1990: 41).

Networks can supply information, add credibility, and lead to exchange relationships with suppliers and customers (Johannisson, 2000: 370). All of these are needed by entrepreneurs who are trying to develop new ventures. Thus, it is not surprising that, as we observe entrepreneurial processes, networks and alliances appear to play prominent roles.

Networks and Alliances

Networks have been defined as "a set of nodes (persons, organizations) linked by a set of social relationships (friendship, transfer of funds, overlapping membership) of a specified type" (Laumann, Galaskiewicz, and Marsden, 1978: 458). Networks are distinct from hierarchical or market relationships in their reliance on reciprocity, collaboration, complementary independence, and an orientation toward mutual gain (Larson, 1992). Developed extensively in sociology, social network analysis has been applied to many management issues, including marketing channels (Podolny, 1994), location decisions (Romo and Schwartz, 1995), acquisitions (Palmer et al., 1995), and organizational adaptation (Baum and Oliver, 1992).

Alliances have been defined as "voluntary arrangements between firms involving exchange, sharing, or co-development of products, technologies, or services" (Gulati, 1998: 293). Among the issues that have been considered are those relating to alliance formation, including motivation, and the influence of company size, geographic location, and innovativeness (Hagedoorn, 1993; Hagedoorn and Schakenraad, 1994). Other topics considered have been governance and alliance evolution, performance of alliances as a whole, and performance of individual firms entering alliances (Gulati, 1998: 294).

Entrepreneurship

We shall consider the activities involved in establishing and developing a new venture, whether it be independent or within an established corporation. The framework to be utilized considers the following topics: (1) idea generation; (2) investigation and development of the idea; (3) assembly of resources; (4) implementation and early operation; (5) performance implications. This framework, for independent and corporate ventures, is presented in figure 10.1.

It should be recognized that the activities involved in starting a business or a corporate venture are not always pursued in order. One study, looking at a number of startup events, found a variety of sequences. For instance, such benchmarks as personal commitment, outside financial support, initial sales, and first hiring occurred in varying sequences (Reynolds and Miller, 1992). It should also be noted that many nascent or "would-be" entrepreneurs try to start companies, but then give up (Carter et al., 1996). In a study of major innovations in a variety of settings, Van de Ven and his co-authors found "the process does not unfold in a simple linear sequence of stages and substages" (Van de Ven et al., 1999: 10).

In reviewing prior research on networks relating to entrepreneurial firms, we shall consider all kinds of new ventures, not only those which are highly innovative. This is because the limited amount of relevant research utilizing a social network framework has considered a variety of kinds of new and small firms. However, published entrepreneurship alliance research has primarily centered upon innovative small firms, particularly in biotechnology. Note that in corporate entrepreneurship, we are focusing upon new venture creation, rather than the more general concepts of corporate renewal or entrepreneurial orientation, which can include dimensions such as innovativeness, proactiveness, and willingness to take risks (Covin and Slevin, 1991; Miller, 1983). As Sharma and Chrisman observe in their review, a variety of definitions of corporate entrepreneurship have been used, some of which are much broader than that considered here (Sharma and Chrisman, 1999). We should also note that there are other ways, not examined here, by which established companies might create or participate in startups, including joint ventures and venture capital investments.

Studies involving the creation of independent new ventures often center upon the network ties of the individual entrepreneur. This is because "In entrepreneurship research, the personal and organizational networks converge" (Zhao and Aram, 1995: 351). Larger-scale ventures often are built around entrepreneurial teams. However, the network ties utilized by such teams in venture creation have not received much attention. Later, as the venture develops, more people usually become involved and the unit of analysis often shifts to the organization.

	Independent entrepreneurship	Corporate entrepreneurship
Idea generation		
Investigation/Development		
Assembly of resources		
Implementation		
Performance implications		

Figure 10.1 Venture creation process

Idea Generation

Sources of ideas for new ventures can originate in a variety of ways. Vesper speaks of three broad approaches: detecting opportunity cues, probing the future, and systematic searching (Vesper, 1993: 5–9). The origins of ideas for new firms have been examined in a number of studies. Sources of ideas in a large-scale study of National Federation of Independent Business members included prior job (43 percent), hobby or interest (18 percent), chance happening (10 percent), or "someone suggested it" (8 percent) (Cooper et al, 1990: 19). New high-technology firms often seem to be closely related to the organization which the entrepreneur left, that being the case for an average of 73 percent of the entrepreneurs studied in seven separate studies (Cooper, 1986: 159).

A social network perspective suggests that information leading to idea generation should come from the interactions entrepreneurs have with people in their networks. Little has been done in tracing how entrepreneurs utilize their networks to develop ideas. However, we might expect that the nature of the entrepreneur's previous job responsibilities would affect the attributes of these networks, the kinds of information gained, and the nature of the ideas which the entrepreneur then develops. For instance, salespeople will have developed ties with distributors and customers, purchasing agents with suppliers, and finance people with bankers. Those in boundary-spanning roles will have been more likely to develop ties with people outside their organizations. Through these ties they may learn of unmet market needs, or promising new technologies, or industry changes which offer entrepreneurial promise. Employees are most likely to develop networks within their industries and thus to learn of opportunities within those industries. Of course, industries vary widely in the extent to which they might offer entrepreneurial opportunities at a given time. For instance, those working in e-commerce are likely to develop more new-venture ideas than those in the steel industry. These processes do not lead to the identification of opportunities in predictable ways. Rather, personal networks "Create unforeseeable business opportunities since they are randomly created by unexpected encounters" (Johannisson, 2000: 377).

It is not only work-related networks that can lead to opportunities. Recall that the

NFIB study reported that hobbies or personal interests had been the source of the idea for 18 percent of founders, chance happenings for 10 percent, and suggestions from others for 8 percent. We might expect that the personal networks of potential entrepreneurs related to their hobbies, families, or friendships would play a role in idea generation. There are some entrepreneurs (probably not many) who engage in deliberate search for new business ideas. Karl Vesper, reporting upon how 100 successful entrepreneurs had come up with their venture ideas, noted that some had systematically contacted people to seek ideas. "One entrepreneur adopted a strategy of calling or visiting at least one person daily who might be able to help him find an opportunity, any opportunity." Another "discovered a successful product by asking purchasing agents what items they were having trouble obtaining" (Vesper, 1992: 79). Entrepreneurs may find that those with whom they have weak ties, with infrequent interactions, have access to information in other networks not normally accessible to them (Aldrich and Zimmer, 1986; Burt, 1992).

In corporate entrepreneurship, some departments, such as R&D and new venture departments, are charged with identifying and exploring opportunities. Sometimes they pursue ideas they have developed themselves and sometimes they take on ideas suggested by operating divisions (Kanter et al., 1991a). Individuals in marketing and purchasing occupy boundary-spanning roles, in which they can bring into the organization information about market needs and new technologies. One study found that about 75 percent of the ideas used in developing product innovations came from outside the organization (Utterback, 1971); another reported that ideas for most new product innovations came from customers (von Hippel, 1988). The extent to which organizational and individual networks were utilized in getting these ideas was not the focus of these studies. However, we might expect that such ties would play an important role.

Whether individuals feel empowered to pursue and develop ideas depends upon the culture and administrative systems within their firms. These include the degree to which there are incentives to develop ideas and whether there are enough slack resources to pursue them. It should not be assumed that the organization will always be supportive. As Kanter observed, "research has tended to demonstrate that entrepreneurship is difficult for established organizations to tolerate, let alone manage, for more than a short period of time" (Kanter, et al., 1991a: 145).

Internal networks may be important. Those who occupy central roles, exchanging information with people in many relevant departments, may be able to see how ideas might fit with the capabilities and goals of different departments (Floyd and Wooldridge, 1999). Those whose network members may interact with senior management may be in a better position to understand how ideas might help the corporation to respond to current challenges. In studies of corporate innovation, Van de Ven and associates noted, "during opportune moments, these champions offered their organizations an idea or project as a vehicle to solve a crisis or exploit a commercial opportunity" (Van de Ven et al., 1999: 27).

It should be recognized that many people interact with others and access information which could be the basis for new venture ideas. However, whether they take that information and try to shape it into an idea for a specific venture idea depends upon their creativity and their motivation. Those who see opportunities "make new connections, both intellectual and organizational; and they stretch boundaries, reaching beyond the limits of their own jobs-as-given." (Kanter, 1983: 212)

There is an extensive literature on creativity indicating that people vary in their ability to generate innovative ideas. There is some evidence that those who become independent entrepreneurs have this ability. One study found that when corporate managers and independent entrepreneurs were presented with ambiguous situations, the entrepreneurs were less likely to perceive problems and more likely to perceive opportunities (Palich and Bagby, 1995). There is also evidence that organizations can create systems which encourage members to propose new venture ideas. Kanter reported that Eastman Kodak's Research Proposal System resulted in more than 700 ideas per year being submitted in the 1980s (Kanter et al., 1991b: 66).

Geographic location may make a difference. Potential entrepreneurs, whether independent or corporate, located in industry clusters may benefit from "technological spillover" from related organizations (Jaffe et al., 1993). Saxenian speaks of Silicon Valley as a place "where dense social networks and local institutions foster the recombination of experience, skill, and technology into new enterprises" (Saxenian, 1990: 96). She notes the mobility of ideas and people: "As individuals move from firm to firm in Silicon Valley their paths overlap repeatedly: a colleague might become a customer or a competitor, today's boss could be tomorrow's subordinate" (Saxenian, 1990: 97). To the extent that a region has this openness and flow of people and information, it can be a fertile setting for the identification of opportunities.

Investigation and Development of the Idea

The idea is only the beginning. The entrepreneur must evaluate the idea and decide whether to move it forward. This may involve developing it more fully, gathering and appraising information, and testing and sometimes modifying the concept. An integral part of this process is the development of a strategy – a way of competing.

Whether a potential entrepreneur commits time, energy, money, and personal credibility to developing an independent venture idea depends upon several factors: (1) the motivation to make a change (many entrepreneurs leave their previous positions because of negative "pushes"); (2) the extent to which the person feels this is something he or she could do (entrepreneurial self-efficacy has been the focus of some research (Krueger and Brazeal, 1994)); and (3) the degree to which the concept seems promising and feasible.

Network ties may play an important role as the entrepreneur asks people for information or requests that they do something on his or her behalf. ("Is this something your customers would buy?" "What would be your estimate of the cost of this component in lots of 500?" "How should I modify this business plan to make it more attractive to investors?") If the entrepreneur (or members of the entrepreneurial team) has embedded ties with knowledgeable people, they are more likely to transfer fine-grained information, information which reflects detailed, mutual understanding and trust (Uzzi, 1997). Network ties can be used to develop other ties, as when a would-be entrepreneur asks others for suggestions about who to approach or whether a commitment should be made to a particular supplier or professional adviser ("Contact this buyer for that chain and mention my name." "Yes, you could use that lawyer, but for this kind of transaction, most people use the firm of . . ."). Resources are borrowed; favors are requested; others are invited to share the dream (Starr and MacMillan, 1990). The personal networks of the entrepreneur might be viewed as major resources which are created and drawn upon as the entrepreneur seeks information and credibility and enters into exchange relationships (Johannisson, 2000).

The seed capital to investigate an idea often comes from personal savings, family, and friends. The personal networks of the entrepreneur are, of course, vital to raising this early-stage, high-risk money. Some is "sentimental money" offered as expressions of personal support. Some is made available because of confidence in the individual, built up through past relationships.

The processes of gathering information and securing tentative commitments are intertwined. Birley found that entrepreneurs tend to gather information as needed and that informal sources are utilized more than formal ones (Birley, 1985). As a venture is moved forward, it might be viewed as a "real option," in which the independent entrepreneur or the corporation can choose to exercise the option or drop it as information develops (McGrath, 1999). Just as investment in a financial option conveys the right to purchase the underlying asset, a real option conveys the opportunity to continue investment. One implication is that investments should be made sequentially, so that further commitments are made only under favorable circumstances.

What are some of the differences between independent and corporate entrepreneurship? For independent entrepreneurs, there is concern for "fit" with that person's personal interests, capabilities, and contacts. The new venture is built around the entrepreneur, so that the right kind of startup for one entrepreneur is not necessarily the right one for another. If a team is being assembled, which often occurs through the personal ties of the founder, then the values, contacts, and skills of that group are critical.

For corporate entrepreneurs, there is concern for "fit" with corporate strategy and with whether a particular new venture concept might receive corporate support. Fit might be viewed as having two dimensions: a relational fit reflecting organizational culture and structure and an economic fit involving venture needs and the resources of the parent (Thornhill and Amit, 2001).

Van de Ven observed "that innovations are not initiated on the spur of the moment, by a single dramatic incident, or by a single entrepreneur. An extended gestation period, often lasting several years, of seemingly random events occurred before concentrated efforts were launched to develop an innovation" (Van de Ven et al., 1999: 196–7). At this point the corporate entrepreneur must shape and test the concept for the venture, developing it to the point where it might receive fuller corporate support. This may involve technical development, market exploration, and estimation of expected costs and investment requirements.

(A good idea) "needs to be turned into something that can be tested and, if successful, integrated into the rest of what a company does, makes, or sells" (Hargadon and Sutton, 2000). It is not necessarily the case that the person who conceives the idea must be the one implementing it. The inventor or the person who conceives the idea may be able to attract a sponsor or "product champion" who provides legitimacy to the project and secures resources from the corporation (Venkataraman et al., 1992). Both the formal and informal networks of those people first involved with the project may be utilized in obtaining information and assistance from other parts of the organization. If the project is clearly sanctioned by the organization, then formal networks, corresponding to the formal organization, may primarily be utilized. However, often the corporate entrepreneur will utilize personal informal networks (often based upon past working relationships or friendships) to persuade people in other parts of the organization to provide assistance, sometimes going well beyond anything they are formally required to do. People in engineering may be asked to develop prototypes or samples. Marketing people may supply market and competitive information. Manufacturing may assist in estimating costs. As the venture gains momentum, various managers may play different roles, including champion, mentor, critic, and institutional leader (Van de Ven et al., 1999: 98–100).

It is by no means assured that the venture will get the help it needs or find the organizational setting which permits it to develop. The corporate context, including the extent to which lower levels of management have credibility and the ability to exercise initiative, will bear upon whether ideas are pursued (Birkinshaw, 1999; Burgelman, 1983). Ventures may be involved with "strategic conflicts of interest involving domain and synergy; administrative conflicts involving unwillingness of other departments to share resources with the new venture or the unwillingness of the venture to use the policies and systems of the established organizations; 'culture' clashes because of the more chaotic nature of innovation; and measurement and reward issues" (Kanter et al., 1990: 417). It helps if the corporate entrepreneur has strong personal ties with managers controlling critical resources. It helps if the venture project is perceived as interesting and if the organization has enough slack to pursue projects with no immediate payoff. It helps if the developing venture is perceived as consistent with corporate strategy.

Information and assistance will be needed from outside organizations, such as suppliers, channels of distribution, and customers. If the corporation has existing ties with organizations, and if trust has developed, then it is more likely that assistance will be forthcoming. Furthermore, a history of interactions means that individuals within the corporation are likely to know the specific people in other organizations to contact. They are then able to draw upon the personal relationships that have developed (Uzzi, 1997).

Assembly of Resources

As a venture is moved forward, resources are needed. Partners or key employees must be attracted. Working models or systems must be developed and tested. Customer reaction must be gauged.

It is not the case that a venture has to own all the assets it utilizes. Stevenson, in discussing the distinguishing attributes of an entrepreneurial orientation, emphasizes that entrepreneurs strive to use resources, rather than own them, and this use is often episodic, as a venture concept is tested or moved through stages (Stevenson et al.,

1994: 3–16). MacMillan and Starr note that one of the major differences between independent and corporate ventures is that independent entrepreneurs often borrow, beg, scavenge, or amplify as they seek to test ideas at the lowest possible cost. They scavenge when they use goods that others do not intend to use and they amplify when they leverage far more value out of an asset than is perceived by its original owner (Starr and MacMillan, 1990). Entrepreneurial ventures often deal with new technologies, new markets, new management teams, and untested strategies. There is great uncertainty, including whether key employees and customers will actually commit and whether enough capital can be raised. Under such conditions, prospective suppliers of resources may be reluctant to invest until all the other parts of the puzzle are in place. If visible and respected parties become involved (such as a promising customer or a respected venture capital firm), others may be reassured by the presence of these "bell cows" (Stevenson et al., 1994: 228). The commitment of respected organizations adds credibility to the new venture (Stuart et al., 1999). Potential contributors of resources may be more likely to commit if they have experience in dealing with firms such as the startup; such experience makes them better able to judge the risks and potential associated with a particular venture. Potential contributors may also be more willing to be involved if they have excess capacity, and if they derive noneconomic benefits or thrills from being involved (Stevenson et al., 1994: 228–30).

Because new independent ventures are built around limited resources and the capabilities of only a few people, there is often a need to leverage these through outsourcing and through forming alliances as much as possible. Thus, some e-commerce startups outsource most of the key functions, such as manufacturing, warehousing, credit checking, and shipping (Amit and Zott, 2000). A challenge may be whether the startup can develop relationships with the "right" firms. If the venture is well funded or viewed as having exciting prospects (such as many e-commerce startups in 1999), then investors and potential alliance partners may be falling over each other to participate. However, in more normal times, the limited resources and uncertain prospects of the startup may mean that major selling jobs are needed to attract resource providers. Entrepreneurs who have strong ties with potential resource providers have an advantage. "Tie strength is based upon the amount of time, the emotional intensity, the mutual confiding and the reciprocal services which characterize the tie" (Rowley et al., 2000: 370–71). Investigation of the ways in which some entrepreneurs are able to develop these strong ties clearly is a promising area for research.

Those who can rely upon ties from past relationships may be able to utilize these to get introductions and to add to their credibility. A study of venture capital financing in the biotech industry found that the professional ties and company connections of entrepreneurs were critical in determining whether the venture received financing. Prior service at a reputable company seemed to suggest competence. The nature of the prior organizational ties appeared to make a difference, with entrepreneurs who had worked for pharmaceutical firms being viewed more favorably than those who had worked for research institutions (Higgins and Gulati, 2000). These references are important because they help the resource provider judge the competence, commitment, and reliability of the entrepreneur.

For the corporate entrepreneur, it is important to be able to frame the proposed venture in ways which fit the corporate strategy and the objectives of individual departments from which help is sought. Because corporate assets will be tapped, the proposed venture is less dependent solely upon the entrepreneur. Often, a senior manager will begin to sponsor the project, thereby adding credibility and the ability to get cooperation from people both inside and outside the corporation. (Some corporations are organized so that new venture departments take over the idea if it is outside the domain of an operating division and then try to develop it (Kanter et al., 1991b).) Starr and MacMillan note that corporate entrepreneurs, even when they have social capital, are less likely to draw upon it to co-opt legitimacy and underutilized assets. They attribute this to the fact that established corporations do not tend to have an asset-parsimonious mindset, and because corporate entrepreneurs are expected to follow established procedures and to follow the rules. They are expected to accomplish the original plan and may not have the time to develop social capital (Starr and MacMillan, 1990).

For both independent and corporate entrepreneurs, geography makes a difference. Ventures located in clusters of similar firms are probably more likely to be able to raise capital. This is because both angel investors and venture capital firms are likely to be located there and both like to be able to monitor and assist the firms in which they have invested. These financing sources can also use their networks in these geographic areas as they engage in "due diligence" and investigate the venture.

If a corporate venture is in a different line of business from the parent corporation, it is an interesting question whether it should be located near corporate headquarters or in a cluster of similar ventures. The former permits the venture to build network ties with key parts of the corporation; the latter permits the venture to build ties outside the organization and benefit from knowledge spillover about technology and market developments within the cluster. Xerox Corporation's Palo Alto Research Center (PARC) illustrated the latter approach. It was the first with such innovations as the mouse and windows technology; however, its distance from corporate headquarters in Rochester, New York, may have been one reason why the corporation never capitalized upon its technology satisfactorily.

Implementation and Early Development

It is as a venture actually begins to be implemented that many questions are answered, including how the product performs and whether customers commit. The cost of testing an idea varies greatly. For some businesses based upon the personal skills of the founder, such as consulting or serving as a sales representative, it may be possible to start on a part-time basis. If orders materialize and customers are satisfied, it may be developed gradually, financing growth from earnings and hiring key employees as the business grows. By contrast, businesses based upon major product development or requiring substantial investment in physical facilities may require large investments before the first sale is made. For instance, an entrepreneur planning to build a hotel cannot build one room, see if he or she can rent it, and then expand.

It is during this time that the venture may form alliances – with suppliers, with distributors, with customers, with licensers, or with firms which provide key functions, such as fulfillment. Such arrangements permit the startup to leverage its limited resources and to concentrate upon what it does best. Often, the alliance partner has complementary resources or specialized knowledge, such as a pharmaceutical firm's sales force or its ability to work with the FDA (Teece, 1986). Use of alliance partners offers further benefits to the independent startup. If alliance partners have complementary assets in place, then the venture may be able to get to market more quickly, vital when first mover advantages are seen to be important. In addition, if the startup does not have to invest in these other assets, then the basic concepts can be tested at lower cost.

As firms begin to work with partners, the relationships can vary from arm's-length transactions to embedded relationships. Often, the initial relationships are lacking in social relationships, but some of these may develop into closer ties. When there is a high degree of embeddedness, firms may invest in specialized assets, develop specific knowledge of their partner's plans and problems, and do more than required by the letter of the contract (Uzzi, 1997: 47).

The independent startup can face special challenges in finding alliance partners. Established firms are more likely to form alliances with companies with which they previously had alliances, presumably because a level of trust has developed between the organizations (Gulati, 1998). However, new companies do not have previously existing alliance partners. Furthermore, they lack credibility (Stinchcombe, 1965). Potential partners do not know whether they can or will do what they say they will do (Niederkofler, 1991).

New firms, which typically do not occupy central positions in networks, may have opportunities to form alliances when their industries experience structure-loosening events, such as major changes in technology or ways of competing (Madhaven et al., 1998). Eisenhardt and Schoonhoven (1996), in examining the alliances formed by new semiconductor firms, showed that the social capital of the top management team also could facilitate alliance formation. The rate of alliance formation was greater for startups whose top management teams were larger and whose members had worked for more previous employers and at higher levels within those organizations.

Larson traced the process by which seven young firms developed close collaborative alliances. Initially there was a trial period in which there was primary economic exchange. Then, a partnership developed, sometimes with information exchanges, transfer of scheduling and forecasting information, and collaborative R&D. The two sides learned about each other and developed trust and norms of reciprocity (Larson, 1992; Larson and Starr 1993). The processes described take time and this particular research did not focus upon how firms with no operating history might achieve close relations with alliance partners. Uzzi's research in the apparel industry suggested that entrepreneurs who had achieved embedded relationships in their prior positions sometimes were able to utilize these relationships in getting assistance as they got started in a new firm. "We never make gifts (i.e., sewing machines, hangers, racks, new lighting) to potential startups unless there is a history of personal contact" (Uzzi, 1997: 52). Specific institutions, such as "The 128 Venture Group" in Boston, can play a role in bringing potential alliance partners together, as can organized forums intended to aid the formation of international alliances (Nohria, 1992; Hara and Kanai, 1994).

If the startup forms an alliance with a larger firm, there may be problems in developing working relationships across the organizations. The agreement may have been negotiated with senior managers of the larger firm. However, whether lower-level managers, engineers, and salespeople will be enthusiastic about working with their counterparts in the startup is not assured. The evolution of the alliance will depend upon whether there is strategic fit and operating fit. The latter must be achieved by middle managers who must deal with the procedural, structural, and cultural differences between organizations (Niederkofler, 1991). There may be differences in alliance experience, differences in objectives to be realized through the alliance, and differences in decision-making processes (Beamish, 1999). Legal agreements are not enough. It is important to build relations through day-to-day exchanges (Larson, 1992). If the firms are to work closely together, differences in decision-making styles and in cultures may create friction.

As firms get established, they vary in the extent to which they develop embedded ties with other organizations. Several studies have examined the factors associated with having closer ties. One study reported that if the founders were still with the small firm, it was more likely to be involved in close ties with suppliers (Lipparini and Sobrero, 1994). Another found that strategies developed by young firms, such as emphasis upon focused product innovation or a broad product line, tended to be associated with ties to particular kinds of organizations (Ostgaard and Birley, 1994). One Norwegian study found that the members of the board of directors may assist in developing contacts, particularly if they have incentives to do so (Borch and Huse, 1993). Sometimes negotiations occur within companies, as those who are the "linking pins" with outside organizations persuade their colleagues to be involved (Hara and Kanai, 1994).

When a startup develops a relationship with an alliance partner, there are risks. To commit with one firm usually means not to commit to another. Both lock-in and lock-out effects can occur (Gulati et al., 2000: 210). Mutual dependency develops. However, the relationship may not be as important to the partner as to the startup. Sometimes the partner misrepresents its abilities or does not follow through or exploits the alliance to learn what the new company has developed. These moral hazard problems have been studied in alliance research. One study of opportunism in research alliances reported that opportunism was less likely to occur if there was congruence between the firms, with the founders having come from organizations similar to the alliance partner. It was also found that the number of active alliances between partners was negatively related to opportunism. There was an inverted U-shaped relationship between age of the relationship and opportunism; for a period of about 4.6 years there was increasing opportunism before it then declined (Deeds and Hill, 1999). If the firms can develop embedded ties, based upon trust and personal friendship, then the agreement is more likely to be mutually rewarding (Uzzi, 1997).

However, even if the alliance partners are performing to the best of their ability, the startup's prospects depend upon the success of the partners and of the network members. If partners fail or are simply less effective than the partners of competitors, then the startup will suffer. Environmental jolts may cause alliance partners to exit, lessening the number of partners with which the venture has relationships (Venkataraman and Van de Ven, 1998).

The corporate venture faces a somewhat different set of challenges in implementing the venture concept and in forming alliance relationships. Like the independent startup, it must put the parts together, test the venture concept, and assemble data that helps to determine the promise of the venture. To secure funding and corporate support, the corporate entrepreneur must demonstrate that the venture is consistent with corporate strategy and that the market potential is enough to be interesting to the corporation. (Independent ventures are not necessarily under the same pressure to develop substantial scale.) Burgelman argues that there is often a variation–selection–retention framework, in which entrepreneurial initiatives compete for resources. Autonomous initiatives at middle and operating levels result in a variety of alternatives. Top management ratifies the outcome of the process, thereby leading to new ventures and greater variety within the organization (Burgelman, 1991). As part of these processes the internal entrepreneur may have to find an existing division or a new venture department sponsor or take on the proposed venture. Unlike the startup, it may be able to make use of assets within the corporation, including people in engineering, manufacturing, and sales. However, in utilizing corporate assets the venture may be handed off to others who then take responsibility for the venture. This can lead to emotional problems for team members as they deal with psychological separation (Van de Ven et al., 1999: 55).

If alliances with external organizations are necessary, the established corporation may be able to benefit from its existing network ties. Using its present relationships it may be able to persuade existing alliance partners to help in developing the new venture. In part, this is because the venturing corporation may be able to provide benefits to the alliance partner in other ways, through transactions and resource sharing involving other lines of business. In addition, alliance partners may view corporate ventures as more attractive because they have the assets of the parent corporation behind them and thus are more likely to be operated at a large scale.

Within the established corporation, the developing venture needs to establish relationships with other organizational units. These relationships may permit the venture to leverage limited resources, to learn, and to establish credibility. One study reported that prior network centrality, perceived trustworthiness, and strategic relatedness affect the rate at which new linkages are created between a new unit and other parts of the organization (Tsai, 2000).

As a venture moves forward, whether it be independent or corporate, it typically operates in an environment of great change. It can be viewed as a nest of options (Luehrman, 1998). The venture can be dropped or further investments can be made as events unfold. For the independent venture, a challenge is to manage cash flows so that uncertainty can be resolved and promise demonstrated before cash runs out. The investors (who might be alliance partners) will often make staged investments, with the option to withdraw if the venture begins to look unattractive (Sahlman, 1992). An established corporation will typically consider its investments in a developing venture in the same way. In addition, the consideration of an individual venture will be affected by changes in overall corporate strategy and the interest or support of influential senior executives (Fast, 1977).

Influences upon Performance

Performance measures relating to networks and alliances can have several focal points. One is to consider the performance of the individual entrepreneur or venture and relate that to network or alliance activity. Another is to examine the success of particular dyads, relationships between entrepreneurial ventures and alliance partners. A third is to consider the implications of membership in a network, including the success of entire networks.

Judging entrepreneurial performance can be challenging. Some ventures require long lead times to get established. Ventures usually have a concentration of risk in only a few products or markets, such that environmental shocks can cause rapid changes in prospects or performance. In corporate entrepreneurship, individual ventures may have various objectives, not all of which are reflected in the economic success of the venture. They may be intended as learning experiences, or as models to change corporate culture, or as vehicles to retain valued employees (Kanter et al., 1991b). Individual alliances also may be set up with various goals in mind. Some are not intended to have long lives, but are intended primarily as vehicles for learning.

We might expect that entrepreneurs reporting larger networks and closer embedded relationships would experience better performance because of the informational and exchange advantages of these ties. We would also suppose that those entering into alliances would benefit because they could concentrate their efforts and leverage their assets as alliance partners take on certain critical functions. Furthermore, the benefits of alliances may vary, depending upon the nature of the alliance partner and the way in which the alliance relationship is managed.

Previous research has considered the extent to which the action set of the entrepreneur (those network members actually involved in some way in the founding) is related to subsequent growth of the new venture. Hansen reported that the size and degree (extent to which network members know and interact with each other) were both related to subsequent new venture growth (Hansen, 1995).

A study of six technology-intensive firms in China reported that higher-growth firms tended to have more total contacts in their networks and interacted more frequently and with more resource exchange with those contacts (Zhao and Aram, 1995).

Startup biopharmaceutical firms demonstrated a positive relationship between number of cooperative relationships and innovation output (number of patents). Furthermore, innovation output did not attract large firm relationships, but rather depended upon them (Shan et al., 1994).

Entry into formal alliances seems to have benefited many small firms. An international survey of manufacturers with fewer than 200 employees reported overall satisfaction rates with alliance experiences of 73 to 96 percent across eight countries (Weaver, 2000: 393). However, as the author notes, many factors may affect whether particular alliances are successful.

A study of 150 semiconductor firms found that young and small firms benefit more from large and innovative strategic alliance partners than do old and large organizations. In part, this is because young and small firms have uncertain prospects. Alliances with respected partners serve as signals which convey recognition and social status (Stuart, 2000).

Baum and co-authors examined the performance of Canadian biotech startups and considered how characteristics of alliance partners impacted startup performance (Baum et al., 2000). They found evidence that a number of kinds of alliances increased initial venture growth; however, industry association membership and government laboratory alliances were associated with lower rates of growth. Alliances which provided access to more diverse information raised several measures of growth. Alliances with potential rival biotech firms experienced lower growth. If the biotech partner had a strong patenting record, this helped the startup; if its patenting record was weak, this hurt the startup. It appears that the particular alliance partners chosen did make a difference.

Young high-technology firms face uncertain prospects, making it difficult for investors to judge how they will do. A study of young biotechnology firms going public found that those with prominent strategic alliance partners and equity investors were able to go public more quickly and earn greater valuations in their IPOs (initial public offerings). There appeared to be a transfer of status between the parties; for the young firms sponsorship by well-known partners substituted for experience and accomplishments (Stuart et al., 1999).

Several studies have examined the conditions under which alliance relationships are more successful. One study focused upon inter-firm agreements involving young high-technology firms. Whether R&D cooperative arrangements related positively or negatively to young firm growth depended upon the background of the management teams. For those with prior industry and technical experience, R&D cooperative agreements were associated with higher growth (McGee and Dowling, 1994). Apparently strong management backgrounds enabled firms to learn and benefit from these alliances.

A study focusing upon the perceived success of individual alliances reported that trust and perceived partner integrity (but not alliance longevity) were associated with alliance success (Meyer et al., 1997).

It is not always the case that the closer the ties the better. Firms seeking bank financing were more likely to get loans and to receive lower interest rates on loans if their network included a mix of embedded ties and arm's-length ties with other banks. This mix led to network complementarity, with the arm's-length ties enabling firms to scan the market for loan prices and structures and with the embedded ties leading to lower interest rates (Uzzi, 1999).

The challenge of trying to prevent opportunistic action, in which partners would seek to take advantage of the young firm, was examined in one study. It was found that opportunism decreased if there was congruence between the partners, if there was more frequent contact between them, if they had a number of active alliances, and if the firms had increased experience with one another. Surprisingly, more alliances between the partners was associated with more (not less) opportunism. These findings were unexpected because, as the authors hypothesized, one would expect that more alliances would have led to more stable relationships. Opportunistic action within one alliance would put all the alliances at risk. The authors did not try to explain this unexpected finding. Relational contacts developed through personal interaction were more important than structural or contractual deterrents (Deeds and Hill, 1999).

In regard to performance of networks, Dyer found that supplier–automaker networks which were more specialized were more successful. Specialization involved alliance partners making investments in assets specific to the relationship. Of course, there are costs and risks associated with such investments, most notably if there is low trust between the partners or if there are large exogenous shocks in the industry (Dyer, 1996).

The effect of alliance governance relationships upon new venture performance has been studied. Alliances formed in functions outside the functional expertise of the new venture (such as an R&D firm forming a marketing alliance) showed somewhat higher growth with contractual, rather than equity ownership agreements (Wisnieski and Dowling, 1997).

In regard to corporate entrepreneurship, we know that new venture creation within established corporations faces major challenges. One study reported that, on average, established firms take twice as long as independent ventures to reach profitability and end up half as profitable (Weiss, 1981). Biggadike's study of corporate new ventures in the PIMS database reported that the average new corporate venture studied took seven years to reach break-even (Biggadike, 1979). The literature using a social network transaction perspective and that focusing upon corporate alliances are both very large. However, much less has been done in examining explicitly how networks and alliances bear upon corporate new venture success.

The extant research on performance implications of network activities for entrepreneurial firms, and particularly for entrepreneurial ventures within established corporations, is limited. The potential benefits from networks include better information, added credibility, and exchange relationships. However, the development and maintenance of networks is not without cost. Many of the studies suggest that involvement with larger and more interconnected networks has a positive effect. However, those who have reviewed the body of existing work are not uniform in their assessments. Johannisson observed, "the empirical support for the proposition that personal networking enhances individual firm survival and growth is not indisputable" (Johannisson, 2000: 378). Nevertheless, Stuart concluded that "the evidence rests heavily on the side that alliances engender superior performance" (Stuart, 2000: 793). In addition, alliance success appears to depend upon the characteristics of alliance partners and upon the ability of the management team of the startup to manage and learn from the relationship.

Conclusion

Entrepreneurs trying to start ventures capitalize upon the social capital they have developed and work to develop new network ties which can help them be successful. Research which examines how these ties have been developed before startup and how they can be developed in the middle of the formation process seems promising. Entrepreneurs entering new industries or new geographic areas face particular challenges. Research examining the process by which they are successful (or are not successful) in developing new ties is needed.

The development of intracorporate networks is relevant to new venture creation within established corporations. Although some work has been done in this area, we know very little about how corporate entrepreneurs with varying degrees of social capital proceed to develop and capitalize upon internal networks to obtain the legitimacy and resources they need.

Corporate ventures usually involve some departure from the traditional business of the corporation. To the extent that this involves developing new external ties, we need to know how entrepreneurs within the corporation proceed to do this. The contrasts in the processes utilized by corporate entrepreneurs versus independent entrepreneurs seem worthy of examination.

Independent ventures based upon new technology often enter into alliances with larger firms which have complementary assets. Sometimes they enter into multiple alliances with different alliance partners, with each agreement relating to a different area of application or specific technology. Many large firms have portfolios of alliances and extensive experience. Gulati quoted one manager: "One thing that also makes it easier for us to enter new alliances is our extensive experience with doing alliances. Forming a new partnership is not a big deal anymore – we have our own formula and we know it works!" (Gulati, 1999). However, new firms, with their limited history, scope, and managerial resources, have little relevant experience. The challenges in safeguarding intellectual capital and in managing multiple relationships appear to be formidable. Research examining how new ventures are and are not successful in doing this is needed.

Johannisson noted that "Personal networking is . . . a basic, existential activity, natural and needed by every human being." Personal contact facilitates the transmission of tacit knowledge and leads to the development of embedded relationships. Therefore, he observes, "personal networking is for practical and emotional reasons spatially concentrated" (Johannisson, 2000: 376–7; 382). It is interesting to consider how new methods of communicating, such as the Internet, may affect the process of creating networks. Will it be more likely that entrepreneurs will develop ties with geographically distant individuals and organizations? Will entrepreneurs be less limited by their geographical locations, so that those in relatively isolated regions may be able to develop the networks they need to succeed? Future research will enable us to consider these interesting questions.

References

Aldrich, H. and Zimmer, C. 1986. Entrepreneurship through social networks. In D. Sexton and R. Smilor (eds), *The art and science of entrepreneurship*: Cambridge, MA: Ballinger Publishing Company, 3–23.

Amit, R. and Zott, C. 2000. Value drivers of e-commerce business models. Working Paper, The Wharton School, University of Pennsylvania.

Baum, J. A. C., Calabrese, T., and Silverman, B. S. 2000. Don't go it alone: Alliance network composition and startup's performance in Canadian biotechnology. *Strategic Management Journal*, 21(3): 267–94.

Baum, J. and Oliver, C. 1992. Institutional embeddedness and the dynamics of organizational populations. *American Sociological Review*, 57: 540–59.

Beamish, P. W. 1999. The role of alliances in international management. In R. W. Wright (ed.), *Research in global strategic management*, vol. 7. Greenwich, CT: JAI Press, 43–61.

Biggadike, R. 1979. The risky business of diversification. *Harvard Business Review*, 57(3): 103–11.

Birkinshaw, J. 1999. The determinants and consequences of subsidiary initiative in multinational corporations. *Entrepreneurship Theory and Practice*, 24(1): 9–36.

Birley, S. 1985. The role of networks in the entrepreneurial process. *Journal of Business Venturing*, 1(1): 107–17.

Borch, O. J. and Huse, M. 1993. Informal strategic networks and the board of directors. *Entrepreneurship Theory and Practice*, 18(1): 23–36.

Burgelman, R. A. 1983. A process model of internal corporate venturing in the diversified major firm. *Administrative Science Quarterly*, 28: 223–44.

Burgelman, R. 1991. Intraorganizational ecology of strategy making and organizational adaptation: Theory and field research. *Organization Science*, 2: 239–62.

Burt, R. 1992. *Structural holes: The social structure of competition.* Cambridge, MA: Harvard University Press.

Carter, N. M., Gartner, W. B., and Reynolds, P. D. 1996. Exploring start-up event sequences. *Journal of Business Venturing*, 11: 151–66.

Cooper, A. C. 1986. Entrepreneurship and high technology. In D. Sexton and R. Smilor (eds), *The art and science of entrepreneurship.* Cambridge, MA: Ballinger Publishing Company, 153–68.

Cooper, A. C., Dunkelberg, W. C., Woo, C. Y., and Dennis, Jr., W. J. 1990. *New business in America: the firms and their owners.* Washington, DC: The NFIB Foundation.

Covin, J. G. and Slevin, D. P. 1991. A conceptual model of entrepreneurship as firm behavior. *Entrepreneurship Theory and Practice*, 16(1): 7–25.

Deeds, D. L. and Hill, C. W. L. 1999. An examination of opportunistic action within research alliances: Evidence from the biotechnology industry. *Journal of Business Venturing*, 14(2): 141–64.

Dyer, J. H. 1996. Specialized supplier networks as a source of competitive advantage: Evidences from the auto industry. *Strategic Management Journal*, 17(4): 271–91.

Eisenhardt, K. M. and Schoonhoven, C. B. 1996. Resource-based view of strategic alliance formation: Strategic and social effects in entrepreneurial firms. *Organization Science*, 7(2): 136–50.

Fast, N. 1977. The evolution of corporate new venture divisions. Doctoral dissertation, Harvard Business School.

Floyd, S. W. and Wooldridge, B. 1999. Knowledge creation and social networks in corporate entrepreneurship: The renewal of organizational capability. *Entrepreneurship Theory and Practice*, 23(3): 123–43.

Gulati, R. 1998. Alliances and networks. *Strategic Management Journal*, 19: 293–317.

Gulati, R. 1999. Network location and learning: The influence of network resources and firm capabilities on alliance formation. *Strategic Management Journal*, 20(5): 397–420.

Gulati, R., Nohria, N., and Zaheer, A. 2000. Strategic networks. *Strategic Management Journal*, 21 (special issue): 203–15.

Hagedoorn, J. 1993. Understanding the rationale of strategic technology partnering: Interorganizational modes of cooperation and sectoral differences. *Strategic Management Journal*, 14(5): 371–85.

Hagedoorn, J. and Schakenraad, J. 1994. The effect of strategic technology alliances on company performance. *Strategic Management Journal*, 15 (4): 291–309.

Hansen, E. L. 1995. Entrepreneurial networks and new organization growth. *Entrepreneurship Theory and Practice*, 19(4): 7–20.

Hara, G. and Kanai, T. 1994. Entrepreneurial networks across oceans to promote international strategic alliances for small businesses. *Journal of Business Venturing*, 9(6): 489–507.

Hargadon, A. and Sutton, R. I. 2000. Building an innovation factory. *Harvard Business Review*, 78(3): 157–66.

Higgins, M. C. and Gulati, R. 2000. The effects of IPO ties on investment bank affiliation and IPO success. Working Paper, Harvard Business School.

Jaffe, A. B., Trajtenberg, M., and Henderson, R. 1993. Geographic localization of knowledge spillovers as evidenced by patent citations. *Quarterly Journal of Economics*, 108(3): 577–98.

Johannison, B. 1990. Economies of overview-guiding the external growth of small firms. *International Small Business Journal*, 9(1): 32–44.

Johannisson, B. 2000. Networking and entrepreneurial growth. In D. L. Sexton and H. Landstrom (eds), *The Blackwell handbook of entrepreneurship*. Malden, MA: Blackwell, 368–86.

Kanter, R. M. 1983. *The change masters*. New York: Simon and Schuster.

Kanter, R. M., North, J., Bernstein, A. P., and Williams, A. 1990. Engines of progress: designing and running entrepreneurial vehicles in established companies. *Journal of Business Venturing*, 5(6): 415–30.

Kanter, R. M., North, J., Richardson, L., Ingols, C., and Zolner, J. 1991a. Engines of progress: Designing and running entrepreneurial vehicles in established companies; Raytheon's new product center, 1969–1989. *Journal of Business Venturing*, 6(2): 145–63.

Kanter, R. M., Richardson, L., North, J. and Morgan, E. 1991b. Engines of progress: Designing and running entrepreneurial vehicles at established companies. The new venture process at Eastman Kodak. *Journal of Business Venturing*, 6(1): 63–82.

Krueger, N. F., Jr., and Brazeal, D. V. 1994. Entrepreneurial potential and potential entrepreneurs. *Entrepreneurship Theory and Practice*, 18(3): 91–104.

Larson, A. 1992. Network dyads in entrepreneurial settings: A study of the governance of exchange relationships. *Administrative Science Quarterly*, (37): 76–104.

Larson, A. and Starr, J. A. 1993. A network model of organization formation. *Entrepreneurship Theory and Practice*, 17(2): 5–15.

Laumann, E. O., Galaskiewicz, J. and Marsden, P. V. 1978. Community structure as interorganizational linkages. *Annual Review of Sociology*, 4: 455–84.

Lipparini, A. and Sobrero, M. 1994. The glue and the pieces: Entrepreneurship and innovation in small-firm networks. *Journal of Business Venturing*, 9(2): 125–40.

Luehrman, T. A. 1998. Strategy as a portfolio of real options. *Harvard Business Review*, 76(5): 89–99.

Madhaven, R., Koka, B. R., and Prescott, J. E. 1998. Networks in transition: How industry events (re)shape interfirm relationships. *Strategic Management Journal*, 19(5): 439–59.

McGee, J. E. and Dowling, M. J. 1994. Using R&D cooperative arrangements to leverage managerial experience: A study of technology-intensive new ventures. *Journal of Business Venturing*, 9(1): 33–48.

McGrath, R. G. 1999. Falling forward: Real options reasoning and entrepreneurial failure. *Academy of Management Review*, 24 (1): 13–30.

Meyer, G. D., Alvarez, S. A., and Blasick, J. 1997. Benefits of technology based strategic alliances. In P. Reynolds, W. D. Bygrave, N. M. Carter, P. Davidsson, W. B. Gartner, C. M. Mason, and P. P. McDougall (eds), *Frontiers of entrepreneurship research, 1997*. Babson Park, MA: Babson College, 629–42.

Miller, D. 1983. The correlates of entrepreneurship in three types of firms. *Management Science*, 29(7): 770–91.

Niederkofler, M. 1991. The evolution of strategic alliances: Opportunities for managerial influence. *Journal of Business Venturing*, 6(4): 237–57.

Nohria, N. 1992. Information and search in the creation of new business ventures: The case of the 128 venture group. In N. Niten and R. G. Eccles (eds), *Networks and organizations: structure, form, and action*. Boston: Harvard Business School, 240–61.

Ostgaard, T. A. and Birley, S. 1994. Personal networks and firm competitive strategy – A strategic or coincidental match? *Journal of Business Venturing*, 9(4), 281–305.

Palich, L. E. and Bagby, D. R. 1995. Using cognitive theory to explain entrepreneurial risk-taking: Challenging conventional wisdom. *Journal of Business Venturing*, 10(6): 425–38.

Palmer, D., Barber, B., Zhou, X., and Soysal, Y. 1995. The friendly and predatory acquisition of large U.S. corporations in the 1960s. *American Sociological Review*, 60: 469–500.

Podolny, J. M. 1994. Market uncertainty and the social character of economic exchange. *Administrative Science Quarterly*, 39: 458–83.

Reynolds, P. and Miller, B. 1992. New firm gestation: Conception, birth, and implications for research. *Journal of Business Venturing*, 7: 405–29.

Romo, F. P. and Schwartz, M. 1995. Structural embeddedness of business decisions: A sociological assessment of the migration behavior of plants between 1960 and 1985. *American Sociological Review*, 60: 874–907.

Rowley, T., Behrens, D., and Krackhardt, D. 2000. Redundant governance structures: An analysis of structural and relational embeddedness in the steel and semiconductor industries. *Strategic Management Journal*, 21 (special issue): 369–86.

Sahlman, W. A. 1992. Aspects of financial contracting in venture capital. In W. A. Sahlman and H. H. Stevenson (eds), *The entrepreneurial venture*. Boston: Harvard Business School, 222–42.

Saxenian, A. L. 1990. Regional networks and the resurgence of Silicon Valley. *California Management Review*, 33(1): 89–112.

Shan, W., Walker, G., and Kogut, B. 1994. Interfirm cooperation and startup innovation in the biotechnology industry. *Strategic Management Journal*, 15(5): 387–94.

Sharma, P. and Chrisman, J. J. 1999. Toward a reconciliation of the definitional issues in the field of corporate entrepreneurship. *Entrepreneurship Theory and Practice*, 23(3): 11–27.

Starr, J. A. and MacMillan, I. C. 1990. Resource co-optation via social contracting: Resource acquisition strategies for new ventures. *Strategic Management Journal*, 11 (special issue): 79–92.

Stevenson, H. H., Roberts, M. J., and Grousbeck, H. I. 1994. *New business ventures and the entrepreneur*, 4th edn. Burr Ridge, IL: Irwin.

Stinchcombe, A. L. 1965. Social structure and organizations. In J. G. March (ed.), *Handbook of organizations*. Chicago: Rand McNally.

Stuart, T. E. 2000. Interorganizational alliances and the performance of firms: A study of growth and innovation rates in a high-technology industry. *Strategic Management Journal*, 21(8): 791–811.

Stuart, T., Hoang, H., and Hybels, R. 1999. Interorganizational endorsements and the performance of new ventures. *Administrative Science Quarterly*, 44: 315–49.

Teece, D. J. 1986. Profiting from technological innovation: Implications for integration, collaboration, licensing and public policy. *Research Policy*, 15: 285–305.

Thornhill, S. and Amit, R. 2001. A dynamic perspective of internal fit in corporate venturing. *Journal of Business Venturing*, 16(1): 25–50.

Tsai, W. 2000. Social capital, strategic relatedness and the formation of organizational linkages. *Strategic Management Journal*, 21(9): 925–39.

Utterback, J. 1971. The process of technological innovation within the firm. *Academy of Management Journal*, 14: 75–88.

Uzzi, B. 1997. Social structure and competition in interfirm networks: The paradox of embeddedness. *Administrative Science Quarterly*, 42: 35–67.

Uzzi, B. 1999. Embeddedness in the making of financial capital: how social relations and networks benefit firms seeking financing. *American Sociological Review*, 64: 481–505.

Van de Ven, A., Polley, D. E., Garud, R., and Venkataraman, S. 1999. *The innovation journey*. New York: Oxford University Press.

Venkataraman, S., MacMillan, I. C., and McGrath, R. C. 1992. Progress in research on corporate venturing. In D. L. Sexton and J. I. Kasarda (eds), *The state of the art in entrepreneurship*. Boston: PWS-Kent, 487–519.

Venkataraman, S. and Van de Ven, A. 1998. Hostile environmental jolts, transaction set, and new business. *Journal of Business Venturing*, 13(3): 231–55.

Vesper, K. H. 1992. New-venture ideas: Do not overlook experience factor. In W. A. Sahlman and H. H. Stevenson (eds), *The entrepreneurial venture*. Boston: Harvard Business School Publications.

Vesper, K. H. 1993. *New venture mechanics*. Englewood Cliffs, NJ: Prentice-Hall.

Von Hippel, E. 1988. *The sources of innovation*. New York: Oxford University Press.

Weaver, M. 2000. Strategies alliances as vehicles for international growth. In D. L. Sexton and H. Landstrom (eds), *The Blackwell handbook of entrepreneurship*. Malden, MA: Blackwell, 387–407.

Weiss, L. 1981. Start-up businesses: A comparison of performance. *Sloan Management Review*, 37–53.

Wisnieski, J. M. and Dowling, M. J. 1997. Strategic alliances in new ventures: Does governance structure affect new venture performance? In P. Reynolds et al. (eds) *Frontiers of entrepreneurship research 1997*. Babson Park, MA: Babson College, 643–55

Zhao, L. and Aram, J. D. 1995. Networking and growth of young technology – intensive ventures in China. *Journal of Business Venturing*, 10 (5): 349–70.

CHAPTER ELEVEN

Small Entrepreneurial Firms and Large Companies in Inter-Firm R&D Networks – the International Biotechnology Industry

John Hagedoorn, Nadine Roijakkers

Introduction

This chapter studies the role played by small entrepreneurial firms and large companies in the international biotechnology industry. The biotechnology industry is one of the main examples of current industries that are characterized by "hypercompetition" (D'Aveni, 1994), with a high degree of uncertainty about the combined effects of both new technologies and new market structures. It is an example of an industry with Schumpeterian competition where revolutionary changes in technology and innovative new products and processes have the potential to threaten the position of existing market leaders and their product-market positions (Liebeskind et al., 1996). It is also a sector where we find a large number of R&D alliances, in particular between large and small companies (Hagedoorn, 1996a; Kenney, 1986; Powell, 1996).

Throughout this chapter we will refer to the biotechnology "industry" although, given the above-mentioned characteristics, this is probably an incorrect term as its status as a separate industrial sector is still somewhat unclear. Strictly taken, biotechnology is not yet a regular industrial sector but a hybrid form of an "industry" with established companies, e.g., from the pharmaceutical sector, and a wide range of new biotechnology companies that are science based and technology driven but still with relatively few regular products and limited manufacturing capabilities (Powell, Koput, and Smith-Doerr, 1996). In other words, when we use the term industry in the following analysis, we recognize that we are mainly analyzing a group of companies that are engaged in R&D, innovation, and the manufacturing of products and processes that can be labeled as biotechnological activities.

Our contribution concentrates on the analysis of inter-firm networks of R&D partnerships and the role played by different groups of companies. This analysis of the role of different groups of companies and the structure of networks in the biotechnology industry follows the suggestion made by Hitt and Ireland (2000) and Shan, Walker, and Kogut (1994) that the study of network structures and the role played by different groups of companies is of importance to understanding emerging sectors such as the biotechnology industry. Within these eminent networks we will pay special attention to the role of small entrepreneurial firms that are known to play such an important role in this industry (Kenney, 1986; Powell et al., 1996).

We have chosen the period from 1985 to 1995 because this period is expected to encompass the end of the first period of the growth of the biotechnology industry with the emergence of a large number of small biotechnology companies during the 1980s and a first phase of some maturation where the commercialization of biotechnology is becoming more important (Arora and Gambardella, 1990; Galambos and Sturchio, 1998). This period also covers the years in which inter-firm partnering has risen rapidly, in this sector as well as in many other fields of technology and sectors of industry (Hagedoorn, 1996a).

In the following, we will first discuss the different roles that large companies and small entrepreneurial firms play in generating innovative output and major technological changes. The perspective that is chosen in our contribution is clearly influenced by the Schumpeterian tradition in the study of innovation. We also pay attention to the complementarities of large and small firms in the networks of R&D partnerships that have become so important in the biotechnology industry. These sections lead us to a set of three research questions that will guide the empirical analysis of this chapter. These research questions focus on the general structure of the inter-firm network of R&D partnerships, changes in the position of small entrepreneurial biotechnology firms, and the role of large pharmaceutical companies. After a description of some methodological issues and an explanation of the data used in our analysis, the second part of the chapter is devoted to an empirical analysis that concentrates on the main issues introduced with the research questions. We first analyse some basic trends in R&D partnerships since the mid-1980s. This is followed by an in-depth analysis of the changes in the inter-firm R&D networks, where attention is paid to groups of companies as well as to the nodal players in the different networks that emerge over time. In the final section of this chapter we discuss our main findings and draw some major conclusions from our contribution.

Innovation – the Role of Both Large Companies and Small Entrepreneurial Firms

Our understanding of the importance of innovation and our perception of the role played by different categories of companies, such as large companies and relatively small entrepreneurial firms, can be clearly placed within the Schumpeterian tradition. We follow Schumpeter (1934) where innovation is described in the context of "new combinations" that replace existing products and markets. As suggested by Hagedoorn (1996b) and others, we understand these Schumpeterian new combinations as "technical" innovations in terms of new products or new quality of products, new methods of production, or new sources of supply of raw materials. These technical innovations have to be distinguished from "market or organizational" innovations which are new combinations in terms of new markets or new industry structures.

For the pharmaceutical industry, modern biotechnology is a clear example of a set of new combinations with new technologies and state-of-the-art scientific understanding that creates a technological discontinuity. In the context of this technological discontinuity, innovations not only affect the introduction of new products and new processes but these technical innovations also come with new "players," i.e., companies that restructure parts of the pharmaceutical industry that has gradually become mature (Powell, 1996; Powell et al., 1996). These new scientific and technical innovations from biotechnology, that are currently introduced, are largely based on immunology and molecular biology, including recombinant DNA technology, whereas the "traditional" pharmaceutical industry and its innovations are largely based on organic chemistry. Some observers understand these changes to be so fundamental that they describe the technological discontinuity in the pharmaceutical industry, as caused by modern biotechnology, as a clear shift in the existing technological paradigm (Orsenigo, 1989; Della Valle and Gambardella, 1993; Walsh and Galimberti, 1993).

When we consider the innovative role played by both large companies and smaller entrepreneurial firms, there is also a strong Schumpeterian flavor to our understanding of the contribution of these different categories of companies. The importance of the entrepreneurial company as a major generator of new innovations is most clearly stressed in the "early" Schumpeter (1934). In this early work, entrepreneurial companies are small, independent companies that act as major agents of change within new industries. These entrepreneurial companies are innovators that successfully introduce new products whose development is expected to be largely financed through external sources and not so much through internal financial resources (cash flow). In modern strategic management terminology: this Schumpeterian entrepreneurship is based on proactive strategies that capitalize on firm-specific advantages and innovative capabilities, financed through bank loans and venture capital. The Schumpeterian entrepreneur is not necessarily a strictly rational, economically maximizing agent, a risk taker or a capitalist, as in the "classical" theories of entrepreneurship by Knight and Say (Marco, 1985), but primarily an agent of change who is searching for new opportunities (Santarelli and Pesciarelli, 1990; Hagedoorn, 1996b).

Many elements of these Schumpeterian entrepreneurial firms are clearly present in the biotechnology industry. In fact both Kenney (1986) and Powell et al. (1996) depict small biotechnology firms as an ideal type of modern entrepreneurial company. As mentioned by Arora and Gambardella (1990), Pisano (1991), Barley, Freeman, and Hybels (1992), and Powell et al. (1996), small new biotechnology companies are frequently financed through venture capital or loans and equity participation of large companies. Originally based on university research that led to major scientific and technological changes, nearly all of the small biotechnology companies also started as new entrants to the pharmaceutical industry (Kenney, 1986; Pisano, 1990; Powell, 1996).

In terms of their organizational setting and their organizational culture, most of the small biotechnology companies are quite different from the "standard" company that one finds in traditional industries. New biotechnology companies seem to be driven by scientific discoveries and innovative performance and not only by regular profit-seeking (Lumerman and Liebeskind, 1997). Also, the "academic culture" within these innovation-driven and loosely organized companies, with their informal, non-hierarchical structures, sets them apart from many other "traditional" companies (Pisano, 1991; Powell, 1996).

If we look at the role of large companies in Schumpeter, we have to understand that there also is an important role for these large companies in many publications by Schumpeter. Specifically the "older" Schumpeter (1942) pictures a world of "modern, trustified capitalism" where large science-based companies dominate the innovative environment and where innovation has become routinized in large research laboratories and R&D departments. It is this particular perspective on the role of large companies that for a long period, during the 1950s, 1960s, and 1970s, dominated the understanding of the role of large companies as the main source of innovation (see Kamien and Schwartz, 1982; Scherer, 1984).

In the combined biotechnology and pharmaceutical industry the role of large companies is most clearly found in the dominant role that these companies play in the more traditional pharmaceutical sub-sectors (Arora and Gambardella, 1990). Large companies, with their extensive R&D activities and their long-term experience with time-consuming clinical trials, have come to dominate the innovation process in the traditional pharmaceutical industry. This dominance is based on their leading role in incremental innovation, exploiting their current organic chemical knowledge base and their ability to expand existing portfolios of pharmaceutical products.

Mutual dependence of large and small companies

Some authors (Hakansson, Kjellberg, and Lundgren, 1993; Kenney, 1986; Rothaermel, 2000) stress the importance of complementarity between small, entrepreneurial firms and large companies, in particular in high-tech industries. The basis for this complementarity is to be found in the variety of resources, capabilities, and complementary innovative expertise such as those described in the above.

During the 1980s, when new biotechnology became relevant to the pharmaceutical industry, a certain degree of mutual dependence developed almost instantaneously between large pharmaceutical companies and a group of relatively small new biotechnology firms (Arora and Gambardella, 1990; Pisano, 1991; Powell, 1996). These small biotechnology companies, most of them US-based, have developed a reputation for their R&D capabilities and applied laboratory research in advanced biotechnology at the scientific and technological frontier. Large pharmaceutical companies were already known for their vast body of engineering know-how necessary for scaling up from a laboratory setting to the actual manufacturing process of new pharmaceutical products. They also have the "deep pockets" that are necessary for the extensive and costly clinical testing required as part of the government regulatory process for new diagnostic products and new therapeutic drugs. Furthermore, large companies are known for their financial resources which enable them to deal with the costs of the final stage of commercialization and the successful worldwide market introduction and distribution of safe and effective pharmaceutical products.

The obvious complementarities between both groups of companies during the early period of modern biotechnology led to a mutual dependence as companies started to collaborate on various projects (Laamanen and Autio, 1996; Slowinski, Seelig, and Hull, 1996). This mutual dependence in cooperative projects consisted of financial support and regulatory know-how provided by large pharmaceutical companies to small entrepreneurial biotechnology companies, in return for which large companies acquired access to the research skills of these small biotechnology companies (Arora and Gambardella, 1990; Pisano, 1991; Barley et al., 1992; Shan et al., 1994; Powell, 1996). With the increasing number of new products based on pharmaceutical biotechnology, collaboration between small entrepreneurial firms and large companies also provides the first group with access to new markets and distribution facilities.

Networks as the locus of innovation

The mutual dependence of large pharmaceutical companies and small entrepreneurial biotechnology firms also meant that the locus of innovation in the pharmaceutical industry has gradually changed. Collaboration by these different companies is part of a broader trend in many industries and technologies where the interdisciplinarity of fields of science and technology, the dependence on a substantial stock of knowledge, and the costs of R&D force even the largest companies to collaborate with others (Hagedoorn, 1993). In the biotechnology industry these general developments, together with sector-specific scientific and technological developments, have led to a situation where large pharmaceutical companies are no longer the sole locus of innovation (Arora and Gambardella, 1990). As in so many other industries and fields of technology, extensive collaboration in this sector has led to rather dense networks of companies that enter into all sorts of alliances with a large number of other companies (Hagedoorn, 1990, 1993; Powell et al., 1996). In the biotechnology industry this mutual knowledge resource dependency between groups of large and small companies has led to dense networks of R&D collaboration between a variety of companies, where small firms play an important role in this new locus of innovation.

Some authors (e.g., Arora and Gambardella, 1990; Oakey, 1993; Saviotti, 1998) mention that the network-like structure of this locus of innovation, with both intensive inter-firm collaboration in general and specific cooperation between large companies and small entrepreneurial firms, could be a temporary phenomenon that coincides with the immaturity of biotechnology as a new technological paradigm developed during the 1980s. As the industry matures, small entrepreneurial companies could be taken over or their services could become redundant. Large companies could become more important for the new biotechnology-based pharmaceutical industry as such, as well as for the inter-firm R&D networks that have developed over time. Others (e.g., Pisano, 1991; Segers, 1992; Powell, 1996; Powell et al., 1996; Senker and Sharp, 1997), however, seem to expect that these networks of R&D collaboration in the biotechnology industry are of a more long-term nature because functionally specialized companies can easily maintain various relations with each other through distinctive transactions. In particular, the "nodal" role of small biotechnology companies, both in terms of their critical role as carriers of new scientific knowledge and in their role as major network players with multiple partnerships, is expected to be a long-term affair that will affect the continuation of a network-like structure of innovation in the biotechnology industry for decades (Powell, 1996; Senker and Sharp, 1997; Galambos and Sturchio, 1998).

Research Questions

As the biotechnology industry gradually became somewhat more mature, some phenomena and patterns, discussed above, that characterized the R&D networks of the 1980s might successively have become less significant during the 1990s while new patterns were emerging. In that context one has to consider in particular the density of networks that followed the growth in R&D cooperation and the role of different groups of companies in these networks. The literature discussed in the above clearly suggests a number of specific research questions that will guide our empirical investigation in the following sections. These research questions are:

- Are inter-firm networks in the biotechnology industry becoming less dense or is their density increasing?
- Is the well-established role of small biotechnology firms as nodal players in these inter-firm networks decreasing over time?
- Are R&D partnerships between large pharmaceutical companies becoming a more important element in these networks of innovation?

Research methodology and data

The core of this chapter is found in the empirical analysis of the evolution of the structure of inter-firm alliance networks in biotechnology and the role played by different categories of cooperating firms. Most attention is paid to measuring variation in network density over time and analyzing the extent to which small entrepreneurial biotechnology firms and/or large pharmaceutical companies play a central role in these networks.

Based on our first research question, which refers to increasing or decreasing density of inter-firm networks, we expect that an increasing or decreasing network density will show up in a growing or declining average number of alliances per firm. To study this aspect of network structure, we calculated the ratio of the total number of R&D alliances between firms to the number of participating companies for each year. The total number of alliances for each year was obtained by counting the number of dyads (relations between two firms) at the level of cooperating firms.

In the present context we do not consider the calculation of standard network density indices as a meaningful alternative to the density indicator that we propose. A standard network density index is defined as the ratio of the actual number of alliances between firms to the possible number of links. Comparing these indices from one year to the next year requires that the calculations be based on a constant number of network participants over time (Barley et al., 1992). One option is to compute density indices on the basis of a constant subset of the most active players. Many small biotechnology firms in our population have engaged in only one alliance during the period of investigation. If we based our analysis on a constant subset of the most active players, many small firms would disappear from the population, which is not a desired outcome in light of our research objectives.

Our second research question considers the role of small entrepreneurial biotechnology firms as major network participants. In that context we compare the partnering behaviour of small firms to large companies. To evaluate these alliance activities, we calculated the number of R&D alliances per employee for both groups of firms. We first classified each of the firms in our population into one of three distinct size categories, based on their number of employees during the period of study. Firms with less than or equal to 500 employees are regarded as small and those having between 501 and 5,000 employees are considered as medium-sized companies. Firms with over 5,001 employees are classified as large companies. We created a separate category for academic or governmental institutions. Due to the small size and/or private status of some firms we could only obtain information on their size for a few years. We classified these firms into one of the three categories on the basis of the available information.

For small entrepreneurial biotechnology firms and large pharmaceutical companies we calculated, for both categories, the ratio of the total number of R&D alliances between companies to the number of cooperating firms for each year. The total number of alliances for each year was obtained by counting the number of dyads at the level of cooperating firms. For both small and large firms, we divided the results obtained by the means of the appropriate employee categories to control for any size effects on alliance activity. We transformed the mean numbers of employees into a logarithmic scale (natural logarithm) to account for size differentials, which are unrelated to technological activities of companies. Small biotechnology firms typically employ mainly R&D specialists and therefore they have, compared to large pharmaceutical firms, lower numbers of employees in many other functional areas, such as production, marketing, sales, etc.

For our third research question, which looks at the role of R&D alliances among large pharmaceutical firms, we examine the distribution of alliances between firms of similar and different size classes. If large firms have come to play a more central role in alliances than small entrepreneurial firms, we expect the number of alliances between large firms to have increased as well. An intensification of R&D partnering between large and small firms would point at ongoing complementarity between both categories of cooperating firms. For each year we calculated the total numbers of dyads between large firms, small firms, and between large and small companies as percentages of the overall numbers of dyads in that year. These overall numbers also include R&D partnerships involving medium-sized firms. However, given the limited role of medium-sized companies (about 10 percent of the population) and the emphasis in our research questions on large and small companies, the group of medium-sized firms receives little or no attention in the following.

In order to provide some further details about the evolution of networks and the role played by small biotechnology firms and large pharmaceutical companies, we will represent these networks using a non-metric multidimensional scaling (MDS) technique. MDS is a data reduction procedure somewhat comparable to principal component analysis and other factor-analytical methods. One of the main advantages of MDS is that it can usually, but not necessarily, fit an appropriate model in two-dimensional pictures. More specifically, MDS offers a scaling of similarity data into points lying in an X-dimensional space. The purpose of this method is to provide coordinates for these points in such a way that distances between pairs of points fit as closely as possible to the observed similarities. In order to facilitate interpretation the solution is given in two dimensions, provided that the fit of the model is acceptable. A stress value indicates the goodness-of-fit of the configuration as this measures the proportion of the variance of the disparities that is accounted for by the MDS model, implying that lower values indicate a better goodness of fit (Hair et al., 1994).

Our analysis is restricted to periods of three years, since it is technically impossible to picture all firms in the network when more than three years of data are added. MDS plots are presented for the periods 1985–7, 1989–91, and 1993–5. Comparing these three periods allows us to add a dynamic perspective to our analysis. To improve the interpretation of the pictures, it is useful to draw lines of different styles and thickness between companies, indicating different degrees of cooperation intensity.

For our analyses we make use of two types of data: firm size data and data on R&D alliances. To describe network participants in terms of their size we collected information on the number of employees of each firm from various sources such as the Institute for Biotechnology Information, the US Securities and Exchange Commission, World Scope Global Researcher, Amadeus, and Dun and Bradstreet's Linkages.

The data on R&D alliances is taken from the MERIT–Cooperative Agreements and Technology Indicators (CATI) information system (see Hagedoorn, 1993). This databank contains information on nearly 10,000 cooperative agreements in various sectors, ranging from high-technology sectors such as IT and biotechnology to less technology-intensive sectors such as chemicals and heavy electrical equipment. Cooperative agreements are defined as mutual interests between independent industrial partners that are not linked through majority ownership. In the CATI database, only those agreements are being recorded that involve either a technology transfer or some form of jointly undertaken R&D. Information is also collected on joint ventures in which new technology is received from at least one of the partners, or on joint ventures having some R&D program. Other types of agreements such as production and marketing alliances are not included. Agreements formed between companies and governmental or academic institutions are generally not included in the database unless they involve at least two commercial companies.

Our present study focuses on those alliances that were established in the period 1985–95. In the CATI databank a total of 720 global R&D agreements involving 475 biotechnology and pharmaceutical companies were recorded during this time frame. Our data includes equity agreements, which comprise joint ventures and minority holdings, as well as non-equity alliances that consist of joint R&D agreements and R&D contracts. The data excludes agreements that are established within the context of national and international, government-sponsored, R&D cost-sharing programs. Our population of 475 participating firms comprises 111 large companies, 308 small ones, and 53 firms of medium size. We include three academic or governmental institutions. For our purpose, the most relevant information for each alliance is the number of companies involved, their names as well as the year in which the agreement was established.

This sample is representative for the biotechnology industry during the period 1985–95. Various sources indicate that during this period there are about 100 large pharmaceutical companies with a clear interest in biotechnology (OECD, 1993; OTA, 1988;

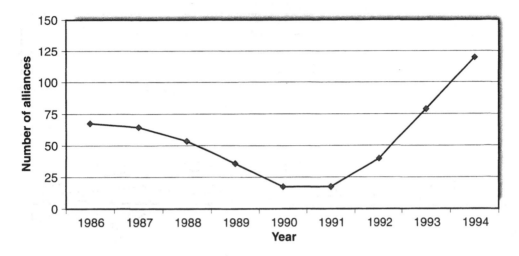

Figure 11.1 Number of newly established R&D alliances, biotechnology, three-year moving averages, 1985–95. *Source*: MERIT-CATI

Walsh and Galimberti, 1993). About two-thirds of the industry during this period consists of small and relatively young firms (Pisano, Shan, and Teece, 1988; Van Vliet, 1998; Walsh, Niosi, and Mustar, 1995).

Trends in R&D partnerships during the period 1985–95

Some general background to the more detailed analysis of the R&D networks in the biotechnology industry is given in figures 11.1 and 11.2. Figure 11.1 demonstrates the importance of pharmaceutical biotechnology in R&D partnering. Over 65 percent of all the biotechnology R&D alliances in the MERIT-CATI database are related to pharmaceutical biotechnology. In the most recent years that we analyze, pharmaceutical biotechnology even reaches a share of over 70 percent of all biotechnology alliances. The dominance of this particular sub-sector in the biotechnology industry, with so few alliances found in other biotechnology sectors, is one of the main reasons why our contribution focuses on the pharmaceutical biotechnology industry.

Figure 11.2 presents the trend in the growth of newly made R&D alliances in pharmaceutical biotechnology during the period 1985–95, as found in the MERIT-CATI database. This development can be characterized as a flattened U-shaped growth pattern. The growth in the number of new R&D alliances drops from about 70 partnerships made annually, as found for the mid-1980s, to about 20 alliances during the early 1990s, after which the growth pattern is restored with a steep increase up to over 100 newly established R&D partnerships during the mid-1990s. This particular growth pattern is quite identical to the pattern found for other industries (Hagedoorn, 1996a). However, to the best of our knowledge, there is no solid explanation in the literature for the specific pattern in the newly established alliances during the period 1985–95.

As a first step in the analysis of the inter-firm R&D networks, and also to assess the

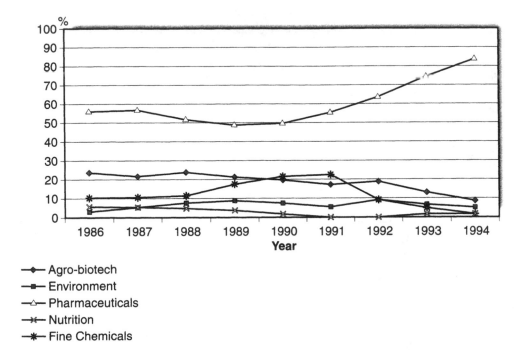

Figure 11.2   Distribution of newly established R&D alliances in various biotechnology-based sectors, three-year moving averages, 1985–95. *Source*: MERIT-CATI

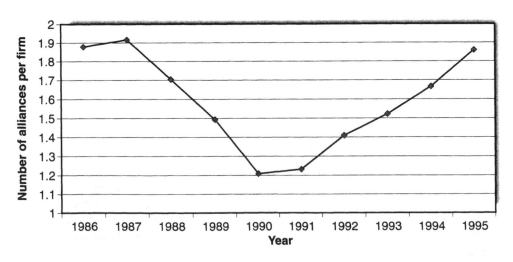

Figure 11.3   Number of newly established R&D alliances per firm, biotechnology, three-year moving averages, 1985–95. *Source*: MERIT-CATI

Table 11.1   Number of newly established R&D alliances and participating firms, biotechnology, 1985–95. *Source*: MERIT-CATI

Year	Alliances	Firms
1985	164	85
1986	158	79
1987	128	75
1988	172	84
1989	76	56
1990	14	13
1991	18	15
1992	78	55
1993	170	106
1994	250	163
1995	332	179

evolution of the network density, we calculated the number of annually, newly made R&D partnerships per firm as they appear in the CATI databank. Information on these numbers of new R&D alliances and participating firms is given in table 11.1. Figure 11.3 shows the total number of newly established alliances per firm in the biotechnology industry for the period 1985–95. These numbers are calculated as three-year moving averages to present the overall trend in the data while correcting for yearly fluctuations. For 1995 we added the actual value to the graph to be able to visualize the strong growth in alliance activity in the last three years of observation.

Figure 11.3 pictures a U-shaped pattern in the average number of newly made R&D partnerships per firm. It demonstrates that, apart from a small increase in 1987, the final years of the 1980s are characterized by a sharp decrease in the number of alliances per firm from 1.9 in 1986 to 1.5 in 1989. The first years of the 1990s show a further decline in the average number of R&D partnerships per firm to a level of 1.2 in 1990. This is followed by a short period of stabilization, which is continued by a sharp rise of new partnerships per firm from 1992 onwards. In 1995 the steep upward trend arrives at a level of 1.85 new alliances per firm.

As an indicator of the magnitude of R&D alliance activities of both small biotechnology firms and large pharmaceutical companies, we computed the number of annually, newly established R&D alliances per employee (logarithmic scale) for both categories of cooperating companies. Figure 11.4 shows the specific trend for the number of new R&D partnerships for these groups of companies. The data in this graph are also shown as three-year moving averages, with the exception of 1995 for which we present the actual values of that year.

We notice that for small firms the average number of new R&D alliances decreased gradually during the final years of the 1980s from about 0.7 in 1986 to fewer than 0.55 in 1989 and this number declined even further to about 0.5 in 1990. In 1991 the number of new R&D alliances was still at a level of around 0.5. From 1992 onwards this number steadily increases and reaches the value of about 0.6 in 1995.

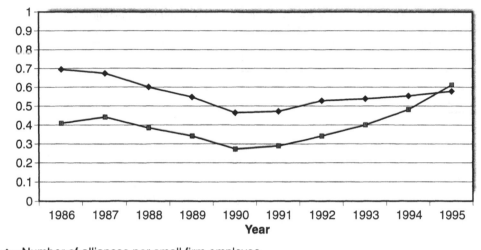

—◆— Number of alliances per small firm employee
—■— Number of alliances per large firm employee

Figure 11.4   Number of newly established biotechnology R&D alliances per employee for small and large firms, mean numbers of employees are log values, three-year moving averages, 1985–95. *Source*: MERIT-CATI

The same pattern of decline in the average number of R&D partnerships during the second half of the 1980s is also found for large firms, albeit at a slightly lower level. Apart from a small increase in 1987, the final years of the 1980s are characterized by a gradual decrease in the average number of alliances from 0.4 in 1986 to fewer than 0.35 in 1989. After a further decline in 1990 to around 0.3 agreements, the number of newly made R&D partnerships took off again during the first half of the 1990s, which is characterized by a rather steep increase to 0.6 in 1995. This number is somewhat higher than the value that we found for small firms in the same year.

To evaluate the importance and magnitude of R&D alliances within and between different categories of companies, we calculated the number of annually, newly established R&D partnerships for large companies, small firms, and combinations of both. Figure 11.5 shows the evolution of the number of newly made alliances between firms of similar and different sizes. All numbers are calculated as three-year moving averages and expressed as percentages of the total number of annually, newly established R&D alliances.

If we consider the specific trend for the share of R&D partnerships between large pharmaceutical firms, we see that during the second half of the 1980s there is a gradual decline from an average share of more than 23 percent in the mid-1980s to around 15 percent in 1989. During the first years of the 1990s the share of R&D partnerships between large firms decreased even further to a level of less than 5 percent in 1992; in 1993 this share reached nearly 7 percent. After this small increase, the downward trend set in again until it arrived at a small share of less than 6 percent in 1994.

During the final years of the 1980s the share of alliances between small biotechnol-

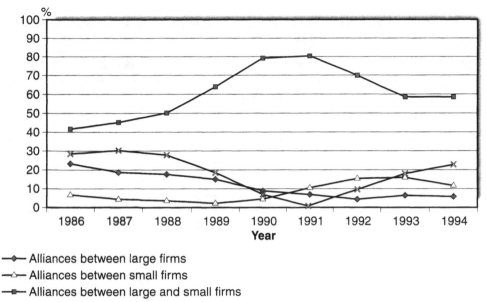

Figure 11.5 Distribution of newly established R&D alliances between firms of similar and different sizes, biotechnology, three-year moving averages, 1985–95. *Source*: MERIT-CATI

ogy firms in all R&D alliances steadily declined from an average of slightly less than 7 percent in 1986 to around 2 percent in 1989. This share reached nearly 5 percent in 1990 after which the upward trend continued until it arrived at a level of more than 16 percent in 1993. In 1994 the share decreased again to slightly more than 12 percent.

Examining the particular trend for the share of R&D alliances between large pharmaceutical firms and small biotechnology companies, we see that during the late 1980s there is a sharp increase from an average share of slightly more than 41 percent in the mid-1980s to nearly 64 percent in 1989. During the first years of the 1990s the average share of R&D alliances between large and small firms stabilized at a level of around 80 percent. After this short period of stabilization in the early 1990s, a sharp downward trend set in from 1992 onwards. It reached a level of less than 59 percent in 1993 and 1994.

The structure of inter-firm R&D networks

After having identified the basic trends in R&D partnering, we now turn to the particular evolution of R&D networks. We examine networks of R&D alliances at two distinct levels. First, we describe the basic characteristics of the overall network, mainly focusing on density in order to evaluate changes in the intensity of alliances between firms. We then evaluate the importance of particular players for the overall structure of the networks by examining the role of the most intense cooperating firms in biotechnology.

Table 11.2   Number of R&D alliances of the 25 most active network participants, 1985–7, 1989–91, and 1993–5. *Source*: MERIT-CATI

1985–7			1989–91			1993–5		
Chiron Corp	Medium	15	Roche Holding Ag	Large	7	Chiron Corp	Medium	19
Roche Holding Ag	Large	14	Smithkline Beecham Plc	Large	5	Smithkline Beecham Plc	Large	19
American Home Products Corp	Large	13	T Cell Sciences Inc	Small	4	Pfizer	Large	16
Eastman Kodak Co	Large	10	Merck and Co Inc	Large	4	Ciba Geigy Ag	Large	14
Pharmacia Ab	Large	10	Sandoz Ag	Large	4	Rhone Poulenc Sa	Large	13
Biogen Inc	Small	10	Glaxo Holdings Plc	Large	3	Hoechst Ag	Large	11
Sumitomo Corp	Large	10	Chiron Corp	Medium	2	Eli Lilly and Co	Large	11
Smithkline Beecham Plc	Large	9	American Home Products Corp	Large	2	Roche Holding Ag	Large	10
Johnson and Johnson	Large	9	Celltech Group Plc	Small	2	Glaxo Holdings Plc	Large	10
Celltech Group Plc	Small	9	Dupont Ei De Nemours and Co	Large	2	Johnson and Johnson	Large	9
Genzyme Corp	Medium	9	Dai Ichi Kangyo Bank Group	Large	2	Merck and Co Inc	Large	9
Procordia Nova Ab	Large	9	Repligen Corp	Small	2	Glaxo Wellcome Plc	Large	9
Hoechst Ag	Large	7	Dow Chemical Co	Large	2	American Home Products Corp	Large	8
Dupont Ei De Nemours and Co	Large	7	Cytel Corp	Small	2	Ligand Pharmaceuticals Inc	Small	8
California Biotechnology Inc	Small	7	Biochem Pharma Inc	Small	2	Warner Lambert Co	Large	8
Ciba Geigy Ag	Large	6	Xenova Group Plc	Small	2	Bristol Myers Squibb Co Inc	Large	7
American Cyanamid Co Inc	Large	6	Solvay and Cie Sa	Large	2	Novo Nordisk As	Large	6
Syntex Corp	Large	6	Telios Pharmaceuticals Inc	Small	2	Allelix Bio-pharmaceuticals Inc	Medium	6
Kyowa Hakko Kogyo Co Ltd	Large	6	Biogen Inc	Small	1	Schering Plough Corp	Large	6
Biotechnology Investments Ltd	Small	6	Sumitomo Corp	Large	1	Pharmacia and Upjohn Inc	Large	6
Centre Applied Microbiology and Research	Ac/gov institution	6	Genzyme Corp	Medium	1	Astra Ab	Large	6
Rhone Poulenc Sa	Large	5	Procordia Nova Ab	Large	1	Corange Ltd	Large	6
Eli Lilly and Co	Large	5	California Biotechnology Inc	Small	1	Zeneca Group Plc	Large	6
Baxter Travenol Labs Inc	Large	5	Ciba Geigy Ag	Large	1	Onyx Pharmaceuticals Inc	Small	6
Amgen Inc	Medium	5	Syntex Corp	Large	1	Eastman Kodak Co	Large	5

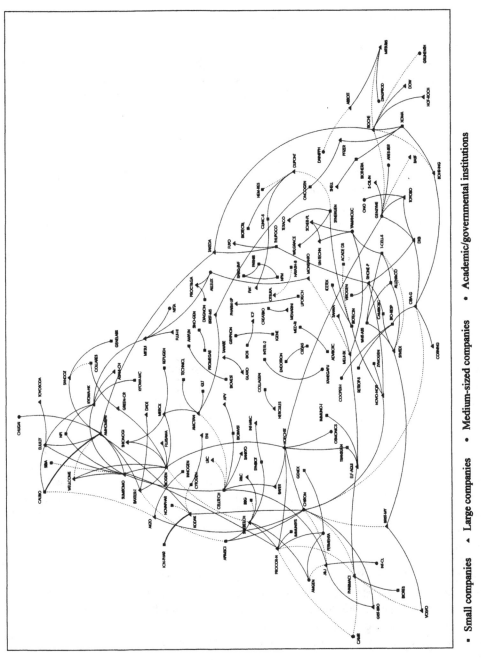

• Small companies ▲ Large companies • Medium-sized companies • Academic/governmental institutions

Figure 11.6 R&D partnerships among cooperating companies in the pharma-biotechnology industry, 1985–7

Figures 11.6–11.8 give us a graphical representation of the R&D alliances in the biotechnology industry in the periods 1985–7, 1989–91, and 1993–5. Solid lines represent one alliance between companies, whereas dotted lines indicate two or three alliances. Thick solid lines indicate four or five alliances. See appendix I for company codes. For all MDS solutions presented in this chapter Kruskal's stress values range from good to very good (Kruskal and Wish, 1978), varying from 0.027 for the period 1985–7 to 0.004 for the period 1989–91.

For an evaluation of the importance of small biotechnology firms and large pharmaceutical companies in R&D partnering, we refer to table 11.2. This table lists the 25 network participants with the most R&D alliances in the biotechnology industry during the periods 1985–7, 1989–91, and 1993–5.

The MDS plot for the period 1985–87 (figure 11.6) shows a rather dense network in which cooperation is not concentrated in any particular part of the network and the multitude of lines connects virtually all the companies in the network, either in a direct or indirect way. Although most firms are connected to at least two other partners, we also see quite a few one-on-one links. Many companies have engaged in at least two R&D alliances with one particular firm. This is illustrative for the growth in the number of alliances per firm during that time period.

If we look at the leading companies of the biotechnology network in the period 1985–7, we see that a number of small biotechnology companies such as Biogen, Celltech Group, and California Biotechnology keep very nodal positions in the network (see figure 11.6). These companies also rank high on the list of most intense cooperating companies (table 11.2). Apparently, many small biotechnology firms are attractive partners for large pharmaceutical corporations. Furthermore, the network is characterized by many strongly tied couples of small and large firms. A few important ties: Biogen and Smithkline Beecham, Celltech Group and American Cyanamid, California Biotechnology and American Home Products. Smithkline Beecham is found in the middle of an R&D network with specialized biotechnology companies such as Applied Immune Sciences and British Biotech, as well as a number of large-sized companies such as Procordia Nova. American Home Products, another leading pharmaceutical company, is mainly connected to large partners such as Eastman Kodak and Sumitomo.

Turning to the next period (1989–91) we find a somewhat different pattern (see figure 11.7). The MDS solution shows an extremely sparse network that involves 75 firms of which the vast majority are part of clusters of firms that are all centered around three focal players: Roche, Smithkline Beecham, and Merck. Although some firms are linked to more than one partner, we observe mostly one-on-one alliances. The majority of firms are connected to one specific partner through no more than one R&D alliance.

In the years 1989–91 the group of most partner-intensive companies in the network for the biotechnology industry covers a number of leading pharmaceutical companies as well as many small biotechnology firms (see table 11.2). We notice that the small biotechnology firms that have already been mentioned changed their positions in the rank order of leading R&D partnering firms, while several new small firms such as T Cell Sciences and Repligen entered the top ranking of cooperating companies. It is obvious that in this period R&D partnering has not led to a dense network and we

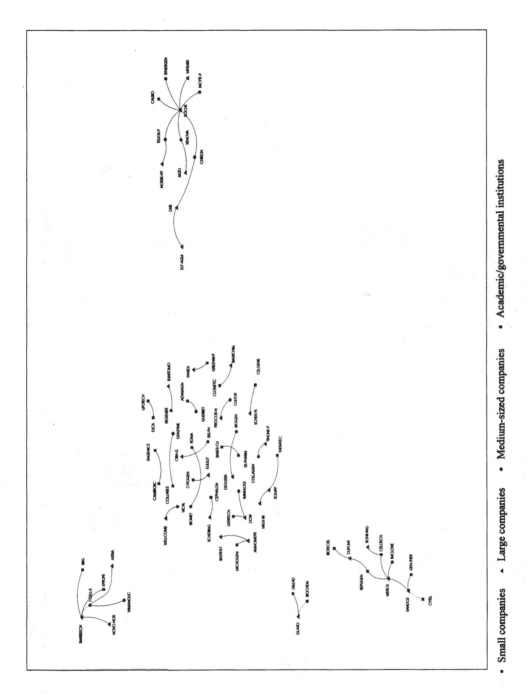

• Small companies   ▲ Large companies   • Medium-sized companies   • Academic/governmental institutions

Figure 11.7   R&D partnerships among cooperating companies in the pharma-biotechnology industry, 1989–91

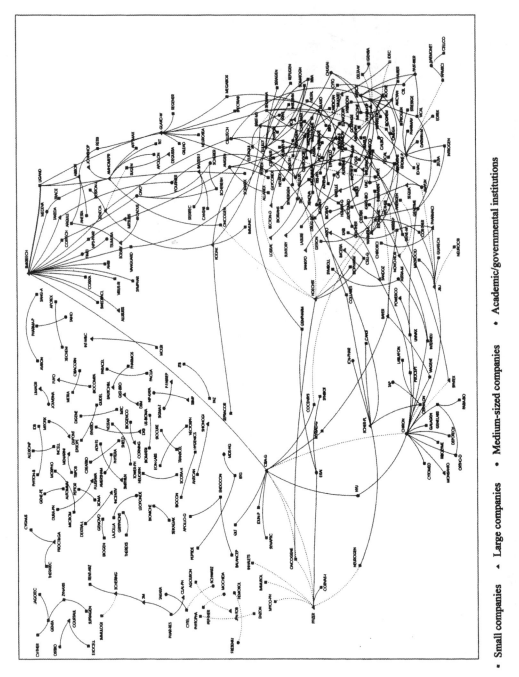

• Small companies   ▲ Large companies   ● Medium-sized companies   ■ Academic/governmental institutions

Figure 11.8 R&D partnerships among cooperating companies in the pharma-biotechnology industry, 1993–5

therefore focus on the somewhat denser clusters of cooperating firms that were found (see figure 11.7).

At the top left-hand side of figure 11.7 we can see one cluster involving a number of small and large cooperating companies, which are all centered around the leading pharmaceutical company Smithkline Beecham. A very nodal position in this cluster is held by T Cell Sciences, which is also closely tied to the core of the cluster. Within this cluster, Smithkline Beecham is mainly connected to small biotechnology firms. Glaxo Holdings is found in the middle of a second, somewhat smaller, R&D network with two specialized biotechnology companies, Biochem Pharma and Gilead Sciences. The strong ties between Glaxo Holdings and Biochem Pharma form the core of this cluster.

A third mixed cluster of small biotechnology firms and large pharmaceutical companies is found at the bottom left-hand side of figure 11.7. The core of this cluster is formed by two large pharmaceutical companies, Merck and Sandoz. If we study this particular cluster, we see that these large firms are mainly tied to a number of small biotech firms such as Celltech Group and Repligen that also hold nodal positions in the network. A large cluster of small and large firms is located at the right-hand side. This cluster is basically centered around the large pharmaceutical company Roche which is found in the middle of an R&D network with many specialized biotech companies. Two nodal biotechnology companies, Xenova Group and Telios Pharmaceuticals, hold important positions in this cluster.

The network density in the biotechnology sector shows a substantial increase if one compares the period 1993–5 (see figure 11.8) with 1989–91. During the period 1993–5, the many newly created R&D alliances between biotechnology companies and pharmaceutical firms resulted in a much denser network structure in which cooperation is mainly concentrated at the right-hand side of figure 11.8. Nearly all companies in this dense part of the network are either directly or indirectly connected to each other. However, as indicated by the network pattern at the left-hand side of figure 11.8, there still are a large number of one-on-one links in other parts of the network. Also, the number of firms that are connected to one particular partner through at least two alliances has increased, which is illustrative for the increase in the number of R&D partnerships per firm during this period.

Small firms that held strong positions in the rank order of most intense cooperating firms during the period 1989–91 have left the group of leading cooperating firms for the period 1993–5. Only two new young biotech firms, Ligand and Onyx, have entered this group (see table 11.2). The top of the network for the biotechnology industry during this time period covers only leading pharmaceutical companies such as Smithkline Beecham, Pfizer, and Ciba Geigy, which all hold nodal positions in the network. Ligand is strongly tied to Smithkline Beecham as well as to other large pharmaceutical firms such as Glaxo Wellcome (see figure 11.8). Onyx is tightly related to large companies such as Eli Lilly and Warner Lambert. Apart from R&D alliances with two nodal biotechnology companies, these large pharmaceutical firms are mainly connected to a wide variety of other small partners. In addition to this, some specific partnerships between large companies can be observed, such as the ties between Smithkline Beecham and Ciba Geigy and Warner Lambert and Basf.

Discussion and Conclusions

Our contribution aims at improving the understanding of the specific evolution of R&D partnerships and the related inter-firm networks in the biotechnology industry. In that context we pay extensive attention to the complementary role of small, entrepreneurial firms and large pharmaceutical companies in these R&D networks.

As also found in previous research (Hagedoorn, 1993; Kenney, 1986; Powell et al., 1996), the widespread collaboration between different groups of cooperating firms in the biotechnology industry has led to rather dense network-like structures of joint innovative activities. Small entrepreneurial biotechnology companies play an important role in these R&D networks. This role for small firms can clearly be understood in the light of the Schumpeterian tradition, where entrepreneurial firms are viewed as important generators of innovative change within new industries. In particular during the 1980s, the nodal role of small, new biotechnology firms coincides with major scientific and technological breakthroughs introduced by many of these new entrants in the pharmaceutical industry (Powell, 1996).

However, as the field of biotechnology has gradually matured, entrepreneurial biotechnology firms could have become less important for the newly developed R&D networks while large companies may have become more dominant. This more dominant role for large science-based firms in a more routinized innovative environment is particularly stressed in the later writings of Schumpeter (1942), see also Scherer (1984). Recent contributions (e.g., Senker, and Sharp, 1997) expect, however, that the nodal role of small biotechnology firms, as major players with multiple partnerships in R&D networks, will not decrease as the technology becomes more mature.

Our analysis reveals that during the second half of the 1980s, the R&D partnership-intensity of small firms was higher than for large companies. The more detailed analysis of the periods 1985–7 and 1989–91 shows that numerous entrepreneurial biotechnology firms kept very nodal positions in R&D networks, albeit next to several large pharmaceutical companies that were also well represented.

One of the other major observations in this chapter is the strong increase in the R&D alliance-intensity for large firms during the first half of the 1990s. At the end of the period this alliance-intensity of large firms exceeds the intensity found for small firms. The changing role of large pharmaceutical companies is also found in the analysis of the overall R&D network of the period 1993–5. This analysis shows that only two young biotechnology firms hold strong positions in the rank order of most intense cooperating firms and that the top positions of the network are mainly taken by leading pharmaceutical companies that hold nodal positions in the overall network.

In congruence with "early" Schumpetarian views, these results are indicative of the significant role played by small entrepreneurial biotechnology firms in innovation, particularly during the 1980s when the new biotechnology first became relevant to the pharmaceutical industry. The early 1990s, however, seem to demonstrate a decreasing importance of these small firms in inter-firm R&D networks if compared to the role of large pharmaceutical companies. These large companies developed into more dominant players with multiple partnerships, a change that is clearly more in line with expectations based on the later writings of Schumpeter.

The complementarity of the innovative capabilities of small, entrepreneurial bio-technology firms and large pharmaceutical companies has formed the basis for numerous R&D partnerships between these two groups of firms. An increasingly dominant role of large firms in all sorts of innovative activities might render these complementarities less obvious. The intensity of specific cooperation between groups of small and large companies, as well as of inter-firm collaboration in general, is then likely to drop off (Arora and Gambardella, 1990; Saviotti, 1998). However, others (Powell, 1996; Senker and Sharp, 1997) expect that entrepreneurial firms will continue to play a critical role in R&D networks with large companies and that intensive R&D collaboration in the biotechnology industry will therefore be of a more long-term nature.

Our analysis of the evolution of inter-firm R&D partnerships in the biotechnology industry reveals that during the first half of the 1990s there is an explosive growth in the number of R&D alliances per firm, accompanied by a strong increase in network density. This latter phenomenon is mainly due to an increase in the number of firms that are connected to one particular partner through at least two R&D alliances. In all of this, R&D alliances between two or more large firms played only a minor role and this share of large–large cooperation was even gradually decreasing. Alliances between large firms and small entrepreneurial companies, however, remained important throughout the period. The detailed analysis of the periods 1985–7, 1989–91 and 1993–5 demonstrates that R&D networks in the biotechnology industry are mainly characterized by many strongly tied couples of entrepreneurial biotechnology firms and large companies.

Our findings suggest that the 1990s have introduced a period of intensified R&D cooperation leading to denser inter-firm networks in the biotechnology industry. In these networks, the dominant role of entrepreneurial biotechnology firms as major players with many partnerships seems to be decreasing. However, as large pharmaceutical firms have increasingly become nodal players in R&D networks, their most preferred partners continue to be small biotechnology firms, implying a continuing mutual dependence between these two groups of firms.

Note

The authors would like to thank the editors of this volume and the participants at the conference on "Creating a new mindset: integrating strategy and entrepreneurship perspectives" for their comments on an earlier version of this paper.

References

Arora, A. and Gambardella, A.1990. Complementarity and external linkages: the strategies of the large firms in biotechnology. *Journal of Industrial Economics*, 38: 361–79.

Barley, S. R., Freeman, J., and Hybels, R. C. 1992. Strategic alliances in commercial biotechnology. In N. Nohria and R. G. Eccles (eds), *Networks and organizations: structure, form, and action*. Boston: Harvard Business School Press, 311–47.

D'Aveni, R. A., 1994. *Hypercompetitive rivalries*, New York: Free Press.

Della Valle, F. and Gambardella, A. 1993. Biological revolution and strategies for innovation in pharmaceutical companies, *R&D Management*, 23: 287–301.

Galambos, L. and Sturchio, J. L. 1998. Pharmaceutical firms and the transition to biotechnology: a study in strategic innovation. *Business History Review*, 72: 250–78.

Hagedoorn, J. 1993. Understanding the rationale of strategic technology partnering: interorganizational modes of cooperation and sectoral differences. *Strategic Management Journal*, 14: 371–85.

Hagedoorn, J. 1996a. Trends and patterns in strategic technology partnering since the early seventies. *Review of Industrial Organization*, 11: 601–16.

Hagedoorn, J. 1996b. Innovation and entrepreneurship: Schumpeter revisited. *Industrial and Corporate Change*, 5: 883–96.

Hair, J. F., Anderson, R. E., Tatham, R. L. and Black, W. C. 1994. *Multivariate data analysis*. New York: Macmillan.

Hakansson, P., Kjellberg, H., and Lundgren, A.1993. Strategic alliances in global biotechnology – a network approach. *International Business Review*, 2: 65–82.

Hitt, M. and Ireland, D. 2000. The intersection of entrepreneurship and strategic management research. In D. L. Sexton and H. Landström (eds), *Handbook of entrepreneurship*. Oxford: Blackwell, 45–63.

Kamien, M. I. and Schwartz, N. L. 1982. *Market structure and innovation*. Cambridge: Cambridge University Press.

Kenney, M. 1986. Schumpeterian innovation and entrepreneurs in capitalism: a case study of the US biotechnology industry. *Research Policy*, 15: 21–31.

Kruskal, J. B. and Wish, M. 1978. *Multidimensional scaling*. Beverly Hills, CA: Sage Publications.

Laamanen, T. and Autio, E. 1996. Dominant dynamic complementarities and technology-motivated acquisitions of new, technology-based firms. *International Journal of Technology Management*, 12: 769–86.

Liebeskind, J., Lumerman, O. A., Zucker, L., and Brewer, M. 1996. Social networks, learning and flexibility: sourcing scientific knowledge in new biotechnology firms, *Organization Science*, 7: 428–43.

Lumerman O. A. and Liebeskind, J. 1997. Three levels of networking for sourcing intellectual capital in biotechnology: implications for studying interorganizational networks. *International Studies of Management and Organization*, 27: 76–103.

Marco, L. V. A. 1985. Entrepreneur et innovation: les sources françaises de Joseph Schumpeter. *Economies et Societés*, 19: 89–106.

Oakey, R. P. 1993. Predatory networking: the role of small firms in the development of the British biotechnology industry. *International Small Business Journal*, 11: 9–22.

OECD. 1993. The OECD in figures: statistics on the member countries. *Supplement to OECD Observer*, no. 182, June–July.

Orsenigo, L. 1989. *The emergence of biotechnology: institutions and markets in industrial innovation*. London: Pinter Publishers.

OTA. 1988. *New developments in biotechnology: US investment in biotechnology*. Government Printing Office, Office of Technology Assessment,Washington, DC.

Pisano, G. P. 1990. The R&D boundaries of the firm: an empirical analysis. *Administrative Science Quarterly*, 35: 153–77.

Pisano, G. P. 1991. The governance of innovation: vertical integration and collaborative arrangements in the biotechnology industry. *Research Policy*, 20: 237–49.

Pisano, G. P., Shan, W., and Teece, D. J. 1988. Joint ventures and collaboration in the biotechnology industry. In D. C. Mowery (ed.), *International collaborative ventures in US manufacturing*, Cambridge, MA: Ballinger, 183–222.

Powell, W. W. 1996. Interorganizational collaboration in the biotechnology industry. *Journal of Institutional and Theoretical Economics*, 152: 197–215.

Powell, W. W., Koput, K. W., and Smith-Doerr, L. 1996. Interorganizational collaboration and the locus of innovation: networks of learning in biotechnology. *Administrative Science Quarterly*, 41: 116–45.

Rothaermel, F. T. 2000. Technological discontinuities and the nature of competition. *Technology Analysis and Strategic Management*, 12: 149–60.

Santarelli, E. and Pesciarelli, E. 1990. The emergence of a vision: the development of Schumpeter's theory of entrepreneurship. *History of Political Economy*, 22: 677–96.

Saviotti, P. P. 1998. Industrial structure and the dynamics of knowledge generation in biotechnology. In J. Senker (ed.), *Biotechnology and competitive advantage: Europe's firms and the US challenge*. Cheltenham: Edward Elgar, 19–43.

Scherer, F. M. 1984. *Innovation and growth – Schumpeterian perspectives*. Cambridge, MA: MIT Press.

Schumpeter, J. A. 1934. *The theory of economic development*. London: Oxford University Press.

Schumpeter, J. A. 1942. *Capitalism, socialism and democracy*. New York: Harper & Row.

Segers, J. P. 1992. Region-specific technology policy in Belgium: the significance of new technology based start-ups. *Small Business Economics*, 4: 133–40.

Senker, J. and Sharp, M. 1997. Organizational learning in cooperative alliances: some case studies in biotechnology. *Technology Analysis and Strategic Management*, 9: 35–52.

Shan, W., Walker, G., and Kogut, B. 1994. Interfirm cooperation and startup innovation in the biotechnology industry. *Strategic Management Journal*, 15: 387–94.

Slowinski, G., Seelig, G., and Hull, F. 1996. Managing technology-based strategic alliances between large and small firms, S.A.M. *Advanced Management Journal*, 61: 42–7.

Van Vliet, R. 1998. Introduction. In J. Senker (ed.), *Biotechnology and competitive advantage: Europe's firms and the US challenge*. Cheltenham: Edward Elgar, 1–5.

Walsh, V. and Galimberti, I. 1993. Firm strategies, globalization and new technological paradigms: the case of biotechnology. In M. Humbert (ed.), *The impact of globalization on Europe's firms and industries*, London: Pinter Publishers, 175–90.

Walsh, V., Niosi, J., and Mustar, P. 1995. Small-firm formation in biotechnology: a comparison of France, Britain and Canada. *Technovation*, 15: 303–27.

Appendix 1 Network Participants Appearing in the MDS Graphs

Company label	Name of the company	Size	Company label	Name of the company	Size
3M	Minnesota Mining And Manufacturing Co	Large	INNOGEN	Innogenetics Sa	Small
ABBOTT	Abbott Laboratories	Large	INSULINM	Insulin Mimetics Ltd	Small
ACADE DS	Acade Diagnostic Systems	Small	INT-CL	Int Clinical Labs Inc	Medium
ADV-TS	Advanced Tissue Sciences Inc	Small	INT-M&C	Int Mineral and Chemical Corp	Large
ADVBIOTC	Advanced Biotherapy Concepts Inc	Small	INTERL-2	Interleukin 2 Inc	Small
ADVMAGN	Advanced Magnetics Inc	Small	INTERNEU	Interneuron Pharmaceuticals Inc	Small
AFFYMAX	Affymax Nv	Small	INTROGEN	Introgen Therapeutics Inc	Small
AGOURON	Agouron Pharmaceuticals Inc	Small	ISIS-PH	Isis Pharmaceuticals Inc	Small

Company label	Name of the company	Size	Company label	Name of the company	Size
AKZO	Akzo Nobel Nv	Large	IXSYS	Ixsys Inc	Small
ALBANY-M	Albany Molecular Research Inc	Small	J&J	Johnson and Johnson	Large
ALEXIONP	Alexion Pharmaceuticals Inc	Small	JAGOTEC	Jagotec Sa	Small
ALKERMES	Alkermes Inc	Small	JOHNSHOP	Johns Hopkins Health System Corp	Large
ALLANEX	Alanex Corp	Small	JOUVEINA	Jouveinal Sa	Medium
ALLELIX	Allelix Biopharmaceuticals Inc	Medium	JPN-TOB	Japan Tobacco Inc	Large
ALLEN&CO	Allen And Co	Small	KABI	Kabi Pharmacia	Small
ALUSUISS	Swiss Aluminium Ltd	Large	KANEGAFU	Kanegafuchi Chemical Industry Co Ltd	Medium
AMBI	Applied Microbiology Inc	Small	KARO-BIO	Karo Bio	Small
AMCYAN	American Cyanamid Co Inc	Large	KODAK	Eastman Kodak Co	Large
AMERSHAM	Amersham International Plc	Medium	KYOWA-HK	Kyowa Hakko Kogyo Co Ltd	Large
AMGEN	Amgen Inc	Medium	KYOWA-MC	Kyowa Medex Co	Small
AMHOMEPR	American Home Products Corp	Large	L'ORÉAL	L'Oréal Sa	Large
AMYLIN	Amylin Pharmaceuticals Inc	Small	LABLAFON	Laboratoire L Lafon	Small
ANERGEN	Anergen Inc	Small	LAJOLLA	La Jolla Pharmaceutical Com	Small
ANESTA	Anesta Corp	Small	LASURE	Lasure and Crawford	Small
ANTICAN	Anticancer Inc	Small	LEOFONDE	Leo Fondet	Medium
APIMSCI	Applied Immune Sciences Inc	Small	LIGAND	Ligand Pharmaceuticals Inc	Small
APOLLO-G	Apollo Genetics Inc	Small	LIMAGR	Limagrain Group	Large
APOLLON	Apollon Inc	Small	LIPOTECH	Liposome Technology Inc	Small
APOTEX	Apotex Inc	Small	LRC	London Rubber Co Int Plc	Large
APV	Apv Plc	Large	LYNX-TH	Lynx Therapeutics Inc	Small
ARES-SER	Ares Serono Ag	Medium	MARKET-B	Martek Biosciences Corp	Small
ARQULE	Arqule Inc	Small	MDS-HG	Mds Health Group Ltd	Medium
ARRIS-P	Arris Pharmaceutical Corp	Small	MED-RI	Medical Research Int Ltd	Small
ASAHI-CH	Asahi Chemical Industry Co Ltd	Large	MEDEVA	Medeva Plc	Medium
ASTRA	Astra Ab	Large	MEDIMMUN	Medimmune Inc	Small
ASTRA-M	Astra Merck Inc	Medium	MEDTRON	Medtronic Inc	Large
ATHENA	Athena Neurosciences Inc	Small	MEGABIOS	Megabios Corp	Small
AUTOIMMU	Autoimmune Inc	Small	MEIJI-SK	Meiji Seika Kaisha Ltd	Large
AVIRON	Aviron	Small	MENARINI	Menarini Industrie Farmaceutiche	Large
BAKER-CU	Baker Cummins Inc	Small	MERCK	Merck and Co Inc	Large

Company label	Name of the company	Size	Company label	Name of the company	Size
BALANCEP	Balance Pharmaceuticals Inc	Small	METRA	Metra Biosystems Inc	Small
BASF	Basf Ag	Large	MI-KASEI	Mitsubishi Kasei Corp	Large
BATELLE	Battelle Memorial Institute Inc	Large	MICROCID	Microcide Pharmaceuticals Inc	Small
BAUSCH&L	Bausch and Lomb Inc	Large	MICROGEN	Microgen Inc	Small
BAXTER-T	Baxter Travenol Labs Inc	Large	MICROM	Micromet GmbH	Small
BAYER	Bayer Ag	Large	MILLENPH	Millennium Pharmaceuticals Inc	Small
BBG	British Biotech Plc	Small	MITOTIX	Mitotix Inc	Small
BECTON-D	Becton Dickinson and Co Inc	Large	MITSUBIS	Mitsubishi Corp	Large
BIO-RESP	Bio Response Inc	Small	MITSUI	Mitsui Group	Large
BIOCHEM	Biochem Pharma Inc	Small	MOCHIDA	Mochida Pharmaceutical Co Ltd	Medium
BIOCOMPA	Biocompatibles Int Plc	Small	MOLBI	Molecular Biosystems Inc	Small
BIOCON	Biocon Inc	Small	MONSANTO	Monsanto Co	Large
BIOCURE	Biocure Holdings Plc	Small	MORPHO	Morphosys GmbH	Small
BIOGEN	Biogen Inc	Small	MYCO-PH	Myco Pharmaceuticals Inc	Small
BIOGENCO	Biosource Genetics Corp	Small	MYRIAD-G	Myriad Genetics Inc	Small
BIOINVST	Bioinvest	Small	NEUREX	Neurex Corp	Small
BIOMATRI	Biomatrix Inc	Small	NEUROCRI	Neurocrine Biosciences Inc	Small
BIOMET	Biomet Inc	Medium	NEUROGEN	Neurogen Corp	Small
BIONICHE	Bioniche Inc	Small	NEUROSEA	Neurosearch As	Small
BIOPHARM	R Biopharm GmbH	Small	NEXAGEN	Nexagen Inc	Small
BIORAD	Bio Rad Laboratories Inc	Medium	NIP-KAYA	Nippon Kayaku Co Ltd	Medium
BIORES	Biores Bv	Small	NITTA	Nitta Gelatin Inc	Medium
BIOS	Bios Corp	Small	NORSK-HY	Norsk Hydro As	Large
BIOTECIN	Biotechnology Investments Ltd	Small	NOVAPHAR	Nova Pharmaceutical Corp	Small
BIOTECRL	Biotech Research LABS	Small	NOVO-NOR	Novo Nordisk As	Large
BIOTHERA	Biotherapeutics Corp	Small	NPI	Newport Pharmaceuticals Int Inc	Small
BIOTRANS	Biotransplant Inc	Small	NPM	Nederlandse Participatie Maatschappij	Small
BIOVEST	Biovest Partners	Small	NPS-PHAR	Nps Pharmaceuticals Inc	Small
BOEHRI-S	Boehringer Sohn Ch	Large	NYU	State University of New York	Ac/gov institu-tion
BOHR-ING	Boehringer Ingelheim	Large	OGS	Oxford Glycosystems Group Plc	Small
BOSTON-L	Boston Life Sciences Inc	Small	OMEGA	Omega Biologicals Inc	Small

Company label	Name of the company	Size	Company label	Name of the company	Size
BRIST-MS	Bristol Myers Squibb Co Inc	Large	ONCOGEN	Oncogen	Small
BRIST-MY	Bristol Myers Co	Large	ONCOGENE	Oncogene Science Inc	Small
BTG	Btg Plc	Small	ONO	Ono Pharmaceutical Co Ltd	Medium
CADUS	Cadus Pharmaceutical Corp	Small	ONYX	Onyx Pharmaceuticals Inc	Small
CALBIO	California Biotechnology Inc	Small	ORTHO-D	Ortho Clinical Diagnostics Inc	Medium
CAMBIOSC	Cambridge Bioscience Corp	Small	OSMONICS	Osmonics Inc	Medium
CAMR	Centre Applied Microbiology and Research	Ac/gov institution	OSTBIO	Osteometer Biotech	Small
CANJI	Canji Inc	Small	OTSUKA	Otsuka Pharmaceutical Co Ltd	Large
CANTAB	Cantab Pharmaceuticals Plc	Small	P-FABREP	Pierre Fabre Participations	Large
CARDICAN	Cardican	Small	PACLIA	Pacific Liaisons	Small
CAT	Cambridge Antibody Technology Group Plc	Small	PARA-BIO	Pharmadigm Biosciences Inc	Small
CELGENE	Celgene Corp	Small	PARACEL	Paracelsian Inc	Small
CELIAS	Celias	Small	PARNIB	Parnib	Small
CELL-G	Cell Genesys Inc	Small	PAST-MER	Pasteur Merieux Msd	Medium
CELLCO	Cellco Inc	Small	PAZ	Paz GmbH	Small
CELLTECH	Celltech Group Plc	Small	PDC	Pharmaceutical Discovery Corp	Small
CELTRIX	Celtrix Pharmaceuticals Inc	Small	PEP-THER	Peptide Therapeutics	Small
CENTAUR	Centaur Pharmaceuticals Inc	Small	PEPTIDE	Peptide Technology Ltd	Small
CENTOCOR	Centocor Inc	Small	PEPTOR	Peptor Ltd	Small
CEPHALON	Cephalon Inc	Small	PFIZER	Pfizer	Large
CHIRON	Chiron Corp	Medium	PHAR-RES	Pharmaceutical Resources Inc	Small
CHIROSCI	Chiroscience Group Plc	Small	PHARM-UP	Pharmacia and Upjohn Inc	Large
CHROMAX	Chromaxome Corp	Small	PHARMA-P	Pharma Patch Plc	Small
CHUGAI	Chugai Pharmaceutical Co Ltd	Medium	PHARMACI	Pharmacia Ab	Large
CIBA-G	Ciba Geigy Ag	Large	PHARMAGE	Pharmagenics Inc	Small
CIBACORN	Ciba Corning Diagnostics Corp	Small	PHARMAV	Pharmavene Inc	Small
CLAL-PH	Clal Israel Ltd	Large	PHARMECO	Pharm Eco Laboratories Inc	Small
CLINIC-S	Clinical Sciences Inc	Small	PHARMOS	Pharmos Corp	Small
CLONETIC	Clonetics Corp	Small	PHYTERA	Phytera Inc	Small
COCENSYS	Cocensys Inc	Small	PHYTON	Phyton Catalytic Inc	Small
COLLAGEN	Collaborative Genetics Corp	Small	PHYTON-B	Phyton Inc	Small

Company label	Name of the company	Size	Company label	Name of the company	Size
COLLARES	Collaborative Research Inc	Small	PHYTOPHA	Phytopharmaceuticals Inc	Small
COOPER-I	The Cooper Companies Inc	Medium	POWERCO	Power Corp of Canada	Large
COR-THER	Cor Therapeutics Inc	Small	PPL-THER	Ppl Therapeutics Plc	Small
CORANGE	Corange Ltd	Large	PROCEPT	Procept Inc	Small
CORIXA	Corixa Corp	Small	PROCOR-N	Procordia Nova AB	Large
CORNING	Corning Glass Works	Large	PROCT&GA	Procter and Gamble Co	Large
CORTECH	Cortech Inc	Small	PROGEN	Progenics Pharmaceuticals Inc	Small
CORVAS-I	Corvas Int Inc	Small	PROMEGAB	Promega Corp	Small
COURTAUL	Courtaulds Plc	Large	QLT	Qlt Phototherapeutics Inc	Small
CREATBIO	Creative Biomolecules Inc	Small	QUIDEL	Quidel Corp	Small
CSL	Csl Ltd	Medium	R&C	Reckitt and Colman Plc	Large
CULTOR	Cultor Oy	Medium	RABO-BVF	Rabobank Biotech Venture Fund	Small
CV-THER	Cv Therapeutics Inc	Small	REGENER	Regeneron Pharmaceuticals Inc	Small
CYGNUS	Cygnus Therapeutic Systems	Small	RENT-ARZ	Dr Rentschler Arzneimittel GmbH and Co.	Small
CYTEL	Cytel Corp	Small	REPLIGEN	Repligen Corp	Small
CYTO	Cytotherapeutics Inc	Small	RESSI	Ressi Group Inc	Small
CYTOGEN	Cytogen Corp	Small	RETROP-S	Retroperfusion Systems Inc	Small
CYTOMED	Cytomed Inc	Small	RHONE-P	Rhone Poulenc SA	Large
DADE	Dade Int Inc	Large	RIBOGENE	Ribogene Inc	Small
DAINIPPH	Dainippon Pharmaceutical Co Ltd	Medium	RIBOZYME	Ribozyme Pharmaceuticals Inc	Small
DARWIN-M	Darwin Molecular Corp	Small	ROCHE	Roche Holding Ag	Large
DEGUSSA	Degussa Ag	Large	S-OIL-N	Amoco Standard Oil of Indiana	Large
DELTA-W	Delta West Pty Ltd	Small	SANDOZ	Sandoz Ag	Large
DEPOTECH	Depotech Corp	Small	SANG-A	Sang A Pharma Co Ltd	Small
DEXTRA-L	Dextra Laboratories	Small	SANKYO	Sankyo Com Ltd	Large
DIAGNON	Diagnon Corp	Small	SANWA	Sanwa Group	Large
DIAGPROD	Diagnostic Products Corp	Medium	SBMP	Snow Brand Milk Products Co Ltd	Large
DIGENE	Digene Corp	Small	SCHEIN-P	Schein Pharmaceutical Inc	Medium
DKB	Dai Ichi Kangyo Bank Group	Large	SCHER-PL	Schering Plough Corp	Large
DOW	Dow Chemical Co	Large	SCHERER	Rp Scherer Corporation	Medium
DRUG-RC	Drug Royalty Corp	Small	SCHERERH	Scherer Healthcare Inc	Small
DSM	Dsm NV	Large	SCHERING	Schering Ag	Large
DUPONT	Dupont E I De Nemours and Co	Large	SCHWARZ	Schwarz Pharma Ag	Medium

Company label	Name of the company	Size	Company label	Name of the company	Size
DURA-PH	Dura Pharmaceuticals Inc	Small	SCOTIA-H	Scotia Holdings Plc	Small
EDITEK	Editek Inc	Small	SEIKAGAK	Seikagaku Kogyo Corp	Small
EISAI	Eisai Co Ltd	Medium	SENSUS	Sensus Drug Development Corp	Small
ELANCORP	Elan Corp Plc	Medium	SEPRACOR	Sepracor Inc	Small
ELF-AQUI	Elf Aquitaine Sa	Large	SEQUA	Sequa Corp	Large
ELILILLY	Eli Lilly and Co	Large	SEQUANA	Sequana Therapeutics Inc	Small
ENDOCON	Endocon Inc	Small	SERAGEN	Seragen Inc	Small
ENDOTRON	Endotronics Inc	Small	SHELL	Shell Nv	Large
ENGENICS	Engenics	Small	SHIELD	Shield Diagnostics Ltd	Small
ENI	Eni Group Ente Nazionale Idrocarburi	Large	SHIONOGI	Shionogi and Co Ltd	Large
ENZON	Enzon Inc	Small	SIBIA	Sibia Neurosciences Inc	Small
EON-LABS	Eon Labs	Small	SIGMA-T	Sigma Tau	Medium
EPITOPE	Epitope Inc	Small	SINO-GEN	Sino Genetic	Small
ESCA	Escagenetics Corp	Small	SMITH&N	Smith and Nephew Plc	Large
ETH-HOLD	Ethical Holdings Plc	Small	SMKBEECH	Smithkline Beecham Plc	Large
EXOCELL	Exocell Inc	Small	SOLVAY	Solvay and Cie Sa	Large
FERMENTA	Fermenta Ab	Medium	SOMATIX	Somatix Therapy Corporation	Small
FIAT	Fiat Spa	Large	SOMATOGN	Somatogen Inc	Small
FIMEI	Fimei Finanziaria Industriale Mob. Ed Immob. Spa	Medium	SPECTRAB	Spectra Biomedical Inc	Small
FOCAL	Focal Inc	Small	SS-PHARM	Ss Pharmaceutical Co Ltd	Medium
FOURNIER	Fournier Industrie et Sante	Medium	STERICEC	Steritech Inc	Small
FRESENIU	Fresenius Ag	Medium	STRESSGE	Stressgen Biotechnologies Corp	Small
FUJI-HI	Fuji Heavy Industries Ltd	Large	SUGEN	Sugen Inc	Small
FUJISAWA	Fujisawa Pharmaceutical Co Ltd	Large	SUMITOMO	Sumitomo Corp	Large
FUYO	Fuyo Group	Large	SUNTORY	Suntory	Large
GALAGEN	Galagen Inc	Small	SUPRAGEN	Supragen Inc	Small
GEN-THER	Genetic Therapy Inc	Small	SWEDBACL	Sbl Vaccin Ab	Small
GENE-M	Genemedicine Inc	Small	SYMBOLL	Symbollon Corp	Small
GENE-PE	Gene Pharming Europe Bv	Small	SYMPHAR	Symphar Sa	Small
GENELABS	Genelabs Technologies Inc	Small	SYNAPTIC	Synaptic Pharmaceuticals Corp	Small
GENEX	Genex Corp	Small	SYNBIOT	Synbiotics Corp	Small
GENOVO	Genovo Inc	Small	SYNERGEN	Synergen Inc	Small
GENPHARM	Genpharm Int	Small	SYNTEX	Syntex Corp	Large
GENSIA	Gensia Pharmaceuticals Inc	Small	SYNTRO	Syntro Corp	Small

Company label	Name of the company	Size	Company label	Name of the company	Size
GENTA	Genta Inc	Small	T-CELL-S	T Cell Sciences Inc	Small
GENZYME	Genzyme Corp	Medium	TAIHO	Taiho Pharmaceutical Co Ltd	Medium
GERITECH	Geritech Inc	Small	TAKARA	Takara Shuzo Co Ltd	Medium
GERON	Geron Corp	Small	TAKEDA	Takeda Chemical Industries Ltd	Large
GILEAD	Gilead Sciences Inc	Small	TANABE	Tanabe Seiyaku Co Ltd	Large
GIST-BRO	Gist Brocades Nv	Large	TAP	Tap Pharmaceuticals Inc	Medium
GLAXO	Glaxo Holdings plc	Large	TBC	Texas Biotechnology Corp	Small
GLAXO-W	Glaxo Wellcome Plc	Large	TECHNICL	Techniclone International Corp	Small
GLIATECH	Gliatech Inc	Small	TELIOS-P	Telios Pharmaceuticals Inc	Small
GLYCOMED	Glycomed Inc	Small	TEXACO	Texaco Inc	Large
GLYCOREX	Glycorex	Small	THERAGEN	Theragen Inc	Small
GREEN-CR	Green Cross Corp	Large	THERATEC	Theratech Inc	Small
GREENW-P	Greenwich Pharmaceuticals Inc	Small	THEREXS	Therexsys	Small
GRUNENTH	Gruenenthal GmbH	Medium	THLIPOCO	The Liposome Co Inc	Small
GRYPHON	Gryphon Ventures	Small	TKT	Transkaryotic Therapies Inc	Small
GRYPHONS	Gryphon Sciences	Small	TOWER-PH	Towers Phytochemical Ltd	Small
GUERBET	Guerbet Sa	Medium	TOYOBO	Toyo Boseki Co Ltd	Large
HAEMONET	Haemonetics Corporation	Medium	TOYOSODA	Toyo Soda Manufacturing Co Ltd	Large
HAUSER	Hauser Chemical Research Inc	Small	TRACE	Trace Computers Plc	Small
HAYASH-B	Hayashibira Biochemical	Small	TRANSCEL	Transcell Technologies Inc	Small
HELIOSYN	Heliosynthese Sa	Small	TRANSGEN	Transgene	Small
HEM-RES	Hem Research Inc	Small	TRIPOS	Tripos Inc	Small
HEMOSOL	Hemosol Inc	Small	TSUMURA	Tsumura Juntendo Inc	Medium
HERCULES	Hercules Inc	Large	UCB	Union Chemique Belge Sa	Large
HEXAL	Hexal Pharma Ag	Small	UN-TECHN	United Technologies Corp	Large
HOECHST	Hoechst Ag	Large	UNC	University Of North Carolina	Ac/gov institution
HOF-ROCH	Hoffmann La Roche and Do Ag	Large	UNIVAX	Univax Biologics Inc	Small
HOUGHTON	Houghton and Co	Small	US-BIOMA	Usbiomaterials Corp	Small
HUMAN-G	Human Genome Sciences Inc	Small	VANGUARD	Vanguard Medica	Small
HYBRIDON	Hybridon Inc	Small	VECTORPH	Vectorpharma International Corp	Small

Company label	Name of the company	Size	Company label	Name of the company	Size
HYGENICS	Hygenics Pharmaceuticals Inc	Small	VERTEX	Vertex Pharmaceuticals Inc	Small
ICF	Icf Inc	Large	VESTAR	Vestar Inc	Small
ICN-PHAR	Icn Pharmaceuticals Inc	Medium	VIAGENE	Viagene Inc	Small
ID-VAC	Id Vaccine Corp	Small	VICAL	Vical Inc	Small
IDB	Idb Holding Spa	Small	VIROGEN	Virogenetics Corp	Small
IDEC	Idec Pharmaceuticals Corp	Small	VIRUS-RI	Virus Research Institute Inc	Small
IDETEK	Idetek Inc	Small	VOLVO	Volvo ab	Large
IDUN-P	Idun Pharmaceuticals Inc	Small	WARNER-L	Warner Lambert Co	Large
IGENE	Igene Biotechnology Inc	Small	WELLCOME	Wellcome Group	Large
IMCERA	Imcera Group Inc	Large	WHIT-ASS	Whitehead Associates	Small
IMCLONE	Imclone Systems Inc	Small	WR.GRACE	Wr Grace and Co	Large
IMMULOGI	Immulogic Pharmaceutical Corp	Small	XECHEM	Xechem International Inc	Small
IMMUNIC	Immunicon Corp	Small	XENOVA	Xenova Group Plc	Small
IMMUNOT	Immunotech Sa	Small	XOMA	Xoma Corp	Small
IMMUNSYS	Immunsystem	Small	YAMANOUC	Yamanouchi Pharmaceutical Co Ltd	Medium
IMMUSOL	Immusol Inc	Small	ZELTIA	Zeltia Sa	Small
IMTC	Imtc Holdings Inc	Small	ZENECA	Zeneca Group Plc	Large
INCELL	Incell Corp	Small	ZTB	Ztb Gmbh	Small
INCENTIV	Incentive Ab	Large	ZYMOGEN	Zymogenetics Inc	Small
INCYTE-P	Incyte Pharmaceuticals Inc	Small	ZYNAXIS	Zynaxis	Small
INHALETS	Inhale Therapeutic Systems Inc	Small			

PART V

International Entrepreneurship

International Entrepreneurship: The Current Status of the Field and Future Research Agenda

Shaker A. Zahra, Gerard George

With the globalization of the world economy, interest in international entrepreneurship has increased rapidly over the past decade (Brush 1993, 1995; Hitt and Bartkus, 1997; Hisrich, et al., 1996). One of the most important features of today's global economy is the growing role of young entrepreneurial new ventures (Almeida and Bloodgood, 1996; Bell, 1995; Clark and Mallory, 1997; Fujita, 1995; Haug, 1991). Through the 1990s, researchers' attention has centered on exploring the motivations for, the pattern of, and the pace of internationalization by new ventures (i.e., firms eight years old or younger). Invoking multiple theoretical perspectives, some researchers suggest that new ventures frequently become active players in the global economy soon after the birth of these firms (e.g., Oviatt and McDougall, 1999; Zahra, Matherne, and Carleton, 2000b). More recently, however, researchers have focused on examining the entrepreneurial activities of established companies (i.e., firms older than eight years), aiming to uncover the key patterns of innovative activities associated with successful internationalization (e.g., Zahra and Garvis, 2000). By doing so, researchers have sought to explain how international entrepreneurship may lead to superior financial performance among established firms.

Recent attempts to develop a well-grounded framework to understand the nature and effect of international entrepreneurship have concentrated mainly on the application of various theoretical perspectives to explain this phenomenon by refuting the applicability of traditional frameworks (e.g., McDougall, Shane, and Oviatt, 1994; Oviatt and McDougall, 1994). While insightful and informative, past research in this emerging area has followed different theoretical and methodological traditions, raising questions about its overall value added. This research has also lacked a unified framework that connects the antecedents, types, and outcomes of entrepreneurial activities pursued by new ventures and established companies (McDougall and Oviatt, 2000; Oviatt and McDougall, 1999). These shortcomings suggest a need to pause and consider the current status and cumulative contributions of research into international entrepreneurship and to discuss ways to enhance future contributions.

In this chapter, we seek to achieve four objectives. First, we analyze the concept of international entrepreneurship and its theoretical domain. We believe that the ambiguity of the international entrepreneurship term has led to confusion in past research and caused researchers to overlook important issues. Our discussion distinguishes between international entrepreneurship activities of new ventures and established companies. Second, we review past empirical work on international entrepreneurship and analyze its theoretical foundations and then arrive at a synthesis of the key factors believed to influence international entrepreneurship. Third, we offer an integrative framework that connects the antecedents, types, and outcomes of international entrepreneurship. This framework recognizes the importance of contextual variables in determining the value some companies derive from pursuing international entrepreneurship. Finally, we outline ways to improve future international entrepreneurship scholarship, hoping to increase its rigor and impact while making it accessible and relevant to the managers of new ventures and well-established companies.

Prior international entrepreneurship scholars have observed the close theoretical link between entrepreneurship and international business (IB) research (Oviatt and McDougall, 1994; McDougall and Oviatt, 2000). One of the most interesting revelations from reading published international entrepreneurship research is the extent to which scholars have made use of existing and emerging strategy theories and frameworks. In many ways, international entrepreneurship research has mirrored published strategy research, while also weaving together IB and entrepreneurship explanations of complex organizational phenomena. We believe this integration offers some important opportunities to develop more realistic and comprehensive frameworks of international entrepreneurship dimensions, antecedents, and effects. Therefore, throughout this chapter we highlight areas of convergence and divergence among international entrepreneurship and strategy scholars. We also discuss ways in which international entrepreneurship researchers can better employ strategy theories.

In the first section of this chapter, we present an overview of early research in international entrepreneurship, explain the growth of interest in this important phenomenon, and highlight key transition points in this research. We then review and critique studies that suggest that international entrepreneurship focuses on young firms. Attention will center on "born global" new ventures, recognizing the merits and shortcomings of this focus. Equally important, we also consider international entrepreneurship in established companies and explore the importance of studying these firms and the distinguishing characteristics of their international entrepreneurship. To move the field forward, we propose a comprehensive definition of international entrepreneurship and make some key distinctions between our definition and those definitions available in extant literature.

In the second section of the chapter, we analyze the contributions and cumulative value added of past international entrepreneurship research. We examine empirical and conceptual contributions, highlighting their theoretical foundations, data collection methods, and major findings. The discussion aims to distill what we know about international entrepreneurship and identify areas that need further research. We pay special attention to the challenges that researchers face in conducting research in international entrepreneurship of new ventures or established companies. Here, we categorize and then analyze the key findings of these studies into organizational, environmental, and strategic factors influencing international entrepreneurship. By doing so, we synthesize past research in a way that we hope will document and better model the relationships between international entrepreneurship and firm performance. The discussion also highlights several areas where strategy and entrepreneurship researchers converge and diverge.

In the third section of this chapter, we present a framework that connects its antecedents, types, and outcomes. Antecedents encompass the firm (e.g., top management team characteristics and firm resources). Types of international entrepreneurship activities refer to the extent, speed, and scope of a firm's international operations. International entrepreneurship outcomes include financial and non-financial (e.g., learning) gains that new ventures and established companies seek from internationalization (Barkema and Vermeulen, 1998). Factors that might affect the payoff from international entrepreneurship (e.g., strategic and environmental factors) are also considered. The proposed model makes use of theories from IB (Dunning, 1988; Craig and Douglas, 1996; Hymer, 1976), global strategy (Hitt, Hoskisson, and Ireland, 1994; Hitt et al., 1995; Hitt, Hoskisson, and Kim, 1997), strategic management (Grant, 1991, 1996, 1998), and entrepreneurship (Katz and Gartner, 1988; Kirzner, 1973). This model highlights the necessity of integrating these views as we seek to better understand the nature and implications of international entrepreneurship.

In the concluding section of this chapter, we discuss ways to improve future international entrepreneurship research by enhancing both its rigor and contribution. The discussion covers theory building and empirical issues, highlighting the potential gains scholars can make by capitalizing on innovative methods applied in the strategic management and IB disciplines. We also identify some emerging issues that deserve greater attention in future international entrepreneurship research.

Definition and Domain of International Entrepreneurship

Recently, researchers have drawn on IB and entrepreneurship theories to define and study international entrepreneurship. Originating in the entrepreneurship literature, a stream of research suggests that some new ventures are "born global" and therefore differ significantly from businesses that become international in scope over time as they accumulate resources or competencies (Oviatt and McDougall, 1994, 1999). Researchers, however, have noted that this phenomenon is not new and has existed in other countries, such as Sweden and Switzerland, and is a function of their resources and the size of their home markets (e.g., Bloodgood, Sapienza, and Almeida, 1996). Indeed, the IB literature provides multiple established theories that explain global expansion through market entry and the creation of new or joint ventures in other countries. Examples are the life cycle (Vernon, 1979) and internationalization (Johanson and Vahlne, 1977) theories. Though some argue that these theories are not applicable due to the unique context of "born global" organizations (Oviatt and McDougall, 1994; McDougall, Shane, and Oviatt, 1994), such conclusions appear to overlook venturing by established firms. Therefore, we believe the larger research issue concerns the incongruence in the definition and scope of international entrepreneurship. This section of the chapter, therefore, defines the concept and domain of international entrepreneurship.

To date, the bulk of international entrepreneurship research has focused on studying the internationalization of new ventures. These past efforts have been limited in their scope, concentrating on international new ventures as an independent entrepreneurial act by an individual. This limited focus has several drawbacks. This focus ignores the fact that entrepreneurial activities are an ongoing process that unfolds over time. These activities reflect the creativity of various members of a new venture's top management team. Members of these teams usually draw upon their innate abilities, skills, and talents as well their experience. Another limitation of prior research is precluding the notion of corporate entrepreneurship or venturing by established firms, especially in international markets. Companies of different age and size often engage in entrepreneurial activities as they venture into international markets (Zahra and Garvis, 2000) and these firms should be included in the study of international entrepreneurship. Similarly, the study of entrepreneurship in multinational firms has received considerable attention in recent IB research (e.g., Bartlett and Ghoshal, 2000; Birkinshaw, 1997), and therefore could provide additional insights into the domain, antecedents, and consequences of international entrepreneurship (Barnevik, 1991; Zahra and Garvis, 2000).

Table 12.1 presents an overview of the evolution of research into international entrepreneurship. The first known reference dates back to Morrow's (1988) discussions of the age of the international entrepreneur. Morrow suggested that advances in technology, coupled with increased cultural awareness, have made once-remote markets accessible to companies, whether new ventures or established companies. McDougall's (1989) study of new ventures' international sales was one of the first empirical efforts in this emerging area. This study has provided rich insights into differences between these firms and those ventures that did not go international.

In the early 1990s, McDougall and Oviatt (and their students) developed a series of case studies that clearly showed that some young ventures have gone international early in their life cycles. These case analyses clarified some of the approaches new ventures have followed in going international. Oviatt and McDougall (1994) followed this effort with an influential paper that defined international entrepreneurship, following the study of "born global" new ventures. This definition was narrower in scope than those offered in the literature. Zahra (1993), for example, suggested that the study of international entrepreneurship should encompass both new firms and established companies. A report by an entrepreneurship panel (Giamartino, McDougall, and Bird, 1993) called for a broader definition of international entrepreneurship. Zahra and Schulte (1994) also observed a need to go beyond the "born international" criterion highlighted in the early work of McDougall and Oviatt.

Wright and Ricks (1994) noted the growing importance of international entrepreneurship as an emerging research issue in IB. These authors also suggested that international entrepreneurship is a firm-level activity that crosses national borders and focuses on the relationship between businesses and the international environments in which they operate. This definition helped to shift attention away from using the age of the

Table 12.1   A chronicle of international entrepreneurship definitions

- McDougall (1989) states:

  "international entrepreneurship is defined in this study as the development of international new ventures or start-ups that, from their inception, engage in international business, thus viewing their operating domain as international from the initial stages of the firm's operation."

- Zahra (1993) defines international entrepreneurship as "the study of the nature and consequences of a firm's risk-taking behavior as it ventures into international markets."

- Giamartino, McDougall, and Bird (1993), heading an entrepreneurship-division-wide panel, suggested that the domain of international entrepreneurship be expanded.

- Oviatt and McDougall (1994) state:

  ". . . a business organization that, from inception, seeks to derive significant competitive advantage from the use of resources and sale of outputs in multiple countries."

- Wright and Ricks (1994) highlighted the growing importance of international entrepreneurship as an emerging research theme. They suggested that international entrepreneurship is a firm-level activity that crosses national borders and focuses on the relationship between businesses and the international environments in which they operate.

- McDougall and Oviatt (1996) state:

  "new and innovative activities that have the goal of value creation and growth in business organization across national borders."

- McDougall and Oviatt (2000) state:

  "A combination of innovative, proactive, and risk-seeking behavior that crosses or is compared across national borders and is intended to create value in business organizations." They note that firm size and age are defining characteristics here. But they exclude nonprofit and governmental agencies.

---

firm or timing of internationalization as the sole criterion to define international entrepreneurship. This definition also included young new ventures *and* established companies as being worthy of study. Wright and Ricks' definition, moreover, highlighted the context in which entrepreneurial activities occur, within new ventures or established corporations. This important insight further helped to set the stage for connecting the antecedents, types, and outcomes of international entrepreneurship. A firm's business environment plays an important role in spurring certain types of entrepreneurial activities (Zahra, 1991, 1993) and determining the payoff from these activities (Zahra and Covin, 1995). Finally, an advantage of the Wright and Ricks (1994) definition was the inclusion of comparative analyses of entrepreneurial activities within the domain of international entrepreneurship. There is much to be gained from conducting comparative analyses of international entrepreneurship in new ventures and established companies (McDougall and Oviatt, 2000; Wright and Ricks, 1994; Zahra and Schulte, 1994). These analyses can improve our understanding of the role of national cultures, national institutional environments, and centers (clusters) of innovations in promoting and shaping international entrepreneurship activities. These analyses can also improve theory development efforts by highlighting the role of contextual variables on relationships of interest.

Recently, Oviatt and McDougall (1999) offered a more inclusive list of topics that fall under the umbrella of international entrepreneurship. These topics included, among others, corporate entrepreneurship research. This research agenda reflected an important change in Oviatt and McDougall's view of international entrepreneurship; it recognized the importance of international entrepreneurship in established firms. McDougall and Oviatt (2000), moreover, suggested a broader definition of the entrepreneurship phenomenon; the study of established companies, and the recognition of comparative (cross-national) analysis. As table 12.1 indicates, McDougall and Oviatt's recent definition appears to accept Miller's (1983) definition of entrepreneurship as an organizational-level phenomenon that focuses on innovation, risk taking, and proactiveness. This definition has been widely used in the literature (Zahra, Jennings, and Kuratko, 1999). This focus links international entrepreneurship research to other research already under way in the field of entrepreneurship. It also makes it easier to follow what firms actually do, rather than attempting to decipher the intent of the individual entrepreneurs.

The inclusion of established companies also corrects an oversight in the entrepreneurship field; namely, the presumption that well-established companies are not innovative and refuse to take risks. Many highly regarded well-established companies work hard to foster innovation, support venturing, and encourage risk taking. To ignore these firms automatically precludes an important and vital part of the US and other economies. International entrepreneurship researchers, therefore, have several important opportunities as they study established companies. We outline some of these opportunities later in the chapter.

Despite the progress made toward defining international entrepreneurship, we remain concerned that the domain of this phenomenon remains vague. Lists that attempt to canvass and define the topics covered within international entrepreneurship also remain broad, raising questions about the unique research questions international entrepreneurship scholars should examine. For example, McDougall and Oviatt (2000) list the following topics as belonging within the domain of international entrepreneurship: cooperative alliances, corporate entrepreneurship, economic development activities, entrepreneur characteristics and motivations, exporting and other market entry modes, new ventures and IPOs, transitioning economies, and venture financing. While we applaud the desire to be inclusive, many of these issues have been the focus of considerable research by entrepreneurship, IB, and strategy scholars. This suggests the question: *What makes international entrepreneurship a distinct area of scholarly inquiry?*

We believe that what makes international entrepreneurship a unique and, indeed, worthwhile topic of research is the interplay between entrepreneurship and internationalization processes. Specifically, the innovativeness and risk taking that firms undertake as they expand (or contract) their international operations is what makes international entrepreneurship an interesting research area. Those insights and acts that bring new perspectives and strategies on how, what, when, and why to interna-

tionalize a business activity give meaning to the international entrepreneurship phenomenon. For instance, an e-commerce venture that goes international instantly at
birth is an interesting organizational form that deserves examination. This can be studied using the theoretical lens from organizational theory, sociology, strategy, entrepreneurship, or IB. The innovativeness by which the firm identifies a market opportunity,
defines (configures) its value chain, selects areas to be internationalized, and identifies
unique ways to reach potential customers in cyberspace is what makes this an international entrepreneurship-type study. Similarly, we can find examples of established firms
that are innovative, make proactive choices, and take risks to enter international markets (Zahra and Garvis, 2000).

Focusing on the innovativeness and entrepreneurial nature of a firm's internationalization has several advantages. It compels us to think about the processes by which
entrepreneurial firms and their managers go about justifying their existence. These
firms exist for many reasons, one of which is to offer a new way of doing things. As
readily acknowledged in the strategy literature, this new way can create value through
efficiency, speed, uniqueness, and/or customization. New ventures continue to exist
due to the inability of other firms to copy or undo the advantages of these firms.
Entrepreneurial firms know that their advantages lie in continuous innovation. The
ability to sustain this entrepreneurial spirit is what makes these organizations viable.
Rivals, large or small, do not easily duplicate this entrepreneurial capability. Thus, it
makes sense to focus on this entrepreneurial capacity as the theoretical engine in studying
international entrepreneurship. New ventures that reach the global market quickly
after their birth might be driven by a set of internal and external forces to do so. What
matters is *how* these firms succeed in the global market, a variable that requires
innovativeness, risk taking and entrepreneurship. As the global strategy literature suggests, some of these arguments apply equally well to established companies (Bartlett
and Ghoshal, 2000). This focus is consistent also with the strategy literature, where
companies that excel in their industries are believed to exhibit a great deal of creativity
and innovativeness in leveraging their core competencies. These companies stretch
and leverage their capabilities to achieve superior value creation for their customers
and other stakeholders (Hamel and Prahalad, 1994).

Focusing on innovativeness as a characteristic of international entrepreneurship has
additional advantages. Innovativeness connects the concept of international entrepreneurship to ongoing research in the broader field of entrepreneurship such as corporate entrepreneurship (Burgelman and Sayles, 1986; Zahra et al., 1999); research into
entrepreneurial orientation (Lumpkin and Dess 1996); and comparative literature that
suggests certain cultures are being more innovative or entrepreneurial (Mitchell et al.,
2000; Shane, 1993; Steensma et al., 2000).

The above discussion leads us to define international entrepreneurship as "*the process of creatively discovering and exploiting opportunities that lie outside a firm's domestic
markets in the pursuit of competitive advantage*". This definition builds on recent writings in the field of entrepreneurship that highlight the importance of opportunity
recognition, discovery, and exploitation as a distinguishing characteristic of entrepreneurship (Shane and Venkataraman, 2000; Zahra and Dess, 2001). Further, the term
"creatively," included in our definition, reinforces the need for innovativeness in the
way a firm discovers and/or exploits opportunities, as discussed above. The definition

also recognizes the fact that opportunities are sometimes discovered by some firms but are exploited by others. This is why we borrow the term competitive advantage from the strategic management literature (Barney, 1991; Collis, 1995). Having a competitive advantage can enable new ventures to create wealth to their owners by expanding internationally. Firms that internationalize their operations in innovative and creative ways stand to achieve significant gains that go beyond superior financial performance. Also, this definition is more inclusive than other definitions because it does not center on the size or age of the firm that pursues internationalization, consistent with McDougall and Oviatt (2000). Next, we review past research on international entrepreneurship literature.

Conceptual and Empirical Treatment of International Entrepreneurship: A Review

In this section, we review the conceptual and empirical studies with international entrepreneurship as their central premise of investigation. Several observations emerge from reviewing the international entrepreneurship research. First, past research has substantially benefited from the application of multiple theoretical foci. These theoretical perspectives include: the resource-based view (Autio et al., 1997; Bloodgood et al., 1996); transaction cost theory (Steensma et al., 2000; Zacharakis, 1997); organizational learning (Autio et al., 2000; Zahra, Ireland, and Hitt, 2000a); and product life cycle theory (Roberts and Senturia, 1996). However, McDougall et al. (1994) suggest that traditional IB theories may not be applicable to "born global" ventures. According to these authors, each of the traditional theories has several assumptions about the nature of the market or the sources of competitive advantages to be derived within certain market structures. McDougall et al. contend that many of these assumptions are not relevant in today's global markets or do not match the characteristics of "born international" new ventures. Similarly, we believe that the acceptance of a narrow definition of the international entrepreneurship domain is likely to have restricted the use of certain theoretical frameworks. Conversely, the expanded definition we have just offered above provides a broader range of issues where theoretical foci can be applied to future studies of international entrepreneurship.

Second, the development of international entrepreneurship has relied to a large extent on samples based in the US (Bloodgood et al., 1996; McDougall, 1989; McDougall and Oviatt, 1996; Zahra et al., 2000a, b; Zahra and Garvis, 2000). However, there are some studies that draw on non-US firms. For example, Autio et al. (2000, 1997) and Holmlund and Kock (1998) analyzed ventures in Finland, Coviello and Munro (1995) studied firms from New Zealand, and Fontes and Coombs (1997) studied Portuguese firms. Unfortunately, these studies and those that use US data have tended to evolve independent of each other. Therefore, there is little congruence and overlap in theory building that would account for the potential differences in international entrepreneurship across countries. A promising development is recent work using multi-country data to compare cross-cultural effects on venture creation and alliance formation (Mitchell et al., 2000; Steensma et al., 2000).

Third, past studies appear to draw thematic conclusions based on case studies or small samples. For example, Autio et al. (2000) suggest learning advantages of newness using a sample of 57 privately held Finnish firms. Bloodgood et al. (1996) examined the antecedents and outcomes of the internationalization of 61 ventures. Similarly, McDougall and Oviatt (1996) draw conclusions on performance implications of internationalization using a sample of 62 firms. Other articles rely on case studies (e.g., Tiessen and Merrilees, 1999). Also, most studies concentrated on high-technology samples, thereby limiting the ability to generalize to samples of low technology or traditional industries (Burgel and Murray, 1998; Fontes and Coombs, 1997; Karagozoglu and Lindell, 1997; Reuber and Fischer, 1997; Zahra et al., 2000a, b). Only a few studies have examined service industries (e.g., Mößlang 1995). To summarize, while we commend prior authors for developing and establishing the domain of a new area of scholarly inquiry, there is a need to develop a stronger theoretical rationale and empirical testing with larger and more representative samples.

Fourth, the lack of longitudinal design is a major weakness of prior international entrepreneurship research. The dominance of cross-sectional research designs in past research has resulted in non-cumulative and inconsistent findings. Even though conducting longitudinal research is a time-consuming and challenging process (Davidsson and Wiklund, 2000), it can improve our understanding of the relationships examined in international entrepreneurship research (Sexton, Pricer, and Nenide, 2000). Such research designs can be especially helpful in identifying the potential causal links among variables of interest.

Limitations aside, the studies just reviewed have helped expand the domain of international entrepreneurship. These studies have tested international entrepreneurship as a multidimensional construct. These dimensions are further explored below. Also, several key relationships such as the factors that determine internationalization or its outcomes have been addressed. We categorize these key issues as organizational factors, environmental factors, and strategic factors. To set the stage for the discussion, the next section of this chapter analyzes the various dimensions of international entrepreneurship explored in prior research.

Dimensions of international entrepreneurship

Prior researchers focused on three key dimensions of international entrepreneurship. In table 12.2, we present these dimensions and identify the studies that examined them. As table 12.2 shows, the majority of prior studies examined the extent (or degree) of a new venture's sales internationalization. Typically, the extent of internationalization was measured by the percent of a firm's sales generated from foreign markets. Some studies also examined the speed by which a new venture internationalized their operations. In these studies, speed was defined as the length of time that elapsed between the year the venture was created and the year of its first foreign sales. Table 12.2 also shows that some studies examined the scope of a new venture's sales internationalization, measured by the number of countries (other than country of origin) in which the new venture generated sales. Finally, two studies investigated the regional scope of a new venture's sales internationalization.

One of the most striking features of past international entrepreneurship research is the fact that it has focused almost exclusively on indicators of internationalization of

Table 12.2 Dimensions of international entrepreneurship

Extent/degree of internationalization	Speed	Scope	
		Countries	Regions
• McDougall (1989)	• Reuber and Fischer (1997)	• Zahra et al. (2000a)	• Reuber and Fischer (1997)
• McDougall et al. (1994)	• Zahra et al. (2000b)	• Roberts and Senturia (1996)	• Roberts and Senturia (1996)
• Brush (1995)	• Roberts and Senturia (1996)	• Burgel and Murray (1998)	
• Bloodgood et al. (1996)	• Fontes and Coombs (1997)		
• McDougall and Oviatt (1996)	• Lindqvist (1997)		
• Karagozoglu and Lindell (1997)	• Burgel and Murray (1998)		
• Reuber and Fischer (1997)			
• Burgel and Murray (1998)			
• Zahra et al. (2000a)			
• Zahra et al. (2000b)			

the firm's operations, both in scope (e.g., regions) and scale (i.e., level of sales derived from international operations). A glaring deficiency in past research is ignoring the internationalization of a firm's value chain or inputs into the production process. As acknowledged by strategy (Porter, 1986) and global strategy (Bartlett and Ghoshal, 2000) researchers, these variables can significantly influence the nature and magnitude of a firm's competitive advantage. International entrepreneurship researchers have also overlooked one of the key areas that can give young and established firms enduring competitive advantages that set them apart from their rivals: the ability to recognize opportunities and pursue them creatively (Kirzner, 1973).

Organizational factors influencing international entrepreneurship

One area that has received some attention in prior studies is the effect of firm-related variables on international entrepreneurship. Researchers examined three sets of variables: top management team (TMT) characteristics, firm resources, and firm-specific variables. These variables have been widely discussed in strategy and entrepreneurship research. Table 12.3a summarizes the key findings from prior research on the effect of the top management team and resources on international entrepreneurship. Table 12.3b presents the results for the effect of firm variables on international entrepreneurship.

Strategy researchers have long maintained that the characteristics of the firm's top management team can spell the difference between its success and failure. These characteristics significantly affect firms' strategic choices (Finkelstein and Hambrick, 1996), such as internationalization (Carpenter and Frederickson, 2001; Calof and Beamish, 1994). In table 12.3a, we note the importance of TMT characteristics such as foreign work experience, foreign education, background, and vision as they relate to internationalization. Exposure to international markets or market practices significantly influences the firm's drive to internationalize. These findings are corroborated through case analyses (Oviatt and McDougall, 1995) and empirical studies (Bloodgood et al., 1996; Burgel and Murray, 1998). This is important because senior managers' international experience is positively related to some indicators of firm performance (Carpenter, Sanders, and Gregersen, 2001; Daily, Certo, and Dalton, 2000).

Strategy researchers have invoked the resource-based theory as a key basis for explaining the various strategic choices companies make (Barney, 1991). Our review also highlights the importance of firm resources as a factor influencing international entrepreneurship (table 12.3a). Particular attention has been given to how the firm's unique assets such as product innovativeness (Burgel and Murray, 1998) influence the internationalization process (Zahra et al., 2000a). Also, intangible assets such as reputation and networks can significantly influence the speed and degree of internationalization (Zahra et al., 2000b). The proposition that unique organizational assets and knowledge bases can influence international entrepreneurship also is supported by case analyses (Oviatt and McDougall, 1995). In turn, international expansion enhances the firm's learning and gives it access to new knowledge bases, as found in the study by Zahra et al. (2000a).

Researchers also have examined the effect of several organizational factors on a firm's international entrepreneurship. Specifically, researchers have examined the effects of

Table 12.3a Influence of organizational factors on international entrepreneurship (TMT and resources)

Variable	Dimension	Findings
Top Management Team	Foreign work experience	• Case analyses showed that new ventures led by managers with foreign work experience were able to quickly internationalize their operations and do so successfully (Oviatt and McDougall, 1995; McDougall et al., 1996). • Found a positive and significant association between managers' foreign work experience and degree of new venture's internationalization (Bloodgood et al., 1996; Burgel and Murray, 1998). • A higher percentage of managers of companies that internationalized worked for a foreign company at home (Burgel and Murray, 1998).
	Education abroad	• Found a positive (not significant) relationship between managers receiving education outside the USA and new ventures' international expansion (Bloodgood et al., 1996) • A higher percentage of managers of companies that internationalized received education abroad than those of startups that did not internationalize (Burgel and Murray, 1998).
	Background	• Firms with principal founders drawn from managerial parental backgrounds were significantly more likely to export than firms with other types of founders (Westhead et al., 1998).
	Global vision	• Case analyses suggested that new ventures led by managers with global visions were able to internationalize quickly and successfully (Oviatt and McDougall, 1995).
Resources	Unique assets	• Case analyses suggested that new ventures with unique intangible assets were able to internationalize quickly and successfully (Oviatt and McDougall, 1995). • Companies that internationalized their operations had products that required significantly less customization and maintenance than those that did not (Burgel and Murray 1998). There were no differences between the two groups in the amount of installation or training required to use their products. • Startup companies that did not internationalize were more likely to describe their products as being less innovative (Burgel and Murray, 1998).
	R&D spending	• Positively (not significant) related to internationalization status, speed, or degree (Zahra et al., 2000b). • Startups that internationalized their operations had higher R&D-to-sales ratio (Burgel and Murray, 1998). • Startups that internationalized their operations had higher ratio of employees who worked 50% or more of their time on new product development as percent of sales than those that did not (Burgel and Murray, 1998).

Network

- Case analyses suggested that new ventures with extensive networks were able to internationalize quickly and successfully (Oviatt and McDougall, 1995).
- Technological networks are positively and significantly associated with status, speed, and degree of internationalization, and this effect is higher for new firms with high R&D spending (Zahra et al., 2000b).
- There were no significant differences between startups that internationalized and those that did not with regard to access to venture or angel capital (Burgel and Murray, 1998).
- Firms that had received industry grants were significantly more likely to export (Westhead et al., 1998).

Reputation

- A reputation for technological superiority is positively and significantly associated with status, speed, and degree of internationalization. This effect is higher for status and degree of internationalization of new firms with high R&D spending (Zahra et al., 2000b). Interaction of reputation and R&D is not significant in the case of speed.

Table 12.3b Influence of organizational factors on international entrepreneurship (firm-related variables)

Variable	Findings
Size	<ul><li>Venture size is positively associated with degree of internationalization (Bloodgood et al., 1996).</li><li>Venture size (time 1) was negatively (not significant) associated with relative market share in time 2 (McDougall and Oviatt, 1996).</li><li>Venture size was positively (not significant) associated with internationalization status, speed, or degree (Zahra et al., 2000b).</li><li>Company size is negatively associated (not significant) with degree of internationalization (Reuber and Fischer, 1997).</li><li>High-tech startups that internationalized were significantly larger in sales and employment than firms that did not internationalize (Burgel and Murray 1998).</li><li>There was no significant difference in employment of exporters vs. non-exporters (Westhead et al., 1998).</li></ul>
Age	<ul><li>Age was negatively (not significant) associated with ROI in time 2 (McDougall and Oviatt, 1996).</li><li>Age is positively associated with degree of internationalization in one equation but negative (not significant) in another (Reuber and Fischer, 1997).</li><li>Startups that internationalized were significantly older than firms that did not internationalize (Burgel and Murray, 1998).</li><li>Venture age was positively (not significant) associated with internationalization status or degree (Zahra et al., 2000b).</li><li>Speed of internationalization was not explored in the analysis.</li><li>There were no significant differences in age between exporters and non-exporters (Westhead et al., 1998).</li></ul>
Location	<ul><li>There was no significant difference between firms that exported and those that did not in rural vs. urban location (Westhead et al., 1998).</li><li>National culture influences the formation of technology alliances by entrepreneurial firms (Steensma et al., 2000).</li></ul>
Origin	<ul><li>Corporate origin was negatively and significantly associated with status. Corporate origin was negatively (not significant) associated with degree and speed of internationalization (Zahra et al., 2000b).</li></ul>
Growth orientation	<ul><li>Firm growth orientation was positively associated with average absolute annual international sales growth (Autio et al., 1997).</li></ul>

Environmental scanning	•	Average amount of environmental scanning was positively and significantly associated with international collaborative relationships which, in turn, was positively and significantly associated with average absolute annual international sales growth (Autio et al., 1997).
	•	Analyses indicated that limited global information-gathering capabilities limited companies' internationalization (Karagozoglu and Lindell, 1997).
Financial strength	•	ROE was positively (but not significant) with internationalization status, positive and marginally significant (p<10) with speed and degree of sales internationalization (Zahra et al., 2000b).
	•	Leverage was positively (not significant) associated with degree of internationalization (Bloodgood et al., 1996).

age and size, speculating that experience and resources (firm size as proxy) intensify international entrepreneurship. As table 12.3b shows, research findings did not support theoretical explanations. A similar conclusion emerged from prior studies on the effect of location, which was believed to give companies unique knowledge and resources that can intensify internationalization. Here too, empirical findings did not support theoretical explanations.

As table 12.3b indicates, researchers have also examined venture origin, defined as whether the firm was established by a corporation or an independent entrepreneur. For example, Zahra et al. (2000b) found that ventures created by established firms were less likely to internationalize their sales. A corporate venture status was not significantly associated with the degree or speed of sales internationalization. Future international entrepreneurship researchers are likely to gain a great deal of insight from examining the effect of intangible assets and resources typically associated with venture origin on different dimensions of internationalization. Some strategy research has already uncovered significant differences between independent and corporate ventures in their resource bases (Shrader and Simon, 1997) and competitive strategies, especially with respect to technological choices (Zahra, 1996). Whether or not these differences manifest themselves in the extent or speed of new ventures' internationalization remains unknown. Also, it is not clear if there are differences among independently owned (private) firms vs. publicly owned and managed companies in internationalization or the gains achieved from this important but complex activity.

Growth orientation   Managers' motivation to achieve growth can influence a firm's international entrepreneurship activities. One study that tested this proposition found that firms that had a high growth orientation were likely to internationalize their operations (Autio et al., 1997). This finding highlighted the importance of managerial attitudes in shaping the strategic direction of their enterprises (Finkelstein and Hambrick, 1996), especially in terms of global expansion. However, the dearth of empirical studies that document the types of attitudes that are conducive to globalization and the direction of the relationship between these attitudes and success in international expansion remains a gap in this emerging research stream.

Environmental scanning   Information about the industry and/or potential foreign markets can spur international entrepreneurship. Evidence indicates that the exposure and ability to gather information from foreign markets is positively associated with internationalization (Autio et al., 1997; Karagozoglu and Lindell, 1997). These findings are consistent with strategic management research that highlights the importance of environmental analysis for the effective selection of the strategies companies pursue (Hambrick 1981; Miles and Snow, 1978). Still, much can be gained from conducting more analyses that examine the various systems and processes by which companies gather information about opportunities in their international markets and how they interpret this information as they craft the strategies they pursue.

Financial strength   Table 12.3b suggests that some researchers have begun to examine the effect of a firm's financial status on its internationalization. This research is guided by a belief that successful past organizational performance creates the slack resources needed to support international expansion. Two aspects of a new venture's financial status were considered in prior studies: past ROE and debt leverage. Zahra et al. (2000b) concluded that past ROE was not significantly associated with the status of internationalization (internationalized vs. not). Past ROE was positively but marginally associated with the speed and degree of sales internationalization. In terms of financial leverage, Bloodgood et al. (1996) reported a non-significant association with the degree of internationalization, raising a question about the potential contribution of past performance to new ventures' internationalization. Perhaps the results are unique to the samples examined to date. Alternatively, financial performance may not play a key role in explaining the internationalization of new ventures' sales. That is, regardless of their financial position, some new ventures expand internationally to achieve a variety of strategic goals. Given that only a few studies have been conducted on this issue to date, however, it would be premature to drop indicators of past financial performance from future studies of international entrepreneurship.

In summary, consistent with long-established tradition in the strategic management field, past empirical research has attempted to gauge the influence of several organizational variables on international entrepreneurship. Some key organizational variables are TMT characteristics, firm resources, and firm-level variables such as size, age, location, origin, growth orientation, environmental scanning, and financial strength. However, as the list of variables examined would suggest, a coherent theoretical framework that explains the potential influence of these variables on internationalization is lacking. Table 12.3b also shows that many of these studies do not provide statistically significant support for these relationships. It is possible that external environmental factors play a more significant role in international entrepreneurship and may serve to lessen the effects of organizational factors on international entrepreneurship. Therefore, we now examine research that links a firm's external environment to its international entrepreneurial activities.

Influence of the external environment on international entrepreneurship

Strategic management and entrepreneurship researchers have long acknowledged the importance of the external environment on a firm's various strategic choices (Boyd, Dess, and Rasheed, 1993; Zahra and Bogner, 2000). Consequently, researchers have explored the effect of a firm's external environment on different aspects of international entrepreneurship. Past empirical studies that have investigated these issues appear in table 12.4. These results suggest that new ventures that internationalize their operations early in their life cycles compete in industries that are perceived as being different in their attributes from those where new ventures do not internationalize as quickly or as broadly. Table 12.4 also shows that the characteristics of a new venture's major industry may determine the gains to be made from internationalization (Roberts and Senturia, 1996; Zahra, Neubaum, and Huse, 1996). That is, the characteristics of the industry may significantly moderate the relationship between international entrepreneurship and the financial gains from these activities, as found by Zahra and Garvis (2000).

One has to be cautious in interpreting prior results on the effect of the environment on international entrepreneurship and a firm's future gains from international

Table 12.4 Influence of the external environment on international entrepreneurship

Variables	Findings
Intensity of domestic competition	• No differences between international and purely domestic new venture; sign is positive (McDougall, 1989). • Domestic market saturation was mentioned by only 26% of responding firms as a motivation for internationalization (Karagozoglu and Lindell, 1998).
Limited domestic growth	• Case studies showed the limited growth of domestic markets was a major reason for the rapid internationalization of high-technology new ventures (Coviello and Munro, 1995). • Insufficiency of domestic sales to achieve competitive levels of R&D was key motivation to internationalization, as mentioned by 35% of responding companies (Karagozoglu and Lindell, 1998).
Intensity of international competition	• International new ventures competed in industries that exhibited significantly higher levels of international competition (McDougall, 1989). • Case studies showed that intensity of global competition in the industry was one important factor in explaining the rapid internationalization of high-technology new firms (Coviello and Munro, 1995).
Restrictive government policies	• International new ventures competed in industries that exhibited significantly higher levels of governmental protection and regulations (McDougall, 1989).
Institutional environment	• Institutional environments significantly influence international entrepreneurship (Mitchell et al., 2000). • Institutional structures in emerging economies facilitate entrepreneurship through effective governance mechanisms (George and Prabhu, 2000).
Economies of scale	• No differences between international and purely domestic new venture; sign is positive (McDougall, 1989).
Retaliation by industry incumbents	• No differences between international and purely domestic new venture; sign is positive (McDougall, 1989).
Industry gross profits	• Is negatively and significantly associated with degree of internationalization (Bloodgood et al., 1996).
Industry sales growth	• Positively (not significant) associated with degree of internationalization (Bloodgood et al., 1996)
Type of Industry	• Service firms tended to internationalize less than manufacturing firms (Burgel and Murray, 1998; Westhead et al., 1998).

entrepreneurship. Only a limited number of studies have explored this issue to date, as becomes evident from reviewing table 12.4. Prior studies have also focused primarily on high-technology industries, probably because these industries have experienced the highest rates of growth in the formation of new ventures. Low technology, both in manufacturing and service industries, has not received as much interest in international entrepreneurship research, raising the possibility that past findings do not generalize equally well to all economic sectors.

Researchers also have failed to examine the specific attributes of the environment on international entrepreneurship variables. This is evident in those studies that collected data from single industries in an effort to control for industry variability. This measurement strategy overlooks the possibility that managers within the same industry may view their environments quite differently, which would lead to significant differences in international entrepreneurship. The same variables may also have different implications for internationalization and the gains to be achieved from this strategy at different points in time in the life of a given industry. Also, different segments of the same industry also may experience significant forces of competition, leading to significant differences in international entrepreneurship patterns and outcomes. Finally, researchers have been inconsistent in measuring industry attributes (whether objective or perceived), making it difficult to compare findings across studies and discern clear patterns in prior results. Other researchers have expressed a similar concern about strategic management research (Boyd et al., 1993) and suggested controlling for industry variables (Dess, Ireland, and Hitt, 1990). We believe that international entrepreneurship researchers would benefit significantly from using these recommendations in designing future empirical studies.

The above observations urge greater caution in interpreting prior research results on the relationships between the characteristics of a firm's business environment and international entrepreneurship. These studies also call attention to the need for greater and better theoretically grounded research. One issue that has escaped attention to date is the configuration of international entrepreneurship activities across business environments. Past researchers have examined individual international entrepreneurship dimensions while ignoring the overall configurations of these activities and their implications for a company's performance. Past research ignores the possibility that the payoff from international entrepreneurship might be determined by the trade-offs or synergies that might exist among these activities.

Influence of strategic factors on international entrepreneurship

International entrepreneurship researchers also have examined the effect of a company's competitive strategies on international entrepreneurship. Therefore, in table 12.5, we summarize the key strategy variables used in prior research and their influence on a firm's international entrepreneurship. Table 12.5 suggests that these variables cover generic strategies, functional strategies, and entry strategy. Below we discuss each of these variables in turn.

Generic strategies Researchers propose that a firm's competitive strategy can spur its international entrepreneurship. Consequently, prior studies have attempted to relate

Table 12.5 Influence of strategic factors on international entrepreneurship

Variables	Findings
Generic strategy • Low cost • Differentiation	• Case analyses suggested that product differentiation was important for rapid internationalization (Oviatt and McDougall, 1995). • Product differentiation is positively associated with degree of internationalization (Bloodgood et al., 1996). • Unique product is important for internationalization (Fontes and Coombs, 1997). • R&D spending positively and significantly associated with international collaborative relationships which were positively and significantly associated with absolute annual international sales growth (Autio et al., 1997). • Product quality is conducive to internationalization that is achieved through networks (Holmlund and Kock, 1998).
Functional strategy • Production • Distribution • Marketing	• International new ventures emphasized a distribution and marketing strategy less than domestic ventures (McDougall, 1989). • Firms that had the majority of their customers located in the same country as those measured six years earlier were significantly less likely to export (Westhead et al., 1998). • Product attributes may have important implications for the pace of new ventures' internationalization (Roberts and Senturia, 1996). • Production competence was conducive to internationalization (Holmlund and Kock, 1996). • A negative sign (marginally significant) between marketing differentiation and degree of internationalization (Bloodgood et al., 1996).
Entry strategy	• International new ventures emphasized grand entry scale significantly more than domestic ventures (McDougall, 1989). • Firms that targeted niche markets composed of advanced clients were prepared to internationalize (Fontes and Coombs, 1997). • Technology alliances by entrepreneurial firms affected by national culture (Steensma et al., 2000).

low-cost strategy and differentiation strategy to internationalization. Past studies found that unique products and product differentiation were positively related to internationalization (Bloodgood et al., 1996; Fontes and Coombs, 1997), thereby highlighting the importance of intangible factors in explaining international entrepreneurship. These findings are consistent with the resource-based theory of the firm, indicating that unique resources can intensify and expedite a firm's international expansion. Also, Autio et al. (1997) emphasized the importance of R&D spending and international collaborative relationships, which were conducive to internationalization. Zahra et al. (2000b) noted that such relationships could give new ventures the knowledge and resources that can expedite international expansion.

Functional strategies   Researchers also emphasized production, distribution, and marketing functions and their relationships with international entrepreneurship. Roberts and Senturia (1996) underscored the importance of product attributes such as uniqueness and customization, while Holmlund and Kock (1998) highlighted the importance of production competence for international entrepreneurship. However, McDougall (1989) and Bloodgood et al. (1996) found that international new ventures de-emphasize a distribution and marketing strategy.

Entry strategy   International new ventures have also been profiled for their entry strategy. McDougall (1989) found that international new ventures have emphasized a large-scale entry strategy significantly more than small ventures. Fontes and Coombs (1997) related the composition of their clientele with internationalization in a niche market. Also, Beamish (1999) theorized that different types of alliances are an appropriate mode of entry choices for international entrepreneurship. Still, more empirical work is needed in this area, especially with regard to entrepreneurial firms.

To date, only a handful of studies have connected competitive strategy variables to international entrepreneurship. The selection of the variables, however, does not appear to follow established theories, even though comprehensive reviews of these theories are easily accessible (Carroll, 1993; Teece et al., 1997; Williamson, 1999). Most prior studies have not linked entry strategies to non-financial gains to be achieved through internationalization such as knowledge and learning. The paucity of prior empirical studies and lack of theoretical grounding also suggest a need to further explore these relationships within an integrated and coherent framework. We broadly categorized past studies into generic, functional, and entry strategies. Clearly, opportunities for future scholarly inquiry abound.

Toward an Integrated Model of International Entrepreneurship

In this section, we propose a model of international entrepreneurship that is consistent with our previously stated definition and review of the literature. As already noted, past research shows a need to develop an integrative framework that can serve as a foundation for future theory building and testing of international entrepreneurship. Figure 12.1 presents a proposed integrative framework.

The model includes three sets of factors that we believe to influence international

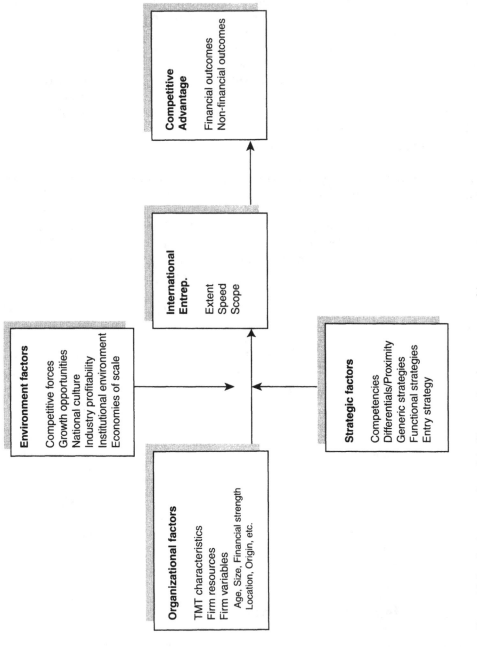

Environment factors

Competitive forces
Growth opportunities
National culture
Industry profitability
Institutional environment
Economies of scale

Organizational factors

TMT characteristics
Firm resources
Firm variables
  Age, Size, Financial strength
  Location, Origin, etc.

International Entrep.

Extent
Speed
Scope

Strategic factors

Competencies
Differentials/Proximity
Generic strategies
Functional strategies
Entry strategy

Competitive Advantage

Financial outcomes
Non-financial outcomes

Figure 12.1 An integrated model of international entrepreneurship

entrepreneurship. It indicates that organizational factors significantly influence a firm's drive to internationalize and therefore are modeled as antecedents of international entrepreneurship, which supports the research summarized in tables 12.3a and 12.3b. These organizational factors include the TMT, firm resources, and firm-related variables (such as age, size, financial strength, location, and origin). Given the formative stage of this stream of research, our list of organizational variables is meant to be representative rather than exhaustive. As research on international entrepreneurship grows, scholars are likely to identify additional organizational variables that significantly determine a firm's drive to internationalize.

Consistent with previous work, figure 12.1 suggests that international entrepreneurship is multidimensional. Figure 12.1 highlights three dimensions of international entrepreneurship: extent, speed, and scope (table 12.2). These three dimensions reveal different facets of international entrepreneurship. Extent would imply the dependence of the firm on international revenues or the number of new markets that a firm has entered. Speed signifies the rate at which the firm enters new markets. Scope could be geographic scope wherein we can possibly consider the economic regions as the unit of analysis or product scope, where we consider the breadth of the product mix that has been effectively internationalized. These dimensions are by no means exhaustive but they provide an adequate launching point for future work.

Next, we list strategic and environmental factors as potential moderators of the relationship between organizational factors and international entrepreneurship dimensions. The strategy literature suggests that a firm's general and task environments significantly influence the motivation or the rate of internationalization (Hitt, Hoskisson, and Kim, 1997). Within the strategic set, we include two variables that were not present in our synthesis of past research. First, we believe that firm competencies are likely to be moderators. Firms that have particular competencies, say in production, can effectively or quickly transfer such capabilities to international markets. These companies, therefore, stand to achieve greater gains from their international expansion. Next, we use the term "differentials" or "proximity" to suggest the amount of difference between the home market and emerging opportunities. These differentials could be, for example, in market practices. For example, distribution systems differ greatly between countries and therefore influence certain dimensions of international entrepreneurship. Other differentials could be in national culture, customer profiles, and habits, among others. The other variables, including generic, functional, and entry strategies listed as potential moderators, have been discussed in the review section (table 12.5).

Though one could argue that environmental factors and strategic factors overlap, we make the distinction in the interest of parsimony and clarity. Environmental factors included in the proposed model are competitive forces (number of competitors, bargaining power, etc.), growth opportunities (rate of market growth, countries with open markets, etc.), regulatory environment, industry profitability, institutional environment, and economies of scale (table 12.4). These factors will act as moderators and determine the strength of the relationship between organizational variables and international entrepreneurship dimensions discussed above. Organizational variables (e.g. senior management's international experience) might affect international entrepreneurship quite differently in different levels of environmental uncertainty (Carpenter and Frederickson, 2001). Research from strategic management highlights the contingent nature of these relationships (Finkelstein and Hambrick, 1996). In particular, the strategic choice approach suggests that certain organizational characteristics may promote (or inhibit) international entrepreneurship activities in different business environments. Thus, a moderating relationship is appropriate when considering the effects of strategic and environmental factors on international entrepreneurship.

Finally, we suggest a set of outcomes from international entrepreneurship. These include outcomes such as financial and non-financial performance indicators. Past empirical research in international entrepreneurship has provided inconclusive results regarding the link between international entrepreneurship and performance. For example, Bloodgood et al. (1996) found a positive and marginally significant relationship between international entrepreneurship and firm income. Whereas Zahra and Garvis (2000) found no relationship between international entrepreneurship and return on assets, McDougall and Oviatt (1996) reported a non-significant relationship. Consequently, future studies would benefit by relating international entrepreneurship to multiple indicators of a company's financial performance. Moreover, few past studies have related international entrepreneurship to non-financial performance. Oviatt and McDougall (1995) connected international entrepreneurship to market share, while Zahra et al. (2000a) related international entrepreneurship to technological learning and acquisition of new knowledge. The importance of non-financial outcomes of international entrepreneurship suggests a need to apply multiple measures to further improve future research in this area.

Future Research in International Entrepreneurship

Our review and analysis suggest that there are tremendous opportunities for research in international entrepreneurship. More recent work in this area has helped provide visibility and underscore the importance of this emerging research stream. Our definition, however, expands the domain of international entrepreneurship to include both new and corporate ventures. By doing so, we hope to expand the boundaries of and domain of the international entrepreneurship phenomenon, providing greater opportunities for discovery and integration. Also, we hope international entrepreneurship scholars draw from the entrepreneurship, strategic management, and IB literatures, thereby enhancing the theoretical rigor and significance of their research. In this section, we outline three areas that may position international entrepreneurship as a prominent and productive research stream: the international entrepreneurship process, the context of international entrepreneurship, and post-internationalization agenda. Below we discuss these issues in turn.

The international entrepreneurship process

The fundamental questions in this area are: "*How, why, and when do entrepreneurial firms discover and exploit opportunities outside their home country?*" These questions raise several interesting secondary research issues. The first issue includes those factors that may influence the firm's desire to search for opportunities beyond its domestic market. Some of these factors have been introduced in our proposed model (figure

12.1). These factors may include TMT characteristics such as ability, exposure, and composition, among others. Managers' creativity and insights may also contribute to this process. Also, factors such as unused or slack firm resources that could be more effectively utilized in alternate market environments. Similarly, financial strength allows the firm the requisite latitude to take calculated risks to expand its market opportunities.

A second research issue involves the characteristics of internationalized firms. We illustrate with the issue of firm size and age. Though past research predominantly considers age as a significant factor in internationalization, it does not necessarily illustrate how age matters in the international entrepreneurship process. To remedy this situation, we suggest going beyond the use of age and size as control variables to address more creative research issues. These issues may include conducting research that determines if small new ventures adopt different strategies than larger corporate ventures. If so, the next step would be to uncover the reasons behind these differences, using traditional theoretical frameworks such as transaction cost economics or resource-based view, to suggest the constraints, benefits, and different configurations adopted by these ventures in the international entrepreneurship process.

Researchers studying new ventures should also recognize that major changes occur in firms' resource and skill base even during the early years of their life cycles. As aptly illustrated by Bantel (1998), for example, startup and adolescent new ventures might adopt different strategies. Presently, it is not clear if and how these differences extend to international entrepreneurship. Future researchers, therefore, would benefit from taking these key organizational transitions as they examine new ventures' international entrepreneurship activities.

A third future research issue centers on the dimensions of international entrepreneurship. We suggest a need to examine the three dimensions of international entrepreneurship: extent, speed, and scope. Though few studies have sought to link firm characteristics to international entrepreneurship dimensions, considerably more work is required in this area. Future research may attempt to better understand the theoretical underpinning of differential relationships between top management, resources, and firm characteristics and international entrepreneurship dimensions. For example, researchers could examine firm-level conditions under which international entrepreneurship is speedier or more geographically dispersed using, say, resource dependence or product life cycle arguments. Future empirical studies along these lines would greatly enhance our understanding of international entrepreneurship processes.

We have proposed a definition of international entrepreneurship as a process of creatively identifying and exploiting opportunities in markets that lie outside the firm's domestic operations. This definition raises additional research questions that center on the sources of creativity associated with opportunity recognition in international markets. These sources may include managerial insights, experience, connections and contacts, network relationships, and informal and formal industry analyses. Sources also include the types of information sources firms use to spot these opportunities, and the approaches companies use to exploit opportunities in international markets. Are these processes shaped by industry conditions? What role does national culture play in this regard (Kogut and Singh, 1988)? How and when are these processes institutionalized? What types of organizational learning occur in and through these processes? How does this learning influence the future entrepreneurial activities of the firm? These and similar questions serve to highlight the range of theoretical and empirical issues that can (and perhaps should) be investigated in future international entrepreneurship research.

The context of international entrepreneurship

The fundamental question here is: "*What contextual factors influence the internationalization of entrepreneurial firms?*" By context of internationalization, we mean those conditions that make internationalization more attractive or lucrative than solely domestic operations. It is critical for future research to account for the context within which international entrepreneurship occurs. We list several environmental and strategic variables within our integrative framework that may guide future work in international entrepreneurship (figure 12.1).

A key research issue concerns the major environmental factors affecting international entrepreneurship. There are other significant factors that merit attention in international entrepreneurship, including industry characteristics, country institutional and regulatory environments, among others (figure 12.1). This area is virtually unexplored because of the number of combinations of factors that can help explain international entrepreneurship. For example, the role of institutions in fostering entrepreneurship and internationalization of these ventures has not been investigated. Recent theoretical work suggests that certain types of institutions provide opportunities for firms to develop their networks and attract international partnerships for expansion (George and Prabhu, 2000). Unexplored areas also include industry characteristics and internationalization processes since many past studies have used small samples.

A second important research issue involves strategic variables that influence international entrepreneurship. Figure 12.1 indicates that firm competencies, strategic differentials, generic, functional, and entry strategies influence international entrepreneurship. How competencies moderate the relationship between organizational factors (such as firm resources) and international entrepreneurship dimensions (such as scope) is an interesting question to explore. Similarly, strategic differentials between home market practices and foreign markets are likely to moderate the relationship between firm resources and the speed of internationalization. Research that explores these issues could develop strong theoretical arguments based on the cognition or industrial-organization literatures.

Post-internationalization processes and outcomes

The fundamental question in this area is "*What happens after internationalization?*" The importance of this area and its overlap with strategy literature is derived primarily on the basis of firm performance. Yet, to date, there are few studies that have explored the relationship between international entrepreneurship and performance, with inconclusive and contradictory results. Our proposed definition of international entrepreneurship suggests that entrepreneurial firms enter international markets in the pursuit of opportunities that lead to competitive advantage that position them to create wealth.

Future research should explore the links between international entrepreneurship and competitive advantage or financial and non-financial performance outcomes.

Similarly, we know little about what these firms do after they enter new markets and how they remain entrepreneurial in their approach. Figure 12.1 suggests a direct link between dimensions of international entrepreneurship and performance, implying a certain set of combinations in which international entrepreneurship may be related to performance. For example, first mover advantages (Mascarenhas, 1997) would suggest that international entrepreneurship speed would be related to competitive advantage while extent of internationalization may be related to non-financial outcomes such as organizational learning or multiple locations of value chain components to reduce transaction costs. Future research can help improve our understanding of these interesting but complex issues.

An area that demands research attention is the type of competitive advantages new ventures vs. established firms gain as they go international. These firms may pursue different goals and utilize different approaches in internationalizing their operations. If this is true, new ventures and established companies might gain very different types of advantages in their global markets. These advantages have implications for firm survival and effective performance. Research into such potential differences would be helpful.

Researchers have begun to examine the effect of international entrepreneurship variables on the non-financial measures of firm performance. Given the few studies completed to date, we do not know the extent to which international entrepreneurship contributes to organizational learning. In particular, we do not know if international entrepreneurship affects a firm's social (Sohn, 1994), technological (Zahra et al., 2000a), or other types of learning (Leonard-Barton, 1995). A noteworthy issue to explore in future studies is whether international entrepreneurship enables established companies to overcome myopia of learning (Levinthal and March, 1993). A related question that requires research attention is whether new ventures have a learning advantage over established companies in international entrepreneurship activities, as has been argued recently in the literature (Autio et al., 2000). The effect of entry strategies on different types of learning is another issue that deserves further attention.

Entrepreneurship (Autio et al., 1997; Larson, 1991; Lipparini and Sobrero, 1994), strategy (Gulati, 1998; Jarrilo, 1988; Keil, Autio, and Robertson, 1997), and IB (Welch and Welch, 1996) have highlighted the importance of networks for successful organizational performance. Some past work has recognized the important role of networks for international entrepreneurship (Autio et al., 1997; Zahra et al., 2000b). Future research should explore the link between networks and international entrepreneurship and how this link affects the speed, scope, and extent of internationalization. Given the diversity of networks that might prevail in an industry, it is especially important to connect the types of resources and information that exist and international entrepreneurship (Hara and Kanai, 1994). Of interest is the effect of networks on a firm's reputation and how this reputation allows the firm to pursue international entrepreneurship opportunities. Reputation is an important strategic asset (Fombrun, 1994; Hall, 1993), especially for young entrepreneurial companies (Bell and McNamara, 1991). A favorable reputation, connection to powerful and established networks, and other invisible assets can profoundly influence the ways companies proceed to position themselves (Itami and Roehl, 1987), especially in foreign markets.

Finally, we need to stress the importance of methodology in future empirical research. As noted earlier, our review indicates a sample bias in many studies. Past studies sampled high-technology firms with little emphasis on traditional industries, or had small sample sizes that may not be entirely representative of the industry. A primary reason is the scarcity of good data. By expanding the domain and providing a framework, we, however, encourage future researchers to include multiple data sources and address issues of sample representativeness. For instance, researchers can access industry- and country-level data from established secondary data sources. Future studies could also be improved by using surveys by partnering with research colleagues in different countries. Such data collection methods would permit drawing generalizable and well-supported conclusions that can improve managerial practice in multiple countries. Second, further work may explore internationalization and successes using longitudinal data and therefore address issues of causality and temporal stability (Sexton et al., 2000). Longitudinal studies of international entrepreneurship processes are especially lacking. Longitudinal studies also allow us to better explain the significance of the results and the relationship between international entrepreneurship variables and future company performance, if any.

In summary, we have highlighted multiple avenues for future scholarly work. We suggest three broad overlapping areas for future research; namely, the process, context, and post-internationalization outcomes of international entrepreneurship. We have also offered examples of how such research would benefit and expand the knowledge that we presently have about international entrepreneurship. Past work has helped us develop a model that we used to suggest specific directions for future research (figure 12.1). We believe that there are numerous opportunities available for further inquiry into international entrepreneurship and hope that scholars will systematically address these issues.

Conclusion

International entrepreneurship is a growing and important research stream, one that offers great opportunities for scholars to employ and integrate theories from multiple disciplines and draw on established theoretical frameworks. Changes in the competitive environment and the interdependence of the global economy make internationalization attractive to entrepreneurial firms. Yet, little is known about the process, context, and outcomes of such internationalization. As our review makes clear, there are several opportunities to conduct meaningful research that both can enrich the development of theory and have significant implications for practicing managers.

In this chapter, we have sought to achieve four objectives. First, we have attempted to expand the definition and domain of international entrepreneurship. Second, we have reviewed past research to identify and consolidate factors that may affect international entrepreneurship. Third, we have advanced an integrative framework that links factors affecting international entrepreneurship and their outcomes. Finally, we also have provided specific directions and suggestions for the future scholarly pursuit of international entrepreneurship. We hope that this chapter and our proposed framework of international entrepreneurship will increase future research in this young but interesting area of the literature.

Notes

The authors gratefully acknowledge the support of the Kauffman Center for Entrepreneurial Leadership as well as the comments of the SMS-Kauffman conference participants. The constructive comments of the editors, especially Michael Hitt, have also improved this chapter significantly. We have received many helpful suggestions from seminar participants in Helsinki University of Technology, Jonkoping International Business School, and Norwegian School of Management.

References

Almeida, J. G. and Bloodgood, J. M. 1996. Internationalization of new ventures: Implications of the value chain. *Frontiers of entrepreneurship research* [electronic edition].

Autio, E., Sapienza, H. J., and Almeida, J. G. 2000. Effects of age at entry, knowledge intensity, and imitability on international growth. *Academy of Management Journal*, 43(5): 909–24.

Autio, E., Yli-Renko, H., and Salonen, A. 1997. International growth of young technology-based firms: A resource-based network model. *Journal of Enterprising Culture*, 5(1): 57–73.

Bantel, K. A. 1998. Technology-based "adolescent" firm configurations: Strategy identification, context, and performance. *Journal of Business Venturing*, 13: 205–30.

Barkema, H. G. and Vermeulen, F. 1998. International expansion through start-up or acquisition: A learning perspective. *Academy of Management Journal*, 41: 7–26.

Barney, J. B. 1991. Firm resources and sustained competitive advantage. *Journal of Management*, 17(1): 9–120.

Bartlett, C. A. and Ghoshal, S. 2000. *Transnational management*. 3rd edn. New York: McGraw Hill.

Beamish, P. 1999. The role of alliances in international entrepreneurship. In R. Wright (ed.), *Research in global strategic management*, 7: 43–61.

Bell, C. and McNamara, J. 1991. *High-tech ventures: The guide for entrepreneurial success*. Reading, MA: Addison-Wesley.

Bell, J. 1995. The internationalization of small computer software firms: A further challenge to stage theories. *European Journal of Marketing*, 29(8): 60–75.

Birkinshaw, J. 1997. Entrepreneurship in multinational corporations: The characteristics of subsidiary initiatives. *Strategic Management Journal*, 18: 207–29.

Bloodgood, J. M., Sapienza, H. J. and Almeida, J. G. 1996. The internationalization of new high-potential US ventures: Antecedents and outcomes. *Entrepreneurship Theory and Practice*, 20(4): 61–76.

Boyd, B. K., Dess, G. G., and Rasheed, A. M. A. 1993. Divergence between archival and perceptual measures of the environment: Causes and consequences. *Academy of Management Review*, 18: 204–26.

Brush, C. G. 1993. Factors motivating small companies to internationalize: The effect of firm age. *Entrepreneurship Theory and Practice*, 17(3): 83–4.

Brush, C. G. 1995. International entrepreneurship: The effect of firm age on motives for internationalization. In Stuart Bruchey (ed.), *Garland studies in entrepreneurship*. New York: Garland.

Burgel, O. and Murray, G. C. 1998. The international activities of British start-up companies in high-technology industries: Differences between internationalisers and non-internationalisers. In P. D. Reynolds, W. D. Byrave, N. M. Carter, S. Manigart, C. M. Mason, G. Meyer and K. Shaver (eds), *Frontiers of entrepreneurship research*. Babson Park, MA: Babson College, 447–63.

Burgelman, R. A. and Sayles, L. R. 1986. *Inside corporate innovation: Strategy, structure, and managerial skills*. New York: Free Press.

Calof, J. and Beamish, P. 1994. The right attitude for international success. *Business Quarterly*, Autumn, 105–10.

Carpenter, M. A. and Fredrickson, J. W. 2001. Top management teams, global strategic posture, and the moderating role of uncertainty. *Academy of Management Journal*, in press.

Carpenter, M. A., Sanders, W., and Gregersen, H. 2001. Bundling human capital with organizational context: The impact of international assignment experience on multinational firm performance and CEO pay. *Academy of Management Journal*, in press.

Carroll, G. R. 1993. A sociological view on why firms differ. *Strategic Management Journal*, 14: 237–50.

Clark, T. and Mallory, G. 1997. The impact of strategic choice on the internationalisation of the firm. In George Chryssochoidis, Carla Millar, and Jeremy Clegg (eds), *Internationalisation strategies*. New York: St. Martin's Press, 193–206.

Collis, D. J. and Montgomery, C. A. 1995. Competing on resources: Strategy in the 1990s. *Harvard Business Review*, 73(4): 118–28.

Coviello, N. E. and Munro, H. J. 1995. Growing the entrepreneurial firm: Networking for international market development. *European Journal of Marketing*, 29(7): 49–61.

Craig, C. S. and Douglas, S. P. 1996. Developing strategies for global markets: An evolutionary perspective. *Columbia Journal of World Business*, 31(1): 70–81.

Daily, C. M., Certo, S. T., and Dalton, D. R. (2000). International experience in the executive suite: The path to prosperity? *Strategic Management Journal*, 21: 515–23.

Davidsson, P. and Wiklund, J. 2000. Conceptual and empirical challenges in the study of firm growth. In D. Sexton and H. Landstrom (eds), *Handbook of entrepreneurship*. Oxford, UK: Blackwell.

Dess, G. G., Ireland, D., and Hitt, M. (1990). Industry effects and strategic management research. *Journal of Management*, 16: 7–27.

Dunning, J. H. 1988. The eclectic paradigm of international production: A restatement and some possible extensions. *Journal of International Business Studies*, 19(1): 1–31.

Finkelstein, S. and Hambrick, D. C. 1996. *Strategic leadership: Top executives and their effects on organizations*. Minneapolis, MN: West Publishing.

Fombrun, C. 1994. *Reputation: Realizing value from the corporate image*. Boston: Harvard Business School Press.

Fontes, M. and Coombs, R. 1997. The coincidence of technology and market objectives in the internationalisation of new technology-based firms. *International Small Business Journal*, 15(4): 14–35.

Fujita, M. 1995. Small and medium-sized transnational corporations: Salient features. *Small Business Economics*, 7: 251–71.

George, G. and Prabhu, G. 2000. Developmental financial institutions as catalysts of entrepreneurship in emerging economies, *Academy of Management Review*, 25(3): 620–30.

Giamartino, G. A., McDougall, P. P., and Bird, B. J. 1993. International entrepreneurship: The state of the field. *Entrepreneurship Theory and Practice*, 18(1): 37.

Grant, R. M. 1991. The resource-based theory of competitive advantage: Implications for strategy formulation. *California Management Review*, 33(3): 114–35.

Grant, R. M. 1996. Prospering in dynamically-competitive environments: Organizational capability as knowledge integration. *Organization Science,* 7: 375–87.

Grant, R. M. 1998. *Contemporary Strategy Analysis,* 3rd edn. Malden, MA: Blackwell.

Gulati, R. 1998. Alliances and networks. *Strategic Management Journal,* 19 (special issue): 293–317.

Hall, R. 1993. A framework linking intangible resources and capabilities to sustainable competitive advantage. *Strategic Management Journal,* 14(8): 607–18.

Hambrick, D. C. 1981. Strategic awareness within top management teams. *Strategic Management Journal,* 2 (3): 263–79.

Hamel, G. and Prahalad, C. K. 1994. *Competing for the future.* Boston: Harvard Business School Press.

Hara, G. and Kanai, T. 1994. Entrepreneurial networks across oceans to promote international strategic alliances for small businesses. *Journal of Business Venturing,* 9(6): 489–507.

Haug, P. 1991. Survey evidence on the international operations of high tech firms. *Management International Review,* 31(1): 63–77.

Hisrich, R., Honig-Haftel, S., McDougall, P., and Oviatt, B. 1996. International entrepreneurship: Past, present and future. *Entrepreneurship Theory and Practice,* 20(4): 5.

Hitt, M. A. and Bartkus B. 1997. International entrepreneurship. In J. Katz (ed.), *Advances in entrepreneurship, firm emergence and growth,* Greenwich, CT: JAI Press, 3: 7–30.

Hitt, M. A., Hoskisson, R. E., and Ireland, R. D. 1994. A mid-range theory of the interactive effects of international and product diversification on innovation and performance. *Journal of Management,* 20(2): 297–326.

Hitt, M. A., Hoskisson, R. E., and Kim, H. 1997. International diversification: Effects on innovation and firm performance in product-diversified firms. *Academy of Management Journal,* 40: 767–98.

Hitt, M. A., Tyler, B. B., Hardee, C., and Park, D. 1995. Understanding strategic intent in the global marketplace. *Academy of Management Executive,* 9(2): 12–19.

Holmlund, M. and Kock, S. 1998. Relationships and the internationalisation of Finnish small and medium-sized companies. *International Small Business Journal,* 16(4): 46–63.

Hymer, S. H. 1976. *The international operations of national firms: A study of foreign direct investment.* Cambridge, MA: MIT Press.

Itami, H. and Roehl, T. W. 1987. *Mobilizing invisible assets.* Cambridge, MA: Harvard University Press.

Jarillo, J. C. 1988. On strategic networks. *Strategic Management Journal,* 9(1): 31–41.

Johanson, J. and Vahlne, J.-E. 1977. The internationalization process of the firm - A model of knowledge development and increasing foreign market commitments. *Journal of International Business Studies,* 8(1): 23–32.

Karagozoglu, N. and Lindell, M. 1998. Internationalization of small and medium-sized technology-based firms: An exploratory study. *Journal of Small Business Management,* 36(1): 44–59.

Katz, J. and Gartner, W. 1988. Properties of emerging organizations. *Academy of Management Review,* 13(3): 429–41.

Keil, T., Autio, E. and Robertson, P. 1997. Embeddedness, power, control and innovation in the telecommunications sector. *Technology Analysis and Strategic Management,* 9(3): 299–316.

Kirzner, I. 1973. *Competition and entrepreneurship.* Chicago, IL: University of Chicago Press.

Kogut, B. and Singh, H. 1988. The effect of national culture on the choice of entry mode. *Journal of International Business Studies,* 19: 411–32.

Larson, A. 1991. Partner networks: Leveraging external ties to improve entrepreneurial performance. *Journal of Business Venturing,* 6(3): 173–88.

Leonard-Barton, D. 1995. *Wellsprings of Knowledge.* Boston: Harvard Business School Press.

Levinthal, D. A. and March, J. G. 1993. The myopia of learning. *Strategic Management Journal*, 14 (special issue): 95–112.

Lindqvist, M. 1991. Infant multinationals: The internationalization of young, technology-based Swedish firms. Unpublished doctoral dissertation, Stockholm School of Economics, Stockholm.

Lipparini, A. and Sobrero, M. 1994. The glue and the pieces: Entrepreneurship and innovation in small-firm networks. *Journal of Business Venturing*, 9(2): 125–40.

Lumpkin, G. and Dess, G. 1996. Clarifying the entrepreneurial orientation construct and linking it to performance. *Academy of Management Review*, 21(1): 135–72

Mascarenhas, B. 1997. The order and size of entry into international markets. *Journal of Business Venturing*, 12(4): 287–99.

McDougall, P. P. 1989. International versus domestic entrepreneurship: new venture strategic behavior and industry structure. *Journal of Business Venturing*, 4: 387–400.

McDougall, P. P. and Oviatt, B. M. 1996. New venture internationalization, strategic change, and performance: A follow-up study. *Journal of Business Venturing*, 11(1): 23–40

McDougall, P. P. and Oviatt, B. M. 2000. International entrepreneurship: The intersection of two paths. Guest Editor's Introduction, *Academy of Management Journal*, 43(5): 902–8.

McDougall, P. P., Shane, S., and Oviatt, B. M. 1994. Explaining the formation of international new ventures: The limits of theories from international business research. *Journal of Business Venturing*, 9(6): 469–87.

Miles, R. E. and Snow, C. C. 1978. *Organizational strategy, structure, and process.* New York: McGraw-Hill.

Miller, D. 1983. The correlates of entrepreneurship in three types of firms. *Management Science*, 29: 770–91.

Mitchell, R. K., Smith, B., Seawright, K., and Morse, E. A. 2000. Cross-cultural cognitions and venture creation decision. *Academy of Management Journal*, 43(5): 974–93.

Morrow, J. F. 1988. International entrepreneurship: A new growth opportunity. *New Management*, 3(5): 59–61.

Mößlang, A. 1995. Internationalization of service companies. *Management International Review*, 37(4): 387–404.

Oviatt, B. M. and McDougall, P. P. 1994. Toward a theory of international new ventures. *Journal of International Business Studies*, 25(1): 45–64.

Oviatt, B. M. and McDougall, P. P. 1995. Global start-ups: Entrepreneurs on a worldwide stage. *Academy of Management Executive*, 9(2): 30–43.

Oviatt, B. M. and McDougall, P. P. 1999. A framework for understanding accelerated international entrepreneurship. In R. Wright (ed.), *Research in global strategic management*, 7: 23–42.

Porter, M. E. 1986. Competition in global industries: A conceptual framework. In M. E. Porter (ed.), *Competition in global industries*. Boston: Harvard Business School Press, 15–60.

Reuber, A. R. and Fischer, E. 1997. The influence of the management team's international experience on the internationalization behaviors of SMEs. *Journal of International Business Studies*, 28(4): 807–25.

Roberts, E. B., and Senturia, T. A. 1996. Globalizing the emerging high-technology company. *Industrial Marketing Management*, 25(6): 491–506.

Sexton, D., Pricer, R., and Nenide, B. 2000. Measuring performance in high growth firms. Presented at the Babson-Kauffman conference, Babson Park, MA.

Shane, S. 1993. Cultural influences on national rates of innovation. *Journal of Business Venturing*, 8: 59–73.

Shane, S. and Venkataraman, S. 2000. The promise of entrepreneurship as a field of research. *Academy of Management Review*, 25(1): 217–26.

Shrader, R. and Simon, M. 1997. Corporate versus independent new ventures: Resource, strategy, and performance differences. *Journal of Business Venturing,* 12: 47–66.

Sohn, J. H. D. 1994. Social knowledge as a control system: A proposition and evidence from the Japanese FDI behavior. *Journal of International Business Studies,* 25: 295–324.

Steensma, K., Marino, L., Weaver, M., and Dickson, P. 2000. The influence of national culture in the formation of technology alliances by entrepreneurial firms. *Academy of Management Journal,* 43(5): 951–73.

Taylor, W. 1991. The logic of global business: An interview with ABB's Percy Barnevik. *Harvard Business Review,* 69(2): 91–105.

Teece, D. J., Pisano, G., and Shuen, A. 1997. Dynamic capabilities and strategic management. *Strategic Management Journal,* 18: 509–33.

Tiessen, J. H. and Merrilees, B. 1999. An entrepreneurial model of SME internationalization: Evidence from six cases. In R. Wright (ed.), *Research in Global Strategic Management,* 7: 131–57.

Vernon, R. 1979. The product cycle hypothesis in a new international environment, *Oxford Bulletin of Economics and Statistics,* 4, 255–67

Welch, D. E. and Welch, L. S. 1996. The internationalization process and networks: A strategic management perspective. *Journal of International Marketing,* 4(3): 11–28.

Westhead, P., Wright, M. and Ucbasaran, D. 1998. The internationalization of new and small firms. In P. D. Reynolds, W. D. Byrave, N. M. Carter, S. Manigart, C. M. Mason, G. D. Meyer and K. G. Shaver (eds), *Frontiers of entrepreneurship research 1998.* Babson Park, MA: Babson College, 464–77.

Williamson, O. E. 1999. Strategy research: Governance and competence perspectives. *Strategic Management Journal,* 20(12): 1087–8.

Wright, R. W. and Ricks, D. A. 1994. Trends in international business research: Twenty-five years later. *Journal of International Business Studies,* 25(4): 687–701.

Zacharakis, A. L. 1997. Entrepreneurial entry into foreign markets: A transaction cost perspective. *Entrepreneurship Theory and Practice,* 21: 23–40.

Zahra, S. 1991. Predictors and financial outcomes of corporate entrepreneurship: An exploratory study. *Journal of Business Venturing,* 6: 259–86.

Zahra, S. A. 1993. Conceptual model of entrepreneurship as firm behavior: A critique and extension. *Entrepreneurship Theory and Practice,* 14(4): 5–21.

Zahra, S. 1996. Technology strategy and performance: A study of corporate-sponsored and independent biotechnology ventures. *Journal of Business Venturing,* 11(4): 289–321.

Zahra, S. and Bogner, W. 2000. Technology strategy and software new venture performance: The moderating effect of the competitive environment. *Journal of Business Venturing,* 15(2): 135–73.

Zahra, S. and Covin, J. G. 1995. Contextual influences on the corporate entrepreneurship-performance relationship: A longitudinal analysis. *Journal of Business Venturing,* 10: 43–58.

Zahra, S. and Dess, G. 2001. Defining entrepreneurship as a scholarly field. *Academy of Management Review,* in press. (Dialogue)

Zahra, S. and Garvis, S. 2000. International corporate entrepreneurship and company performance: The moderating effect of international environmental hostility. *Journal of Business Venturing,* in press.

Zahra, S. A., Ireland, D. R., and Hitt, M. A. 2000a. International expansion by new venture firms: International diversity, mode of market entry, technological learning and performance. *Academy of Management Journal,* 43(5): 925–50.

Zahra, S. A., Jennings, D. F., and Kuratko, D. 1999. Guest Editors' Introduction: Corporate entrepreneurship in a global economy. *Entrepreneurship Theory and Practice,* 24(1): 5–8.

Zahra, S., Matherne, B. and Carleton, J. 2000b. Leveraging technological resources for competitive advantage: The case of Software New Ventures. Proceedings of the 2nd Annual McGill University Conference on Globalization, in press.

Zahra, S., Neubaum, D. and Huse, M. 1996. The effect of the environment on the firm's export intensity. *Entrepreneurship: Theory and Practice*, 1997, 22(1): 25–46.

Zahra, S., Nielsen, A. and Bogner, W. 1999. Corporate entrepreneurship, knowledge and competence development. *Entrepreneurship Theory and Practice*, 23(3): 169–89.

Zahra, S. and Schulte, W. 1994. International entrepreneurship: Beyond folklore and myth. *International Journal of Commerce and Management*, 4(1/2): 85–95.

CHAPTER THIRTEEN

What Sort of Top Management Team is Needed at the Helm of Internationally Diversified Firms?

Harry Barkema, Oleg Chvyrkov

Globalization is one of the most important trends of the last decade (Hitt, Keats, and De Marie, 1998), and many firms are now in varying stages of internationalization. What sort of CEOs and TMTs are needed at the helm of internationally diversified firms? Do these firms need different executives as compared to less internationalized firms? *If* executives at internationalized firms are different, *how* are they different? These questions formed the starting point for the present study.

A large number of prior studies have explored the relationship between CEO and TMT characteristics and a firm's level of technological and administrative innovation (Bantel and Jackson, 1989), changes in strategy (Boeker, 1997a, 1997b; Finkelstein and Hambrick, 1990; Grimm and Smith, 1991; Hambrick, Cho, and Chen, 1996; Wiersema and Bantel, 1992), and so on. However, only a few studies have explored how CEO and TMT characteristics vary with a firm's degree of international diversification (Carpenter and Fredrickson, 2001; Roth, 1995; Sambharya, 1996; Sanders and Carpenter, 1998).

In this chapter, we develop and test novel theory in this respect, merging insights from upper echelons theory (e.g., Eisenhardt and Schoonhoven, 1990; Hambrick and Mason, 1984), research on internationalizing firms (e.g., Birkinshaw and Hood, 1998; Hedlund, 1994), and structural hole theory (Burt, 1992). We argue that highly internationalized firms, with their many different groups (departments, geographical units, divisional units, etc.), require *"entrepreneurial"* executives (cf. Burt, 1992; Burt, Hogarth, and Michaud, 2000) who are able to link loosely connected groups, as well as handle the many other complexities associated with running such firms. This leads to hypotheses on how a variety of CEO and TMT characteristics are related to a firm's degree of international diversification. The hypotheses are tested on panel data on 25 firms that internationalized over a period of more than three decades (1966–98).

From a methodological perspective, our study adds to prior work by examining panel data and by using a better measure of international diversification, i.e., an entropy measure (cf., Hoskisson et al., 1993), than most previous studies have done. The results corroborate a key notion of our theory: that internationally diversified firms are indeed run by a different sort of executive (than less internationalized firms): CEOs with relatively long tenure and TMTs of considerable tenure, heterogeneity, and size.

The chapter is structured as follows. In the next section, we review prior work on TMT demographic characteristics and on internationalizing firms. Our theory and hypotheses are then presented. The sample, methodology, and empirical results are discussed next. The chapter ends with conclusions and suggestions for further research.

Background

Upper echelons theory

Upper echelons theory (Hambrick and Mason, 1984) essentially argues that the value created by executives is due to their exercise of discretion. How they use this discretion, for instance, what strategic decisions are made, is subject to bounded rationality, which implies information search and decision heuristics (Simon, 1945). These processes depend on the managers' cognitive basis and values, which in turn are shaped by their past experiences. A key assumption of upper echelons theory is that these individual attributes can usefully be captured by a manager's demographic characteristics, such as functional and educational background, tenure, and other observable demographic characteristics (Hambrick and Mason, 1984; Pfeffer, 1983).

Perhaps the most often studied demographic characteristic is CEO or TMT (mean) *tenure*. Upper echelons theory argues that, over time, executives become "rigid" and "inert," and more inclined to rely on routines when gathering and processing information. In the words of Miller (1991), they become "stale in the saddle," which reduces the likelihood of strategic innovation and change. Consistent with this theory, Bantel and Jackson (1989) found that long-tenured executives led firms with lower levels of technological innovation than short-tenured executives did. Further empirical support came from studies which found that TMT tenure is positively associated with strategic conformity and commitment to the status quo (Finkelstein and Hambrick, 1990; Hambrick, Geletkanycz, and Fredrickson, 1993), and negatively related to the likelihood and scope of strategic action (Boeker, 1997b; Grimm and Smith, 1991; Hambrick, Cho and Chen, 1996). However, Wiersema and Bantel (1992) found that strategic change was associated with considerable team tenure.

Other studies have explored the relationship between a CEO's and TMT's level of *formal education* and the strategy of their firms. High levels of education are associated with a high capacity for information processing and an ability to discern patterns and discriminate among a variety of stimuli (Schroder, Driver, and Streufert, 1967). Educated individuals are more likely to engage in boundary spanning, to tolerate ambiguity, and to show an ability to "integrate complexity" (Dollinger, 1984). Consistent with these ideas, Bantel and Jackson (1989) found that the level of education was positively related to a firm's level of technological innovation. Further support came from Hambrick, Cho, and Chen (1996) and Wiersema and Bantel (1992), who found a positive relationship between education and propensity for action.

Hitt and Tyler (1991) did not find a relationship between the level of education (or a direct measure of cognitive complexity) and strategic decisions. Their study also casts doubt on the validity of education as a measure of cognitive complexity (r= 0.07), although Wally and Baum (1994) found a correlation of 0.5 between educational level and a direct measure of cognitive complexity. Hence, the evidence in favor of a relationship between executive education and strategy appears to be weaker than the evidence in favor of tenure – discussed above – possibly because the validity of education as a measure of cognitive ability and complexity is not high.

Prior research has not only studied the (mean) *level* of demographic attributes of CEOs and top teams, such as tenure and education, but also the diversity or *heterogeneity* in TMT characteristics. This research assumes that heterogeneity in TMT characteristics captures cognitive diversity, defined in terms of differences in beliefs and preferences held by upper-echelon executives of a TMT (Miller, Burke, and Glick, 1998). As these authors argue, cognitive diversity is positively related to the comprehensiveness of strategic decision making and the extensiveness of strategic planning. A greater diversity in views and opinions, both directly and through the implied lower level of cohesion and increased challenging of other viewpoints, leads to more discussions, more resources spent on analyses and consultants, and so on. While Miller, Burke, and Glick (1998) did not observe the predicted effects of diversity, Hambrick et al. (1996) found positive relationships between TMT tenure diversity and educational diversity and the likelihood for strategic action; other results consistent with these ideas were found by Boeker (1997b) and Wiersema and Bantel (1992).

Likewise, Michel and Hambrick (1992) found that heterogeneously tenured teams were found in firms with complex, interdependent corporate structures. However, other researchers have argued that higher levels of heterogeneity (eventually) lead to less communication and higher levels of dispute and disagreement within a TMT, which may hurt the process of reaching solutions, and eventually firm performance. Perhaps this explains why evidence on the relationship between demographic diversity and firm performance is mixed (for overviews, see Finkelstein and Hambrick, 1996; Miller et al., 1998).

Finally, *top team size* is believed to capture TMT diversity as well, since larger teams are more likely to encompass a variety of views, cause–effect relationships, educational and functional backgrounds, and so on. Larger teams are also believed to have greater capacity for information processing. Indeed, various studies have found a positive relation between TMT size and complex turbulent environments (Barkema and Vermeulen, 1998a; Eisenhardt and Schoonhoven, 1990; Haleblian and Finkelstein, 1993).

In view of the importance of globalization in recent decades, surprisingly little research has explored demographic characteristics in the international setting (Carpenter and Fredrickson, 2001). Earlier research has primarily addressed international experience of top management teams. For instance, a positive relation was found between the amount and diversity of TMT international experience and a firm's global strategic posture (Carpenter and Fredrickson, 2001; Sambharya, 1996). Roth (1995) found that a CEO's international experience contributed to firm performance in case of highly interdependent subsidiaries. Furthermore, Sanders and Carpenter (1998) found a positive relationship between TMT size and a firm's degree of international diversification, while Carpenter and Fredrickson (2001) found a positive relationship between TMT educational and tenure heterogeneity and a firm's global strategic posture. The latter result is consistent with the idea that TMTs in internationally diversified firms require more diverse network ties, skills, and world views; that top team diversity promotes trust and perceptions of procedural justice among a firm's different product and geographic unit managers, as well as inter-unit cooperation and coordination. Finally, Barkema and Vermeulen (1998a) found that TMT size and heterogeneity contributed to an MNC's ability to learn from its foreign experience, particularly, from foreign failures.

Managing multinational corporations

Running a large, internationally diversified corporation is a highly complex task. In early stages of internationalization, firms have only a few foreign subsidiaries, which typically serve as "appendices" of the firm, involved in marketing, selling, and distributing home-grown products and services in the particular foreign country or region (Malnight, 1995, 1996). Command structures are "top down." However, in later stages of internationalization, subsidiaries often acquire other tasks as well, for instance, the development or testing of new products. Theoretical and empirical (inductive) research by Malnight (1995) and Birkinshaw and colleagues (Birkinshaw, 1997; Birkinshaw and Hood, 1998) suggests that subsidiaries may even compete internally to win the opportunity to develop or coordinate the testing of a new product for the whole firm. A foreign subsidiary may also acquire a world mandate for a product or process (Birkinshaw and Hood, 1998), or develop toward a regional center for many of the firm's operations (Ghauri, 1990). Hence, managers of subsidiaries can also be entrepreneurs, in the sense that they wish to build an important subsidiary, compete with other subsidiaries to fulfill roles like coordinating (worldwide) the development or testing of a new drug, and so on.

Horizontal streams of data, ideas, people, and other resources are much more common in full-fledged multinational corporations (MNCs) than in firms at early stages of internationalization (Bartlett and Ghoshal, 1989; Hedlund, 1994; Malnight, 1995, 1996). Top teams of MNCs, rather than aggressively expanding overseas and breaking home-grown organization cultures and structures to incorporate foreign operations as in early stages of internationalization (Bartlett, 1981), are more heavily involved in balancing the various powers within the firm, for instance, of functional, divisional, and regional managers (Bartlett, 1981). These TMTs can create value in various ways: by facilitating the vast horizontal streams of knowledge and people within their firm (Bartlett and Ghoshal, 1989; Hedlund, 1994; Malnight, 1995), by monitoring a wide variety of subsidiaries in many countries and cultures, by deciding which firm is awarded the development of a new product or other responsibility (Birkinshaw and Hood, 1998), etc. In addition to these internal challenges, these TMTs also meet many external opportunities and threats in terms of governments, customers, suppliers, and competitors in a variety of cultural and institutional settings (Barkema, Bell, and Pennings, 1996). All of this adds to the complexity of managing a highly internationalized firm.

We are now ready to develop theory and hypotheses on which CEO and TMT characteristics fit internationally diversified firms and are more likely to be encountered at the top of full-fledged MNCs as compared to less internationalized firms.

Theory and Hypotheses

Prior research in the domain of upper echelons theory has emphasized that, over time, job tenure promotes inertia and rigidity; information gathering and processing is increasingly governed by routines, and fewer alternatives are considered when searching for solutions. In other words, executives become "stale in the saddle" (Miller, 1991). Consistent with these ideas, many studies have found that "tenure" is negatively associated with the likelihood and scope of strategic change (Boeker, 1997b; Finkelstein and Hambrick, 1990; Grimm and Smith, 1991; Hambrick, Cho and Chen, 1996; Hambrick, Geletkanycz, and Fredrickson, 1993).

However, we believe that the lack of strategic change may also, at least in part, be caused by something else. Over time, executives develop "social exchange relationships" (Homans, 1961) with increasing numbers of managers in their firm, which implies mutual "gift giving" in terms of time, effort, information, and perhaps even friendship. These exchange relationships endow CEOs with power (over the time, effort, and information of their subordinates), but also obligate them. CEOs who have been in office for a long time may have developed strong exchange relationships with many managers, in particular if they appointed these managers to their present positions. This network encapsulates long-tenured CEOs in a diffuse network of obligations and general commitments, but also endows them with social networks and information networks, the information and power to sway decisions in their own direction, and the option to establish non-redundant links between different groups within their firm.

The concept of "structural holes" (Burt, 1992) is particularly appropriate in this setting. Structural hole theory emphasizes that "entrepreneurial" managers (cf. Burt, 1992; Burt, Hogarth, and Michaud, 2000) who actively combine different and otherwise loosely connected groups are particularly powerful and may be particularly valuable to their firm. People, departments, and subsidiaries have a tendency to focus on their immediate tasks to the exclusion of adjacent tasks. As a result, "structural holes" emerge in the organization: groups lose track of other groups within the firm or of the external environment. Hence, large benefits are possible for managers who act as brokers – of information, people, and other resources – between sparsely connected groups; these managers are much more beneficial for their firms than managers who run their organizations on purely bureaucratic grounds. Prior research has confirmed such success for American managers, as well as for French managers (e.g., Burt, Hogarth, and Michaud, 2000). Social ties may even develop with managers several layers down in the organization as, for example, a successful CEO such as Lou Gerstner demonstrated at various companies he worked for (Finkelstein and Hambrick, 1996).

In highly complex organizations such as MNCs, it appears particularly important to link different, otherwise loosely connected units and serve as a broker between them. MNCs may have many different geographical, divisional, and functional "kingdoms" which tend to focus on their own activities rather than on the activities of others or their environment, and where horizontal and informal flows of people, information, and resources are crucial for the firm's success (Bartlett and Ghoshal, 1989; Hedlund, 1994). With increasing tenure, site-visits of foreign subsidiaries, and so on, CEOs may develop dense networks with a variety of functional, divisional, and geographic managers. Over time, they may also acquire the experiential knowledge to effectively run a variety of national, functional, and perhaps industry cultures (Argyres, 1996; Johanson and Vahlne, 1977), as well as the political savvy to engage in arbitrage between different political factions (Sutcliffe, 1994). They may also learn about the abilities of many individual managers and subsidiaries to develop products and take on responsibilities, which in turn helps them to make good decisions when distributing world mandates and other responsibilities among subsidiaries (cf. Birkinshaw and Hood, 1998). All of this may accumulate with on-the-job experience and become increasingly important as companies become more internationalized. We therefore hypothesize:

H1a: CEO tenure is positively related to the degree of international diversification of the firm.

For similar reasons, we expect that at internationally diversified firms, tenure is important for other members of the TMT as well (i.e., the implied networks with a variety of groups within the MNC, the experiential knowledge to connect subsidiaries in a variety of national cultures, etc.).

In early stages of internationalization, cognitive and strategic frame-breaking in terms of going beyond national settings is needed (Barkema and Vermeulen, 1998a), and younger teams of managers with short tenure and less established routines are more likely to break the mold, venture into the unknown, and meet and handle unprecedented opportunities and threats (Hambrick and Mason, 1984; Keck, 1997; Thomas, Litschert, and Ramaswamy, 1991; Wiersema and Bantel, 1992). In other words, a different sort of "entrepreneur" may be needed than the sort of entrepreneurial executive (cf. Burt, 1992) needed at highly internationalized firms. In the latter firms, a strong culture of veteran teams promotes incremental learning and change (Huy, 1999) which is more congruent with managing a full-fledged MNC with its complex web of relationships between subsidiaries and with headquarters; vast horizontal streams of ideas, knowledge, people, products, services, and so on. Greater TMT tenure also promotes social cohesion and a strong group identity (Bantel and Jackson, 1989; Boeker, 1997b; Finkelstein and Hambrick, 1996; Hambrick and Mason, 1984; Keck, 1997; Michel and Hambrick, 1992; Pfeffer, 1983). This helps the top team to counterbalance the various political powers within the MNC, to advance their own corporate agenda, and to meet the vast information processing needs (Roth, 1995) which managing a highly complex firm requires (Sanders and Carpenter, 1998). Hence, we expect that:

H1b: TMT (mean) tenure is positively related to the degree of international diversification of the firm.

Managing a large, internationally diversified firm is inherently more complex than running a domestic company. Combining the complexities of balancing many different political factions within the MNC, managing many subsidiaries in a variety of cultural and institutional settings, and meeting the challenge of competitors in a variety of national and regional settings is a highly complex task from a cognitive perspective (Roth, 1995; Sambharya, 1996; Sanders and Carpenter, 1998). Consistent with this idea, Calori, Johnson, and Sarnin (1994) found that executives of internationally diversified firms have more complex mental maps than those at domestic firms. A number of studies have found that cognitive complexity, i.e., the ability to discern patterns and distinguish between objects, is positively related to amount of formal education (see Finkelstein and Hambrick, 1996; Wally and Baum, 1994). Consistent with this theory (i.e., cognitive theory and traditional upper echelons theory), we therefore hypothesize a positive relationship between formal education, as a proxy of cognitive complexity, and a firm's degree of international diversification.

There is reason for caution since there also are studies such as Hitt and Tyler (1991) that did not find a relationship between cognitive complexity and strategic decisions. Their study also casts doubt on the validity of formal education as a measure of cognitive complexity, although Wally and Baum (1994) found more support. It could also be argued that there is considerable screening of managers before any of them is promoted to the top team and it is therefore unlikely that managers who are not cognitively complex will be selected. Nevertheless, we hypothesize that – in relative terms – executives at internationally diversified firms will show a tendency to be *more* cognitively complex than executives at less internationalized firms, and that (consistent with traditional upper echelons theory) formal education is a useful measure to capture such differences. Formally:

H2a: The amount of formal education of the CEO is positively related to the degree of international diversification of the firm.
H2b: The (mean) formal education of the TMT is positively related to the degree of international diversification of the firm.

While, in general, greater tenure of CEOs and TMT members is relatively favorable at internationally diversified firms (in terms of developing networks and knowledge over time), we also expect, *ceteris paribus*, that *heterogeneity* in team tenure is favorable, for a variety of reasons. First, managers who entered the top team at different points in time have a greater variety of social networks within and outside the firm. Executives who joined the TMT relatively recently are more likely to complement the networks of executives who joined (much) earlier in terms of connecting otherwise loosely connected groups, departments, divisions, geographic regions, and different layers in the MNC. This implies fewer "structural holes" within the company and consequently fewer missed opportunities for beneficial combinations. Moreover, executives who joined the top team at different points in time are more likely to represent a variety of experiences (including recent hands-on experience with major or rising divisions or regional centers) and knowledge structures. We expect that this helps them handle the complexities of running an MNC (Carpenter and Fredrickson, 2001).

So far we have discussed TMT heterogeneity in tenure. We also expect that heterogeneity in educational background – engineering, law, or business administration, etc. – makes it more likely that a TMT connects different functional, divisional, and geographic units, encompasses a variety of experiences and cognitive structures, and enhances informal and horizontal flows of ideas, data, and people within the firm. All of this becomes more important at higher levels of international diversification. Formally:

> *H3a: TMT tenure heterogeneity is positively related to the degree of international diversification of the firm.*
> *H3b: TMT educational heterogeneity is positively related to the degree of international diversification of the firm.*

Finally, we expect a positive relationship between TMT size and a firm's degree of international diversification. Larger teams are more likely to link otherwise loosely connected functional, divisional, or geographic units simply because more TMT members implies more social ties with the rest of the firm. Larger teams are also more likely to contain a variety of experiences and knowledge structures and have more information-processing capacity, all of which makes them more likely to match the needs of running a highly complex MNC (Sanders and Carpenter, 1998). Larger teams can also benefit from task division and specialization of members (Eisenhardt and Schoonhoven, 1990; Haleblian and Finkelstein, 1993; Hambrick and Mason, 1984; Smith et al., 1994). Congruent with these ideas, Sanders and Carpenter (1998) found a positive relationship between TMT size and the degree of internationalization of the firm, using 1992 cross-section data on 258 US firms (and using a composite measure of diversification based on foreign sales, foreign production, and geographic dispersion). We expect to find the same relationship using panel data on Dutch firms over a period of three decades and an entropy measure of international diversification. Hence, the last hypothesis to be tested in this study is:

> *H4: TMT size is positively related to the degree of international diversification of the firm.*

Method

Sample and variables

Hypotheses were tested on a sample of 25 large, listed, non-financial Dutch firms from a variety of industries which internationalized between 1966 and 1998 – the time frame of the study. Data came from annual reports of these companies.

Top team   In Dutch companies, the team of top executives is formally defined as the *Raad van Bestuur* (i.e., executive board) and therefore easily identifiable. Hence, the *TMT Size* variable is readily available from Dutch annual reports. In contrast to US practice and reflecting low power distance and reliance on teamwork commonly found in Dutch companies, there were times – especially in the socially oriented 1970s – and companies, where the CEO position (i.e., Chairperson of the Raad van Bestuur) was not formally defined in the annual report. The Chairperson was then typically the first individual on the list of executives. However, in a few cases, top managers were simply listed in alphabetical order. In those cases, we were unable to enter data for CEO-related variables. In a few cases, we observed two Chairperson titles on the team. We then based our analysis on the average scores of the demographic variables for the two CEOs.

Education   Following Wiersema and Bantel (1992) and Boeker (1997b), education of executives was coded according to their titles. "Drs" (doctorandus – Dutch title for university graduates in Economics and Social Sciences), "MR" (Dutch university degree in Law), and "IR" (degree in Engineering) are different university degrees. "Dr" and "Dr.Ir" are doctorates. Managers without a university degree had typically completed a vocational training program; they were categorized as "no degree".

Educational level was captured in terms of executives having a university degree or not. (The US classification in terms of BA, MBA, etc., did not apply during the window of analysis.) Hence, CEO educational level was captured by a dummy variable (i.e., university training or not), while the educational level of TMTs was captured by the percentage of the team members with a university degree.

Heterogeneity in educational type of the TMT was captured by the Herfindahl-Hirshman index:

$$H = \sum_{i=1}^{n} S_i^2$$

where H is the homogeneity index, S the percentage of TMT members with dominant educational track i, and n the number of different educational backgrounds. Subtraction from unity yields Blau's heterogeneity index (Wiersema and Bantel, 1992).

Executive tenure   Tenure (including CEO tenure) was measured as tenure with the TMT. Mean tenure and tenure heterogeneity were both used in the analysis. *Tenure heterogeneity* was computed as the coefficient of variation; the standard deviation divided by the mean (Wiersema and Bantel, 1992; Boeker, 1997b).

Degree of internationalization   Designed to capture the industry diversification of firms, the Jacquemin-Berry entropy measure (Acar and Sankaran, 1999; Boeker, 1997b; Hoskisson et al., 1993; Palepu, 1985; Wiersema and Bantel, 1992) has recently been used to measure geographic diversification as well (e.g., Hitt, Hoskisson, and Kim, 1997).

$$\sum_{i=1}^{N} P_i \ln(1/P_i)$$

Originally (e.g., Palepu, 1985) P_i indicated the percentage of a firm's total sales in the ith business, with N as the number of businesses. Barkema and Vermeulen (1998b) used the entropy measure of geographic diversification at the level of cultural blocks (cf. Ronen and Shenkar, 1985). The number of ventures was used to capture presence in a region instead of sales. Following Barkema and Vermeulen (1998b), we developed a more sophisticated measure that accounts for diversification patterns at the country level. Hence, subscript i indicates the country and P_i, the share of a firm's subsidiaries located in country i. Our entropy measure of international diversification

Table 13.1 Descriptive statistics and correlations

	Min	Max	Mean	S.D.	N	1	2	3	4	5	6	7	8	9	10
1. Entropy	0.00	3.34	1.4312	0.8208	796	1.000									
2. Firm size (ln assets)	10.10	17.04	13.8945	1.1567	634	0.488	1.000								
3. Product diversity	3.00	54.00	16.6189	9.9976	753	-0.034	0.206	1.000							
4. Team size	1.00	17.00	4.2581	1.8651	775	0.070	0.039	-0.113	1.000						
5. Mean team tenure	1.00	18.50	7.7397	3.1172	775	0.190	0.304	0.118	-0.052	1.000					
6. Tenure diversity	0.00	1.56	0.6312	0.2964	768	0.121	0.099	0.040	0.094	-0.033	1.000				
7. % Team members with degree	0.00	1.00	0.5896	0.3468	796	0.071	0.284	-0.084	-0.202	0.075	0.084	1.000			
8. Education diversity	0.00	0.75	0.4365	0.2238	765	-0.047	0.239	-0.001	-0.064	-0.060	0.024	0.451	1.000		
9. CEO tenure	1.00	31.00	11.1226	6.4303	742	0.196	0.199	-0.042	0.170	0.606	0.325	0.014	-0.041	1.000	
10. CEO degree	0.00	1.00	0.6624	0.4678	742	0.108	0.252	-0.049	-0.183	0.026	0.148	0.691	0.328	-0.025	1.000

takes a value of zero if all units are located in one country and increases with even distribution of subsidiaries across countries.

The problem with this measure is that it does not account for the size of ventures (i.e., we do not have data on the size of the ventures). There is no reason to believe that this limitation causes any bias. If the size of the subsidiaries varies significantly with time or across firms, time and firm dummies will capture (and control for) these effects.

Control variables   Bigger firms are likely to have larger TMTs. We therefore included the logarithm of assets as a measure of *firm size* in all regressions.

Product diversification adds to decision-making constraints imposed by geographic diversification (Hitt et al., 1997; Barkema and Vermeulen, 1998b; Tallman and Li, 1996). Product diversity is measured by the number of three-digit SBI industries (the Dutch analog of SIC codes). Descriptive statistics and correlations of variables used in our study are presented in table 13.1.

Analysis

Although several statistical procedures may be used for the analysis of panel data, this study used a simple version of Fixed Effects: the LSDV (Least Squares Dummy Variable) model. We chose the Fixed Effects procedure because it is consistent under a wide set of assumptions, for example, it helps to avoid cross-sectional heteroscedasticity (Greene, 1997). The structure of our data set, i.e., an unbalanced panel with a relatively small number of firms, made the LSDV procedure particularly convenient. To make our results more robust, we also included year dummies in the regressions; hence, we have a Fixed-Firm-and-Time-Effects model.

Results

Results of the regression analyses are presented in table 13.2. Model 1 contains only the control variables. As expected, firm size correlates positively with international diversification. The negative relationship between product diversification and international diversification is consistent with the idea that the governance scope of product-diversified firms may leave little cognitive capacity to handle the complexity of international interdependence (Barkema and Vermeulen, 1998b; Hitt, Hoskisson, and Ireland, 1994; Hitt, Hoskisson, and Kim, 1997).

Model 2 adds the CEO variables: tenure and level of formal education. Consistent with H1a, the effect of CEO tenure is positive and significant ($p < 0.05$). However, H2a, concerning the effect of the level of CEO education, is not corroborated.

Model 3 captures the TMT variables. Consistent with H1b, the effect of TMT (mean) tenure is positive and highly significant ($p < 0.001$). The hypothesized effect of the mean level of education of the TMT (H2b) is not corroborated. However, both hypothesized heterogeneity effects, that of TMT tenure (H3a) and education (H3b), are strongly corroborated ($p < 0.001$ and $p < 0.01$, respectively). The hypothesized influence of TMT size (H4) is supported as well ($p < 0.001$). Finally, Model 4 shows that when both CEO and TMT variables are included in the model, the CEO effects disappear.

Table 13.2   LSDV regression results. Dependent: entropy measure of international diversification

Variable[a]	Model 1 (N = 626)	Model 2 (N = 598)	Model 3 (N = 612)	Model 4 (N = 585)
Constant	−2.548***	−2.533***	−2.996***	−3.051***
Controls				
Firm size	0.222***	0.209***	0.212***	0.208***
Product diversity	−3.216E−03	−1.258E−02**	−6.422E−03†	−1.536E−02***
Team structure				
Team size			3.907−02***	3.763E−02***
Mean tenure			2.530E−02***	2.304E−02***
Tenure diversity			0.115**	0.111*
Percent of members with degree			2.519E−03	−1.528E−02
Educational diversity			0.309***	0.409***
CEO traits				
CEO tenure		5.603E−03*		−1.088E−03
CEO with degree		5.060E−02		−4.193E−02
Model fit				
F-value	52.164***	51.610***	51.034***	50.140***
R square	0.849	0.859	0.861	0.869
Adj. R square	0.833	0.842	0.844	0.851

[a] Firm dummies not shown
*** $p < 0.001$ ** $p < 0.01$ * $p<0.05$ † $p<0.10$ (one-tailed if hypothesized, two-tailed if not)

In order to study the direction of causal effects, in a follow-up analysis we tested the models with TMT and CEO characteristics lagging international diversification by 1 and 2 years. Results were very similar to those presented above, yet with higher significance of explanatory variables and better model fit. These findings suggest that in our sample, international diversification of the firm shapes TMT composition, rather than the other way around.

Discussion and Conclusions

A key notion of our chapter is that internationally diversified firms require "entrepreneurial" (cf. Burt, 1992; Burt et al., 2000) executives who are able to link loosely connected groups within their firms to enhance (beneficial) informal flows of data, ideas, people, and other resources. These executives also face highly complex internal and external environments (i.e., governments, subsidiaries, suppliers, customers, and competitors in a variety of cultural and institutional environments). Hence, internationally diversified firms require CEOs and TMTs with well-developed social networks and large information-processing capacity. Implications of our theory were tested using panel data on 25 firms over a period of more than three decades (1966–98). Consistent with predictions, we found that CEO and TMT *tenure* were positively related to a firm's degree of international diversification. Further support came from positive relationships between TMT *heterogeneity (of tenure and education)* and TMT *size*, and the degree of international diversification. Finally, predictions about CEO and TMT *level of education* were not corroborated.

Our study adds to prior work in several ways. Our theory – anchored in upper echelons theory, research on internationalizing firms, and structural holes theory – was consistent with the idea that internationally diversified firms require entrepreneurial executives (cf. Burt, 1992; Burt et al., 2000) who are able to bridge "structural holes" within their firms through non-redundant ties between otherwise loosely connected groups. Perhaps these executives differ from the sort of entrepreneurial executives needed at early stages of internationalization (see also Lu and Beamish, 2001). The task of these executives is to "break the mold" (i.e., domestic mindsets) and venture into the unknown (i.e., foreign countries) – the sort of strategic change typically associated with executives at low levels of tenure (Boeker, 1997b; Finkelstein and Hambrick, 1990; Grimm and Smith, 1991; Hambrick et al., 1993; Hambrick et al., 1996). The implication of all this would be, consistent with the evidence in this chapter, that firms require different sorts of entrepreneurial managers at different stages of internationalization; this is perhaps one of the most exciting ideas stemming from our chapter.

Our study (based on panel data on Dutch firms) also adds at a more empirical level to the small but growing literature on what sort of top managers are needed in international corporations. Prior studies have found strong support for the idea that international experience (level and heterogeneity) is important for the TMTs of MNCs. Based on a different measure of diversification, data from a different culture (the Netherlands instead of the US) and panel data, our study confirms earlier results on TMT heterogeneity and size, and firm internationalization (cf. Carpenter and Fredrickson, 2001; Sanders and Carpenter, 1998).

Moreover, we add evidence on the relationship between *CEO* characteristics and international diversification. Interestingly, with TMT variables included, the CEO effects disappeared in our empirical model. Prior studies have suggested mixed support for the idea that studying TMT characteristics adds to studying the influence of the CEO (see Finkelstein and Hambrick, 1996; Miller et al., 1998). Our results suggest (cf. Finkelstein and Hambrick, 1996) that the TMT does add to the CEO; in fact, our results suggest an even stronger conclusion: that the CEO title does not matter much beyond being a TMT member (i.e., CEOs are also included in the TMT). However, we should be careful when generalizing this particular result in view of the Dutch governance system in which CEOs are chairpersons of the "Raad van Bestuur" (i.e., the executive board) and act more like "first among equals" than their US counterparts (i.e., CEOs) do.

Finally, no support was found for the two hypotheses about the *level* of education (of the CEO and the TMT). Interestingly, these were the only hypotheses that were exclusively anchored in cognitive complexity theory and *not* also anchored in structural holes theory (i.e., all other hypotheses were anchored in structural hole theory and sometimes in cognitive complexity theory). In addition, this hypothesis assumed that the level of formal education was a valid measure of cognitive ability or complexity. This suggests that either cognitive complexity theory or a formal education measure is not valid in the context of internationally diversified firms, or both. In fact, prior research by Calori et al. (1994) has provided direct evidence consistent with the idea that executives at internationally diversified firms have more complex cognitive maps than their counterparts at less internationalized firms. This casts additional doubt on "education level" as a measure of cognitive complexity and ability (cf. Hitt and Tyler, 1991). However, more research is needed to make more definitive conclusions.

Obviously, this study has limitations as well. Empirical support from a non-US sample and using panel data in itself add to prior work that has found similar empirical outcomes. However, the empirical results from this study might be predicated on the particular culture in which the firms in our sample were rooted (as in any other study). Future work using data from different cultures would add to our study. Further, our study examined the relationship between CEO and TMT characteristics and a firm's degree of international diversification in order to determine what sort of CEOs and TMTs are needed at highly internationalized firms (as opposed to less internationalized firms). Future studies may examine interesting *contingencies:* the relationship between TMT characteristics and international diversification in turbulent and stable environments (Keck, 1997; Murray, 1989) or low–high interdependence (Michel and Hambrick, 1992) of the components of the firm, for instance, in the context of varying degrees of product diversification (cf. Barkema and Vermeulen, 1998b; Hitt et al., 1997; Tallman and Li, 1996). Carpenter and Fredrickson's 2001 study, which explores how the influence of heterogeneity on international diversification is moderated by uncertainty, is an interesting example in this respect.

More generally, we currently understand very little about what sort of top managers and top teams are needed at the helm of MNCs (i.e., highly complex organizational structures – according to some, internal networks in themselves, cf. Hedlund (1994) – with many different factions, regional and divisional units, etc.). There is very little systematic knowledge (theory and evidence) on what sort of managers are needed in this position as compared to the sort of managers needed in firms in early stages of internationalization. The issue of how the demands on the top team – and hence the optimal composition of the TMT – change as firms internationalize over time is extremely interesting, both from a theoretical and from a practical perspective, and we therefore strongly encourage the development of such dynamic theory.

References

Acar, W. and Sankaran, K. 1999. The myth of unique decomposability: Specializing the herfindahl and entropy measures: *Strategic Management Journal*, 20: 969–75.

Argyres, N. 1996. Capabilities, technological diversification and divisionalization. *Strategic Management Journal*, 17: 395–410.

Bantel, K. A., and Jackson, S. E. 1989. Top management and innovations in banking: Does the composition of the top team make a difference? *Strategic Management Journal*, 10 (special issue): 107–24.

Barkema H. G., Bell, J. H. J., and Pennings, J. M. 1996. Foreign entry, cultural barriers, and learning. *Strategic Management Journal*, 17: 151–66.

Barkema, H. G. and Vermeulen, F. 1998a. Sloughing the old: The learning process of internationalizing firms. Paper presented at the annual meeting of the Academy of Management in San Diego.

Barkema, H. G. and Vermeulen, F. 1998b. International expansion through start-up or acquisition: a learning perspective. *Academy of Management Journal*, 41: 7–26.

Bartlett, C. A.1981. Multinational structural change: Evolution versus reorganization. In L. Otterbeck (ed.), *The management of headquarters-subsidiary relationships in multinational corporations*. London, Gower, 121–45.

Bartlett, C. A. and Ghoshal, S. 1989. *Managing across borders: the transnational solution*. London: Hutchinson Business Books.

Birkinshaw, J. 1997. Entrepreneurship in multinational corporations: The characteristics of subsidiary initiatives. *Strategic Management Journal*, 18: 207–30.

Birkinshaw, J. and Hood, N. 1998. Multinational subsidiary evolution: Capability and charter change in foreign-owned subsidiary companies. *Academy of Management Review*, 23: 773–95

Boeker, W. 1997a. Executive migration and strategic change: the effect of top manager movement on product market entry. *Administrative Science Quarterly*, 42: 231–36.

Boeker, W. 1997b. Strategic change: the influence of managerial characteristics and organizational growth. *Academy of Management Journal*, 40: 152–70.

Burt, R. S. 1992. *Structural holes*. Cambridge, MA: Harvard University Press.

Burt, R. S., Hogarth, R. M., and Michaud, C. 2000. Organization science – The social capital of French and American managers. *Organization Science*, 11: 123–47.

Calori, R., Johnson, G., and Sarnin, P. 1994. CEO's cognitive maps and the scope of the organization. *Strategic Management Journal*, 15: 437–57.

Carpenter, M. A. and Fredrickson, J. W. 2001. Top management teams, global strategic posture, and the moderating role of uncertainty. *Academy of Management Journal*, in press.

Dollinger, M. 1984. Environmental boundary spanning and information processing effects on organizational performance. *Academy of Management Journal*, 27: 351–68.

Eisenhardt, K. M., and Schoonhoven C. B. 1990. Organizational growth: linking founding team, strategy, environment, and growth among US semiconductor ventures, 1978–1988. *Administrative Science Quarterly*, 35: 504–29.

Finkelstein, S. and Hambrick, D. C. 1990. Top-management-team tenure and organizational outcomes: The moderating role of managerial discretion. *Administrative Science Quarterly*, 35: 484–503.

Finkelstein S. and Hambrick D. C. 1996. *Strategic leadership: Top executives and their effects on organizations*. Minneapolis/St.Paul: West.

Ghauri P. N. 1990. Emergence of new structures in Swedish multinationals. In S.B. Prasad (ed.), *Advances in international comparative management*, Greenwich, CT: JAI Press.

Greene, W. H. 1997. *Econometric Analysis*, 3rd edn. Upper Saddle River, NJ: Prentice Hall.

Grimm, C. M. and Smith, K. G. 1991. Management and organizational change: a note on the railroad industry. *Strategic Management Journal*, 12: 557–62

Haleblian J. and Finkelstein S. 1993. Top management team size, CEO dominance and firm performance: the moderating roles of environmental turbulence and discretion. *Academy of Management Journal*, 36: 844–63.

Hambrick, D. C., Cho, T. S., and Chen, M.-J. 1996. The influence of TMT heterogeneity on firms' competitive moves. *Administrative Science Quarterly*, 41: 659–84.

Hambrick, D .C., Geletkanycz, M. A., and Fredrickson, J. W. 1993. Top executive commitment to the *status quo*: Some tests of its determinants. *Strategic Management Journal*, 14: 401–18.

Hambrick, D. C. and Mason P. A. 1984. Upper echelons: The organization as reflection of its top managers. *Academy of Management Review*, 9: 193–206.

Hedlund, G. 1994. A model of knowledge management and the N-form corporation. *Strategic Management Journal*, 15: 73–90.

Hitt, M. A., Hoskisson, R. E., and Ireland, R. D. 1994. A mid-range theory of the interactive effects of international and product diversification on innovation and performance. *Journal of Management*, 20: 297–326.

Hitt, M. A., Hoskisson, R. E., and Kim, H. 1997. International diversification: Effects on innovation and firm performance in product-diversified firms. *Academy of Management Journal*, 40: 767–98.

Hitt, M. A., Keats, B. W., and DeMarie, S. M. 1998. Navigating in the new competitive landscape: Building strategic flexibility and competitive advantage in the twenty-first century. *Academy of Management Executive*, 12: 22–43.

Hitt, M. A., and Tyler, B. B. 1991. Strategic decision models: Integrating different perspectives. *Strategic Management Journal*, 12: 327–51.

Homans, G. C. 1961. *Social behaviour: its elementary forms*. London: Routledge and Kegan Paul.

Hoskisson, R. E., Hitt, M. A., Johnson, R. A., and Moesel, D. D. 1993. Construct validity of an objective (entropy) categorical measure of diversification strategy. *Strategic Management Journal*, 14: 215.

Huy, Q. N. 1999. Emotional capability, emotional intelligence, and radical change. *Academy of Management Review*, 24: 325–45.

Johanson, J., and Vahlne, J.-E. 1977. The internationalization process of the firm – a model of knowledge development and increasing foreign market commitment. *Journal of International Business Studies*, 8: 23–32.

Keck, S. L. 1997. Top management team structure: differential effects by environmental context. *Organization Science*, 8: 143–56.

Lu, J. W. and Beamish, P. W. 2001. The internationalization and performance of SMEs. *Strategic Management Journal*, in press.

Malnight, T. M. 1995. Globalization of an ethnocentric firm: an evolutionary perspective. *Strategic Management Journal*, 16: 119–41.

Malnight, T. M. 1996. The transition from decentralized to network-based MNC structures: an evolutionary perspective. *Journal of International Business Studies*, 27: 43–65.

Michel, J. G. and Hambrick, D. C. 1992. Diversification posture and TMT characteristics. *Academy of Management Journal*, 35: 35.

Miller, C. C., Burke, L. M., and Glick, W. H. 1998. Cognitive diversity among upper-echelon executives, implications for strategic decision process. *Strategic Management Journal*, 19: 39–58.

Miller, D. 1991. Stale in the saddle: CEO tenure and the match between organization and environment. *Management Science*, 37: 34–52.

Murray, A. I. 1989. Top management group heterogeneity and firm performance. *Strategic Management Journal*, 10: 125–41.

Palepu, K. 1985. Diversification strategy, profit performance and the entropy measure. *Strategic Management Journal*, 6: 239–55.

Pfeffer, J. 1983. Organizational demography. In L. L. Cummings and B. M. Staw (eds.), *Research in organizational behavior*, 5. Greenwich, CT: JAI Press, 299–357.

Ronen, S. and Shenkar, O. 1985 Clustering countries on attitudinal dimensions: a review and synthesis. *Academy of Management Review*, 10: 435–54.

Roth, K. 1995. Managing international interdependence: CEO characteristics in a resource-based framework. *Academy of Management Journal*, 38: 200–31.

Sambharya, R. B. 1996. Foreign experience of TMTs and international diversification strategies of US multinational corporations. *Strategic Management Journal*, 17: 739.

Sanders, G. Wm. and Carpenter, M. A. 1998. Internationalization and firm governance: Roles of CEO compensation, top team composition, and board structure. *Academy of Management Journal*, 41: 158–78.

Schroder, H. M., Driver M. J., and Streufert, S. 1967. *Human information processing: individuals and groups functioning in complex social situations*. New York: Holt, Rinehart, and Winston.

Simon, H. A. 1945. *Administrative Behaviour*. 2nd edn. New York: Free Press.

Smith K. G., Smith, K. A., Olian, J. D., Sims, H. P., Bannon, O' Jr. D. P., and Scully, J. A. 1994. Top management team demography and process: the role of social integration and communication. *Administrative Science Quarterly*, 39: 412–38.

Sutcliffe, K. M. 1994. What executives notice: Accurate perceptions in TMT. *Academy of Management Journal*, 37: 1360–78.

Tallman, S. and Li J. 1996. Effects of international diversity and product diversity on the performance of multinational firms. *Academy of Management Journal*, 39: 179–96.

Thomas, A. S., Litschert, R. J., and Ramaswamy, K. 1991. The performance impact of strategy–managerial coalignment: an empirical examination. *Strategic Management Journal*, 12: 327–51.

Wally, S. and Baum, J. R. 1994. Personal and structural determinants of the pace of strategic decision making. *Academy of Management Journal*, 37: 932–56.

Wiersema, M. F. and Bantel, K. 1992. Top management team demography and corporate strategic change. *Academy of Management Journal*, 35: 91–121.

PART VI

Strategic Leadership and Growth

CHAPTER FOURTEEN

The Entrepreneurial Imperatives of Strategic Leadership

Jeffrey G. Covin, Dennis P. Slevin

The phenomenon of leadership has been the focus of systematic social science research since the early 1930s (House and Aditya, 1997). However, it wasn't until approximately the mid-1980s that social scientists began to widely recognize the distinctiveness and significance of that portion of the leadership domain known today as strategic leadership (Finkelstein and Hambrick, 1996), defined by Hitt, Ireland, and Hoskisson (2001: 489) as "the ability to anticipate, envision, maintain flexibility, and empower others to create strategic change as necessary." It's not that the "new" phenomenon of strategic leadership emerged in the mid-1980s. Rather, the unique domain of strategic leadership started to clarify during this time period. Specific ways in which general managers must be leaders, not simply administrators, were increasingly recognized and debated.

The general manager's role in processes of organizational innovation, for example, became a prominent topic within the management literature (e.g., Drucker, 1985; Burgelman and Sayles, 1986). General management effectiveness was increasingly portrayed as a function of how well the manager could serve as an architect of change, and this required leadership skills and insights that were not always well defined within the traditional general management paradigm. Organizational transformation and strategic renewal processes came to be recognized as vital responsibilities of the general manager. These change-related responsibilities demanded that general managers exhibit proficient strategic leadership. Unfortunately, the vast majority of leadership research conducted through the 1970s focused on lower- and middle-level managers and their relationships with their immediate subordinates (House and Aditya, 1997). The nature of strategic leadership challenges and the determination of how these challenges should be met represented fertile ground for academic theory and research.

As the twenty-first century begins, the domain of strategic leadership is still being defined. Hitt, Ireland, and Hoskisson (2001) have argued compellingly that this domain has at least six components: (1) determining strategic direction, (2) exploiting and maintaining core competencies, (3) developing human capital, (4) sustaining an effective organizational culture, (5) emphasizing ethical practices, and (6) establishing balanced organizational controls. Recent research by Hagen, Hassan, and Amin (1998) has verified that general managers do, in fact, view these six activities as important aspects of strategic leadership.

Strategic leadership also has an entrepreneurial component that is implicit in much of the writing on the topic, but heretofore not well articulated. It is arguable that effective strategic leaders have an entrepreneurial mindset that results in their constant and conscious attempts to achieve growth and/or supernormal profits for their firms through the recognition and exploitation of value creating opportunities. McGrath and MacMillan (2000: 1) define an entrepreneurial mindset as a way of thinking about business that "captures the benefits of uncertainty" in that individuals with this mindset consciously search for and try to exploit high potential opportunities that are often associated with uncertain business environments.

An entrepreneurial mindset may be either an individualistic or a collective phenomenon. When manifest as a collective phenomenon that is shared by members of the upper management echelon and, perhaps, by other members of the organization, an entrepreneurial mindset is conceptually equivalent to what Meyer and Heppard (2000a) recently labeled an entrepreneurial dominant logic. According to these authors, an entrepreneurial dominant logic exists when "the firm and its members interpret, value, and act on information on the basis of the potential of value creation and profitability for the firm" (2000a: 2). Thus, it is correct to view entrepreneurship as a phenomenon that may be framed around both individuals and firms.

The presence of an entrepreneurial dominant logic suggests that the tasks associated with the six components of effective strategic leadership identified by Hitt, Ireland, and Hoskisson (2001) might be approached with a bias toward entrepreneurial thought and behavior. Identifying the ways in which an entrepreneurial dominant logic may impact the execution of Hitt, Ireland, and Hoskisson's (2001) six components of effective strategic leadership is beyond the intended scope of this chapter. Nonetheless, a premise of this chapter is that the presence of an entrepreneurial dominant logic will facilitate the effective practice of strategic leadership in the long run.

Likely benefits that may accrue to organizations whose members and, in particular, strategic leaders embrace an entrepreneurial dominant logic include increased flexibility and adaptability to environmental demands, the emergence of a strong capacity for internal innovation, an enhanced ability to preempt competitors in the exploitation of product-market opportunities, and greater receptivity to the adoption of novel yet promising business models (Meyer and Heppard, 2000b). Most fundamentally, the embracing of an entrepreneurial dominant logic should facilitate an organization's ability to create long-term shareholder wealth. Consistent with the arguments of McGrath and MacMillan (2000) and Rowe (2001), the position taken here is that a firm's sustained viability depends on its ability to regularly convert business opportunities into revenue and profits that form the basis for shareholder wealth. This conversion will be best assured when the firm's strategic leaders recognize and act in accordance with an entrepreneurial dominant logic.

The purpose of this chapter is to identify those "entrepreneurial imperatives" that follow from an entrepreneurial dominant logic. Entrepreneurial imperatives are herein defined as *those aspects of effective strategic leadership that are inherently entrepreneurial in that they relate to the recognition and/or exploitation of opportunity.* These entrepreneurial aspects of strategic leadership are "imperatives" since they have been, or can be, presented as essential to competitive success in what Bettis and Hitt (1995) have labeled the "new competitive landscape." Some entrepreneurial imperatives are obvious and explicit in the strategic leadership literature. Others are less obvious in this literature, or are more evident in the new venture, corporate entrepreneurship, or competitive strategy literatures. Given the diversity of the theoretical arenas from which entrepreneurial imperatives might be inferred, and the fact that this broad literature base does not always clearly recognize what is "entrepreneurial" about any stated managerial prescriptions, the entrepreneurial component of strategic leadership can be difficult to discern. This chapter will attempt to clarify this component.

The following section delineates several entrepreneurial imperatives of strategic leadership. The imperatives identified in this section are not assumed to be exhaustive but, rather, are presented as representative of an effective strategic leader's entrepreneurial tasks and obligations. This section is followed by a comparison of the traditional general management paradigm with an enhanced strategic leadership paradigm that recognizes a leader's entrepreneurial imperatives. The final section of this chapter identifies some of the challenges likely to confront strategic leaders as they heed the entrepreneurial imperatives. It also offers insights that may enable strategic leaders to overcome some of the more manageable initial obstacles to the institutionalization of an entrepreneurial dominant logic within their firms.

The Entrepreneurial Imperatives

Strategic leadership effectiveness will be promoted when leaders exhibit behavior consistent with six entrepreneurial imperatives. Specifically, it is argued here that strategic leaders must (1) nourish an entrepreneurial capability, (2) protect innovations that threaten the current business model, (3) make opportunities make sense for the organization, (4) question the dominant logic, (5) revisit the "deceptively simple questions," and (6) link entrepreneurship and business strategy. These entrepreneurial imperatives are briefly summarized in table 14.1 and presented in more detail below.

Nourish an entrepreneurial capability

Capabilities exist when an integrated set of organizational resources has the capacity to work together in the performance of a task (Hitt, Ireland, and Hoskisson, 2001). An entrepreneurial capability exists when an organization exhibits a systematic capacity to recognize and exploit opportunity. The resources that collectively and integratively comprise an entrepreneurial capability may be quite varied. Some resource sets will primarily impact the opportunity recognition function (e.g., those related to market and technology forecasting proficiency), while other resource sets will primarily impact the opportunity exploitation function (e.g., those related to decision-making speed and organizational flexibility). The presence of an effective entrepreneurial capability requires both types of resource sets.

It is, perhaps, self-evident that strategic leaders should nourish an entrepreneurial

Table 14.1   The entrepreneurial imperatives of strategic leadership

Nourish an entrepreneurial capability	The capacity for entrepreneurship can and should be deliberately developed within organizations. This imperative facilitates both the recognition and the exploitation of opportunity.
Protect innovations that threaten the current business model	Disruptive innovations hold the promise of strategic renewal by potentially enabling the organization to transition from less to more effective business models. This imperative primarily facilitates the exploitation of opportunity.
Make opportunities make sense for the organization	The opportunity "radar screen" must be explicitly defined for organizational members. This imperative primarily facilitates the recognition of opportunity.
Question the dominant logic	Key industry and market assumptions must be periodically reviewed and tested to ascertain their validity. This imperative primarily facilitates the recognition of opportunity.
Revisit the "deceptively simple questions"	A clearer, expanded, or otherwise different sense of purpose can emerge when the most basic business questions are revisited. This imperative primarily facilitates the recognition of opportunity.
Link entrepreneurship and business strategy	Strategy should define appropriate arenas for planned innovations, yet autonomous inventions and discoveries must be capable of impacting the content of future strategy. This imperative primarily facilitates the exploitation of opportunity.

capability. However, ambiguity over what an entrepreneurial capability is, where it resides (in an organizational sense), and how it can be nourished precludes many strategic leaders from taking a proactive stance with respect to its management. Too often, strategic leaders simply assume that entrepreneurial ideas and initiatives will automatically surface within the organization as a natural by-product of organizational operations. Entrepreneurial processes may not be regarded as amenable to managerial manipulation, or they may be confused with and considered equivalent to planned innovation processes. The result of such limited thinking about entrepreneurship is failure to unleash the entrepreneurial potential of the organization.

There is much room for discussion and debate over what, exactly, constitutes an entrepreneurial capability. For purposes of the current discussion, it is useful to conceive of an entrepreneurial capability as a result of certain *organizational qualities* that facilitate the recognition and exploitation of opportunity. Alvarez and Barney (2000) identify agility, creativity, ingenuity, and foresight as entrepreneurial capabilities. We take a slightly different approach by proposing that these are organizational qualities that facilitate the development of an entrepreneurial capability.

From a strategic leadership perspective, the key challenge is determining how to promote such organizational qualities. Meeting this challenge requires that strategic leaders recognize that *individuals* are the source of entrepreneurship in organizations. Human capital, defined as "the knowledge and skills of a firm's entire workforce" (Hitt, Ireland, and Hoskisson, 2001: 501), forms the basis for the development of entrepreneurial capital within organizations. A key task of strategic leaders is, therefore, to create an organizational context that encourages the exhibition of an entrepreneurial mindset and behavior by and among individuals. According to Miles et al. (2000), such a context may be created through a "package" that includes (1) a top management strategic vision that is conducive to entrepreneurial action, (2) an organizational form composed of systems or routines that allow strategy and entrepreneurship to emerge throughout the organization, and (3) a human investment philosophy that recognizes the potential of all organizational members to contribute to the realization of the entrepreneurial strategic vision. The specifics of how to create the type of context that nourishes entrepreneurial capabilities are beyond the intended scope of this chapter. However, details on this topic can be found in the excellent writings of, for example, Peters (1990, 1991), Quinn (1985), and Sathe (1989).

Protect innovations that threaten the current business model

Business models are defined by the choices and assumptions managers make regarding such things as who their firms' customers are, what these customers want, what their firms' unique value propositions should be, and how their firms should deliver on these propositions. Managers often have an interesting way of responding to product, process, administrative, market, or technological innovations that represent potential threats to current business models: they ignore them, or they discount them, or they try to kill them. This pattern of response plays out within individual organizations as well as across industries (Cooper and Schendel, 1976; Cooper and Smith, 1992). A manager's natural inclination seems to be to protect the firm against such "disruptive" innovations. What is at stake, after all, is the rent-generating capacity of the current business model.

The tendency of managers and other organizational members to view disruptive innovations as threats may be a function of the performance of their firms. The managers of high-performing firms often cite the performance of their companies as evidence of the inherent correctness of their business models (Miller, 1992). A belief in the appropriateness of a current business model can blind managers to the vulnerabilities of the model and cause these managers to search for future growth and profits exclusively within the model or within a minimally reconfigured model. The possibility that the current "successful" model may eventually need to undergo a major redesign or, perhaps, even be scrapped may never be seriously considered, and evidence in support of these possibilities may be routinely discredited and dismissed.

The tendency to view disruptive innovations as threats may also be a function of the maturity of the product-market arenas in which a firm competes. In particular, the managers of firms competing in mature product-market arenas may more commonly view disruptive innovations as threats. In such arenas, successful business models will be more broadly recognized, and managers may exhibit reluctance to embrace any disruptive innovation that could result in deviation from an accepted industry recipe (Spender, 1989).

Thus, while disruptive innovations will generally be viewed as threatening (e.g., Bower and Christensen, 1995; Christensen, Bohmer, and Kenagy, 2000), the extent to which a disruptive innovation is perceived as threatening may be affected by firm- and industry-specific factors.

Enlightened, entrepreneurial strategic leaders have a different mindset regarding business models and disruptive innovations. These leaders do not view innovations that may redefine the rent-generating dynamics of the current business model as threats; they view them as potential opportunities. Moreover, such strategic leaders recognize that even though they may perceive such innovations as opportunities, other members of their organizations may not. These other organizational members may regard any potentially disruptive innovation, whether externally or internally originating, as a virus to the current business model (McGrath and MacMillan, 2000). Strategic leaders must, therefore, protect potentially disruptive innovations. Such innovations hold the promise of strategic renewal for the organization and should be selectively embraced, not rejected out of hand. The challenge faced by strategic leaders when confronting potentially disruptive innovations is eloquently described by Christensen (1997) as managing "the innovator's dilemma" – that is, by staying close to their customers, in accordance with the current business model, managers will regularly reject innovations that may become central to viable future business models.

Two insights may be particularly valuable in enabling strategic leaders to heed the entrepreneurial imperative of protecting innovations that threaten the current business model. First, comparative analyses of financial returns likely to be generated by further investments in the current business model versus the new business model will nearly always favor the current model. Therefore, strategic leaders should not frame decision scenarios as "should we make investments that will allow us to extract further value from our current products, markets, or technologies *or* should we make investments that may allow us to extract value from new product, market, or technological innovations?" Rather, the second question should be treated as a separate question. Marginal returns on investment are predictably more uncertain for investments in new innovations. Thus, the seemingly valid financial logic of comparing marginal returns on investment will often result in a failure to embrace innovations on which new business models can be built.

Second, unique organizational architectures are consciously developed and autonomously emerge around individual business models. These architectures are composed of a more or less coherent set of organizational elements sometimes summarized as the "7 S's" of strategy, structure, systems, staff, skills, style, and shared values (Bradach, 1996). Self-renewing organizational architectures contain within them the entrepreneurial seeds of creative destruction. A principal strategic leadership task is to balance the architecture-related needs of the current business model with the architecture-related needs of any innovation-driven, emerging business model.

However, evidence suggests it may be unrealistic to assume that well-established architectures will evolve to embrace business models based on radical product, process, administrative, market, or technological innovations. They are simply too geared toward making the current business model "work." According to McGrath and MacMillan (2000: 302), "The problem with launching new business models is that everything about a new business model is likely to be out of whack with the business model of your existing core business." Consistent with Bower and Christensen's (1995) prescription for the successful management of disruptive technologies, strategic leaders may be well advised to create separate organizations in which entrepreneurial innovations that favor new business models can be nourished.

Make opportunities make sense for the organization

The recognition of opportunity requires that an event, trend, concept, or possibility fall within a person's opportunity "radar screen." Strategic leaders must explicitly define this radar screen, thereby making opportunities identifiable as such by the organization's members. This is not an easy task to fulfill. It requires that strategic leaders manipulate how organizational members think about the organization's business and their roles within the domain of business activity.

Three techniques may be useful in enabling strategic leaders to make opportunities make sense for the organization. First, strategic leaders might communicate a broadened definition of their firm's business. For example, the CEO of a company that manufactures liquid crystal displays (LCDs) might choose to define the "business" of the firm, in a product sense, as the opto-electronic devices rather than LCDs. This would enable and encourage organizational members to look beyond their firm's immediate product domain for business opportunities in related product, market, or technology arenas in which the firm's core competencies may be particularly valuable.

Second, strategic leaders might challenge the organizational members to define the firm's opportunities from the perspective of an innovation model other than that which is dominant for the firm. Most firms innovate around products, markets, or technologies. That is, they see themselves as offering a certain type of product and think in terms of product innovation, with issues of market and technology choice being secondary. Or they see themselves as serving particular markets with choices of products and technologies following from the decision to serve those markets. Or they see themselves as technology driven and focus on how they might best leverage their technological competencies through operations in logical product and market arenas. The provision of a new lens for viewing innovation can facilitate recognition of previously overlooked entrepreneurial opportunities. Thus, for example, an entrepreneurial strategic leader of a market-driven company might encourage his or her firm's members to ask not only "How can we best serve this market?" but also "What other markets might value our products?" (the type of question asked by a product-driven company) and "What new products are we uniquely positioned to develop given our technological competencies?" (the type of question asked by a technology-driven company).

A third technique strategic leaders might employ to make opportunities make sense for the organization is to openly and regularly articulate alternative and plausible future scenarios for their firm. These scenarios should be defined in terms of key organizational, environmental, and strategic variables that currently represent major uncertainties for the firm. The articulation of such scenarios can counter the tendency of organizational members to think in terms of a single, fatalistic future in which opportunities are defined for the business by exogenous events. Across alternative scenarios, organizational members should be able to recognize distinct entrepreneurial opportunities that are context specific. In short, the articulation of alternative and plausible future scenarios holds the promise of expanding the opportunity radar screen for an organization's members.

Question the dominant logic

Prahalad and Bettis (1986) proposed the concept of dominant logic to refer to the way managers conceptualize their business and make major resource allocation decisions. Dominant logic was proposed as an organizational-level variable reflecting schemas, mindsets, or, more generically, cognitive frames that are shared among an organization's members. These shared cognitive frames are said to be based largely on the organizational members' experiences and are often unrecognized by these members. Because their genesis is in past experience, dominant logics reflect the learning that has occurred within the organization over time. Herein lies a problem. An existing dominant logic may cause the organization's members to interpret information from a historical perspective that is no longer relevant or valid in the current business environment. What is needed, according to Bettis and Prahalad (1995), is the capacity to unlearn an existing logic so that a newer, more temporally and contextually appropriate logic can take hold within the organization. On this point, Amit, Brigham, and Markman (2000) have recently argued that competitive success in the new competitive landscape will require that firms employ entrepreneurial management, and such management demands that firms question the existing dominant logic. Likewise, Hitt and Reed (2000) have argued that a dynamic dominant logic – one that changes over time – is needed to ensure that managers' conceptualizations of their firms evolve as environmental conditions change.

In the interests of clarity, it should be pointed out that organizational members can change how they collectively filter and interpret information, thus exhibiting a dynamic dominant logic, all the while persisting with an entrepreneurial mindset or entrepreneurial dominant logic as this latter concept is described by Meyer and Heppard (2000a). An entrepreneurial dominant logic "leads a firm and its members to constantly search and filter information for new product ideas and process innovations that will lead to greater profitability" (Meyer and Heppard, 2000a: 2). Thus, an entrepreneurial dominant logic simply refers to the exhibition of a collective entrepreneurial mindset within a firm's overall dominant logic. Consistent with Meyer and Heppard (2000a), we believe this proposed entrepreneurial element within the dominant logic is valuable and will prove increasingly so as the rate of environmental change, broadly speaking, accelerates. Nonetheless, the broader information filters and interpretive lenses that comprise the traditionally defined dominant logic and that may have once well served the organization can be expected, for reasons articulated above, to yield diminished utility over time. This is why strategic leaders must question the larger dominant logic. In short, the position taken here is that a firm's long-term viability will be best assured when its dominant logic is continuously challenged and evolves in manners consistent with a collective entrepreneurial mindset.

The creation of a dynamic dominant logic through regularly questioning the existing dominant logic, as advocated above, is an inherently entrepreneurial undertaking. It requires that strategic leaders consciously challenge their perceptions of the rules of the game of business, which can lead to the recognition and exploitation of opportunity. Enlightened strategic leaders know that historical precedence doesn't make a routine or practice "right," and they also know that the rules of the game of business should not be accepted as givens but are, at least partially, socially contrived artifacts that are amenable to "reinvention." Strategic leaders can often successfully choose for their firms to play different competitive games, creating business models that break with conventional wisdom and existing industry recipes for success. This is the essence of what Markides (1997, 1998) has referred to as strategic innovation, defined as "a fundamental reconceptualization of what the business is all about that, in turn, leads to a dramatically different way of playing the game in an existing business" (1998: 32). Kim and Mauborgne (1997, 1999) have similarly noted that entrepreneurial companies employ the strategic logic of "value innovation" wherein the firm challenges conventional definitions of where and how value is created in markets. Strategic innovation and value innovation are both consistent with an entrepreneurial mindset.

The techniques of strategic innovation and value innovation should prove useful in enabling strategic leaders to create appropriate dynamic dominant logics in their firms. These techniques are well presented in the writings of Markides (1997, 1998) and Kim and Mauborgne (1997, 1999), respectively, and will not be repeated here. Recognition of the subtlety of existing dominant logics, however, is one area in which the proposed techniques are somewhat lacking. Without a good sense of what the current dominant logic is, strategic leaders will not be adequately prepared to challenge that logic through strategic innovation or value innovation. Moreover, the longer the duration over which a dominant logic has been entrenched, the more invisible it is to organizational members. Therefore, the optimal use of strategic innovation and value innovation techniques for the purpose of instilling within the organization a dynamic dominant logic is arguably contingent upon how well strategic leaders can "surface" the existing dominant logic.

Toward this end, the cognitive science-based technique of assumption analysis (see Mason and Mitroff, 1981) may hold much promise as a strategic leadership tool. Briefly, in assumption analysis, structured debates in which facts or data are interpreted from opposing points of view are used to surface the hidden beliefs and assumptions that underlie individuals' positions on strategic issues. When supported by appropriate group process norms, conflicts among identified beliefs and assumptions are then constructively resolved to yield a new understanding of the appropriateness of various alternative positions, such as those that might follow from particular dominant logics.

Revisit the "deceptively simple questions"

The "deceptively simple questions" are those asked most earnestly and often at the time of a firm's inception. They may never be consciously asked again. Or, tentative answers to these questions may be inferred through observation of a firm's pattern of behavior over time without the questions ever having been consciously asked. The deceptively simple questions are the "clean slate" questions. They include questions like: What business are we in?; What is our reason for existence?; What is the essential purpose of our business?; What is our vision for the future?; and How do we define success? The deceptively simple questions are clearly at the core of strategic management. They are the most basic questions a strategic leader can ask of his or her firm, yet they are characteristically the most difficult questions to answer adequately. Any executive can tell you what his or her firm does (e.g., "We make widgets!"), but much deeper, more basic questions frequently generate stock responses that reflect a superficial and often flawed view of the firm. "To maximize shareholder value," for example, is as likely to be identified as a firm's mission as it is the desired result of fulfilling the mission.

Revisiting the deceptively simple questions is an entrepreneurial imperative of strategic leadership because what one identifies as an opportunity is determined by how one answers these questions. Opportunities and the appropriateness of past and intended strategic behavior become apparent when the deceptively simple questions are seriously considered or reconsidered. Unfortunately, revisiting the deceptively simple questions may be discouraged within organizations because simply "thinking" about basic business issues is often interpreted as a sign of executive inactivity or indecisiveness (Levitt, 1991). Overt decisions and observable behavior are more favorably viewed than reflective processes. Effective managers are said to exhibit a strong bias toward action (Kotter, 1982; Mintzberg, 1973). Time spent revisiting past decisions or implicit choices may be equated to time wasted or counterproductive second-guessing. Consequently, many fundamental business questions may never be seriously or adequately contemplated. Equally troublesome, many fundamental business questions may be asked only once, the assumption being that "the answer" is everlasting.

A problem with not deeply contemplating the deceptively simple questions is that without their serious consideration organizational members may, for example, conceptualize their firm's business in an overly narrow sense, focusing on what the firm does and the means used to achieve the ends of business rather than questioning what their firm can do or should do, or what those business ends should be. Without organizational members having a strong sense that their business is, or should be, more than what they see, there may be little perceived need and opportunity for members to engage in entrepreneurial behavior that reinvents the firm or helps to fulfill its essential purpose.

A problem with asking the deceptively simple questions only once is that the half-life of even thoughtful, appropriate answers seems to be decreasing. Regarding the fundamental purpose of a business, McTavish has argued that, "harsher economic circumstances are forcing companies to realize that they must *regularly* [emphasis added] think about their essential purposes. . ." (1995: 59). Similarly, arguments by Ireland and Hitt (1999) suggest that the realities of the new competitive landscape (e.g., the rapid diffusion of technology throughout industries, shortening product life cycles, the increasing importance of knowledge as a factor of production) demand that companies periodically revisit the fundamental business questions whose answers were once thought immutable over the span of any typical organization life cycle.

Thus, it is essential that executives take the time needed to consciously and collaboratively identify and review the deceptively simple questions. As noted by Levitt (1991: 3), "[f]ew things are more important for a manager to do than ask simple questions. . . ." The objective of this exercise is not to identify "correct" answers. Rather, the objective should be to facilitate a widespread awareness of fundamental strategic issues and choices and to encourage organizational members at all levels to embrace an entrepreneurial mindset.

Link entrepreneurship and business strategy

The business environment of the twenty-first century is requiring that organizations become more entrepreneurial in their outlook and operations. However, the objective of firms should not simply be to become more entrepreneurial. The objective should be to become more *strategically* entrepreneurial. This demands that strategic leaders forge an appropriate linkage between entrepreneurial processes and strategy in their firms.

Entrepreneurial processes are herein defined as those processes by which business opportunities are defined and support is garnered for their exploitation within an organizational setting. Product concept testing, venture "bootlegging," product championing, and business model experimentation, for example, might be considered entrepreneurial processes. The activities entailed by these types of processes can occur with or without having been sanctioned by a firm through its "formal" business strategy. That is, entrepreneurial processes can be either intended or emergent.

When an established organization "acts entrepreneurially," it can and, we would argue, must do more than just pursue planned innovations. It must also assess the potential strategic relevance of autonomous innovations that emerge as a "by-product" of the firm's daily operations (Burgelman, 1984). Such unplanned, autonomous innovations can represent major growth opportunities for the firm, but without some mechanism for strategically rationalizing these innovations and integrating them into the future strategic fabric of the organization, the firm will be in no position to benefit from their discovery. In short, acting entrepreneurially involves taking advantage of foreseen opportunities through planned innovations as well as unforeseen opportunities through ex post strategic rationalization processes.

Therefore, an appropriate linkage between entrepreneurship and strategy is one in which entrepreneurial processes and strategy are reciprocally related. That is, strategy affects and is affected by entrepreneurial processes. However, this latter linkage, where emergent entrepreneurial processes impact strategy, is often weak or nonexistent in organizational contexts. Many firms seem to have difficulty dealing with the more autonomous aspects of entrepreneurship. Effective strategic leaders know that to fully appropriate value from any entrepreneurial capability within their organizations, they must find a way to allow unforeseen opportunities to become part of the formal strategic agenda. Part of the strategic leadership challenge involves creating an organizational infrastructure, funding mechanisms, and value system that encourage rather than ignore or discourage the pursuit of unforeseen opportunities. Strategic leaders must then combine planned initiatives and unplanned initiatives that emerge from the pursuit of unforeseen opportunities in a package that makes strategic sense for their organizations.

If strategic leaders are successful at executing the preceding entrepreneurial imperatives, they will have helped to create self-renewing organizations, which is argued to be the ultimate general management challenge (see Bartlett and Nanda, 1996). As stated by McGrath and MacMillan (2000: 301), "Your most important job as an entrepreneurial leader is not to find new opportunities or to identify the critical competitive insights. Your task is to create an organization that does these things for you as a matter of course." As detailed below, a new paradigm of effective general management practice appears to be emerging.

Traditional General Management vs. Entrepreneurial Strategic Leadership: A Comparison of Beliefs and Philosophies

The preceding observations suggest that effective strategic leaders will have managerial beliefs and philosophies that may diverge considerably from those associated with conventional assumptions about effective general management practice. Table 14.2 summarizes several areas discussed above, as well as a few additional areas, in which differences exist between what will be referred to as the "traditional general management" (TGM) and "entrepreneurial strategic leadership" (ESL) paradigms. The individual entries of table 14.2 are briefly discussed below.

Organizational resources and capabilities Under the TGM paradigm, good managers are expected to protect the organization's resources and capabilities. Being a steward of stability and insulating the organization's overall resource base from potentially undermining forces have traditionally been depicted as high callings for the general manager (Rowe, 2001; Nadler and Tushman, 1999). Entrepreneurial strategic leaders, on the other hand, recognize that many resources and capabilities have finite life spans over which they can generate value for the organization. While these leaders appreciate that an organization's resources and capabilities should be valued, they also know that an unquestioning belief in the enduring value of some resources and capabilities may lead to a false sense of security. Changes in technologies, markets, and industry success factors can quickly erode the value of resources and capabilities. Unless a firm's resource base can be continuously adapted to meet the demands of an evolving business environment, those who oversee the firm may find themselves protecting a worthless set of organizational assets. In short, entrepreneurial strategic leaders view their firms as bundles of resources and capabilities that must evolve rather than be maintained "as is."

The firm's "business" and "purpose" Conventional wisdom within the TGM paradigm holds that general managers must set the course for their organizations, then work to ensure that their organizations stay the course, making only slight navigational corrections when needed. Those fundamental questions regarding the business and purpose of the firm are assumed to have relatively enduring answers. Once the firm is "defined" by its management, it more or less stays so defined. Under the ESL paradigm, definitions of the firm's business and purpose are open to regular review and reassessment. Strategic leaders are, in fact, expected to redefine, reinvent, and renew their firms as an essential part of maintaining competitiveness. Nadler and Tushman (1999: 53) have recently observed that "Today, and in coming decades, leaders of complex organizations should enter their jobs with the expectation that they might well be required to reinvent their organizations three, four, or even more times over the course of their tenure."

Business strategy The TGM paradigm admonishes managers to play the strategy game better than their rivals in competitor firms. The rules of engagement are, for the most part, understood as a set of externally determined requirements that are simply part of doing business in a particular industry arena. The rules may sometimes be bent, but they are seldom, if ever, jettisoned. The ESL paradigm makes no such assumptions about the immutability of the rules. If a firm cannot play the prevailing strategy game

Table 14.2 Traditional general management vs. entrepreneurial strategic leadership: a comparison of beliefs and philosophies

Attitude toward . . .	Traditional general management	Entrepreneurial strategic leadership
Organizational resources and capabilities	Resources and capabilities should be protected	Resources and capabilities should be valued but challenged
The firm's "business" and "purpose"	Definitions of "business" and "purpose" are relatively enduring	Definitions of "business" and "purpose" should be periodically reexamined
Business strategy	Play the game better than competitors	Play the game better than competitors *or* play your own game
Organizational architecture	Designed to optimize implementation of the strategy	Designed to allow for strategic flexibility
Meeting customer needs	Stay "close to the customer"	Stay "close to the customer," but also invest in promising innovations that don't currently meet expressed needs
Entrepreneurial activity within the organization	Entrepreneurial activity should follow from strategy	Entrepreneurial activity should lead to as well as follow from strategy
Organizational learning	Institutionalize knowledge to avoid having to relearn business lessons	Institutionalize a questioning attitude such that learning and unlearning can coexist

better than its competitors, a new strategy game that favors the initiating firm may need to be considered. Effective strategic leaders recognize that strategy, like the firm's purpose or overall business model, is subject to reinvention at the leader's discretion.

Organizational architecture Strategy is the starting point for the design of an organization's architecture under the TGM paradigm. A principal concern of general managers is the creation of an architecture in which the structure, systems, processes, resources, and other organizational system elements are mutually supportive and chosen to optimize implementation of the firm's strategy. Under the ESL paradigm, creating an organizational architecture that exhibits strategic *fit* is regarded as less important than creating one that allows for strategic *flexibility* – the ability to strategically adapt to the various and changing demands of an uncertain competitive environment (Sanchez, 1995). The constant search for perfect alignments among an organizational system's elements, including fit with the firm's strategy, is considered a dysfunctional obsession. Instead, given the dynamism of markets and industries, effective strategic leaders seek to create more robust architectures that can effectively accommodate modest-to-moderate changes in strategy without losing their fundamental integrity. According to

Sanchez and Mahoney, such robust architectures exhibit a high degree of "modularity," defined as "a special form of design which intentionally creates a high degree of independence or "loose coupling" between component designs by standardizing component interface specifications" (1996: 65).

Meeting customer needs Ever since the publication of Peters and Waterman's (1982) classic management book *In Search of Excellence*, many managers have assumed that staying "close to the customer" is an inherently desirable organizational goal. The TGM paradigm reflects this belief. Under the ESL paradigm, it is recognized that the customer is sometimes wrong. This may sound like heresy to "old school" marketing pundits. However, current customers often provide flawed feedback regarding the potential of emerging markets and technologies (Christensen and Bower, 1996). These customers can often not see far beyond *their* current needs. Competing for the future demands that strategic leaders consider the intersections of market and technology trajectories, and selectively invest in promising innovations that may not currently meet expressed needs (Hamel and Prahalad, 1994). Thus, to borrow Slater and Narver's (1998) terms, entrepreneurial strategic leaders are "market-oriented" rather than "customer-led."

Entrepreneurial activity within the organization The TGM paradigm has had surprisingly little to say on the matter of entrepreneurial activity within the firm, at least if one defines entrepreneurial activity as more than just intended investments in innovation-focused initiatives. Innovation, which forms the core of all entrepreneurial activity (Stevenson and Gumpert, 1985), is discussed more from a rational, planned perspective than from a serendipitous, emergent perspective. As such, one might infer under the TGM paradigm that entrepreneurial activity should follow from strategy. However, unless those who oversee the organization create mechanisms for allowing unforeseen opportunities to be formally recognized, these opportunities will seldom, if ever, help to define the strategic agenda, and the organization will not be fully leveraging its entrepreneurial capability. Under the ESL paradigm, strategic leaders appreciate that the sustainability of a firm's competitiveness requires that entrepreneurial activity lead to as well as follow from strategy.

Organizational learning Much of the identifiable discrepancy between what have been presented as the TGM and ESL paradigms seems to be rooted in different top management attitudes toward organizational learning. Under the TGM paradigm, business-related knowledge is held as "the truth." Once the truth is learned, it becomes incumbent upon effective general managers to try to institutionalize it. To not do so will result in having to continually relearn the lessons of business. Under the ESL paradigm, what is true today may not be so tomorrow. The lessons of business must be learned *and* unlearned because they change. Therefore, strategic leaders strive to institutionalize a questioning attitude. According to Bartlett and Nanda, an organizational leader's biggest challenge "lies in institutionalizing a process that leads those deep in the organization to continually question, test, and evaluate conventional wisdom and accepted practice" (1996: 3).

Concluding Observations: Toward Embracing an Entrepreneurial Dominant Logic

Entrepreneurial imperatives were defined as those aspects of effective strategic leadership that are inherently entrepreneurial in that they relate to the recognition and/or exploitation of opportunity. The entrepreneurial imperatives identified in this chapter were (1) nourish an entrepreneurial capability, (2) protect innovations that threaten the current business model, (3) make opportunities make sense for the organization, (4) question the dominant logic, (5) revisit the "deceptively simple questions," and (6) link entrepreneurship and business strategy. These imperatives represent behaviors consistent with how an entrepreneurial strategic leader might act. This list is certainly incomplete. On the other hand, a list of, say, 30 imperatives – that is, 30 major entrepreneurship-related tasks and obligations – would border on the absurd. Admittedly, the imperatives presented here are also potentially overlapping, therefore not as distinct as one might wish such a list to be. The imperatives "revisit the deceptively simple questions" and "make opportunities make sense for the organization," for example, could involve some of the same behaviors. Nonetheless, it is hoped that strategic leaders and those who study their behavior will find the list of imperatives presented here thought provoking.

Many factors might keep individuals from recognizing a strategic leader's entrepreneurship-related tasks and obligations. Entrepreneurial behavior has historically been associated with new venture phenomena and has not long been discussed as pertinent in other business contexts. Failure to broadly recognize what defines the essence of entrepreneurial behavior (the recognition and exploitation of opportunity) has also contributed to such behavior not being seen as inherent to the strategic leadership role. However, even if and when strategic leaders and those who study them develop a better appreciation of the role of entrepreneurship within the strategic leadership domain, it will not necessarily be easy to heed what are accepted as the entrepreneurial imperatives. Among those factors that could make it difficult to heed any entrepreneurial imperatives accepted as valid are an organization's culture, the presence of strategic inertia, and the absence of a transition plan that addresses how to promote a collective entrepreneurial mindset.

Much of the difficulty a strategic leader might experience when trying to facilitate the emergence of an entrepreneurial dominant logic relates to the presence of those factors that limit "managerial discretion" or "latitude of action." As noted by Finkelstein and Hambrick (1996), leaders are not equally well positioned to impact organizational outcomes. Rather, there are factors inherent to the organization's task environment, internal environment, and the leader him- or herself that influence how much the leader can affect an organization's outcomes. For example, the presence of external legal constraints, large organization size, and weak political skills, among other factors, are assumed to have a negative impact on managerial discretion. Discretion-inhibiting factors explain much of why a series of leaders has had trouble reinventing such large American icons as General Motors and Sears, Roebuck and Co. In short, their predictably will be mental blocks to practicing entrepreneurial strategic leadership, but there are also very real limits to any given leader's ability to act like an entrepreneur and create a climate conducive to sustaining entrepreneurship within the organization.

Moreover, the task of heeding the strategic imperatives would, realistically, not be as simple as this chapter may seem to suggest. Acting in complete accordance with each of the imperatives would entail a change process whose adequate description is well beyond the scope of this chapter.

The preceding observations beg the question "What, then, might be presented as fundamental insights of potential value to any strategic leader who believes in the inherent value of an entrepreneurial mindset and who strives to create a deeply entrepreneurial firm?" This chapter concludes with three such insights. These insights are framed as broad implementation guidelines that should facilitate the occurrence of entrepreneurial behaviors and initiatives throughout the organization, as would be consistent with the presence of an entrepreneurial dominant logic.

First, strategic leaders should "act as if. . . ." That is, they should think of what opportunities their firm would pursue, what value proposition(s) their firm would offer, how they would organize their firm's operations, what their firm's essential competencies would be, etc., *if they were leading a new venture*. It is probable that much of what keeps strategic leaders from thinking and acting entrepreneurially is of their own psychological construction. By "acting as if. . ," the real limits to the recognition and pursuit of opportunity will be more easily identified and tested. The trappings of "what is" will always bias an individual's perception of "what can be." The psychological removal of these trappings can facilitate entrepreneurial thinking on the part of the strategic leader and the exhibition of entrepreneurial behavior as a firm-level phenomenon (Covin and Slevin, 1991).

Second, strategic leaders should "focus on the software." The strategy, structure, systems, and operating procedures of a firm represent much of the "hardware." These are the contextual variables that formally frame a firm's business activity and are amenable to direct and immediate managerial manipulation. The hardware variables can have a strong impact on individual and group action since people take their behavioral cues, in part, from the formal contexts in which they operate. Not surprisingly, the hardware is often the first target of attack in large-scale planned organizational change efforts.

Still, considerable anecdotal evidence suggests a focus on the hardware will not enable strategic leaders to unleash the entrepreneurial potential of their firms. To do so requires a focus on the software – the more subtle and informal aspects of an organization's architecture including shared values, behavioral norms, and general perceptions, beliefs, attitudes, and assumptions. An organization's culture and climate comprise much of the software. Importantly, it is here where entrepreneurship is either fundamentally embraced or rejected. Strategic leaders cannot simply choose or declare that entrepreneurial activities permeate their organizations. The institutionalization of entrepreneurship in its various manifestations requires that it *emerge* as a shared value. This can only be accomplished through focusing on the software.

Third, strategic leaders should "share the load." Great leaders are able to tap into the greatness of their followers. Likewise, entrepreneurial strategic leaders find ways of accessing the latent entrepreneur in all organizational members. "Sharing the load" means that strategic leaders must recognize that they will never be wise enough, energetic enough, resourceful enough, or committed enough to single-handedly create deeply entrepreneurial organizations. Individuals working at all levels of the organization are the ultimate source of entrepreneurship. Therefore, strategic leaders must work to ensure the existence of a shared sense of responsibility for entrepreneurship within the firm. To quote Professor Grant Miles, "One of the first steps in developing entrepreneurial competencies and strategies is to include all of the people in the organization. . . It is important to find ways to unleash the entrepreneurial potential that is already there" (quoted in Meyer and Heppard, 2000b: 15). Only when all levels of the organization feel empowered and obliged to think and act like entrepreneurs will the self-renewing organization become a reality (McGrath and MacMillan, 2000).

In conclusion, there is a consensus building within the popular business press as well as the academic literature that a firm's long-term viability will increasingly hinge upon its ability to exhibit entrepreneurial behavior (Zahra, Nielsen, and Bogner, 1999). Well-considered managerial prescriptions and technologies intended to address this need are increasingly being offered (see, for example, Eisenhardt, Brown, and Neck, 2000; Nadler and Tushman, 1999; Whitney, 1996). While exceptions certainly exist, and the literature is still quite fragmented, the collective writing on this topic reflects a remarkable consistency of thought. Nonetheless, the strategic leader's tasks and obligations with respect to the recognition and pursuit of opportunity and, more specifically, the creation of the self-renewing, entrepreneurial organization are topics about which the literature has been largely silent. This chapter has focused on identifying these entrepreneurship-related tasks and obligations, hopefully promoting a greater appreciation of the role, manifestations, and overall scope of entrepreneurship within the strategic leadership domain.

References

Alvarez, S. and Barney, J. B. 2000. Entrepreneurial capabilities: A resource-based view. In G. D. Meyer and K. A. Heppard (eds), *Entrepreneurship as strategy*. Thousand Oaks, CA: Sage Publications, 63–81.

Amit, R. H., Brigham, K., and Markman, G. D. 2000. Entrepreneurial management as strategy. In G. D. Meyer and K. A. Heppard (eds), *Entrepreneurship as strategy*. Thousand Oaks, CA: Sage Publications, 83–99.

Bartlett, C. A. and Nanda, A. 1996. *The GM's leadership challenge: Building a self-renewing organization*. Harvard Business School Note 9–397–023, Boston: Harvard Business School Publishing.

Bettis, R. and Hitt, M. A. 1995. The new competitive landscape. *Strategic Management Journal*, 16 (summer special issue): 7–19.

Bettis, R. and Prahalad, C. K. 1995. The dominant logic: Retrospective and extension. *Strategic Management Journal*, 16: 5–14.

Bower, J. L. and Christensen, C. M. 1995. Disruptive technologies: Catching the wave. *Harvard Business Review*, 73(1): 43–53.

Bradach, J. 1996. *Organizational alignment: The 7–S model*. Harvard Business School Note 9–497–045. Boston: Harvard Business School Publishing.

Burgelman, R. A. 1984. Designs for corporate entrepreneurship in established firms. *California Management Review*, 26(3): 154–66.

Burgelman, R. A. and Sayles, L. R. 1986. *Inside corporate innovation: Strategy, structure, and managerial skills.* New York: Free Press.

Christensen, C. M. 1997. *The innovator's dilemma: When new technology causes great firms to fail.* Boston: Harvard Business School Press.

Christensen, C. M. and Bower, J. L. 1996. Customer power, strategic investment, and the failure of leading firms. *Strategic Management Journal,* 17(3): 197–218.

Christensen, C. M., Bohmer, R., and Kenagy, J. 2000. Will disruptive innovations cure health care? *Harvard Business Review,* 78(5): 102–11.

Cooper, A. C. and Schendel, D. 1976. Strategic responses to technological threats. *Business Horizons,* 19(1): 61–9.

Cooper, A. C. and Smith, C. G. 1992. How established firms respond to threatening technologies. *Academy of Management Executive,* 6(2): 55–70.

Covin, J. G. and Slevin, D. P. 1991. A conceptual model of entrepreneurship as firm behavior. *Entrepreneurship Theory and Practice,* 16(1): 7–25.

Drucker, P. 1985. *Innovation and entrepreneurship.* New York: Harper & Row.

Eisenhardt, K. M., Brown, S. L., and Neck, H. M. 2000. Competing on the entrepreneurial edge. In G. D. Meyer and K. A. Heppard (eds), *Entrepreneurship as strategy.* Thousand Oaks, CA: Sage Publications, 49–62.

Finkelstein, S. and Hambrick, D. 1996. *Strategic leadership: Top executives and their effects on organizations.* St. Paul, MN: West.

Hagen, A. F., Hassan, M. T., and Amin, S. G. 1998. Critical strategic leadership components: An empirical investigation. *S.A.M. Advanced Management Journal,* 63(3): 39–44.

Hamel, G. and Prahalad, C. K. 1994. *Competing for the future.* Boston: Harvard Business School Press.

Hitt, M. A., Ireland, R. D., and Hoskisson, R. E. 2001. *Strategic management: Competitiveness and globalization,* 4th edn. Cincinnati, OH: South-Western College Publishing.

Hitt, M. A. and Reed, T. S. 2000. Entrepreneurship in the new competitive landscape. In G. D. Meyer and K. A. Heppard (eds), *Entrepreneurship as strategy.* Thousand Oaks, CA: Sage Publications, 23–47.

House, R. J. and Aditya, R. M. 1997. The social scientific study of leadership: Quo vadis? *Journal of Management,* 23(3): 409–73.

Ireland, R. D. and Hitt, M. A. 1999. Achieving and maintaining strategic competitiveness in the 21st century: The role of strategic leadership. *Academy of Management Executive,* 13(1): 43–57.

Kim, W. C. and Mauborgne, R. 1997. Value innovation: The strategic logic of high growth. *Harvard Business Review,* 75(1): 103–13.

Kim, W. C. and Mauborgne, R. 1999. Creating new market space. *Harvard Business Review,* 77(1): 83–93.

Kotter, J. P. 1982. *The general managers.* New York: Free Press.

Levitt, T. 1991. *Thinking about management.* New York: Free Press.

Markides, C. 1997. Strategic innovation. *Sloan Management Review,* 38(3): 9–23.

Markides, C. 1998. Strategic innovation in established companies. *Sloan Management Review,* 39(3): 31–42.

Mason, R. O. and Mitroff, I. I. 1981. *Challenging strategic planning assumptions.* New York: John Wiley and Sons.

McGrath, R. G. and MacMillan, I. 2000. *The entrepreneurial mindset: Strategies for continuously creating opportunity in an age of uncertainty.* Boston: Harvard Business School Press.

McTavish, R. 1995. One more time: What business are you in? *Long Range Planning,* 28(2): 49–60.

Meyer, G. D. and Heppard, K. A. 2000a. Entrepreneurial strategies: The dominant logic of entrepreneurship. In G. D. Meyer and K. A. Heppard (eds), *Entrepreneurship as strategy.*

Thousand Oaks, CA: Sage Publications, 1–22.

Meyer, G. D. and Heppard, K. A. 2000b. *Entrepreneurship as strategy*. Thousand Oaks, CA: Sage Publications.

Miles, G., Heppard, K. A., Miles, R. E., and Snow, C. C. 2000. Entrepreneurial strategies: The critical role of top management. In G. D. Meyer and K. A. Heppard (eds), *Entrepreneurship as strategy*. Thousand Oaks, CA: Sage Publications, 101–14.

Miller, D. 1992. The Icarus Paradox: How exceptional companies bring their own downfall. *Business Horizons*, 35(1): 24–35.

Mintzberg, H. 1973. *The nature of managerial work*. New York: Harper & Row.

Nadler, D. A. and Tushman, M. L. 1999. The organization of the future: Strategic imperatives and core competencies for the 21st century. *Organizational Dynamics*, 28(1): 45–60.

Peters, T. 1990. Get innovative or get dead. *California Management Review*, 32(1): 9–26.

Peters, T. 1991. Part two: Get innovative or get dead. *California Management Review*, 33(2): 9–23.

Peters, T. and Waterman, R. H., II. 1982. *In search of excellence*. New York: Harper & Row.

Prahalad, C., and Bettis, R. 1986. The dominant logic: A new link between diversity and performance. *Strategic Management Journal*, 7: 485–501.

Quinn, J. B. 1985. Managing innovation: Controlled chaos. *Harvard Business Review*, 63(3): 73–84.

Rowe, W. G. 2001. Creating wealth in organizations: The role of strategic leadership. *Academy of Management Executive*, 15(1): 81–94.

Sanchez, R. 1995. Strategic flexibility in product competition. *Strategic Management Journal*, 16 (summer special issue): 135–59.

Sanchez, R. and Mahoney, J. T. 1996. Modularity, flexibility, and knowledge management in product and organization design. *Strategic Management Journal*, 17 (winter special issue): 63–76.

Sathe, V. 1989. Fostering entrepreneurship in the large, diversified firm. *Organizational Dynamics*, 18(10): 20–32.

Slater, S. F. and Narver, J. C. 1998. Customer-led and market-oriented: Let's not confuse the two. *Strategic Management Journal*, 19: 1001–6.

Spender, J. C. 1989. *Industry recipes: The nature and sources of managerial judgment*. Oxford: Blackwell.

Stevenson, H. H. and Gumpert, D. 1985. The heart of entrepreneurship. *Harvard Business Review*, 85(2): 85–95.

Whitney, J. O. 1996. Strategic renewal for business units. *Harvard Business Review*, 74(4): 84–98.

Zahra, S. A., Nielsen, A. P., and Bogner, W. C. 1999. Corporate entrepreneurship, knowledge, and competence development. *Entrepreneurship Theory and Practice*, 23(3): 169–89.

CHAPTER FIFTEEN

Entrepreneurship as Growth: Growth as Entrepreneurship

Per Davidsson, Frédéric Delmar, Johan Wiklund

Introduction

An increasing number of scholars identify themselves as "entrepreneurship research-ers" (and educators), and would refer to the field of research they are affiliated with as "entrepreneurship research." Many of these researchers would also have a second home in some other application area such as small business, family business, or innovation; in a business sub-discipline like marketing, finance, or strategic management; or in a discipline such as psychology, sociology, or economics. Apart from occasionally mak-ing it into mainstream journals, the North American members of this community of scholars would regard *Journal of Business Venturing* and *Entrepreneurship Theory and Practice* as primary outlets for their research as well as important reading for their professional development (Romano and Ratnatunga, 1997). Further, they are likely regulars at the *Babson College/Kauffman Foundation Entrepreneurship Research Con-ference* and/or members of the *Entrepreneurship Division* of the Academy of Manage-ment. In other parts of the world other journals, conferences, and associations could be added, but the North American ones would not be entirely disregarded.

Entrepreneurship – the concept as well as the phenomenon – certainly attracts at least occasional interest also from researchers who do not fit the above description. However, it is the (admittedly heterogeneous) community of researchers described above, and their research, that we have in mind when in the following, we refer to "entrepreneurship researchers" and "entrepreneurship research".

Within this rapidly expanding field, *business growth* has become a major theme. Gartner (1990) showed that "growth" was one out of eight themes that professional users commonly associated with the entrepreneurship concept. Livesay (1995) chose "En-trepreneurship and Growth" as the title for his two-volume collection of essential readings in the field. In 1997, growth was chosen as the theme for the Babson/Kauffman Conference. It may further be noted that 26 studies in Delmar's (1997) methodologi-cal review of research on firm growth were published in either *Journal of Business*

Venturing or *Entrepreneurship Theory and Practice.* Thirteen of the studies had some variant of the word "entrepreneur" in the title. In his partly overlapping review of 53 studies on growth, Wiklund (1998) included 20 that were published in these two journals, and another twelve appearing in other publications that were clearly identifiable as outlets for entrepreneurship research, such as *Entrepreneurship and Regional Development* or *Frontiers of Entrepreneurship Research.* Again, thirteen of the studies had some variant of the word "entrepreneur" in the title.

This shows that many researchers evidently associate "growth" with "entrepreneurship" and vice versa. However, entrepreneurship researchers are not alone in showing an interest in business growth. Rather, growth is a major theme both in economics and management studies (Acs and Audretsch, 1990; Evans, 1987; Greiner, 1972; Kazanjian and Drazin, 1989; Penrose, 1959). For the young and formative field of entrepreneurship research this gives reason to reflect seriously upon a number of issues. Firstly, there is the risk that entrepreneurship researchers reinvent worse versions of wheels that are already in operation in other fields, thus failing to make a meaningful contribution. Secondly, there is the risk that they over-extend their own field, thus creating obstacles rather than contributions to a clear and thorough understanding of entrepreneurial processes. To avoid these risks, entrepreneurship researchers have reasons to ask themselves:

- Are there particular aspects of business growth that fall naturally within the domain of entrepreneurship?
- If so, is interest in these issues unique to entrepreneurship research (suggesting potential for unique contribution) or do other fields of research share them (suggesting potential for fruitful collaboration)?

The purpose of this chapter is to attempt to answer these questions. We will approach this task by first asking "Is entrepreneurship growth?" Starting from a number of contemporary and influential definitions of entrepreneurship, we discuss the possible inclusion or exclusion of growth implied by these definitions. We then turn to the converse question: "Is growth entrepreneurship?" We will argue that specific types or stages of firm growth do satisfy theoretical criteria to qualify as "entrepreneurship." Having identified the aspects of business growth that fall naturally within the domain of entrepreneurship, we broaden our discussion, exploring the potential for making a unique contribution. We argue that entrepreneurship research should deal not only with the growth of the "firm" or the "organization," but also with the growth of specific *economic activities* regardless of their organizational affiliations. In the concluding section we recapitulate and further discuss our main points.

As a background, we should mention that all three authors wrote their doctoral dissertations on entrepreneurship and small firm growth (Davidsson, 1989, Delmar, 1996; Wiklund, 1998). In addition, all three authors have subsequently been personally involved in conceptual and methodological work on the topic of growth, as well as in several longitudinal empirical studies, ranging from growth aspirations during the pre-start-up phase of independent new ventures to acquisition-based expansion of large corporations (e.g., Davidsson and Delmar, 1997, 1998; Davidsson and Wiklund, 2000; Delmar, 1997; Delmar and Davidsson, 1998, 1999; Wiklund and Davidsson, 1999;

Wiklund et al., 1997). This chapter is best regarded as the result of a process of wrestling between theory and data that has been going on with greater or lesser intensity for well over a decade. Our early conceptual views affected which questions the studies were designed to address. Various results of the studies in turn affected our conceptual views. Although the present paper is conceptual, we will draw upon and occasionally make reference to our earlier empirical work as well.

Is Entrepreneurship Growth?

Having set the stage we can now turn to our first main question: "Is entrepreneurship growth?" We have mentioned already that Gartner (1990) showed that growth was one out of eight themes that professional users commonly associated with the entrepreneurship concept. However, his study also made clear that not all would agree on that issue. This suggests that a discussion of whether or not entrepreneurship entails growth has to start with the definition of entrepreneurship.

This, of course, is no small part of the problem we are addressing. Through history, the words "entrepreneur," "entrepreneurial," and "entrepreneurship" have been associated with many different specific economic (and other) roles and phenomena (cf. Hebert and Link, 1982; Kirzner, 1983). Contemporary academic usage of the terms is somewhat more restricted, but this does not mean that researchers are anywhere near a consensus as to what is the legitimate use of the concept "entrepreneur" and its derivatives.

If we selectively pick one definition, the problem we are addressing could be made simple enough. For example, Cole (1949) defined entrepreneurship as a purposeful activity to initiate, maintain, and grow ("aggrandize") a profit-oriented business. Here, growth is part of the very definition. Cole (1949: 88) included mere "maintenance" of a business while stressing "freedom of decision." Still today, much research that is presented under the entrepreneurship label deals with any management issues in small, owner-managed businesses, thereby implicitly adopting a view of entrepreneurship similar to Cole's. Recent conceptual discussion of entrepreneurship, however, has favored a view where issues related to small firms or family-owned businesses do not automatically qualify as dealing with entrepreneurship. At the same time, these views may include processes in organizations that are not owner-managed in the concept of entrepreneurship.

In table 15.1 we have compiled the modern conceptualizations that, arguably, have attracted the most interest and following. As a detailed examination will reveal, a common characteristic of these conceptualizations is that they make no mention of firm size. Neither do they restrict the entrepreneurship domain to owner-managed firms.

In other respects the definitions differ. Gartner's view – which he is careful to present as a suggestion for redirection rather than a formal "definition" – is that entrepreneurship is the creation of new organizations. This choice of focus has two origins. One was a perceived lack of treatment of organizational emergence in organization theory. Somehow organizations were assumed to exist; theories started with existing organizations (cf. Katz and Gartner, 1988). The other was a frustration with the preoccupation that early entrepreneurship research had with personal characteristics of

Table 15.1 Different views on entrepreneurship

Scholar(s)	Definition or conceptualization of entrepreneurship	Role of entrepreneurship research
Gartner (1988)	"Creation of new organizations" (p. 18)	Answer the question "How do organizations come into existence?" (p. 26); in particular "what individuals do" (p. 27) to make this happen
Low and MacMillan (1988)	"Creation of new enterprise" (p. 141)	"[E]xplain and facilitate the role of new enterprise in furthering economic progress" (p. 141)
Stevenson and Jarillo (1990), cf. Stevenson and Gumpert (1985), Stevenson et al. (1985), Stevenson and Sahlman (1986)	"The process by which individuals – either on their own or inside organizations – pursue opportunities without regard to the resources they currently control" (p. 23).	Study the process of pursuit of opportunity from a behavioral perspective (implicit main focus)
Venkataraman (1997), cf. Shane and Venkataraman (2000)	"[T]he discovery and exploitation of profitable opportunities for private wealth, and as a consequence for social wealth as well" (p. 132)	"[T]o understand how opportunites to bring into existence future goods and services are discovered, created, and exploited, by whom, and with what consequences" (p. 120)

entrepreneurs. For these reasons, Gartner (1988) suggested that entrepreneurship research ought to be the behavioral study of organizational emergence. Conceptually, this does not leave room for including growth in the concept of entrepreneurship. Growth is a different organizational phenomenon, requiring other theoretical explanations (Gartner, forthcoming; Gartner and Brush, 1999).

The other definitions are broader and/or less precise. Low and MacMillan (1988) share with Gartner (1988) the view that entrepreneurship research should be more process-oriented. Their suggested definition of the field is "creation of new enterprise." In their wish to include aspects of what most researchers associated with the term "entrepreneurship" at the same time as they try to give the field at least some firm direction, Low and Macmillan remain somewhat vague about exactly what is to be included under their definition. However, they consistently use "new venture" and "new enterprise" rather than "new firm" or "new organization" when they outline their own thoughts. They explicitly discuss pursuit of opportunities within existing firms, and say that they are interested in "*all* entrepreneurial phenomena that impact economic progress" (1988: 151, original emphasis). Our understanding of this is that their suggested main focus of entrepreneurship research is the *creation of new economic activity,* regardless of what type of organization introduces it. Low and MacMillan (1988) do not explicitly address growth, but increases of the size of an existing organization resulting from its successful internal efforts to establish "new enterprise" would, by implication, be entrepreneurship manifesting itself as growth.

Stevenson and his collaborators (see table 15.1) start from experiences with large, established organizations and the relative lack of capacity for novelty that they sometimes show. These authors share with Gartner (1988) the view that entrepreneurship research should focus on behavior, although their emphasis is on entrepreneurship within existing organizations. Their main argument is pursuit of opportunity regardless of current resources vs. getting a safe return on resources already owned or controlled. Opportunity is the central concept, and especially opportunities for *new economic activities.* Stevenson and Jarillo state that "[A]n opportunity is, by definition, something beyond the current activities of the firm. . ." (1990: 23). Further, they explicitly include growth as they say that "Entrepreneurship is the function through which growth is achieved (thus not only the act of starting new businesses)" (1990: 21) and describe entrepreneurial behavior as "the quest for growth through innovation" (1990: 25).

Venkataraman's (1997) view is influenced by thoughts from economics and somewhat more macro-oriented than the previous ones. It shares with Stevenson and Jarillo (1990) the strong focus on opportunity. Importantly, opportunities to enhance the efficiency of [the production of] existing goods are *not* regarded as entrepreneurial. Entrepreneurship deals with opportunities for *future* goods and services (Shane and Venkataraman, 2000, p.220). Again, we would hold that *new economic activity* is a reasonable summary descriptive term. With respect to growth, it is important to note that Venkataraman (1997, cf. Shane and Venkataraman, 2000) includes not only *discovery* in his delineation of the field, but also *exploitation.* While it may be argued that discovery (or opportunity recognition) is the fundamental and distinguishing feature of entrepreneurship relative to management (Fiet, 1996; Gaglio, 1997; Kirzner, 1973), an inevitable counter-argument is that without action toward making creative ideas become real it would be awkward indeed to maintain that any entrepreneurship has been carried out. Schumpeter (1934, ch. 2) already made this argument quite forcefully. If exploitation is included in the definition of entrepreneurship, it must logically follow that the growth that results from a better exploitation strategy of a given opportunity (relative to a worse exploitation strategy) is entrepreneurship manifested as growth.

Based on this discussion of definitions we would argue that the contemporary discourse on the meaning of "entrepreneurship" offers two main alternatives (cf. Sharma and Chrisman, 1999). The first, most clearly articulated by Gartner (1988), holds that *entrepreneurship is the creation of new organizations.* This view certainly has a lot to commend it. It has a clearly defined focus, thereby avoiding the risk of over-extending the field. It addresses an ecological void that has been given only cursory treatment in economics and management studies. This has also led other scholars to adopt it (Aldrich, 1999; Sharma and Chrisman, 1999; Thornton, 1999) although some would exchange "creation" for "emergence," thus de-emphasizing behavioral and strategic aspects.

The main problem with Gartner's (1988) approach is why the area of interest he delineates should be called "entrepreneurship" rather than "organization creation."

While pointing out an important and clearly defined arena for research, Gartner's (1988) definition in fact disregards most of the themes that users of the concept associate with entrepreneurship (Gartner, 1990). There is no explicit consideration of innovation or new combinations (Schumpeter, 1934, p. 66) and his approach disregards the possibility of alternative modes of exploitation for given opportunities (Shane and Venkataraman, 2000; Van de Ven, Angle, and Poole, 1989). Therefore, if an independent inventor chooses to commercialize his or her invention through starting a new firm, this is entrepreneurship under Gartner's definition. If s/he already has a firm and uses that vehicle instead, or if an existing firm buys the invention and employs the inventor as product champion, no entrepreneurship has occurred. Conceptually, this perspective does *not* include growth.

The second view, emerging as a common theme in the other three conceptualizations offered in table 15.1, is that *entrepreneurship is the creation of new economic activity*. This view includes relatively more of the connotations professional users associate with the entrepreneurship concept, and it is also more in line with a classical authority like Schumpeter (1934). The downside is that it is more vague and possibly more difficult to apply consistently in empirical work. The approach could also be criticized for not giving enough consideration to the different resource conditions facing independent startups and internal ventures, respectively.

Let us here define more precisely what we do and do not include in "new economic activity." By this concept we mean an activity that is new to the firm *and* which also changes the product or service offerings that are available on a market. The "new to the firm" criterion requires that either an entirely new organization is created, or an existing organization starts to carry out activities that are distinctly different from what it has carried out so far. While this is a necessary criterion, it is not sufficient. The creation of a new organization for other purposes than the carrying out of new economic activity would not constitute entrepreneurship. Neither would a spin-off, nor a management buy-out, nor internal reorganization of an existing organization suffice as long as the organization merely continues to provide the market with the same supply as existed prior to the internal changes. It is when such changes also lead to changes in what is offered to the market that the criteria for "new economic activity" are fulfilled. Our requirements for newness to the market are relatively mild, though. As we see it, less spectacular forms of entrepreneurship are imitative, but increase competition and therefore the incentives for all actors to improve themselves. Entrepreneurship of higher degrees is exemplified by the introduction of genuinely innovative products or services, which may shift consumption patterns and attract follower entrants, thus restructuring industries or creating a new one.

As a minimum, then, entrepreneurship understood as the creation of new economic activity requires that a new or established firm introduces what internally is a new activity and appears at the same time as a new imitator in a market. At the high end of the spectrum, we would find the global introduction of radical innovation. According to this view, an opportunity to establish new economic activity can be pursued either within an existing organization or by establishing a new one. Both would constitute entrepreneurship. Thus, when an organization grows as a result of developing new activities, the growth is a reflection of the firm's entrepreneurship. When new economic activities are added to old ones in existing organizations, this is entrepreneurship manifested as growth rather than as the creation of new organizations. Hence, under this view of entrepreneurship the question in the heading of this section can be answered affirmatively: entrepreneurship is (sometimes) growth.

We have discussed advantages and disadvantages associated with the two views. On balance, although we regard both as important areas for research, we should make it no secret that as conceptualization of entrepreneurship we prefer the latter alternative, *creation of new economic activity*. However, we will discuss also the "creation of new organizations" view in the remainder of this chapter.

Admittedly, the two views we focus on do not fully capture all aspects of all contemporary definitions of entrepreneurship. A couple of exclusions should be mentioned. Although related to Schumpeter's (1934) theorizing, our definition of "new economic activity" deviates from his description of types of economic development – often cited as his "definition of entrepreneurship" – in that we are less willing to accept innovation regarding resource input and resource transformation (new raw materials, process innovation) as instances of entrepreneurship *per se*. We hold that it is when such internal changes affect what is offered in the market that "new economic activity" is introduced. Kirzner (1973, 1983) would accept the discovery of any opportunity to make a profit as "entrepreneurship." Some such discoveries might lead neither to the creation of a new organization nor to a new economic activity as we have defined it. While narrow in other respects, Kirzner's view is therefore in this regard broader than both of the views we deal with here.

In this section we have argued that the contemporary discourse on entrepreneurship presents two main views on entrepreneurship: entrepreneurship as *creation of new organizations* or as *creation of new economic activities*. "Entrepreneurship is growth" is not a conceptually valid statement under the former view, whereas it is so under the latter view given that new economic activities add to the size of an established organization.

Is Growth Entrepreneurship?

If it were accepted that entrepreneurship is (sometimes) growth, the vice versa must also be true: growth is (sometimes) entrepreneurship. When we first addressed this question we thought it was rather simple. Davidsson (1989: 7) expressed it as follows: "[I]s growth entrepreneurship? The answer to that question is contingent on to which extent the manager is free to choose. If economic behavior is discretionary, pursuing continued development of the firm is the more entrepreneurial choice when refraining from doing so is another feasible alternative, just like founding a firm is more entrepreneurial than not doing so." While this still seems to us a reasonable line of argumentation we have since then in other contexts shown conceptually and empirically that the issue of business growth is very complex and multifaceted. In fact, business growth may perhaps best be conceived of as a collective term for several rather different phenomena, requiring separate methods of inquiry as well as separate theoretical explanations (Davidsson and Wiklund 2000; Delmar, 1997; Delmar and Davidsson, 1998). In the present context, then, the question becomes: *what* growth can justifiably be regarded as manifestations of entrepreneurship?

As regards Gartner's (1988) organization creation view of entrepreneurship we have noted that conceptually, growth is not part of his definition. Empirical evidence suggests that the large majority of independent startups start very small and remain one- to three-person entities throughout their entire existence (Davidsson, Lindmark, and Olofsson, 1998; Delmar and Davidsson, 1999). Consistent with this, Katz and Gartner (1988) separate characteristics of the person from those of the organization also for one-person businesses. However, such results suggest that restricting entrepreneurship to the study of the gestation process of "normal" or "average" startups only up to the point when they first start trading or first make a profit may be too restrictive. Growth up to some arbitrary level after a firm first starts as a sole trader may be necessary if it is to be meaningful to talk at all of the creation of "organizations" as they are conceived of in organization theory, and thus fill the gap Gartner (1988) pointed out. It may thus be advisable for research under this paradigm to include in the concept of "emergence" or "creation" also what other researchers might call "early growth." The starting point in terms of time and size would thus determine whether or not "growth is entrepreneurship."

For the "entrepreneurship is new economic activity" view, the form of growth comes to the fore. Although exceptions exist (e.g., Amit, Livnat, and Zarowin, 1989; Penrose, 1959), the growth literature surprisingly rarely shows a strong interest in *how* or in *which form* firms expand. Examples of growth trajectories and their causes can be found in the literature dealing with related topics such as mergers or acquisitions (Chatterjee and Wernerfelt, 1991; Hoskisson, Johnson, and Moesel, 1994; Markides, 1995) or innovation and technological change (Tushman and Anderson, 1986). A limitation of this research – for our purposes – is that the samples investigated are often composed of large firms in relatively mature industries. Furthermore, this literature is not predominantly interested in growth *per se*, but in how the phenomena under scrutiny change the behavior or financial performance of organizations.

Nevertheless, they do suggest different factors that might explain why firms come to grow through acquisition or by growing organically. Research on innovation and technological change focuses on the creation and diffusion of new products and services and how they affect the environmental conditions that determine the selection of firms for survival. Here, it is argued that the introduction of a new product or service leads to discontinuities, increased turbulence, and uncertainty on the market. Initiators of such changes grow more rapidly than other firms (Tushman and Anderson, 1986). It is implicitly clear that it is organic growth the authors have in mind, and their perspective is very close to the "entrepreneurship as new economic activity" view.

Markides and Williamson (1996) adopt a resource-based view, and suggest that acquisition or mergers are used in order to acquire and exploit resources or assets owned by other companies, to make the same resources unavailable to its rivals at a competitive cost, or both. Penrose (1959) of course preceded them. In her original formulation of the resource-based view, Penrose suggested that firms that exhibit organic growth have the ability to detect emerging expansion opportunities and to recombine existing resources in new ways so as to take advantage of these opportunities. In other words, Penrose argues that "entrepreneurial resources" (or "entrepreneurial capability") are crucial for organic growth. Acquired growth is a different process. In this case Penrose (1959) holds that the financial strength of the firm and its access to managerial slack are more important. Barney (1988) also argues that the reason organizations choose to grow through acquisitions often is excessive cash flow. Both financial and managerial slack is related to the size of the firm. This would suggest that the firm's acquisition growth is determined by the size of its resource pool rather than by its determination to develop new economic activities.

In one of our earlier studies we tested these predictions and found that firm size was indeed positively and significantly associated with acquisition growth, whereas a firm's degree of entrepreneurial strategic orientation (cf. Miller and Friesen, 1982) was positively and significantly related to organic growth (Wiklund and Davidsson, 1999). In another project we performed an analysis of high-growth firms broken down by firm size and age. We found very strong empirical relationships, suggesting that organic growth dominated among young and small firms whereas old and large firms grew almost exclusively through acquisition (Davidsson and Delmar, 1998). This suggests that "growth is entrepreneurship" is a reasonable generalization for young and small firms, but not for large and old ones.

We have argued already that when a firm grows as a consequence of adding new activities, we have a case of entrepreneurship manifested as growth. The short review above reinforces our view that this type of *organic* growth could justifiably be counted as entrepreneurship, while growth through *acquisition* could usually not. Returning to the definitions in table 15.1, we find that Venkataraman's (1997) focus on "future goods and services" rules out growth through acquisition when the latter means moving existing production of goods and services from one organization to another. We would hold that the gist of Stevenson and Jarillo's (1990) argument also rules out acquisition growth. As suggested by Barney (1988) and Markides and Williamsson (1996), acquisitions are often financial investments or serve to either protect or get synergy out of existing resources. This is in Stevenson and Jarillo's conceptualization typical "trustee" behavior – the opposite of entrepreneurship. In our earlier discussion we found that the opportunities these authors have in mind are typically opportunities for starting new activities. This is also how we understand Low and MacMillan (1988). While their "new enterprise" does not necessarily mean "new to the world" it does not suffice that the activity is new only to the firm, as when existing activity is transferred from one organization to another.

From the "entrepreneurship is new economic activity" view, then, the distinction between organic and acquired growth appears crucial for whether firm growth can be regarded as entrepreneurship or not. But what about cases where organic growth does not involve addition of new activities, but only growth in volume of an existing activity of the firm? Regarding entrepreneurship not as a dichotomous but a continuous phenomenon, Venkataraman's (1997) emphasis on discovery *and* exploitation provides some justification for regarding organic growth as a reflection of entrepreneurship even when it is "mere" volume growth based on the original activity. The quality of the discovery – how radical a break with current practices it represents and how large a relative advantage it creates – determines its growth potential (Rogers, 1995; Tushman and Anderson, 1986). The quality of the exploitation determines, in turn, how much of that potential is realized. Therefore, organic growth in volume can be regarded as a (admittedly less than perfect) measure of the "amount" of entrepreneurship that a particular instance of new economic activity represents.

We would be the first to admit that reality is not so simple that organic growth of firms always means they have engaged in new economic activity and that growth achieved through acquisition is never associated with genuinely new activity. In some cases, organic growth could be the result of mere volume growth of a producer of a commodity product who has just had the luck to be picked among equal alternatives by a large and growing customer. Acquisitions may in some instances reflect an aggressive strategy to rapidly buy an "infrastructure" to be filled by the acquiring firm's own, growing activities. By and large, however, we would argue that it is reasonable to suggest that if particular firms were analyzed more closely, cases of organic growth would be much more likely to fulfill the criteria for qualifying as "new economic activity" than would cases of acquisition growth.

In summary, we have argued in this section that when doing empirical work based on Gartner's definition of entrepreneurship it would be advisable to include what other researchers might call "early growth" into the operationalization of "organizational creation." When entrepreneurship is viewed as new economic activity it is reasonable to assume that growth of firms represents entrepreneurship when the growth is achieved organically, whereas growth through acquisition does normally not represent entrepreneurship. As empirical results suggest that young and small firms grow organically, whereas old and large firms grow through acquisition, there is in practice considerable overlap between the two perspectives as concerns when "growth is entrepreneurship" appears to be a reasonable assumption.

Beyond the Firm Level

So far, our discussion has concerned the growth of firms or organizations. We have concluded that under the "new economic activity" definition, organic growth of firms is a legitimate interest for entrepreneurship research. However, an interest in the growth of firms is not unique to entrepreneurship research. It would seem natural for researchers in strategic management to share the interest in organic growth through the introduction of new economic activities, as one aspect of a more general interest in organizational growth (cf. Amit et al., 1989). As we have noted, it seems to be the case that also within the field of strategic management very little research has been conducted with this specific focus. Hence, this should be an area for fruitful exchange between the two sub-disciplines or interest groups.

In other respects the interests of these two lines of research differ. Although Gartner's definition focuses on the creation of a new firm (or "organization"), the other definitions in table 15.1 are not focused on the firm level of analysis at all. This is clearly distinct from definitions of strategic management, which presuppose the existence of a firm (or organization) and an interest in its fate (Barney, 1997; Schendel and Hofer, 1979). The entrepreneurship definitions we favor instead point out the *new economic activity* as the unit of focal interest; the core interest in entrepreneurship is the emergence and growth of specific new activities.

From this perspective organic firm growth remains a proxy for entrepreneurship as long as we do not know in more detail the extent to which it represents either the introduction of new economic activity or the quality of the discovery and exploitation of opportunity for such activity. Consequently, entrepreneurship researchers should design studies where the new activity is explicitly used as the unit of analysis (cf. Davidsson and Wiklund, 2000; Davidsson and Wiklund, forthcoming).

Ideally, the growth of such new activities should be studied at two levels. First, it is of interest to follow the growth of the original effort, which may equal the growth of a new organization, a unit within an existing organization, or a unit which changes its organizational affiliation and/or its human champions one or more times during the course of the study. Second, we share with Venkataraman (1997), Low and MacMillan (1988), and many other entrepreneurship researchers an explicit interest in wealth creation also on the social level (see table 15.1). From that point of view it would be of great interest to study how the new activity grows externally through imitation and – in some cases – gives rise to new populations of organizations or of practices. This interest has a large overlap with ecological or evolutionary approaches in organization theory (Aldrich, 1999) as well as with research on the diffusion of innovations (Rogers, 1995).

Conclusion

Is entrepreneurship growth? Is growth entrepreneurship? In this chapter we have given conditional affirmative answers to these questions. There is, however, one fundamental problem with associating entrepreneurship with growth that we have as yet not addressed. An organization or an activity can only grow if it is successful. If success is included in the concept of entrepreneurship, it follows that whether something constitutes "entrepreneurship" or not can only be determined in retrospect. As a consequence, it would be difficult to study entrepreneurship in real time. As a resolution to this dilemma we suggest that entrepreneurship *as an economic phenomenon* only occurs if value is created and that entrepreneurship is ultimately measured by what effect an attempted new organization or new activity has. Entrepreneurship *as a scholarly domain*, however, needs to study also failed attempts, and to do so in real time. Otherwise, censoring would lead to a biased view of entrepreneurship as an economic phenomenon.

We have examined two major views of entrepreneurship that were derived from definitions suggested by influential contemporary scholars: entrepreneurship as *creation of new organizations* and entrepreneurship as *creation of new economic activity*. We have argued that without any consideration of growth, entrepreneurship is reduced to a dichotomous empirical variable whose content does not fully reflect any of these definitions. Most startups never create much of an organization. In addition, new activities are no doubt undertaken within existing organizations, adding to their size. This suggests that entrepreneurship cannot be operationalized solely as startup vs. non-startup of independent new firms. Irrespective of which of the two main perspectives is chosen, some aspects of growth should be regarded as part of the entrepreneurship phenomenon.

If entrepreneurship is (sometimes) growth it follows that growth must (sometimes) be a reflection of entrepreneurship. From the "organization creation" perspective, we have argued that empirical studies are well advised to include also what other researchers might call "early growth" into the operationalization of emergence, and perhaps to over-sample high-potential startups. Otherwise the research cannot fill the perceived gap between organizational non-existence and organizations as they usually appear in organization theory. From the "new economic activity" perspective, we argued that organic firm growth is much more likely to satisfy the criteria for qualifying as entrepreneurship. Empirical research has shown that among young and small firms that expand, almost all the growth is organic. By contrast, in larger and older firms all or almost all the growth was attributable to acquisitions. Growth may thus be a reasonable indicator of entrepreneurship in the former groups, but not in the latter.

We concluded that organic growth of firms should also be a fruitful area for cross-fertilization with strategic management research. A range of research issues of mutual interest presents itself. For example, is it reasonable after a closer look to say that organic growth is entrepreneurial whereas acquisition growth is not? Under what circumstances is an organic growth strategy conducive to firm performance? Why is it that young and small firms grow organically whereas old and large firms grow through acquisitions? Is it that larger firms run out of entrepreneurial steam? If so, what structures and processes of larger organizations deter their creation of new economic activities, and what can be done to overcome these obstacles? Alternatively, is it young and small firms' lack of financial and managerial resources that forces them to grow organically although acquisition growth would be more profitable or less risky? If so, what can firms do to overcome these liabilities of smallness and newness that prevent them from growing via acquisitions? These are questions that are of interest from both perspectives.

From the perspective of entrepreneurship research, however, even organic firm growth remains a proxy for the dependent variable that represents the real preference. We have argued that if entrepreneurship is defined as "new economic activity," it follows that entrepreneurship researchers should also try to use the new economic activity itself as the unit of analysis in empirical research. Needless to say, studies using the activity itself as unit of analysis may be difficult to carry out (cf. Van de Ven et al., 1989; Van de Ven et al., 1999). Would it be possible to define "new economic activity" in a precise enough manner to make sampling possible? How could the universe of "new economic activities" be determined, so that representative samples could be drawn? Would the sampled units maintain a clear identity over time, so that longitudinal studies could follow units that can meaningfully be regarded "the same" despite all the changes they go through? Are there enough theoretical concepts and established operationalizations of these available for this level of analysis? If not, could such be developed?

Clearly, tough challenges await the empirical researcher who sets out to study the growth of "new economic activities" over time. However, several of these problems apply to the firm level of analysis as well, although researchers have learnt to habitually disregard them (Davidsson and Wiklund, 2000). Moreover, we would argue that the potential for entrepreneurship research and for individual researchers to make more of a unique contribution might be much greater if these challenges are accepted.

Note

We gratefully acknowledge support from the Knut and Alice Allenberg's Foundation, the Swedish Foundation for Small Business Research (FSF), the Swedish Council for Work Life Research (RALF), and the Board for Industrial and Technical Development (NUTEK). We would also like to thank Dieter Boegenhold, S. Michael Camp, Michael Hitt, Duane Ireland, and Donald Sexton for valuable comments on earlier versions of this manuscript. The responsibility for any remaining errors and omissions is, of course, entirely the authors'.

References

Acs, Z. J. and Audretsch, D. B. 1990. The determinants of small-firm growth in US manufacturing. *Applied Economics*, 22(2): 143–53.

Aldrich, H. 1999. *Organizations evolving*. Newbury Park, CA: Sage Publications.

Amit, R., Livnat, J., and Zarowin, P. 1989. The mode of corporate diversification: Internal ventures versus acquisitions. *Managerial and Decision Economics*, 10: 89–100.

Barney, J. B. 1988. Returns to bidding firms in mergers and acquisitions: Reconsidering the relatedness hypothesis. *Strategic Management Journal*, 9: 71–8

Barney, J. B. 1997. *Gaining and sustaining competitive advantage*. Reading, MA: Addison-Wesley.

Chatterjee, S. and Wernerfelt, W. 1991. The link between resources and the type of diversification: Theory and evidence. *Strategic Management Journal*, 12, 33–48.

Cole, A. H. 1949. Entrepreneurship and entrepreneurial history. Harvard University Research Center in Entrepreneurial History, *Change and the entrepreneur*, Cambridge, MA: Harvard University Press, 88–107. Reprinted in H. C. Livesay (ed.), 1995. *Entrepreneurship and the growth of firms*, vol. 1. Aldershot, UK: Edward Elgar, 100–22.

Davidsson, P. 1989. *Entrepreneurship and small firm growth*. Stockholm: The Economic Research Institute (diss.).

Davidsson, P. and Delmar, F. 1997. High-growth firms: Characteristics, job contribution and method observations. *RENT XI Conference*, Mannheim, Germany.

Davidsson, P. and Delmar, F. 1998. Some important observations concerning job creation by firm size and age. *Recontres St. Gall*, Elm, Switzerland, University of St. Gallen.

Davidsson, P., Lindmark, L., and Olofsson, C. 1998. The extent of overestimation of small firm job creation: an empirical examination of the "regression bias". *Small Business Economics*, 10: 87–100.

Davidsson, P. and Wiklund, J. 2000. Conceptual and empirical challenges in the study of firm growth. In D. Sexton and H. Landström (eds), *The Blackwell Handbook of Entrepreneurship*. Oxford and Malden, MA: Blackwell, 26–44.

Davidsson, P. and Wiklund, J. (forthcoming). Levels of analysis in entrepreneurship research: current practice and suggestions for the future. *Entrepreneurship Theory and Practice*.

Delmar, F. 1996. *Entrepreneurial behavior and business performance*. Stockholm: The Economic Research Institute (diss.).

Delmar, F. 1997. Measuring growth: Methodological considerations and empirical results. In R. Donckels and A. Miettinen (eds), *Entrepreneurship and SME research: On its way to the next millennium*. Aldershot, UK and Brookfield, VA: Ashgate, 190–216.

Delmar, F. and Davidsson, P. 1998. A taxonomy of high-growth firms. *Frontiers of entrepreneurship research 18*. Wellesley, MA: Babson College, 399–403.

Delmar, F. and Davidsson, P. 1999. Firm size expectations of nascent entrepreneurs. *Frontiers of entrepreneurship research 19*. Wellesley, MA: Babson College, 90–104.

Evans, D. S. 1987. Test of alternative theories of firm growth. *Journal of Political Economy*, 95: 657–74.

Fiet, J. 1996. The informational basis on entrepreneurial discovery. *Small Business Economics*, 8: 419–30.

Gaglio, C. M. 1997. Opportunity identification: Review, critique and suggested research directions. In J. Katz and J. Brockhaus (eds), *Advances in entrepreneurship, firm emergence, and growth*. Greenwich, CT: JAI Press, 3: 139–202.

Gartner, W. B. 1988. 'Who is an entrepreneur?' is the wrong question. *American Small Business Journal* (spring): 11–31

Gartner, W. B. 1990. What are we talking about when we are talking about entrepreneurship? *Journal of Business Venturing*, 5: 15–28.

Gartner, W. B. (forthcoming). Is there an elephant in entrepreneurship research? Blind assumptions in theory development. *Entrepreneurship Theory and Practice*.

Gartner, W. B. and Brush, C. B. 1999. Entrepreneurship as organizing: Emergence, newness, and transformation. Paper presented at Academy of Management Entrepreneurship Division Doctoral Consortium, Chicago.

Greiner, L. E. 1972. Evolutions and revolutions as organizations grow. *Harvard Business Review*, 50(4): 37–46.

Hebert, R. F. and Link, A. N. 1982. *The entrepreneur: Mainstream views and radical critiques*. New York: Praeger.

Hoskisson, R. E., Johnson, R. A., and Moesel, D. D. 1994. Corporate divestiture intensity in restructuring firms: Effects of governance, strategy, and performance. *Academy of Management Journal*, 37(5): 1207–51.

Katz, J. and Gartner, W. B. 1988. Properties of emerging organizations. *Academy of Management Review*, 13(3): 429–41.

Kazanjian, R. K. and Drazin, R. 1989. An empirical test of stage of a growth progression model. *Management Science*, 35(12): 1489–503.

Kirzner, I. 1973. *Competition and entrepreneurship*. Chicago, IL: University of Chicago Press.

Kirzner, I. M. 1983. Entrepreneurs and the entrepreneurial function: a commentary. In J. Ronen (ed.), *Entrepreneurship*. Lexington, MA: Lexington Books, 281–90.

Livesay, H. C. (ed.) 1995. *Entrepreneurship and the growth of firms*, vols 1–2. Aldershot, UK: Edward Elgar.

Low, M. B. and MacMillan, I. C. 1988. Entrepreneurship: past research and future challenges. *Journal of Management*, 14: 139–61.

Markides, C. C. 1995. Diversification, restructuring and economic performance. *Strategic Management Journal*, 16: 101–18.

Markides, C. C. and Williamson, P. J. 1996. Corporate diversification and organizational structure: A resource-based view. *Academy of Management Journal*, 39(2): 340–67.

Miller, D. and Friesen, P. H. 1982. Innovation in conservative and entrepreneurial firms: two models of strategic momentum. *Strategic Management Journal*, 3: 1–25.

Penrose, E. 1959. *The theory of the growth of the firm*. New York: John Wiley.

Rogers, E. M. 1995. *Diffusion of innovations*. New York: Free Press.

Romano, C. and Ratnatunga, J. 1997. A citation classics analysis of articles in contemporary small enterprise research. *Journal of Business Venturing*, 12: 197–212.

Schendel, D. and Hofer, C. W. 1979. Introduction. In D. E. Schendel and C. W. Hofer (eds.), *Strategic management: A new view of business policy and planning*. Boston: Little, Brown and Company.

Schumpeter, J. 1934. *The theory of economic development*. Cambridge, MA: Harvard University Press.

Shane, S. A. and Venkataraman, S. 2000. The promise of entrepreneurship as a field of research. *Academy of Management Review*, 25(1): 217–26.

Sharma, P. and Chrisman, J. J. 1999. Toward a reconciliation of the definitional issues in the field of corporate entrepreneurship. *Entrepreneurship Theory and Practice*, 24: 11–27.

Stevenson, H. H. and Gumpert, D. E. 1985. The heart of entrepreneurship. *Harvard Business Review*, 63(2): 85–94.

Stevenson, H. H. and Jarillo, J. C. 1990. A paradigm of entrepreneurship: Entrepreneurial management. *Strategic Management Journal*, 11: 17–27.

Stevenson, H. H., Roberts, M. J., and Grousbeck, H. I. 1985. *New business and the entrepreneur*. Homewood, IL: Irwin.

Stevenson, H. H. and Sahlman, S. 1986. Importance of entrepreneurship in economic development. In R. Hisrisch (ed.), *Entrepreneurship, intrapreneurship and venture capital*. Lexington: D. C. Heath, 3–26.

Thornton, P. H. 1999. The sociology of entrepreneurship. *Annual Review of Sociology*, 25: 19–46.

Tushman, M. L. and Anderson, P. 1986. Technological discontinuities and organizational environments. *Administrative Science Quarterly*, 31: 439–65.

Van de Ven, A., Angle, H. L., and Poole, M.S. (eds) 1989. *Research on the management of innovation: The Minnesota studies*. New York: Harper & Row.

Van de Ven, A. H., Polley, D., Garud, R., and Venkataraman, S. 1999. *The innovation journey*. Oxford: Oxford University Press.

Venkataraman, S. 1997. The distinctive domain of entrepreneurship research: An editor's perspective. In J. Katz and J. Brockhaus (eds), *Advances in entrepreneurship, firm emergence, and growth*. Greenwich, CT: JAI Press, 3: 119–38.

Wiklund, J. 1998. *Small firm growth and performance: Entrepreneurship and beyond*. Jönköping, Sweden, Jönköping International Business School (diss).

Wiklund, J. and Davidsson, P. 1999. A resource-based view on organic and acquired growth. Paper presented at the Academy of Management Pre-conference. Chicago, August.

Wiklund, J., Davidsson, P., Delmar, F., and Aronsson, M. 1997. Expected consequences of growth and their effect on growth willingness in different samples of small firms. In P. D. Reynolds, W. D. Bygrave, N. M. Carter, P. Davidsson, W. B. Gartner, C. M. Mason, and P. P. McDougall, *Frontiers of Entrepreneurship Research 17*. Wellesley, MA: Babson College.

Author Index

Porter, M. E. **2, 26, 48**, 81, 155, 160, 174, 181, 182, 265
Powel, W. W. 223, 224, 225, 226, 227, 228, 242, 243
Prabhu, G. 280
Prahalad, C. K.
  and Bettis (1986) 31, 161
  Bettis and (1995) 28, 316
  Conner and (1996) 96, 154
  Hamel and (1989) 179, 193
  and Hamel (1990) 108, 174, 175
  Hamel and (1993) 175, 179
  Hamel and (1994) 48, 261, 322
  Hamel and (1996) 31
Preisendorfer, P. 50
Pricer, R. 263
Prusa, T. J. 54

Quinn, J. B. 313

Ramanujam, V. 29
Ramaswamy, K. 294
Randle, Y. 109
Ranft, A. 168
Rangan, U. S. 166
Rao, H. 70, 73–4
Rasheed, A. M. A. 271
Ratnatunga, J. 328
Reddy, S. 166
Reed, T. S. 316
Reuber, A. R. 263, *264, 268*
Revang, O. 30
Reynolds, P. 204
Reynolds, P. D. 21
Ricart i Costa, J. E. 57
Ricks, D. A. 258–9, *259*
Ridderståle, J. 30
Roberts, E. B. 262, *264,* 271, *274,* 275
Roberts, M. *22*
Robertson, P. 281
Robinson, R. 29
Rockart, J. F. 47
Roehl, T. W. 282
Rogers, E. M. 151, 336, 338
Romano, C. 328
Romer, P. 98
Romo, F. P. 203
Ronen, S. 297
Roos, D. R. 187
Roth, K. 289, 291, 295

Rothaermel, F. T. 9, 226
Rowe, W. G. 310, 320
Rowley, T. 210
Rumelt, R. P.
  (1974) 176, 181
  (1984) 114, 123n, 174
  (1987) *22,* 23, 90, 98, 106, 109, 110
  and Lippman (1982) 71, 99
  Schendel and Teece (1995) 26
Russo, M. V. 155

Sahlman, S. *331,* 332
Sahlman, W. A. 59, 214
Sambharya, R. B. 289, 291, 295
Sanchez, R. 26, 108, 114, 175, 176, 321, 322
Sandberg, W. R. 19, 27, 28, 32
Sanders, G. Wm. 289, 291–2, 294, 295, 296, 301
Sanders, W. 265
Sankaran, K. 297
Santarelli, E. 225
Sapienza, H. 23, 92, 257
Sarnin, P. 295
Sarasvathy, S. D. 2
Sathe, V. 313
Saviotti, P. P. 227, 243
Sawhney, M. 176, 181, 182
Saxenian, A. L. 207
Sayles, L. R. 152, 261, 309
Schakenraad, J. 204
Schechter, S. M. 29
Schein, E. 148
Schendel, D. E. 22, 23, 26, 27, 36, 173, 175, 313, 337
Scherer, F. M. 226, 242
Schindehutte, M. 1
Schmitz, J. A., Jr. 54
Schoemaker, P. J. H. 4, 122, 154, 174, 190
Schoonhoven, C. B. 23, 212, 289, 291, 296
Schroder, H. M. 290
Schulte, W. 258, 259
Schumpeter, J. 5, 25, 61, 69, 97, 136, 141, 142, 223
  (1934) 20, *22,* 24, 90, 94, 95–6, 98, 101, 102, 129, 224, 225, 332, 333, 334
  (1942) 24, 129, 130, 135, 145, 149n, 157, 226, 242
Schwartz, M. 203
Schwartz, N. L. 226
Scott, W. R. 72

Subject Index